DATE DUE

PRINTED IN U.S.A.

Authors & Artists for Young Adults

ISSN 1040-5682

Authors & Artists for Young Adults

VOLUME 20

Thomas McMahon
Editor

GALE

DETROIT • NEW YORK • TORONTO • LONDON

Thomas McMahon, *Editor*

Joyce Nakamura, *Managing Editor*

Hal May, *Publisher*

Diane Andreassi, Ken Cuthbertson, David Johnson, Ronie-Richele Garcia-Johnson, Marian C. Gonsior, Janet L. Hile, Motoko Huthwaite, David P. Johnson, J. Sydney Jones, Nancy Rampson, Megan Ratner, Susan Reicha, Pamela L. Shelton, Kenneth R. Shepherd, and Kathleen Witman,
Sketchwriters/Contributing Editors

Victoria B. Cariappa, *Research Manager*
Cheryl L. Warnock, *Project Coordinator*
Gary J. Oudersluys, *Research Specialist*
Tamara C. Nott and Norma Sawaya, *Research Associates*
Laura C. Bissey and Sean R. Smith, *Research Assistants*

Susan M. Trosky, *Permissions Manager*
Maria Franklin, Edna M. Hedblad, Michele Lonoconus, and Shalice Shah, *Picture Permissions Associates*

Mary Beth Trimper, *Production Director*
Deborah Milliken, *Production Assistant*

Randy Bassett, *Image Database Supervisor*
Sherrell Hobbs, *Macintosh Artist*
Robert Duncan and Mikal Ansari, *Imaging Specialists*
Pamela A. Hayes, *Photography Coordinator*

∞™ The paper used in this publication meets the minimum requirements of American National Standard for Information Sciences—Permanence Paper for Printed Library Materials, ANSI Z39.48-1984.

Library of Congress Catalog Card Number 89-641100
ISBN 0-7876-1136-0
ISSN 1040-5682

10 9 8 7 6 5 4 3 2 1

Printed in the United States of America

Contents

Introduction

Authors and Artists for Young Adults is a reference series designed to serve the needs of middle school, junior high, and high school students interested in creative artists. Originally inspired by the need to bridge the gap between Gale's *Something about the Author,* created for children, and *Contemporary Authors,* intended for older students and adults, *Authors and Artists for Young Adults* has been expanded to cover not only an international scope of authors, but also a wide variety of other artists.

Although the emphasis of the series remains on the writer for young adults, we recognize that these readers have diverse interests covering a wide range of reading levels. The series therefore contains not only those creative artists who are of high interest to young adults, including cartoonists, photographers, music composers, bestselling authors of adult novels, media directors, producers, and performers, but also literary and artistic figures studied in academic curricula, such as influential novelists, playwrights, poets, and painters. The goal of *Authors and Artists for Young Adults* is to present this great diversity of creative artists in a format that is entertaining, informative, and understandable to the young adult reader.

Entry Format

Each volume of *Authors and Artists for Young Adults* will furnish in-depth coverage of twenty to twenty-five authors and artists. The typical entry consists of:

—A detailed biographical section that includes date of birth, marriage, children, education, and addresses.

—A comprehensive bibliography or filmography including publishers, producers, and years.

—Adaptations into other media forms.

—Works in progress.

—A distinctive essay featuring comments on an artist's life, career, artistic intentions, world views, and controversies.

—References for further reading.

—Extensive illustrations, photographs, movie stills, cartoons, book covers, and other relevant visual material.

A cumulative index to featured authors and artists appears in each volume.

Compilation Methods

The editors of *Authors and Artists for Young Adults* make every effort to secure information directly from the authors and artists through personal correspondence and interviews. Sketches on living authors and artists are sent to the biographee for review prior to publication. Any sketches not personally reviewed by biographees or their representatives are marked with an asterisk (*).

Highlights of Forthcoming Volumes

Among the authors and artists planned for future volumes are:

Greg Bear	Robert Frost	Terry McMillan
Janet Bode	Virginia Hamilton	Wilson Rawls
David Brin	Keith Haring	Conrad Richter
Michael Cadnum	Frank Herbert	Jon Scieska
James Fenimore Cooper	Jan Hudson	Sir Walter Scott
Stephen Crane	Kristin Hunter	Neal Shusterman
Sharon Creech	Robin Klein	Lane Smith
Linda Crew	Katherine Kurtz	Ivan Southall
Jenny Davis	Barry Levinson	Bram Stoker
Farrukh Dhondy	David Macauley	Rita Williams-Garcia
Alexandre Dumas	Gregory Maguire	Jacqueline Woodson
Dick Francis	Carson McCullers	Cheryl Zach

Contact the Editor

We encourage our readers to examine the entire *AAYA* series. Please write and tell us if we can make AAYA even more helpful to you. Give your comments and suggestions to the editor:

BY MAIL: The Editor, *Authors and Artists for Young Adults*, Gale Research, 835 Penobscot Building, 645 Griswold St., Detroit, MI 48226-4094.

BY TELEPHONE: (800) 347-GALE

BY FAX: (313) 961-6599

BY E-MAIL: CYA@Gale.com@GALESMTP

Authors & Artists for Young Adults

Louisa May Alcott

■ Writings

Flower Fables, George W. Briggs, 1855.

Hospital Sketches (also see below), James Redpath, 1863.

The Rose Family: A Fairy Tale, James Redpath, 1864.

On Picket Duty, and Other Tales, James Redpath, 1864.

Moods, A. K. Loring, 1865, revised edition, Roberts Brothers, 1882.

Nelly's Hospital, U.S. Sanitary Commission, 1865.

The Mysterious Key, and What It Opened, Elliott, Thomes & Talbot, 1867.

Morning-Glories, and Other Stories, Horace B. Fuller, 1868.

Kitty's Class Day (also see below), A. K. Loring, 1868.

Aunt Kipp (also see below), A. K. Loring, 1868.

Psyche's Art (also see below), A. K. Loring, 1868.

Louisa May Alcott's Proverb Stories (also see below; contains *Kitty's Class Day, Aunt Kipp,* and *Psyche's Art*), A. K. Loring, 1868.

Little Women, or, Meg, Jo, Beth and Amy, two volumes, Roberts Brothers, 1868-69; volume 2 republished in England as *Little Women Wedded,* Low, 1872, as *Little Women Married,* Routledge, 1873, and as *Nice Wives,* Weldon, 1875; both volumes republished in England as *Little Women and Good Wives,* Nisbet, 1895.

Hospital Sketches [and] *Camp and Fireside Stories,* Roberts Brothers, 1869.

An Old-Fashioned Girl, Roberts Brothers, 1870.

Will's Wonder Book, Horace B. Fuller, 1870.

■ Personal

Also wrote under name A. M. Barnard; born November 29, 1832, in Germantown, PA; died March 6, 1888, in Boston, MA; buried in Sleepy Hollow Cemetery, Concord, MA; daughter of Amos Bronson (an educator and philosopher) and Abigail (a teacher and social worker; maiden name, May) Alcott. *Education:* Tutored by her father until the age of sixteen; later studied under Henry David Thoreau, Ralph Waldo Emerson, and Theodore Parker.

■ Career

Author of novels, short stories, and poems. In her youth, held a variety of jobs, including teacher, seamstress, and domestic servant; nurse at Union Hospital, Georgetown, District of Columbia, 1861-63; editor of *Merry's Museum* (children's magazine), 1867.

■ Awards, Honors

Lewis Carroll Shelf award, 1969, for *Little Women,* illustrated by Jessie Wilcox.

(Under pseudonym A. M. Barnard) *V. V.; or, Plots and Counterplots*, Thomes & Talbot, c. 1870.

Little Men: Life at Plumfield with Jo's Boys, Roberts Brothers, 1871.

Aunt Jo's Scrap-Bag, Roberts Brothers, Volume 1: *My Boys, Etc.*, 1872, Volume 2: *Shawl-Straps, Etc.*, 1872, Volume 3: *Cupid and Chow Chow, Etc.*, 1874, Volume 4: *My Girls, Etc.*, 1878, Volume 5: *Jimmy's Cruise in the Pinafore, Etc.*, 1879, and Volume 6: *An Old-Fashioned Thanksgiving, Etc.*, 1882.

Work: A Story of Experience, Roberts Brothers, 1873.

Something to Do (contains *Proverb Stories*), Ward, Lock & Tyler, 1873.

Eight Cousins; or, The Aunt-Hill, Roberts Brothers, 1875.

Silver Pitchers [and] *Independence, a Centennial Love Story*, Roberts Brothers, 1876.

Rose in Bloom: A Sequel to "Eight Cousins," Roberts Brothers, 1876.

(Published anonymously) *A Modern Mephistopheles* (also see below), Roberts Brothers, 1877.

Under the Lilacs, Roberts Brothers, 1878.

Meadow Blossoms, Crowell, 1879.

Water Cresses, Crowell, 1879.

Sparkles for Bright Eyes, Crowell, 1879.

Jack and Jill: A Village Story, Roberts Brothers, 1880.

Spinning-Wheel Stories, Roberts Brothers, 1884.

Lulu's Library, Roberts Brothers, Volume 1: *A Christmas Dream*, 1886, Volume 2: *The Frost King*, 1887, Volume 3: *Recollections*, 1889.

Jo's Boys and How They Turned Out: A Sequel to "Little Men," Roberts Brothers, 1886.

A Garland for Girls, Roberts Brothers, 1887.

A Modern Mephistopheles [and] *A Whisper in the Dark*, Roberts Brothers, 1889.

Louisa May Alcott: Her Life, Letters and Journals, edited by Ednah D. Cheney, Roberts Brothers, 1889.

Comic Tragedies Written by "Jo" and "Meg" and Acted by the Little Women, Roberts Brothers, 1893.

A Round Dozen: Stories, edited by Anne Thaxter Eaton, Viking, 1963.

Glimpses of Louisa: A Centennial Sampling of the Best Short Stories by Louisa May Alcott, edited by Cornelia Meigs, Little, Brown, 1968.

Behind a Mask: The Unknown Thrillers of Louisa May Alcott, edited by Madeleine B. Stern, Morrow, 1975.

Louisa's Wonder Book: An Unknown Alcott Juvenile, edited by Stern, Central Michigan University/ Clark Historical Library, 1975.

Plots and Counterplots: More Unknown Thrillers of Louisa May Alcott, edited by Stern, Morrow, 1976.

Diana and Persis, edited by Sarah Elbert, Ayer Company, 1978.

Transcendental Wild Oats, Harvard Common Press, 1981.

The Selected Letters of Louisa May Alcott, edited by Joel Myerson and Daniel Shealy, Little, Brown, 1987.

The Works of Louisa May Alcott, 1832-1888, Reprint Services Corp., 1987.

A Double Life: Newly Discovered Thrillers of Louisa May Alcott, edited by Stern, Little, Brown, 1988.

Alternative Alcott, edited by Elaine Showalter, Rutgers University Press, 1988.

The Journals of Louisa May Alcott, edited by Myerson and Shealy, Little, Brown, 1989.

Louisa May Alcott's Fairy Tales and Fantasy Stories, edited by Shealy, University of Tennessee Press, 1992.

Louisa May Alcott Unmasked: Collected Thrillers, edited and with an introduction by Stern, Northeastern University Press, 1995.

The Inheritance, Dutton, 1996.

Numerous stories published in books, both individually and in collections. *Little Women* has been republished in dozens of editions. Author of several unproduced melodramas, including *The Bandit's Bride* and *The Moorish Maiden's Vow*. Also contributor of "sensational" fiction, appearing in periodicals and dime novels anonymously or under pseudonyms. Contributor to numerous periodicals. Works translated in numerous foreign languages. Alcott family papers collected at Houghton Library, Harvard University.

■ Adaptations

Several film and television adaptations have been made of Alcott's work, including *Little Women*, Famous Players, Lasky Corp., 1919, RKO, 1933, Metro-Goldwin-Mayer, 1949, CBS-TV, 1950, British Broadcasting Corporation, 1970, Movie International Co. (series of cartoon films), 1981, Harmony Gold, Ltd. (feature-length cartoon), 1983, and Columbia Tristar, 1994; *Little Men*, Mascott, 1934, and RKO, 1940; and *An Old-Fashioned Girl*, Pathe Industries, 1949. Several sound recordings of Alcott's work have also been made, including *Little Women*, Caedmon, 1975 and 1991; Mind's Eye, 1979; Random House, 1986 and 1994; Penguin Audio, 1995.

■ Sidelights

If longevity is any benchmark for literary greatness, then Louisa May Alcott would qualify. Her novel *Little Women*, published in 1868, still attracts legions of readers well over a century after publication and inspires both popular movies and scholarly volumes of criticism. Alcott was one of the first authors for young readers to be taken seriously by critics, to write stories that entertained rather than simply preached. Her novels "set a new standard for excellence in full characterization, both of the attractive and unattractive qualities of children," noted Ruth K. MacDonald in *Dictionary of Literary Biography*. In her day, the novels Alcott wrote in the "Little Women" series were hugely popular, making Alcott a well-off, independent writer. Fashions change, but the popularity of *Little Women* remains; even in the age of feminist criticism, there are things to like about her books, according to some critics and scholars. In her *Reinventing Womanhood*, Carolyn G. Heilbrun declared *Little Women* to be "one of the most revolutionary voices in American fiction about family roles and the expectations of girls. . . ." The Alcott industry, is, in fact, in full bloom, which would have pleased the practical dollars-and-cents side of Alcott. The discovery and thorough publication of Alcott's thriller fiction—which she wrote pseudonymously—has also increased her critical stature. According to Sarah Elbert in *AB Bookman's Weekly*, this alternate fiction is "evidence of Alcott's rise from 'minor' writer to 'great' author in the canon of American literature."

Alcott wrote her own life; lightly veiled autobiography is what she served up to a readership that was seldom disappointed. As she noted in a journal entry at the time of publication of *Little Women*, the book was not a "bit sensational, but simple and true, for we really lived most of it; and if it succeeds that will be the reason for it." It is the word "most" that needs underlining, for if the fictional Jo's life in *Little Women* was an idealized version of domestic life for readers, it was also partly so for the author herself. Alcott's was not an idyllic upbringing.

A Transcendental Education

Born in Germantown, Pennsylvania, on November 29, 1832, Alcott was the second of four daughters (a son died at birth) of Amos Bronson Alcott and Abigail May. Bronson was a noted transcendentalist philosopher, son of an English pioneering family that was among the first settlers of New England. The Alcott's were successful—hard-working and industrious—but Bronson managed to escape the world of manual labor for a life of the mind. Praised and sponsored by such luminaries as Ralph Waldo Emerson and Henry David Thoreau, Bronson set out as a teacher, promulgating what were in his day revolutionary methods: a focus on spiritual, physical, and creative development, and a complete avoidance of rote memorization of dates and facts. In short, it was an education for the "whole" child. Bronson Alcott wanted to create critical thinking in his pupils without destroying their emotional side; he encouraged individuality and originality. Of course he was doomed to failure.

The Alcott household consisted of older sister Anna, then Louisa, and two younger sisters, Elizabeth and May. Hard work mixed with heady thinking was a staple at the Alcott's. Alcott and her mother were very close, and it was from her that Louisa won encouragement to write. Indeed, each of the children fostered a special artistic skill—painting, sculpting, drama, music. Together, the children would put on plays and musical productions. Theirs was a peripatetic life, always on the move from one school to another as the father tried to eke out a living under hostile conditions. It did not help that Bronson Alcott was also staunchly abolitionist in a town like Boston which was pro-slavery. Parents, at first charmed by Bronson Alcott, would later yank their children out of his schools when they displayed independent thought. Bronson Alcott's own children were educated in these schools and at home, but the living was precarious. The Germantown school folded shortly after Louisa's birth, and there followed a series of other such failures. A six-year residency in Boston at the Masonic Temple School came to an end over an abolitionist pamphlet that Bronson wrote. Then followed the disastrous experiment in communal living at Fruitlands near Harvard, Massachusetts. This commune lasted a bare seven months and almost succeeded in ripping the family apart. "I was very unhappy," the young Alcott wrote in her journal, "and prayed God to keep us all together." It was a formative experience for her. The family moved to Concord with the help of Emerson, but the father was never again to be counted on as breadwinner.

Four sisters from a close-knit family learn the value of hard work and self-reliance in this 1868 classic.

Louisa May saw it all with the open eyes of youth. She recognized the inspiration of her father's idealism, but also experienced the financial effects such idealism had on the family. It was then she resolved that she would help to keep the family together by becoming the breadwinner. She was twelve at the time.

Though money was in short supply, ideas were decidedly not. The Alcott children had an education to be envied. Emerson, who became Alcott's hero, was a close friend and neighbor. Louisa, as

tutor to Emerson's daughter, had free access to the man's excellent library, reading literary classics as well as philosophy. Thoreau was her botany teacher, and there was a constant stream of influential thinkers in the household: Margaret Fuller, Elizabeth Peabody, Julia Ward Howe, and James Russell Lowell among others. Nathaniel Hawthorne was a reclusive neighbor, though the Alcott children played with the Hawthorne children. The girls were taught the virtue of hard work and of play, as well. They each kept journals, which the parents regularly read—for such journals were meant to be a record of pure if not noble thoughts. It was a close-knit, self-reliant household. High ideals were always foremost, and the support of reform causes such as abolition, coeducation, vegetarianism, and women's suffrage were a given.

From Concord the family moved back to Boston, and even tighter financial times with the mother doing social work and the children tutoring and taking in sewing. However, the family still found time for volunteer work. By 1850, Alcott was teaching and beginning to write with the intention of publication. Her early efforts included sentimental short stories and gothic thrillers, written largely under the pseudonym of A. M. Barnard for such publications as the *Saturday Evening Gazette, Frank Leslie's Illustrated Paper,* and even the *Atlantic Monthly.* She soon discovered that she could turn out such stories quickly and earn a reasonable return for her efforts, some of the later ones earning $40 each. Publication of her first book came in 1855, a collection of fairy tales she had written for young Ellen Emerson whom she had tutored. The collection, *Flower Fables,* won some notice because it was sponsored by Mrs. Nathaniel Hawthorne. The work earned Alcott $32, though her editor advised her stick to teaching instead of writing. Heavily didactic, the fairy tales deal with flowers, children, animals, and fairies, and through the course of each tale, the protagonist learns some lesson: being selfless, controlling your temper, and the like. "The themes are all ordinary," MacDonald noted in *Dictionary of Literary Biography,* "commonplaces of literature for children at the time, and the collection is altogether undistinguished." Publication of the book, however, encouraged Alcott, both with her potboilers and with two novels for adults on which she was laboring.

From Youth to Womanhood

In 1858, Alcott's sister Elizabeth died after a long illness. Alcott herself had provided much of the care during this time. In her diary of March 14, 1858, Alcott wrote: "My dear Beth died at three this morning, after two years of patient pain. . . . Saturday she slept, and at midnight became unconscious, quietly breathing her life away till three; then, with one last look of the beautiful eyes, she was gone." The next month she noted, "Death, never seemed terrible to me, and now is beauti-ful; so I cannot fear it, but find it friendly and wonderful." Not long after this, the oldest sister, Anna, married, marking the end of the cohesive family unit. Alcott continued to work on her stories and two adult novels, but with the coming of the Civil War in 1861, she volunteered for nursing work at the Union Hospital in Washington, D.C. Though the nursing experience would only last seven weeks, it was another turning point in her life. A bout of typhoid fever ended Alcott's service, and its treatment with mercury would affect her the rest of her days, causing her to take to her bed for protracted periods of time.

Alcott also sent letters home to her family during her short sojourn in Washington. These she soon edited and published as *Hospital Sketches,* a book that won her some degree of renown. The public was anxious for any information it could get on the soldiers, and thus the book sold well in the North. Alcott's lightness of tone also helped to make the book a success. As she noted in the introduction to the book, she wanted to "send home cheerful reports even from the saddest of scenes," and to "make the best of everything." Tribulation Periwinkle, the author's persona in the book, is a realist who describes the horrors of the hospital in clear speech, depicting suffering with a degree of nobility in the sufferer and also with a degree of humor. The success of the book and its realistic style—as opposed to the florid passages of some of her thriller fiction—surely was influential in Alcott's development. Here were all the elements that would later inform her "Little Women" books: a plain almost colloquial style, good local color and sense of scene, solid characterization, and a wry sense of humor.

The success of *Hospital Sketches* encouraged Alcott to finish one of her adult novels, and in 1865 *Moods* was published. Though this would remain Alcott's favorite book, it was not well received. With the proceeds from these two books, however, and working as a companion to an invalid, Alcott was able to travel to Europe, visiting Paris and London. Returning to Concord in 1866, she resumed writing her gothic thrillers to earn money for the family. She took over editorship of a children's magazine, *Merry's Museum,* for which she wrote a short story about four girls who give away their Christmas breakfast to a poor immigrant family. Alcott's editor at Roberts Brothers, publishers of her earlier books, encouraged her to write a novel for girls, but Alcott was not initially enthused about the project.

Little Women

The carrot of success, however, drove Alcott on, and soon she was determined to base her novel on her own family life. Discussing it with her mother and sisters, she won their approval. "So I plod away, though I don't enjoy this sort of thing," she wrote in her journal of the time. "Never liked girls or knew many, other than my sisters; but our queer plays and experiences might be interesting, though I doubt it." Within six weeks she had the completed manuscript of what would become part one of *Little Women,* and still both she and her editor were less than sanguine about its qualities. Yet once published, the book was an instant success, sending Alcott back to her desk to dash off in two months a sequel, at first titled *Good Wives* and changed to *Little Women or, Meg, Jo, Beth, and Amy, Part Second.* The two have ever since been published in one volume.

Little Women traces the lives of the four sisters in the March family from adolescence to early adulthood. Often compared to John Bunyan's classic *Pilgrim's Progress,* the book teaches the difficult lessons of life such as hard work and obedience as it follows the sisters through various episodic situations and adventures. Often blatantly sentimental, the novel does provide a relatively realistic look at mid-nineteenth century domestic life. Part one of the novel deals with about one year in the life of the March family, consisting of Meg, Jo, Beth, and Amy, as well as the mother—Marmee—and an absent father off serving as a chaplain in the Civil War. There is also the servant Hannah who often provides a voice of reason and common sense. The characters are clearly drawn from life: Anna is the fictional Meg, the oldest and the one who carries the responsibility for the younger children. But Meg, like Anna, also longed for another world, one free from financial distress and full of the finer things in life. Jo is clearly a recreation of Alcott herself, the rebellious one in the family, the writer who retreats to the attic to scribble away. The tomboy, she publishes her sensational stories for money and pokes fun at piousness in all its guises. The fictional Beth is drawn from the real Elizabeth, and like her is of frail health and dies young. Shy and of good cheer, she is the pure one of the family. The youngest March is Amy, based on May, and is artistic as well as conventional and at times trying. Binding the family together is Marmee, the mother, a rock who is always there for her children; unflappable, predictable, steady, and understanding. In short, everyone's ideal mother. It is significant that the March father is absent throughout most of part one, off with the Union Army, just as Bronson Alcott was absent in many spiritual and material ways from his family.

Beginning with a Christmas breakfast, the story follows the March sisters through four seasons of growth. Jo grows as a writer and tutor to young children; Meg fights her resentment at the family's difficult financial position; Beth is supportive and very much a do-gooder in the community; and young Amy tries to understand the world of womanhood her sisters are entering. The sisters adopt the young man next door, Laurie, allowing him to join their dramatic Pickwick Club. Laurie and Jo form a special friendship, an androgynous twinning of sorts, in which each gains attributes the other possesses. Meg, meanwhile, has also formed an attachment for Mr. Brooke, Laurie's tutor. The girls are always busy with chores, sewing and cooking and folding bandages for the soldiers. Throughout the year the four girls have consciously improved on their personal faults. Marmee is called away suddenly to nurse her husband, wounded at the front, and then Beth falls ill with scarlet fever. The doctor gives up hope, but Marmee, alerted by Laurie, returns and nurses her daughter back to health, though Beth never fully recovers. Part one ends with the second Christmas and the surprise return of the father.

Four years elapse between part one and part two of the novel. Autobiography is now replaced with more fictional techniques. Meg and Mr. Brooke marry, an echo of the real-life sister Anna's marriage, and the girls continue with their various pursuits, both artistic and domestic. Meg now has a house of her own, and Jo is working as a governess in New York. Young Amy, meanwhile is off on a grand tour of Europe with Aunt March. Laurie is still at college, and then goes off to Europe for a time to find himself—much at the instigation of Jo—and his friendship for her has turned into real affection. However, when he asks Jo to marry him, she refuses. Instead he marries Amy. Beth dies—another real event—but in the end Jo does marry, something that Alcott never did. Alcott the writer obviously had her eye on marketability when she had Jo join with Professor Bhaer, a poor German intellectual, knowing that the conventional happy ending for a young woman was marriage rather than career. Bhaer, in fact, insists that Jo stop her sensational writing—a demand to which she acquiesces. Together the two start a school and have two sons. Though married, hers is not the traditional sort of marriage her sisters Meg and Amy have opted for.

A financial success at publication, the books forming *Little Women* were also warmly received by critics. A reviewer in the *Nation* noted that the book was "not only very well adapted to the readers for whom it is especially intended but may also be read with pleasure by older people."

This tale, the followup to Alcott's classic first novel, *Little Women*, follows Jo, Meg, Amy, and Beth into young adulthood.

From the outset, the reception of the books was influenced by the strong individuality displayed by each of the four sisters, even though they are at times irreverent and use not only slang words but also "mild curses," as MacDonald pointed out. *Harper's*, reviewing part two of the novel, noted that it was a "rather mature book for the little women, but a capital one for their elders." It is partly this refusal on Alcott's part to talk down to her young readers that has insured the lasting popularity of *Little Women*. And it has endured, never having gone out of print since its original publication and now published in over a dozen languages.

With the book's centenary in 1968 came a flotilla of new criticism, followed close upon by feminist revision. Some modern critics, such as Brigid Brophy, writing in the *New York Times Book Review*, found the novel worked in spite of the heavy sentimentalizing. Brophy called Jo "one of the most blatantly autobiographical yet most fairly treated heroines in print." Lavinia Russ, however, in *Horn Book* felt that Brophy was wrong, noting that girls all over the world love the book not because of its sentimentality, but because it makes them realize that "life is not going to hold a neat, happy ending for her. . . . [Girls] are right to love *Little Women*, every word of it, because it is a story about *good* people." The critic Elizabeth Janeway, writing in *Only Connect: Readings on Children's Literature*, while conceding that *Little Women* is "dated and sentimental and full of preaching and moralizing," also commented that the character of Jo is what makes the book continue to be read. "Jo is a unique creation," Janeway wrote, "the one young woman in nineteenth-century fiction who maintains her individual independence, who gives up no part of her autonomy as payment for being a woman." Other critics have focussed on the portrayal of family life in the novel and have concluded, like Constantine Georgiou in *Children and Their Literature*, that "As a family chronicle, this plotless story honestly reveals everyday happenings with accurate details that mark the account as a social history of the nineteenth century."

Yet not all critics saw the work as a positive achievement. In her 1977 biography of Alcott, *Louisa May*, Martha Saxton contended that *Little Women* was an artistic sell-out for the author, a simplistic tale full of moralizing, and that Alcott had backed away from serious fiction as a result of the cool reception of her adult novel, *Moods*. Other critics wrote of Jo's masochism for both cutting off her hair to earn money for her mother's journey to Washington to nurse her husband, and in cutting off her artistry when she agreed to stop writing her sensational stories at the request of her own husband. However, Stephanie Harrington in the *New York Times* countered many of these arguments by calling *Little Women* "a feminist tract," which depicted a "liberated" woman for her time. That Alcott's novel provides so many possible interpretations is part of the reason for its longevity. As Alison Lurie noted in the *New York Review of Books*, "From a mid-nineteenth-century perspective, *Little Women* is both a conservative and a radical novel. . . . In contemporary terms, [Jo] has it all: not only a husband and children but two careers and she doesn't have to do her own housework and cooking."

An Author of Note

Alcott's was a household name after the publication of both parts of *Little Women*. She was also a wealthy woman, well able to support herself and the remaining members of her family. Never marrying, Alcott lived a somewhat independent life of a novelist, though she continued to bear the financial burden for the family until her death. She followed up the success of the March family in 1869 with *An Old-Fashioned Girl*, serialized in the *Merry Museum* and then published in two parts in 1870. The juvenile novels of Alcott's middle years are often grouped together as the "Little Women" series, though in fact the March family figures in only two further books, *Little Men* and *Jo's Boys*. However, Alcott employed many of the same techniques in other novels such as *An Old-Fashioned Girl*: a flawed but likeable main character who tries to better herself; a realistic depiction of scene; and a simplicity of language and clarity of style that presents a moral and still avoids being merely preachy.

The old-fashioned girl of the title is Polly Milton, fourteen, off to visit the wealthy Shaws and their three children. A foreshadowing of such families in the twentieth century, the Shaws have material possessions but are not happy. Mr. Shaw is too busy making money to be with his children who are generally left to their own devices, while Mrs. Shaw is a nervous wreck who takes to her bed.

This 1871 work describes the efforts of Jo Bhaer to teach a group of orphan boys at her Plumfield school.

The Shaws are blithely ignorant of the trials and tribulations of those less fortunate economically than they, and are snobbish when it comes to Polly trying to earn her own way by teaching music. The Shaws are a foil to the March family—whereas the latter made the most of the least in terms of material possession, the Shaws are unsatisfied even with all their money. Polly later becomes something of a model for the Shaws, and in particular for her friend Fanny, when the family loses its money. Polly is not the strong character that Jo is, but the book does make telling comments about the inadequacy of the curriculum for young women in schools.

The book secured Alcott's reputation, selling 27,000 copies within the first month after publication. "Let whoever wishes to read a bright, spirited, wholesome story get the *Old-Fashioned Girl* at once!" declared a reviewer for the *Athenaeum* in its 1870 review, and a critic in the *Atlantic Monthly* commented that it is "a pretty story, a very pretty story; and almost inexplicably pleasing." MacDonald in *Dictionary of Literary Biography* noted that the book revolved around its main character, just as did *Little Women*. But where Jo was a character of many parts, "Polly is too good to be true," MacDonald wrote, noting also that *An Old-Fashioned Girl* did not have the same "vibrancy or vigor" of the first novel.

In fact, Alcott replayed many of the same themes for the rest of her writing life. Employing the *Little Women* formula, she succeeded in turning out two more March family books and several other juvenile novels that had lively characters and fast-paced, episodic story lines. However, most critics agree that Alcott's best work for younger readers was her first. Money was suddenly no problem for Alcott and her family because of such writing. Off in Europe in 1870 with her younger sister May, she learned of the death of Anna's husband, John Pratt. She at once decided to write a novel, the proceeds of which should go to providing for Anna and her family. What came of this resolve was a sequel to *Little Women* titled *Little Men*.

In this book Alcott gave free rein to her views on educational reform, as the book is set at Plumfield, the house which Aunt March gave to Jo and which she set up with her husband as a school. Like *Little Women*, the novel is framed by the seasons, and *Little Men* develops an agricultural metaphor, beginning with the planting in the spring by Jo and Professor Bhaer, as if to say they are also planting the seeds of improvement in their students. There are pillow fights and picnics and much philosophizing about the proper form of education for young boys. Reviewing the book at the time, a critic in *Harper's New Monthly Magazine* commented that "The description of an actual boarding-school, with its humdrum life, would be as tedious as any thing that can well be conceived of, and that Miss Alcott is able to invest a story . . . with any interest must be taken as one of the evidences of her genius." Jo, in this installment, has become not only a famous educator but also a famous writer for children, as well as super-mom to her kids and a supportive and loving wife to her husband. The Alcott scholar, Madeleine B. Stern, noted in the *New England Quarterly* that *Little Men* does not have the depth of its predecessor: "The boys . . . lack the three-dimensional qualities of the March girls. . . . To each the author endowed one glaring fault awaiting correction by the Plumfield methods." Other critics have pointed out that underneath the sweet atmosphere of the book is another possibly darker one, as depicted in the attachment between Jo and one of her wayward students, Dan Kean, "one that Alcott describes in peculiarly sexual terms," according to MacDonald in *Dictionary of Literary Biography*. After *Little Men*, Alcott wrote no children's books for four years, finishing instead an adult novel, *Work: A Story of Experience*, that she had been laboring on for years.

Other mid-career juvenile books by Alcott include *Eight Cousins, Rose in Bloom, Under the Lilacs, Jack and Jill*, and the collections, *Aunt Jo's Scrap-Bag* and *Lulu's Library*. According to MacDonald in *Writers for Children*, "Of all [Alcott's] books for children, *Under the Lilacs* (1878) is Alcott's least satisfactory." This was perhaps, in part due to the fact Alcott was both ill herself and nursing her dying mother at the time of its writing. *Eight Cousins*, and its sequel, *Rose in Bloom*, are interesting in that Alcott wrote them both as less episodic novels than her others, and told them from the point of view of only one main character, Rose Campbell, as she goes through the sort of educational development that Bronson Alcott would have liked established for all young people. Many of these books and stories follow relatives of the March family, or residents of the same sort of New England town in which *Little Women* was set. The themes of individual development, self-worth, and educational reform as well as family life are all explored and reintroduced, and Alcott's loving portrayal of life in nineteenth-century America makes these books accessible even today.

Toward the end of her life, in 1886, Alcott published a long-awaited third-volume in the March saga, *Jo's Boys, and How They Turned Out*. In fact, Alcott had begun work on this final volume several years before, but her own ill health, her father's stroke and declining health, and her sister May's death in child-birth all delayed the writing. More outspoken now in her beliefs about women's rights, Alcott even includes in this last novel a female physician who is quite content to remain single without any disparagement of spinsterhood thrown her way. But Alcott seems to have been less than content with her creation, driven now by public demand rather than inner need. Angela M. Estes and Kathleen M. Lant, writing in *Children's Literature,* pointed out that the "crime" of Alcott's loss of her own artistic vision runs right through the "Little Women" books. Evidence of it is plain to see, they contend, in *Jo's Boys* where Jo is described by Alcott as "a literary nursery-maid providing moral pap for the young." According to Estes and Lant, "Alcott has, at this very moment, lost even her own fervid joy in the young woman who promised so much, who shone so brightly for so many readers young and old, but who could not grow into adulthood as herself, as Jo." *Jo's Boys* is generally considered the least compelling and successful of the series, though sales at the time would deny such an assertion.

Posthumous Alcott

Alcott died on March 6, 1888, just two days after her father, Bronson Alcott, passed away. The Alcott estate left provision for nieces and nephews by her sisters; Alcott had no children of her own. Quickly upon her death, the Alcott industry began, with posthumous publications of letters, journals, and sketches. Alcott became known as the Children's Friend, and *Little Women* entered the canon of the most popular children's books of all time. Her readers, however, had an inkling of another Alcott during the writer's lifetime when she published a previously anonymous piece of sensational fiction under her own name. *A Modern Mephistopheles* was filled with exotic descriptions and utilized references to both mesmerism and hashish to convey its thrills. Readers of the time were somewhat shocked, but were in the end tolerant of such a diversion. Readers of the twentieth century, however, learned that such a novel was not merely a diversion for Alcott. As early as the 1940s some more of Alcott's sensationalist magazine fiction appeared in print under her name, but from the late 1970s several volumes have appeared, giving a quite different picture of Alcott the writer.

Alcott's magazine thriller fiction has been ably tracked down and compiled in several volumes by Madeleine B. Stern, who has also written extensively on the Concord author. With publication of the first of these, *Behind a Mask: The Unknown Thrillers of Louisa May Alcott,* in 1975, a *Publishers Weekly* critic announced that "Never again will

If you enjoy the works of Louisa May Alcott, you may want to check out the following books and films:

Susan Cahill, *Among Sisters,* 1989.
Geri Ciebel Chavis, *Family: Stories from the Interior,* 1987.
The "Sebastian Sisters Quintet" by Susan Beth Pfeffer, including *Claire at Sixteen,* 1989.
Sense and Sensibility, Columbia, 1995.

you have quite the same image of this particular 'little woman.'" Here were stories of intrigue with sensational plots, and of women who do not always bow to conventions as Jo March ultimately does. "Marital sadism, inherited madness, murder and drug abuse" are among the elements of many of these stories, according to Jonathan Keates in the *Times Literary Supplement.* Reviewing the fifth of such volumes of reprints, *From Jo March's Attic: Stories of Intrigue and Suspense,* a contributor in *Publishers Weekly* noted that "Virtue always wins at least a moral victory, but not before rousing melodramas have revealed the sizzling passions surging under the laces and jewels worn by Alcott's characters."

Long stories such as *Taming a Tartar* have received much attention as a proto-feminist tract, while Alcott's recovered manuscript, *A Long Fatal Love Chase,* became a million-dollar bestseller in 1995, spending weeks on the *New York Times* bestseller list and garnering a huge paperback printing. Alcott had suddenly become beach reading, a posthumous career shift that would have amazed no one more than the author herself. Written in 1866, the suspense novel was rejected at the time as being too sensational. Young Rosamund Vivian, living alone with her grandfather on an English island, falls in love with the first stranger to come along, Philip Tempest, a man old enough to be her father. Eloping with him, she soon discovers he is married and is perhaps even a murderer. She flees to Paris, and Tempest proceeds to stalk her across Europe.

"This romantic cliffhanger about a woman pursued by her ex-lover, a relentless stalker, seems sprung from today's headlines," announced a *Publishers Weekly* critic, adding that Alcott's portrayal of Tempest shows "strong psychological insights" and that its publication should revise "our image of a complex and, it is now clear, prescient writer." Keates however, in the *Times Literary Supplement*, felt that rather than being the major work touted by its publisher and editor, the novel was merely a prelude to better things in Alcott's career. Despite its "irrepressible adrenalin-flow," Keates noted that "We enjoy this kind of thing less because of its factitious revamping of Gothic stereotypes than because we know its author could do better and did." *Little Women* appeared two years after the writing of *A Long Fatal Love Chase.*

If longevity is one mark of a great writer, another is shelf space. When an author has more—many more in this case—volumes written *about* her than she wrote, that author has arrived. More than a century after her death, Louisa May Alcott continues to intrigue and perplex. Whether taken as early feminist or conventional reinforcer of family values, one thing remains true: Alcott created characters in the March family, Jo in particular, that have stood the test of time, that still keep readers turning the page. She made the topic of family a lasting feature of children's literature; she created characters with warts and all, which was something new for children's fiction. And above all, she broke the moralizing tyranny of the children's fiction of her time, penning stories that not only educated, but also entertained.

■ Works Cited

Alcott, Louisa May, *Hospital Sketches* [and] *Camp and Fireside Stories*, Roberts Brothers, 1869.

Alcott, Louisa May, *Jo's Boys, and How They Turned Out*, Roberts Brothers, 1886.

Alcott, Louisa May, *Louisa May Alcott: Her Life, Letters and Journals*, edited by Ednah D. Cheney, Roberts Brothers, 1989.

Review of *Behind a Mask: The Unknown Thrillers of Louisa May Alcott*, *Publishers Weekly*, May 5, 1975, p. 89.

Brophy, Brigid, "A Masterpiece, and Dreadful," *New York Times Book Review*, January 17, 1965, pp. 1, 44.

Elbert, Sarah, "Challenging the Canon of American Literature," *AB Bookman's Weekly*, July 18-25, 1988, pp. 221-27.

Estes, Angela M., and Kathleen M. Lant, "Dismembering the Text: The Horror of Louisa May Alcott's *Little Women*," *Children's Literature*, Volume 17, Yale University Press, 1989, pp. 98-122.

Review of *From Jo March's Attic: Stories of Intrigue and Suspense*, *Publishers Weekly*, September 20, 1993, p. 62.

Georgiou, Constantine, *Children and Their Literature*, Prentice-Hall, 1969, p. 338.

Harrington, Stephanie, "Does 'Little Women' Belittle Women?," *New York Times*, June 10, 1973, section II, p. 9.

Heilbrun, Carolyn G., "Marriage and Family," *Reinventing Womanhood*, Norton, 1979, pp. 190-91.

Janeway, Elizabeth, "Meg, Jo, Beth, Amy, and Louisa," *Only Connect: Readings in Children's Literature*, edited by Sheila Egoff, G. T. Stubbs, and L. F. Ashley, Oxford University Press, 1969, pp. 286, 288, 290.

Keates, Jonathan, "Heaven Bless Hashish," *Times Literary Supplement*, November 10, 1995, p. 40.

Review of *Little Men*, *Harper's New Monthly Magazine*, August, 1871, p. 458.

Review of *Little Women*, *Nation*, October 22, 1868, p. 335.

Review of *Little Women*, *Harper's*, August, 1869, pp. 455-56.

Review of *A Long Fatal Love Chase*, *Publishers Weekly*, July 17, 1995, p. 218.

Lurie, Alison, "She Had It All," *New York Review of Books*, March 2, 1995, pp. 3-5.

MacDonald, Ruth K., "Louisa May Alcott," *Dictionary of Literary Biography*, Volume 42: *American Writers for Children before 1900*, Gale, 1985, pp. 18-36.

MacDonald, Ruth K., "Louisa May Alcott," *Writers for Children*, edited by Jane M. Bingham, Scribner's, 1988, pp. 1-6.

Review of *An Old-Fashioned Girl*, *Atlantic Monthly*, June, 1870, pp. 752-3.

Review of *An Old-Fashioned Girl*, *Athenaeum*, June 18, 1870, p. 803.

Russ, Lavinia, "Not to Be Read on Sunday," *Horn Book*, October, 1968, pp. 524, 526.

Stern, Madeleine, B., "Louisa M. Alcott: An Appreciation," *New England Quarterly*, December, 1949, pp. 475-98.

■ For More Information See

BOOKS

Bedell, Madelon, *The Alcotts*, Clarkson Potter, 1981.

Burke, Kathleen, *Louisa May Alcott*, Chelsea House, 1988.

Delamar, Gloria T., *Louisa May Alcott and "Little Women": Biography, Criticism, Critique*, McFarland, 1990.

Elbert, Sarah, *A Hunger for Home: Louisa May Alcott and Little Women*, Temple University Press, 1984.

Green, Carol, *Louisa May Alcott: Author, Nurse, Suffragette*, Children's Press, 1984.

Gulliver, Lucille, *Louisa May Alcott: A Bibliography*, B. Franklin, 1973.

MacDonald, Ruth K., *Louisa May Alcott*, Twayne, 1983.

Meigs, Cornelia, *Invincible Louisa: The Story of the Author of Little Women*, Little, Brown, 1968.

Payne, Alma J., *Louisa May Alcott: A Reference Guide*, G. K. Hall, 1980.

Santrey, Laurence, *Louisa May Alcott, Young Writer*, Troll Associates, 1986.

Saxton, Martha, *Louisa May: A Modern Biography of Louisa May Alcott*, Houghton Mifflin, 1977.

Stern, Madeleine B., *Louisa May Alcott*, University of Oklahoma Press, 1950.

Stern, Madeleine B., editor, *Critical Essays on Louisa May Alcott*, G. K. Hall, 1984.

PERIODICALS

American Literary Realism, Winter, 1973, pp. 27-45.
Children's Literature Association Quarterly, Winter, 1986, pp. 192-6; Winter, 1992, p. 42.

Contemporary Review, February, 1971, pp. 99-104.
Feminist Studies, Summer, 1979, pp. 369-70, 381-83.
Holiday, November, 1968, pp. 18, 22, 25-26.
Journal of General Education, no. 22, 1970, pp. 81-92.
Journal of Popular Culture, Winter, 1975, pp. 583-92.
Library Bulletin, May, 1975, pp. 647-50.
Library Journal, January, 1988, p. 86; December, 1993, p. 124; April 15, 1995, p. 118; August, 1995, p. 113.
Lion and the Unicorn, Fall, 1977, pp. 91-97; December, 1994, pp. 143-53.
Mademoiselle, December, 1973, p. 40.
New Republic, October 22, 1924, p. 204.
New Yorker, December 26, 1994, p. 49.
New York Times Book Review, November 9, 1969, p. 65; November 3, 1974, p. 27; July 25, 1976, p. 7; November 14, 1982, p. 49; January 14, 1990, p. 31.
Novel: A Forum on Fiction, Fall, 1972, pp. 36-51; Fall, 1976, pp. 6-26.
Publishers Weekly, January 13, 1997, p. 54.
Redbook, December, 1975, pp. 149-50.
School Library Journal, March, 1988; December, 1993, p. 78.
Times Literary Supplement, April 6, 1989, p. 332; June 7, 1991, p. 11.
Washington Post, November 3, 1968, p. 34.*

—Sketch by J. Sydney Jones

Rudolfo Anaya

■ Personal

Full name, Rudolfo Alfonso Anaya; born October 30, 1937, in Pastura, NM; son of Martin (a cattle and sheep rancher) and Rafaelita (Mares) Anaya; married Patricia Lawless (a writer), 1966. *Education:* Attended Browning Business School, 1956-58; University of New Mexico, B.A., 1963, M.A., 1968, M.A., 1972.

■ Addresses

Home—5324 Canada Vista, N.W., Albuquerque, NM 87120.

■ Career

Writer and educator. Junior high and high school teacher in Albuquerque, NM, 1963-70; University of Albuquerque, Albuquerque, director of counseling, 1971-73, associate professor of creative writing and Chicano literature, 1974-88, professor, 1988-1993. Lecturer at various universities around the world, including Universidad Anahuac, Mexico City, Mexico, summer, 1974; University of Haifa, Israel, 1986; University of Bordeaux, 1986; University of New Mexico Scholars Exchange Program with Trujillo, Spain, 1988; St. John's College, 1988; Fort Lewis College, 1988; University of Colorado, 1988; Colorado College, 1988; Pike's Peak Community College, 1988; Clark County Community College, 1989; California State University at Los Angeles, 1989; Texas A & M University, 1989; Chico State University, 1989; Yale University; University of Michigan; Michigan State University; University of California at Los Angeles; University of Indiana; University of Texas at Houston. Instructor or lecturer at various seminars and conferences around the world, including New Mexico Writers' Workshop, summers, 1977-79; Quebec Writers Exchange, Trois Riviéres, 1982; Brazil International Seminar, 1984; Southwest Regional Conference of English Language Arts, Albuquerque, NM. The Loft, Minneapolis, MN, writer-in-residence, 1989. *Member:* Rio Grande Writers Association, founder and first president.

■ Awards, Honors

Premio Quinto Sol literary award, 1971; literary award, University of New Mexico Mesa Chicana, 1977; award, City of Los Angeles, 1977; Governor's Public Service Award, New Mexico, 1978, 1980; fellowships, National Chicano Council on Higher Education, 1979, 1980; fellowship, National Endowments for the Arts, 1979; book award, Before Columbus Foundation, 1980, for *Tortuga;*

Governor's Award for Excellence and Achievement in Literature, New Mexico, 1980; literature award, Delta Kappa Gamma, New Mexico, 1981; Script Development award, Corporation for Public Broadcasting, 1982, Award for Achievement in Chicano Literature, Hispanic Caucus of Teachers of English, 1983; fellowship, Kellogg Foundation, 1983-85; Mexican Medal of Friendship, Mexican Consulate of Albuquerque, New Mexico, 1986; New Mexico Eminent Scholar, 1989; PEN Center West Award for fiction, for *Alburquerque*; honorary doctorates from universities including University of Albuquerque, 1981, and Marycrest College, 1984.

■ Writings

NOVELS

Bless Me, Ultima, Tonatiuh International, 1972, published in Spanish as *Bendiceme, Ultima*, translated by Alicia Smithers, Warner, 1994.

Heart of Aztlán, Editorial Justa, 1976.

Tortuga, Editorial Justa, 1979.

The Legend of La Llorona, Tonatiuh/Quinto Sol International, 1984.

Lord of the Dawn: The Legend of Quetzacoatl, University of New Mexico Press, 1987.

Alburquerque, University of New Mexico Press, 1992.

Zia Summer, Warner Books, 1995.

Jalamanta: A Message from the Desert, Warner Books, 1996.

Rio Grande Fall, Warner Books, 1996.

PLAYS

The Season of Llorona (one-act play) first produced in Albuquerque, NM, at El Teatro de la Compañía de Albuquerque, October 14, 1979.

Who Killed Don José?, first produced in Albuquerque, NM, at La Compañía Menval High School Theatre, July, 1987.

The Farolitos of Christmas, first produced in Albuquerque, New Mexico, at La Compañía Menval High School Theatre, December, 1987.

Also author of plays, *Matachines* and *Billy the Kid*. Author of "Rosa Linda," an unproduced play written for the Corporation for Public Broadcasting; author of the Visions Project, unpublished and unproduced dramas for KCET-TV in Los Angeles.

SHORT STORIES

"The Place of the Swallows," *Voices from the Rio Grande*, Rio Grande Writers Association Press, 1976.

"Requiem for a Lowrider," *La Confluencia*, Volume 2, number 2-3, 1978.

"A Story," *Grito del sol*, Quinto Sol Publications, 1979.

"B. Traven Is Alive and Well in Cuernavaca," *Escolios*, May-November, 1979; *Cuentos Chicanos*, revised edition, University of New Mexico Press, 1984.

The Silence of the Llano (collected short stories), Tonatiuh/Quinto Sol International, 1982.

"The Road to Platero," *Rocky Mountain Magazine*, April, 1982.

"The Captain," *A Decade of Hispanic Literature*, Revista Chicano-Riqueña Press, 1982.

"The Village Which the Gods Painted Yellow," *Nuestro*, January/February, 1983.

"In Search of Epifano," *Wind Row*, Spring, 1987; *Voces*, El Norte-Academia, 1987.

"The Farolitos of Christmas" (for children), *New Mexico Magazine*, 1987.

"Children of the Desert," published as "Figli del Deserto," *L'Umana Avventura*, Editorial Jaca, 1989.

Also author of "The Gift," *2 Plus 2, A Collection of International Writing*, edited by James Gill, Mylabriss Press.

EDITED WORKS

(With Jim Fisher, and contributor) *Voices from the Rio Grande*, Rio Grande Writers Association Press, 1976.

(With Antonio Márquez) *Cuentos Chicanos: A Short Story Anthology*, University of New Mexico Press, 1980.

(With Simon J. Ortiz) *A Ceremony of Brotherhood, 1680-1980*, Academia Press, 1981.

Voces: An Anthology of Nuevo Mexicano Writers, University of New Mexico Press, 1987.

Tierra: Contemporary Fiction of New Mexico (short story collection), Cinco Puntos, 1989.

(With Francisco Lomeli) *Aztlán: Essays on the Chicano Homeland*, El Norte, 1989, University of New Mexico Press, 1991.

Blue Mesa Review, Volume 8: Approaching the Millennium, Blue Mesa Review/Creative Writing Center, University of New Mexico, 1996.

OTHER

Bilingualism: Promise for Tomorrow (screenplay), Bilingual Educational Services, 1976.

(Contributor) Charlotte I. Lee and Frank Galati, editors, *Oral Interpretations*, 5th edition, Houghton, 1977.

(Contributor) *New Voices 4 in Literature, Language and Composition*, Ginn, 1978.

(Author of introduction) Sabine Ulibarri, *Mi abuela fumaba puros*, Tonatiuh International, 1978.

(Contributor) *Anuario de letras chicanas*, Editoral Justa, 1979.

(Translator) *Cuentos: Tales from the Hispanic Southwest, Based on Stories Originally Collected by Juan B. Rael*, edited by José Grieto y Maestas, Museum of New Mexico Press, 1980.

The Adventures of Juan Chicaspatas (epic poem), Arte Público, 1985.

A Chicano in China (nonfiction), University of New Mexico Press, 1986.

The Farolitos of Christmas (a children's book), illustrated by Edward Gonzales, Hyperion, 1995.

Selected from "Bless Me, Ultima," Literary Volumes of New York City, 1989.

(Contributor) Ulibarri, Sabine R., *Flow of the Rivers: Corre el Rio* (translated by Jesus Guzman), Hispanic Culture Foundation, 1992.

(Author of foreword) *Growing Up Chicana-O: An Anthology*, edited by Tiffany A. Lopez, William Morrow, 1993.

(Author of introduction) Bryan Howard, *The Incredible Elfego Baca*, Clear Light Publishers, 1993.

(Contributing author) *Man on Fire: Luis Jimenez/El hombre en llamas*, translated by Margarita B. Montalvo, The Albuquerque Museum, 1994.

(Author of foreword) *Writing the Southwest*, edited by David K. Dunaway, NAL/Dutton, 1995.

The Anaya Reader, Warner Books, 1995.

(Author of introduction) David L. Witt, *Spirit Ascendant: The Art and Life of Patrocino Barela*, Red Crane Books, September, 1996.

Maya's Children (children's book), illustrated by Maria Baca, Hyperion, 1997.

Contributor of short stories, articles, essays, and reviews to periodicals in the United States and other countries, including *La Luz, Bilingual Review-Revista Bilingüe, New Mexico Magazine, La Confluencia, Contact II, Before Columbus Review, Literatura Uchioba*, and *New York Times Book Review*; contributor to *Albuquerque News*. Anaya's manuscripts are held at the Zimmerman Museum, University of New Mexico, Albuquerque. Coordinating Council of Literary Magazines, vice-president, 1974-80; *Blue Mesa Review*, editor; *American Book Review*, associate editor, 1980-85; *Escolios*, associate editor; *Viazlán*, regional editor; *International Chicano Journal of Arts and Letters*, regional editor; *Puerto Del Sol Literary Magazine*, member of advisory board. Work has been translated into German and Polish.

■ Sidelights

The sixteen-year-old boy laughed with his friends as he approached an irrigation-ditch pool for a swim. But as Rudolfo Anaya dove into the water, "the world disappeared." When he finally came to, he could not move. "I felt a panic I had never felt before. Death was coming for me, and I could not move in protest. . . . I knew I was about to drown. But my instinct for survival had been sharpened too well for me to give up without a struggle. It was not my time to die."

The teen-aged Anaya was right—he would not die. Yet the accident and resulting paralysis, from which he eventually recovered, changed his life forever. As Anaya recalled in *Contemporary Authors Autobiography Series* (*CAAS*), it was this accident that made him "determined to do more than my more abled friends had ever done. I fished, scaled the mountains of Taos, hunted with Cruz from the pueblo, finished high school, entered the university, married, and began to travel. I climbed mountains and crossed oceans and deserts in foreign places my old friends back home didn't know existed."

That was not all. Anaya grew up to become a celebrated American writer. His first novel, *Bless Me, Ultima*, brought a new voice, a fresh perspective, and another range of concerns to American literature; it revealed a part of the physical and cultural landscape of America that had been little noticed before. Furthermore, as Antonio Márquez, writing in *The Magic of Words*, has explained, Anaya became "the most acclaimed and the most popular and universal Chicano writer, and one of the most influential voices in contemporary Chicano literature" whose work "has inspired the largest body of criticism in contemporary Chicano literature." Finally, Anaya became a protector and promoter of Chicano culture. Each of his works, wrote Kevin McIlvoy of *Los Angeles Times Book Review*, is a "'fiesta,' a ceremony preserving but reshaping old traditions that honor the power within the land and *la raza,* the people."

Growing up in New Mexico

"People ask me why I became a writer," Anaya commented in *CAAS.* "My answer is that I became a writer in my childhood. . . . The characters of my childhood, the family, friends, and neighbors that made up my world, they and their lives fed my imagination." Anaya spent the first part of his childhood in Santa Rosa, New Mexico, near the Pecos River. There he roamed about the *llano,* the plains, with his friends, hunting, exploring the river, swimming, and fishing. At home, with his mother and sisters, he learned the catechism in Spanish, and as he explained in *CAAS,* "was molded into a good Catholic." Still, Anaya "kept asking the sisters and the priest uncomfortable questions." When Anaya went to school, he learned English, despite the fact that "[m]oving from a world of Spanish into a world of English was shocking." "My mother was fanatic about school, not one day was to be lost," he explained. "She knew the value of education."

Anaya's life began to change when during his adolescent years. He began to notice, for the first time, how racial prejudice could divide friends. His family moved to Albuquerque, and he began to cope with urban life. He played football and baseball, and worked hard to avoid gangs and trouble. He was in high school when the dive into the irrigation ditch fractured two vertebrae in his neck and paralyzed him. The help of doctors, nurses, his friends and family, along with Anaya's own determination to walk again, helped him to recover.

Anaya completed high school with good grades, and went on to study business to become an accountant. Finding this vocation unfulfilling, he enrolled at the University of Albuquerque. He worked and went to classes during the day and studied at night. While working his way through college was difficult enough, Anaya had other obstacles to overcome. There was little at the University that informed students about Mexican American and Indian history and culture. Anaya, along with other Mexican American students, were "unprepared by high school to compete as scholars. . . . The thought was still prevalent in the world of academia that we were better suited as

janitors than scholars." Anaya and his friends often had difficulty with English which "was still a foreign language to us," and their speech patterns were regarded as wrong and were corrected. He explained in *CAAS,* "We were different and we were made to feel different. It was a lonely time; many of us did not survive."

The Recreation of Ultima

Despite the obstacles he faced, Anaya developed a love for literature in a freshman English class. He read avidly and began to write poetry and novels. Much of his early work concerned his loss

In this 1972 work, a young boy's life is forever changed through the teachings of a *curandera,* or healer, named Ultima.

of faith in God that came about as a result of his university studies and after a broken relationship. Anaya later destroyed much of this early work and then began again. He later graduated from college and began a teaching career. He also married Patricia Lawless, "the one person who truly believed" that Anaya could become a writer, and the person who would serve Anaya as both an editor and a mentor. Anaya not only wrote after school (he worked as a junior high and high school teacher during this time), he wrote in "a vacuum." He lamented in *CAAS*, "I had no Chicano models to read and follow, no fellow writers to turn to for help."

It was during this time, in the 1960s, that Anaya began work on what would eventually become *Bless Me, Ultima*. He wrote every day, rewriting and reworking versions of the novel for seven years. *Bless Me, Ultima* recalls the wonder of Ultima, la Grande, a *curandera*, or healer, who heavily influenced Anaya as a child. According to Anaya in *CAAS*, Ultima also appeared to Anaya while he was writing his novel. "Ultima opened my eyes and let me see the roots of my soul." *Bless Me, Ultima* begins when Ultima comes to stay with a six-year-old boy's family. The boy (Antonio Juan Márez y Luna) becomes Ultima's friend and apprentice; through her he learns to see the llano with new eyes, and how to use its plants to help people. Yet Ultima's arrival also brings change. When she heals one of Antonio's uncles, a man beset by witches' curses, the witches' father vows revenge. Much of the suspense in the novel comes from this man's evil intentions, Utima's spiritual battle with him, and Antonio's desparate attempts to protect Ultima.

Bless Me, Ultima also follows the boy's development over the course of the few years that Ultima stays with the family. It is an exciting time for Antonio. His brothers are coming home from the battle fields of World War II, and Antonio is about to start school. But he is also worried about his destiny: will he become a wandering *vaquero*, like his father's people the Márez, or a farmer in harmony with the earth, like his mother's brothers the Lunas? Will he make his mother's dream come true, and be a priest? Will he become, as Ultima says, a man of letters? In his first year of catechism, Antonio also ponders the nature of God and wonders why God lets bad things happen to good people. After seeing a majestic, golden carp and hearing a story that the carp is a god, he wonders if there is more than one god. Finally, Antonio wonders why Ultima's magic prevails where the work of the Catholic church has failed. Antonio's tender, young faith is beset with questions and doubts; his worst fears take expression in the dream sequences included in each chapter.

The Glorious Reception of *Bless Me, Ultima*

At first, Anaya had difficulty getting his work published. "I approached dozens of publishers, the result was always the same. I collected enough form letter rejections to wallpaper the proverbial room, but I was undaunted," Anaya wrote in *CAAS*. Finally, he noticed a call for manuscripts from the editors of a magazine called *El Grito*. Anaya sent them a letter, and when they finally responded, it was with an offer to publish his novel.

When *Bless Me, Ultima* won the Premio Quinto Sol Award for the best Chicano novel of 1972, Anaya and his novel attracted a great deal of criticism, much of it positive. Antonio Márquez wrote in *The Magic of Words* that while "some critics were irritated" by its "'affectations'" and "'artistic naivete,'" *Bless Me, Ultima* was generally "well-received and enthusiastically acclaimed in some quarters." Although, according to Márquez, some critics gave the work too much praise by calling it "'an American classic,'" the book "was deservedly praised for its fine storytelling, superb craftsmanship, and the artistic and philosophic dignity that it brought to Chicano literature." "Anaya offers a valuable gift to the American scene" with his "American novel," wrote Scott Wood in *America*.

Anaya was famous: the publication of *Bless Me, Ultima* had turned him into a Chicano leader as well as a writer. "Anaya gives every indication of invigorating the cultural growth of his people and of verifying the existence of an inner force and power in their daily lives," explained Daniel Testa in *Latin American Literary Review*. In 1974, Anaya took a position in the English Department at the University of New Mexico to teach creative writing. He also began to serve on the board of the Coordinating Council of Literary Magazines, where he met other important American writers from a variety of ethnic backgrounds. Although he was working, and playing a part in the emergent Chicano movement by traveling, speaking, and meeting other Chicano writers, Anaya none-

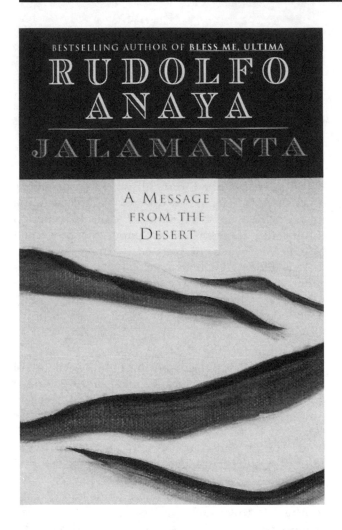

After being banished to the desert for thirty years, a man returns to his village to share the knowledge and wisdom he has acquired.

theless continued to write. He was inspired by his growing understanding of the wrongs in society, and by his travels around the country and in Mexico (where he was exploring his ancient, Mesoamerican roots). As he related in *CAAS*, he felt his pride renewed by a resounding message that was changing the society he'd grown up in: "It is good to be a Chicano!"

Heart of Aztlán, Anaya's next novel, reflects his continuing recovery of his Mesoamerican heritage with all of its precious symbols, myths, and legends. It is also a political novel that demonstrates what can happen to a people once they have been forced to leave their land. The novel begins as the Chavez family realizes that the land they've farmed for generations is depleted. They have no

other option but to move to a barrio in Albuquerque. There, the dislocated family is gradually torn apart. The children fall prey to the dangers of urban poverty, including gangs and drugs, while their father attempts to lead the people of the barrio to confront those who oppress them. According to Marvin A. Lewis in *Revista Chicano-Riqueña*, the book is "thematically concerned with a people's struggle to reconcile their myths and legends with present day realities."

Given the success of *Bless Me, Ultima*, critics often compare other works of Mexican American fiction to it—including Anaya's later novels. Lewis asserted that *Heart of Aztlán* "lacks the depth" that *Bless Me, Ultima* possesses, and that while the "principal ingredients for an outstanding work of Chicano fiction" are present in the novel, "Anaya is not able to reconcile literarily all of his thematic concerns." Another critic, Carter Wilson of *Ploughshares*, wrote that *Heart of Aztlán* "is more patiently wrought and, in that sense at least, a better piece of fiction" than *Bless Me, Ultima*.

Tortuga draws upon Anaya's experiences after his diving accident. In this novel, a teenage boy lies in a hospital, partially paralyzed and confined in a body cast. He hears the screams, cries, and tales of the children in a hospital, yet he cannot move. In despair, the boy, nicknamed "Tortuga," or turtle, because of the cast, tries to kill himself. It is only the wisdom of a terminally ill boy that allows him to appreciate the value of his own life. "Anaya works at the level of myth, dreams, and fantasy. Indeed, the principal strategy of the novel is to infuse every incident with myth," explained Angelo Restivo in *Fiction International*. In the opinion of Antonio Márquez in *The Magic of Words*, "there is an integrity and cohesiveness to *Tortuga* that were lacking in *Heart of Aztlán*. Apart from containing the rudiment of Anaya's fiction—a mythopoeic cluster of images and symbols, it discloses sharper insight and accommodation of realistic situations. . . . *Tortuga* . . . is in several respects Anaya's most accomplished novel."

Together, *Bless Me, Ultima*, *Heart of Aztlán*, and *Tortuga* make up a trilogy that traces the experience of Chicanos over several decades. Yet if these novels are about more than the Chicano experience, it is because Anaya is more than a novelist. Anaya told William Clark in a *Publishers Weekly* interview that although he thinks of himself "as a novelist . . . from the beginning, I wanted to try many things." After the publication of his first three novels, Anaya began to publish diverse works, including plays, essays, edited collections of stories, an epic poem (*The Adventures of Juan Chicaspatas*), a travel journal (*A Chicano in China*), and even a children's book (*The Farolitos of Christmas: A New Mexican Christmas Story*). Two novels, *The Legend of La Llorona* and *Lord of the Dawn: The Legend of Quetzacoatl*, are Anaya's interpretations and revisions of traditional folktales. These last projects are especially important to Anaya, who vowed in *CAAS*, "I will not rest until the people of Mexican heritage know the great cultures and civilizations they are heirs to from that country to the south."

Anaya has also published a number of short stories. Ten of these are collected in *The Silence of the Llano*. As Cordelia Candelaria noted in *Dictionary of Literary Biography*, three of the stories are excerpts from Anaya's trilogy of novels. The seven others "primarily deal with either the subject of mythmaking and the nature of fiction, or with the llano's silence." Two stories, "The Silence of the Llano" and "The Road to Platero," according to Candelaria, are tales of incest. Other stories, such as "Place of the Swallows," examine "mythmaking and the nature of fiction and its relation to lived experience." In Candelaria's opinion, "The Apple Orchard," about a boy's practical joke in school and a female teacher's surprising response, demonstrates Anaya's "chronic problem in portraying women credibly."

Alburquerque Brings Renewed Fame

In the early 1990s, Anaya began to publish a quartet of novels; each takes place in a different season. *Alburquerque*, the first of these novels, is set in New Mexico's largest city (tellingly, in the title of the book Albuquerque is spelled as it was before a sign painter dropped an "r" out of the name). While *Alburquerque* is the story of a young man who is searching for his identity, it is also the story of the maintenance and recovery of Mexican American culture, myth, and tradition in Albuquerque. Furthermore, according to Kevin McIlvoy in the *Los Angeles Times Book Review*, the work is "a tribute to how storytelling traditions should be allowed to change and develop."

Alburquerque begins after Abran Gonzalez's career as a boxer has ended and he learns that he was

adopted. He meets his real mother (a wealthy, beautiful, and acclaimed painter of Hispanos) as she is dying. Abran spends the rest of the novel learning about his deceased mother, falling in love with her nurse Lucinda, and searching for his father. As the novel progresses, an exciting mayoral contest ensues. Although McIlvoy found the depiction of the mayoral race to be "predictable melodrama," he did not think it marred the "exhilarating fiesta" or "splendid reading experience" *Alburquerque* provides. While Antonya Nelson of *New York Times Book Review* observed that Anaya had too much going on in one novel, she wrote that the work provides "moments of genuine surprise." She also especially appreciated "a series of mystical experiences," which are "wonderfully told and mesmerizing. . . . I only wish more of 'Alburquerque' were as bewitching." *Alburquerque* won the PEN Center West Award for Fiction.

Anaya's series continued with *Zia Summer*, a novel which introduces Mexican American detective Sony Baca and engages him in an effort to stop the illegal disposal of hazardous nuclear waste. *Zia Summer* was followed by *Rio Grande Fall*, in which Baca must call upon his spiritual power to solve a mystery involving the death of his cousin and the murderer of a balloonist. In the words of a critic for *Library Journal*, the novel is "a thrilling adventure." Anaya revealed to Clark in *Publishers Weekly* that the fourth novel in this series may portray another of Baca's encounters with the eco-terrorist from *Zia Summer*.

During his twenty-five year career as a prize-winning author, Anaya has described the beautiful and lonely lands of his home in New Mexico, revealed the complexities and wonders of Mexican American culture in New Mexico, and examined the themes of dislocation and recovery. His work has formed a major part of a canon of Mexican American literature that allows Mexican American students of all ages to educate themselves about their culture, heritage, and history. As Anaya has continued his own career as a writer, he has advanced the fight for the rights of people—workers, teachers, students, and Chicanos. He has also worked to make the Chicano voice more accessible in published form, and has thus paved the way for other Mexican American writers to follow his example. Given all of these contributions, we may well agree with Antonio Márquez who, writing in *The Magic of Words*, exclaimed that Anaya has received "the honor and the task of leading Chicano literature into the canons of world literature."

■ Works Cited

Anaya, Rudolfo, autobiographical sketch in *Contemporary Authors Autobiography Series*, Volume 4, Gale, 1986, pp. 15-28.

Candelaria, Cordelia, "Rudolfo A. Anaya," *Dictionary of Literary Biography*, Volume 82: *Chicano Writers*, Gale, 1989, pp. 24-35.

Clark, William, "Rudolfo Anaya: 'The Chicano Worldview,'" *Publishers Weekly*, June 5, 1995, pp. 41-42.

Lewis, Marvin A., "Heart of Aztlán,'" *Revista Chicano-Riqueña*, Summer, 1981, pp. 74-76.

Márquez, Antonio, "The Achievement of Rudolfo A. Anaya," *Magic of Words: Rudolfo A. Anaya and His Writings*, edited by Paul Vassallo, University of New Mexico Press, 1982, pp. 33-52.

McIlvoy, Kevin, "Celebrating the Old Ways," *Los Angeles Times Book Review*, August 30, 1992, p. 8.

Nelson, Antonya, "Turf Wars in New Mexico," *New York Times Book Review*, November 29, 1992, p. 22.

Restivo, Angelo, "Rudolfo A. Anaya, 'Tortuga'," *Fiction International*, Number 12, 1980, pp. 283-84.

Review of *Rio Grande Fall*, *Library Journal*, September 1, 1996, p. 213.

Testa, Daniel, "Extensive/Intensive Dimensionality In Anaya's 'Bless Me, Ultima'," *Latin American Literary Review*, Spring-Summer, 1978, pp. 70-78.

Wilson, Carter, "Magical Strength in the Human Heart," *Ploughshares*, Volume 4, number 3, 1978, pp. 190-97.

Wood, Scott, "Book Reviews: 'Bless Me, Ultima'," *America*, January 27, 1973, pp. 72-74.

■ For More Information See

BOOKS

Bruce-Nova, John David, *Chicano Authors: Inquiry by Interview*, University of Texas Press, 1980.

Gonzalez, Cesar A., *Rudolfo Anaya: Focus on Criticism*, Lalo Press, 1990.

Lomelí, Francisco A. and Donaldo W. Urioste, *Chicano Perspectives in Literature: A Critical and Annotated Bibliography*, Apparition, 1976.

PERIODICALS

Booklist, February 1, 1996, p. 915.

Entertainment Weekly, June 16, 1995, p. 56.

Horn Book, November-December, 1995, p. 727.

Library Journal, February 1, 1996, p. 64.

Nation, July 18, 1994, p. 98.

New York Times Book Review, July 2, 1995, p. 15; December 17, 1995, p. 28.

Publishers Weekly, May 25, 1992, p. 36.

School Library Journal, December, 1992, p. 36.

World Literature Today, Spring, 1979.*

—Sketch by Ronie-Richele Garcia-Johnson

Maya Angelou

■ Personal

Surname is pronounced "Ahn-ge-low"; given name, Marguerite Annie Johnson; born April 4, 1928, in St. Louis, MO; daughter of Bailey (a doorman and naval dietician) and Vivian (a registered nurse, professional gambler, and a rooming house and bar owner; maiden name, Baxter) Johnson; married Tosh Angelos, 1950 (divorced); married Paul Du Feu, December, 1973 (divorced, 1981); children: Guy. *Education:* Attended public schools in Arkansas and California; studied music privately, dance with Martha Graham, Pearl Primus, and Ann Halprin, and drama with Frank Silvera and Gene Frankel; studied cinematography in Sweden.

■ Addresses

Home—Winston-Salem, NC. *Agent*—c/o Dave La Camera, Lordly and Dame, Inc., 51 Church Street, Boston, MA 02116.

■ Career

Author, poet, scriptwriter, playwright, composer. *Arab Observer* (English-language newsweekly), Cairo, Egypt, associate editor, 1961-62; University of Ghana, Institute of African Studies, Legon-Accra, Ghana, assistant administrator of School of Music and Drama, 1963-66; freelance writer for *Ghanaian Times* and Ghanaian Broadcasting Corporation, 1963-65; *African Review,* Accra, feature editor, 1964-66. Harpo Productions, *Brewster Place* (television series), writer.

Appeared in *Porgy and Bess* on twenty-two nation tour sponsored by the U.S. Department of State, 1954-55; appeared in Off-Broadway plays, *Calypso Heatwave,* 1957, and Jean Genet's *The Blacks,* 1960; produced and performed in *Cabaret for Freedom,* Off-Broadway, 1960; appeared in *Mother Courage* at University of Ghana, 1964; appeared in *Medea* in Hollywood, 1966; television narrator, interviewer, and host for African American specials and theater series, 1972—; made Broadway debut in *Look Away,* 1973; directed film, *All Day Long,* 1974; appeared in television miniseries *Roots,* 1977; directed play, *And Still I Rise,* Oakland, CA, 1976; directed play, *Moon on a Rainbow Shawl,* by Errol John, London, 1988; appeared as Aunt June in film, *Poetic Justice,* 1993; appeared as Lelia Mae in television film, *There Are No Children Here,* 1993; appeared in advertising for the United Negro College Fund, 1994; appeared as Anna in film, *How to Make an American Quilt,* 1995.

Lecturer at University of California, Los Angeles, 1966; writer-in-residence at University of Kansas, 1970; distinguished visiting professor at Wake Forest University, Wichita State University, and California State University, Sacramento, 1974; Reynolds Professor of American Studies at Wake Forest University, 1981—; visiting professor, universities in the United States; lecturer at various locations in the United States.

Southern Christian Leadership Conference, northern coordinator, 1959-60; appointed member of American Revolution Bicentennial Council by President Gerald R. Ford, 1975-76. *Member:* American Film Institute (member of board of Trustees, 1975—), Directors Guild of America, Equity, American Federation of Television and Radio Artists, Women's Prison Association (member of advisory board), National Commission on the Observance of International Women's Year, Harlem Writer's Guild.

■ Awards, Honors

National Book Award nomination, 1970, for *I Know Why the Caged Bird Sings;* Yale University fellow, 1970; Pulitzer Prize nomination, 1972, for *Just Give Me a Cool Drink of Water 'fore I Diiie;* Tony Award nomination, 1973, for performance in *Look Away;* Rockefeller Foundation scholar in Italy, 1975; named Woman of the Year in Communications, *Ladies' Home Journal,* 1976; Emmy Award nomination, 1977, for performance in *Roots;* appointed first Reynolds Professor of American Studies at Wake Forest University, 1981; Matrix Award in the field of books, Women in Communication, Inc., 1983; North Carolina Award in Literature, 1987; Langston Hughes Award, City College of New York, 1991; Horatio Alger Award, 1992; Inaugural poet for President Bill Clinton, 1993; Grammy, Best Spoken Word Album, 1994, for recording of "On the Pulse of Morning"; etiquette award, National League of Junior Cotillions, 1993; Medal of Distinction, University of Hawaii Board of Regents, 1994; recipient of fifty honorary degrees from institutions including Smith College, 1975, Mills College, 1975, and Lawrence University, 1976.

■ Writings

AUTOBIOGRAPHY

I Know Why the Caged Bird Sings, Random House, 1974.
Gather Together in My Name, Random House, 1974.

Singin' and Swingin' and Gettin' Merry Like Christmas, Random House, 1976.
The Heart of a Woman, Random House, 1981.
All God's Children Need Traveling Shoes, Random House, 1986.
I Know Why the Caged Bird Sings [and] *The Heart of a Woman* (selections), Literacy Volunteers of New York City, 1989.

POETRY

Just Give Me a Cool Drink of Water 'fore I Diiie, Random House, 1971.
Oh Pray My Wings Are Gonna Fit Me Well, Random House, 1975.
And Still I Rise, Random House, 1978.
Shaker, Why Don't You Sing?, Random House, 1983.
Poems: Maya Angelou, four volumes, Bantam, 1986.
Now Sheba Sings the Song (a single, illustrated poem) illustrations by Tom Feelings, Dutton, 1987.
I Shall Not Be Moved, Random House, 1990.
On the Pulse of Morning, Random House, 1993.
Wouldn't Take Nothing For My Journey Now (short essays), Random House, 1993.
The Complete Collected Poems of Maya Angelou, Random House, 1994.
A Brave & Startling Truth, Random House, 1995.
Phenomenal Woman: Four Poems Celebrating Women, Random House, 1995.
(Contributor) Mary Higgins Clark, *Mother,* Pocket Books, 1996.

Also author of *The Poetry of Maya Angelou,* 1969. Contributor of poems in *The Language They Speak Is Things to Eat: Poems by Fifteen Contemporary North Carolina Poets.*

CHILDREN'S PICTURE BOOKS

Mrs. Flowers: A Moment of Friendship (selection from *I Know Why the Caged Bird Sings*), illustrations by Etienne Delessert, Redpath Press, 1986.
Life Doesn't Frighten Me (a poem), edited by Sara Jane Boyers, illustrated by Jean-Michel Basquiat, Stewart, Tabori & Chang, 1993.
(Contributor) *Soul Looks Back in Wonder,* illustrated by Tom Feelings, Dial, 1993.
My Painted House, My Friendly Chicken, & Me, photographs by Margaret Courtney-Clarke, designed by Alexander Isley Design, Crown, 1994.

Kofi and His Magic, photographs by Margaret Courtney-Clarke, Crown, 1996.

PLAYS

(With Godfrey Cambridge) *Cabaret for Freedom* (musical revue), first produced in New York City at Village Gate Theatre, 1960.

The Least of These (two-act drama), first produced in Los Angeles, 1966.

(Adapter) Sophocles, *Ajax* (two-act drama), first produced in Los Angeles at Mark Taper Forum, 1974.

(And director) *And Still I Rise* (one-act musical), first produced in Oakland, CA, at Ensemble Theatre, 1976.

(Author of lyrics with Alistair Beaton) *King*, book by Lonne Elder III, music by Richard Blackford, London, 1990.

Also author of a drama, *The Best of These*, a two-act drama, *The Clawing Within*, 1966, a two-act musical, *Adjoa Amissah*, 1967, and a one-act play, *Theatrical Vignette*, 1983.

FILM AND TELEVISION

Georgia, Georgia (screenplay), Independent-Cinerama, 1972.

(And director) *All Day Long* (screenplay), American Film Institute, 1974.

(Writer of script and musical score) *I Know Why the Caged Bird Sings*, Columbia Broadcasting System (CBS-TV), 1979.

Sister, Sister (television drama), National Broadcasting Co., Inc. (NBC-TV), 1982.

(Writer of poetry) John Singleton, *Poetic Justice* (motion picture), Columbia Pictures, 1993.

Composer of songs, including two songs for movie, *For Love of Ivy*, and composer of musical scores for both her screenplays. Author of "Black, Blues, Black," a series of ten one-hour programs, broadcast by National Educational Television (NET-TV), 1968. Also author of "Assignment America," a series of six one-half-hour programs, 1975, and of "The Legacy" and "The Inheritors," two Afro-American specials, 1976. Other documentaries include *Trying to Make It Home* (Byline series), 1988, and *Maya Angelou's America: A Journey of the Heart* (also host). Public Broadcasting Service Productions include *Who Cares about Kids,*

Kindred Spirits, Maya Angelou: Rainbow in the Clouds, and *To the Contrary.*

RECORDINGS

Miss Calypso (audio recording of songs), Liberty Records, 1957.

The Poetry of Maya Angelou (audio recording), GWP Records, 1969.

An Evening with Maya Angelou (audio cassette), Pacific Tape Library, 1975.

I Know Why the Caged Bird Sings (audio cassette with filmstrip and teacher's guide), Center for Literary Review, 1978, abridged version read by Angelou, Random House, 1986.

Women in Business (audio cassette), University of Wisconsin, 1981.

Making Magic in the World (audio cassette), New Dimensions, 1988.

On the Pulse of Morning (audio production), Ingram, 1993.

Wouldn't Take Nothing For My Journey Now (audio production), Ingram, 1993.

Phenomenal Woman (audio production), Ingram, 1995.

OTHER

Conversations with Maya Angelou, edited by Jeffrey M. Elliot, Virago Press, 1989.

(Author of forward) Rosamund Grant, *Caribbean & African Cooking*, Interlink, 1993.

Double Stitch: Black Women Write about Mothers & Daughters, HarperCollins, 1993.

(Author of forward) Patricia M. Hinds, editor, *Essence: 25 Years Celebrating Black Women*, Harry N. Abrams Inc., 1995.

Maya Angelou (four-volume boxed set), Ingram, 1995.

(Contributor) Jontyle T. Robinson, *Bearing Witness: Contemporary Works by African American Women Artists*, Rizzoli International Publications, 1996.

(Contributor) Jack Smedley, *The Journey Back: A Survivor's Guide to Leukemia*, Rainbow's End Company, 1996.

Co-author (with Charlie Reilly and Amiri Baraka) *Conversations with Amiri Baraka*. Short stories are included in anthologies such as *Harlem* and *Ten Times Black*. Contributor of articles, short stories, and poems to national periodicals, including *Harper's, Ebony, Essence, Mademoiselle, Redbook, La-*

dies' Home Journal, Black Scholar, Architectural Digest, New Perspectives Quarterly, Savvy Woman, and *Ms. Magazine.*

■ Adaptations

I Know Why the Caged Bird Sings was adapted as a television movie by Columbia Broadcasting System, Inc. (CBS-TV), 1979. *And Still I Rise* was adapted as a television special by Public Broadcasting Service (PBS-TV), 1985. *I Know Why the Caged Bird Sings,* produced for audio cassette and compact disk, Ingram, 1996.

■ Overview

Standing before the church congregation, little Marguerite Johnson realized that everyone was looking at her, and that she wasn't a white girl with long blonde hair. As she remembered that she was a girl with dark skin, a gap between her teeth, and kinky dark hair, she struggled to remember the words of the poem she'd memorized for Easter. It was no use. As Marguerite ran towards the door of the church, "a green persimmon, or it could have been a lemon, caught me between the legs and squeezed. I tasted the sour on my tongue and felt it in the back of my mouth. Then . . . the sting was burning down my legs and into my Sunday socks." Marguerite Johnson—the girl who would grow up to become a performer who flaunted her beauty, power and grace on stages all over the world—the girl who would become a writer whose work would inspire thousands and thousands of readers of all races and genders and ages—had wet herself. Yet that was just the beginning of a traumatic childhood, as the girl would recall in her most famous work, *I Know Why the Caged Bird Sings.*

As a young black woman growing up in the South, and later, in war-time San Francisco, Johnson (who changed her name to Maya Angelou at the beginning of her stage career) faced racism from whites and poor treatment from most men (she was raped when she was seven years old). She found that, in this position, she had few career options, and little chance of leading a fruitful life; she gave birth out of wedlock at seventeen, experimented with drugs, and worked as a madam and prostitute. Instead of letting forces beyond her control overcome her, Angelou began

to forge art from her early experiences and change the world as she'd once known it. She became a singer, dancer, actress, composer, and director (Hollywood's first female black director). She became a writer, editor, essayist, playwright, poet, and screenplay-writer. She became known, as Annie Gottlieb wrote in the *New York Times Book Review,* as a person who "writes like a song, and like the truth. The wisdom, rue and humor of her storytelling are borne on a lilting rhythm completely her own."

Angelou also became a civil rights activist (who worked at one time for Dr. Martin Luther King and once staged a protest at the United Nations) and an educator. By 1975, wrote Carol E. Neubauer in *Southern Women Writers: The New Generation,* "Angelou had become recognized not only

This 1969 autobiography details Angelou's painful childhood and her struggle to achieve independence.

as a spokesperson for blacks and women, but also for all people who are committed to raising the moral standards of living in the United States." How had this woman—who had done some things that many would consider immoral—become a leader with a moral agenda? She did so by writing about herself, by fighting for civil and women's rights, and by providing an amazing example of the human potential to rise above defeat. Angelou explained this herself in an interview with George Plimpton in the *Paris Review:* "In all my work, in the movies I write, the lyrics, the poetry, the prose, the essays, I am saying that we may encounter many defeats—maybe it's imperative that we encounter the defeats—but we are much stronger than we appear to be, and maybe much better than we allow ourselves to be."

Much of what we know about Angelou's life comes from her autobiographies. Angelou was born in St. Louis, Missouri, and lived her early years in Long Beach, California. As she related in *I Know Why the Caged Bird Sings,* she was just three years old when her parents decided to divorce. Her father sent Angelou and her four-year-old brother alone by train to the home of his mother in Stamps, Arkansas. In Stamps, a segregated town, "Momma" (as Angelou and her brother Bailey called their grandmother) took care of the children and ran a lunch business and a store. The children were expected to stay clean and sinless, and to do well in school. Although she followed the example of her independent and strong-willed grandmother, and was a healthy child, Angelou felt ugly and unloved. When her mother, who lived in St. Louis, requested a visit from the children, Angelou was shocked by her mother's paler complexion, and by the red lipstick her grandmother would have thought scandalous. Angelou was almost as overwhelmed by her mother's wildness and determination as she was by her beauty.

Life in St. Louis was different from that in Stamps; Angelou was unprepared for the rushing noises of city life and the Saturday night parties. Then, when she was just seven and-a-half years old, something terrible happened. In one of the most evocative (and controversial) moments in *I Know Why the Caged Bird Sings,* Angelou described how she was first lovingly cuddled, and later raped by her mother's boyfriend. When the man was murdered by her uncles for his crime

Angelou felt responsible, and she stopped talking. She and her brother were sent back to Stamps. Angelou remained mute for five years, but she developed a love for language and the spoken word. She also read and memorized books. She read the works of black authors and poets, like Langston Hughes, W. E. B. Du Bois, and Paul Lawrence Dunbar. Even though she and Bailey were discouraged from reading the works of white writers at home, Angelou read and fell in love with the works of William Shakespeare, Charles Dickens, and Edgar Allan Poe. When Angelou was twelve and a half, Mrs. Flowers, an educated black woman, finally got her to speak again. Mrs. Flowers, as Angelou recalled in *Mrs. Flowers: A Moment of Friendship,* emphasized the importance of the spoken word, explained the nature of and importance of education, and instilled her with a love of poetry. Maya graduated at the top of her eighth-grade class.

When race relations made Stamps a dangerous place for Angelou and her brother, "Momma" took the children to San Francisco, where Angelou's mother was working as a professional gambler. World War II was raging, and San Franciscans prepared for air raids that never came. Angelou prepared for the rest of her life by attending George Washington High School and by taking lessons in dance and drama on a scholarship at the California Labor School. When Angelou, just seventeen, graduated from high school and gave birth to a son, she began to work as well. She worked as the first female and black street car conductor in San Francisco. As she explained in *Singin' and Swingin' and Gettin' Merry Like Christmas,* she also "worked as a shake dancer in night clubs, fry cook in hamburger joints, dinner cook in a Creole restaurant and once had a job in a mechanic's shop, taking the paint off cars with my hands." For a time, Angelou also managed a couple of prostitutes.

Angelou married a white ex-sailor, Tosh Angelos, in 1950. Yet the pair did not have much in common, and Angelou began to take note of the reaction of people (especially African Americans) to their union. After they separated, Angelou continued her study of dance in New York City. She returned to San Francisco and sang in the "Purple Onion" cabaret. There, Angelou (who had changed her name to fit Bailey's nickname for her, "My," "Mya," and finally "Maya," combined with her ex-husband's last name) garnered the attention of talent scouts. From 1954 to 1955, she was a member of the cast of *Porgy and Bess;* she visited twenty-two countries before leaving the tour to return to her son. During the late 1950s, Angelou sang in West Coast and Hawaiian nightclubs. After some time living in a houseboat commune in Sausalito, California, she returned to New York.

In New York, Angelou continued her stage career with an appearance in an Off-Broadway show, *Calypso Heatwave* (1957). Then, with the encouragement of writer John Killens, she joined the Harlem Writers Guild and met James Baldwin and other important writers. It was during this time that Angelou had the opportunity to hear Dr. Martin Luther King speak. Inspired by his message, she determined to become a part of the struggle for civil rights. So, with comedian Godfrey Cambridge, she wrote, produced, directed, and starred in *Cabaret for Freedom* in 1960, a benefit for Dr. King's Southern Christian Leadership Conference (SCLC). Given the organizational abilities she demonstrated as she worked for the benefit, she was offered a position as the northern coordinator for Dr. King's SCLC in 1961. That same year, she appeared in Jean Genet's play, *The Blacks,* which won an Obie Award.

Angelou began to live with Vusumzi Make, a South African freedom fighter; with Angelou's son Guy, they relocated to Cairo, Egypt. There, Angelou found work as an associate editor at the *Arab Observer.* As she recalled in *The Heart of a Woman,* she learned a great deal about writing there, but Vusumzi could not tolerate the fact that she was working. After her relationship with him ended, Angelou went on to Ghana, in West Africa, in 1962. She later worked at the University of Ghana's School of Music and Drama as an assistant administrator. She worked as a freelance writer and was a feature editor at *African Review.* As she related in *All God's Children Need Traveling Shoes,* Angelou also played the title role in *Mother Courage* during this time.

Angelou returned to the United States in the mid-1960s and found a position as a lecturer at the University of California in Los Angeles in 1966. She also played a part in the play *Medea* in Hollywood. In this period, she was encouraged by author James Baldwin and Random House publishers to write an autobiography. Initially, Angelou declined offers, and went to California for the production of a series of ten one-hour programs

THE INAUGURAL POEM

ON THE PULSE OF MORNING

MAYA ANGELOU

Angelou recited this poem at the inauguration of U.S. President Bill Clinton in January 1993.

that she'd written, "Black, Blues, Black," which were broadcast in 1968. Fortunately, however, Angelou changed her mind and wrote *I Know Why the Caged Bird Sings.* The book, which chronicles Angelou's childhood and ends with the birth of her son Guy, bears what Selwyn R. Cudjoe in *Black Women Writers* calls a burden: "to demonstrate the manner in which the Black female is violated . . . in her tender years and to demonstrate the 'unnecessary insult' of Southern girlhood in her movement to adolescence." *Caged Bird* won immediate success and a nomination for a National Book Award.

Although Angelou did not write *I Know Why the Caged Bird Sings* with the intention of writing other autobiographies, she eventually wrote four more, which may be read with *Caged Bird* as a series. Most critics have judged the subsequent autobiographies in light of the first, and *Caged Bird* remains the most highly praised. *Gather Together in My Name* begins when Angelou is seventeen and a new mother; it describes a destructive love affair, Angelou's work as a prostitute, her rejection of drug addition, and the kidnaping of her son. *Gather Together* was not as well received by critics as *Caged Bird*. As Mary Jane Lupton reported in *Black American Literature Forum*, in this 1974 autobiography, "the tight structure" of *Caged Bird* "appeared to crumble; childhood experiences were replaced by episodes which a number of critics consider disjointed or bizarre." Lupton asserted, however, that there is an important reason why Angelou's later works are not as tight as the first, and why they consist of episodes: these "so-called 'fragments' are reflections of the kind of chaos found in actual living. In altering the narrative structure, Angelou shifts the emphasis from herself as an isolated consciousness to herself as a Black woman participating in diverse experiences among a diverse class of peoples."

Singin' and Swingin' and Gettin' Merry Like Christmas is Angelou's account of her tour in Europe and Africa with *Porgy and Bess*; much of the work concerns Angelou's separation from her son during that time. In *The Heart of a Woman*, Angelou described her acting and writing career in New York and her work for the civil rights movement. She recalled visits with great activists Dr. Martin Luther King and Malcolm X, and the legendary singer Billie Holiday. She also told of her move to Africa, and her experiences when her son was injured in a serious car accident; the book ends with Guy's move into a college dormitory at the University of Ghana. "Angelou's message is one blending chorus: Black people and Black women do not just endure, they triumph with a will of collective consciousness that Western experience cannot extinguish," wrote Sondra O'Neale in *Black Women Writers*. *All God's Children Need Traveling Shoes* once again explores Guy's accident; it moves on from there to recount Angelou's travels in West Africa and her decision to return, without her son, to America.

Angelou's poetry is praised more for its content (praising black beauty and the strength of women, lauding the human spirit, criticizing the Vietnam War, demanding social justice for all) than for its poetic virtue. Yet *Just Give Me a Cool Drink of Water 'fore I Diiie*, which was published in 1971, was nominated for a Pulitzer Prize in 1972. This volume contains thirty-eight poems, some of which were published in *The Poetry of Maya Angelou*.

According to Carol Neubauer in *Southern Women Writers*, "the first twenty poems describe the whole gamut of love, from the first moment of passionate discovery to the first suspicion of painful loss." In the other poems, "Angelou turns her attention to the lives of black people in America from the

---

If you enjoy the works of Maya Angelou, you may want to check out the following books and films:

The poetry of Gwendolyn Brooks, including *Annie Allen*, 1949.
Toni Morrison, *Beloved*, 1987.
Rita Williams-Garcia, *Blue Tights*, 1988.
Jacqueline Woodson, *The Dear One*, 1991.
The Color Purple, Warner Brothers, 1985.

---

time of slavery to the rebellious 1960s. Her themes deal broadly with the painful anguish suffered by blacks forced into submission, with guilt over accepting too much, and with protest and basic survival." In *Oh Pray My Wings Are Gonna Fit Me Well*, dedicated to her husband at the time, Paul Du Feu, Angelou discussed the plight of the human race, the American potential, and the problems plaguing American Blacks. While Sandra M. Gilbert noted in *Poetry* that Angelou is a "stunningly talented prose writer," she commented that this collection is so "painfully untalented . . . that I can't think of any reason, other than the Maya Myth, for it to be in print."

And Still I Rise, which was published in 1978, contains thirty-two poems. Carol Neubauer explained in *Southern Women Writers* that "this series of poems covers a broader range of subjects than the earlier two volumes and shifts smoothly from issues such as springtime and aging to sexual awakening, drug addiction, and Christian salvation. The familiar themes of love and its inevitable loneliness and the oppressive climate of the South are still central concerns. But even more striking than the poet's careful treatment of these subjects is her attention to the nature of woman and the importance of family." "Phenomenal Woman," wrote Neubauer, displays Angelou's "poetic style, the lines . . . terse and forcefully, albeit irregularly rhymed." *Shaker, Why Don't You Sing,* dedicated to Angelou's son and grandson, "moves gracefully from the promise of potential strength to the humor of light satire, at all times bearing witness to a spirit that soars and sings in spite of repeated disappointment."

As Angelou wrote her autobiographies and poems, she continued her career in film and television. She was the first black woman to get a screenplay (*Georgia, Georgia*) produced in 1972. She was honored with a nomination for an Emmy award for her performance in *Roots* in 1977. In 1979, Angelou helped adapt her book, *I Know Why the Caged Bird Sings,* for a television movie of the same name.

■ Update

In the early 1990s, when Angelou was in her sixties, she returned to live in the American South, in what Catherine S. Manegold in the *New York Times* described as a "trim brick house in Winston-Salem." Manegold described Angelou as a woman with broad features, "like chunks of clay collected roughly on a frame," "dancer's feet," a voice with "a swoop, a lingering vowel, an octave dropped for emphasis," and "the innate and compelling grace of a woman who has constructed a full life, one lived without concession or false excuse." Although Angelou suffersfrom arthritis, she leads a very busy life. She taught literature at Wake Forest University in Winston-Salem, and is "in great demand on the lecture circuit, making about 80 appearances a year."

Angelou was especially productive in the late 1980s and early 1990s. According to Neubauer, *All God's Children Need Traveling Shoes*, Angelou's fifth autobiography (published in 1986), "swept Angelou to new heights of critical and popular acclaim." Angelou wrote the poetry for the film, *Poetic Justice* (1993) and played the role of Aunt June. She also played Lelia Mae in the 1993 television film, *There Are No Children Here,* and appeared as Anna in the feature film *How to Make an American Quilt* in 1995. Also in 1995, Angelou's poetry helped commemorate the fiftieth anniversary of the United Nations. She had elevated herself to what Richard Grenier in *National Review* called a "dizzying height of achievement." As a title from an article by Freda Garmaise in *Gentleman's Quarterly* proclaimed, "Maya-ness" was "next to godliness."

A Poem for the President

One of the most important sources of Angelou's fame in the early 1990s was President Bill Clinton's invitation to write and read the first inaugural poem in decades. Americans all across the country watched the six-foot-tall, elegantly-dressed woman as she read her poem for the new president on January 20, 1993. "On the Pulse of Morning," which begins "A Rock, A River, A Tree," calls for peace, racial and religious harmony, and social justice for people of different origins, incomes, genders, and sexual orientations. It recalls the civil rights movement, and Dr. Martin Luther King's famous "I have a dream" speech as it urges America to "Give birth again/To the Dream" of equality. Angelou challenged the new administration and all Americans to work together for progress: "Here, on the pulse of this new day,/ You may have the grace to look up and out/And into your sister's eyes, and into/Your brother's face, your country/And say simply/Very simply/ With hope—Good morning."

While some may see President Clinton's selection of Maya Angelou as a tribute to her, and in thanks for her lifelong contribution to civil rights and the arts, Angelou had her own ideas. She told Catherine S. Manegold in an interview the evening before the inauguration, "In all my work, what I try to say is that as human beings we are more alike than we are unalike." She added, "It may be that Mr. Clinton asked me to write the inaugural poem because he understood that I am the kind of person who really does bring people together."

During the early 1990s, Angelou contributed more poetry and work for children than autobiographical work. *Now Sheba Sings the Song* is just one poem inspired by the work of artist Tom Feelings; the lines or phrases are isolated on each page with eighty-four of Tom Feelings' sepia-toned and black-and-white drawings of black women. *I Shall Not Be Moved* is a collection which takes its title from a line in one of the book's poems. *Phenomenal Women*, a collection of four poems, takes its title from a poem which originally appeared in *Cosmopolitan* magazine in 1978; the narrator of the poem describes the physical and spiritual characteristics and qualities that make her attractive.

Angelou dedicated *Wouldn't Take Nothing for My Journey Now,* a collection of twenty-four short essays, to Oprah Winfrey, the television talk-show hostess who celebrated Angelou's sixty-fifth birthday with a grand party. The essays in this book contain declarations, complaints, memories, opinions, and advice on subjects ranging from faith to jealousy. Genevieve Stuttaford, writing in *Publishers Weekly,* described the essays as "quietly inspirational pieces." Anne Whitehouse of the *New York Times Book Review* observed that the book would "appeal to readers in search of clear messages with easily digested meanings." Yet not all critics appreciated this collection. Richard Grenier of the *National Review* concluded that the book "is of a remarkably coherent tone, being from first page to last of a truly awesome emptiness."

Books for Children

Although Angelou's autobiographies are written, in part, for young people, they are beyond the comprehension of most young children. With the publication of *Mrs. Flowers: A Moment of Friendship* (1986) with selections from *Caged Bird,* children can access the world Angelou describes in her autobiography. Like *Now Sheba Sings the Song,* the text of *Life Doesn't Frighten Me* consists of one poem. Each line or phrase is accompanied by the dynamic, abstract and colorful paintings of the late artist Jean-Michel Basquiat (who died when he was just twenty-seven).

In *My Painted House, My Friendly Chicken & Me,* with photographs by Margaret Courtney-Clarke, a young African girl introduces herself and discusses her life. She tells about her friend, a pet chicken to whom she tells all of her best secrets. She displays her beautiful home, and explains how her mother has carefully painted it. The girl also explains how, although she must go to school wearing uniforms her father has purchased in town, she loves to wear her traditional beads and clothing. She expresses a wish that she and the reader can be friends despite the physical and cultural distance that separates them.

Kofi and His Magic is a picture book which allows young readers to get to know an African child, another culture, and another worldview. Through Angelou's text and Courtney-Clarke's colorful photographs, a West African boy named Kofi shows off his beautiful earth-toned home and tells of his life. Kofi's town, Bonwire, is famous for its Kente cloth production. He explains how,

This 1995 work collects four poems, including "Still I Rise," which celebrate the beauty of women.

even though he is still quite young, he is a trained weaver of Kente cloth. Then, Kofi takes readers on a journey to visit other nearby towns and people, and finally, to see the ocean (which he initially thinks is a big lake). At the end of the book, after Kofi returns to Bonwire, he reveals why he calls himself a magician—Kofi's magic involves allowing the reader to imagine that she or he can visit Kofi and become his friend—the reader must only close her eyes and open her mind for the magic to work.

Assessing Her Life and Work

As Angelou has been busy furthering her career, critics and scholars have attempted to keep up with her, and to interpret her continuing work. While many critics have pointed out that the message in Angelou's prose is universal, Mary Jane Lupton has called attention to the theme of motherhood in Angelou's work. In five volumes of autobiography, Angelou "moves forward: from being a child, to being a mother; to leaving the child; to having the child, in the fifth volume, achieve his independence." In her interview with George Plimpton in the *Paris Review,* Angelou agreed with him that the love of her child was a "prevailing theme" in her autobiographical work.

Some critics have argued that Angelou's poetry is inferior to her prose. Unlike her autobiographical work, Angelou's poetry has not received much of what William Sylvester of *Contemporary Poets* would call "serious critical attention." In Sylvester's opinion, however, Angelou's poetry is "sassy." When "we hear her poetry, we listen to ourselves." In addition, as Lynn Z. Bloom pointed out in *Dictionary of Literary Biography,* "Angelou's poetry becomes far more interesting when she dramatizes it in her characteristically dynamic stage performances." Colorfully dressed, Angelou usually recites her poems before spellbound, if crowded, audiences.

Angelou takes her writing very seriously. She told Plimpton, "Once I got into it I realized I was following a tradition established by Frederick Douglas—the slave narrative—speaking in the first-person singular talking about the first-person plural, always saying "I" meaning "we." And what a responsibility. Trying to work with that form, the autobiographical mode, to change it, to make it bigger, richer, finer, and more inclusive in the twentieth century has been a great challenge for me. . . . I really hope . . . that people *read* my work."

While many critics have described Angelou's ability to write beautiful prose as a natural talent, Angelou has emphasized that she must work very hard to write the way she does. As she has explained to Plimpton and others, very early each morning she goes to a sparse hotel room to concentrate, to lie on the bed and write. She spends the morning on first draft work, and goes home in the afternoon to shower, cook a beautiful meal, and share it with friends. Later that night, she looks at what she's written, and begins to cut words and make revisions. Critics that suggest writing is easy for her, Angelou explained to Plimpton, "are the ones I want to grab by the throat and wrestle to the floor because it takes me forever to get it [a book] to sing. I *work* at the language."

■ Works Cited

Angelou, Maya, *Singin' and Swingin' and Gettin' Merry Like Christmas,* Random House, 1976.

Angelou, Maya, *I Know Why the Caged Bird Sings,* Bantam, 1993.

Angelou, Maya, "On The Pulse of Morning," printed in the *Washington Post,* January 21, 1993, p. A25.

Angelou, Maya, and George Plimpton, "The Art of Fiction CXIX: Maya Angelou," *Paris Review,* Fall, 1990, pp. 145-67.

Bloom, Lynn Z., "Maya Angelou," *Dictionary of Literary Biography,* Volume 38: *Afro-American Writers after 1955: Dramatists and Prose Writers,* edited by Thadious M. Davis and Trudier Harris, Gale, 1985, pp. 3-12.

Cudjoe, Selwyn R., "Maya Angelou and the Autobiographical Statement," *Black Women Writers (1950-1980): A Critical Evaluation,* edited by Mari Evans, Anchor Press/Doubleday, 1984, pp. 3-37.

Garmaise, Freda, "Maya-ness Is Next to Godlinesss," *Gentlemen's Quarterly,* July, 1995, p. 33.

Gilbert, Sandra M., review of *Oh Pray My Wings Are Gonna Fit Me Well, Poetry,* August, 1976.

Gottlieb, Annie, review of *Gather Together in My Name, New York Times Book Review,* June 16, 1974.

Grenier, Richard, review of *Wouldn't Take Nothing for My Journey Now, National Review,* November 29, 1993, p. 76.

Lupton, Mary Jane, "Singing the Black Mother: Maya Angelou and Autobiographical Continuity," *Black American Literature Forum,* Summer, 1990, pp. 257-76.

Manegold, Catherine S., "A Wordsmith at Her Inaugural Anvil," *New York Times,* January 20, 1993, pp. C1, C8.

Neubauer, Carol E., "Maya Angelou: Self and a Song of Freedom in the Southern Tradition," *Southern Women Writers: The New Generation,* edited by Tonette Bond Inge, University of Alabama Press, 1990, pp. 114-42.

O'Neale, Sondra, "Reconstruction of the Composite Self: New Images of Black Women in Maya Angelou's Continuing Autobiography," *Black Women Writers (1950-1980): A Critical Evaluation,* edited by Mari Evans, Anchor Press/Doubleday, 1984, pp. 25-37.

Stuttaford, Genevieve, review of *Wouldn't Take Nothing for My Journey Now, Publishers Weekly,* September 27, 1993, pp. 53-54.

Sylvester, William, "Maya Angelou," *Contemporary Poets,* edited by Thomas Riggs, St. James Press, 1996, pp. 24-26.

Whitehouse, Anne, review of *Wouldn't Take Nothing for My Journey Now*, *New York Times Book Review*, December 19, 1993, p. 18.

■ For More Information See

BOOKS

Bloom, Harold, editor, *Maya Angelou's I Know Why the Caged Bird Sings*, Chelsea House, 1995.

King, Sarah E., *Maya Angelou: Greeting the Morning*, Millbrook Press, 1994.

Lisandrelli, Elaine Slivinski, *Maya Angelou: More Than a Poet*, Enslow Publishers, 1996.

Spain, Valerie, *Meet Maya Angelou*, Random House, 1994.

PERIODICALS

Essence, December, 1992, pp. 48-52.
Five Owls, September, 1995, p. 2.
Library Journal, October 1, 1995, p. 102.
Los Angeles Times Book Review, April 13, 1986, p. 4.
Mother Jones, May-June, 1995, pp. 22-25.
New York Times Book Review, June 5, 1994, p. 48.
Publishers Weekly, March 23, 1990, p. 69.
School Library Journal, October, 1987, p. 146; May, 1995, p. 57.
Voice of Youth Advocates, August, 1986, p. 170.*

—Sketch by Ronie-Richele Garcia-Johnson

T. Ernesto Bethancourt

■ Personal

Name originally Thomas E. Passailaigue; name changed to Tom Paisley; born October 2, 1932, in Brooklyn, NY; son of Aubrey Ernesto (a truck driver) and Dorothy (Charest) Passailaigue; married Nancy Yasue Soyeshima, May 9, 1970; children: Kimi, Dorothea. *Education:* Attended City College of the City University of New York. *Politics:* Registered Democrat. *Hobbies and other interests:* Old cars, old movies.

■ Addresses

Home and office—P.O. Box 787, Alta Loma, CA 91701.

■ Career

Writer, singer, musician, composer, lyricist, actor, and critic. Biographer of recording artists, RCA records and CBS records, 1969-76; staff lyricist, Notable Music, 1970-71. Has held various odd jobs, including a stint as an undercover claims investigator for the New York office of Lloyd's of London. *Military service:* U.S. Navy, served in Korean War, 1950-53. *Member:* PEN International, American Society of Composers, Authors, and Publishers, Mystery Writers of America, Writers Guild of America—West, Authors Guild, Authors League of America, American Federation of Musicians, Southern California Council on Literature for Children and Young People, The Bank Dicks (W. C. Fields fan club).

■ Awards, Honors

American Society of Composers, Authors and Publishers Popular Division Award, 1970-71, for "Cities"; named "Kentucky Colonel" by governor of Kentucky, 1976; *Tune in Yesterday* was named a Notable Children's Book in the Field of Social Studies, National Council on Social Studies—Children's Book Council, 1978; "Author of the Year Award," University of California at Irvine, 1978; American Library Association "Best of the Best Books, 1970-83" citation, for *Tune in Yesterday;* Excellence in a Series award, Southern California Council on Literature for Children and Young People, 1983, for "Doris Fein" series; Central Missouri State University Distinguished Body of Work award, 1984; Children's Choice Award for *Nightmare Town.*

■ Writings

JUVENILE NOVELS; UNDER PSEUDONYM T. ERNESTO BETHANCOURT

New York City Too Far From Tampa Blues, Holiday House, 1975.
The Dog Days of Arthur Cane, Holiday House, 1976.
The Mortal Instruments, Holiday House, 1977.
Tune in Yesterday, Holiday House, 1978.
Dr. Doom: Superstar, Holiday House, 1978.
Instruments of Darkness, Holiday House, 1979.
Nightmare Town, Holiday House, 1979.
Where the Deer and the Cantaloupe Play, Oak Tree, 1981.
T.H.U.M.B.B.: The Hippest Underground Marching Band in Brooklyn, Holiday House, 1983.
The Tomorrow Connection, Holiday House, 1984.
The Great Computer Dating Caper, Crown, 1984.
The Me Inside of Me, Lerner Publications, 1985.

"DORIS FEIN" SERIES; UNDER PSEUDONYM T. ERNESTO BETHANCOURT

Doris Fein: Superspy, Holiday House, 1980.
Quartz Boyar, Holiday House, 1980.
Phantom of the Casino, Holiday House, 1981.
The Mad Samurai, Holiday House, 1981.
Deadly Aphrodite, Holiday House, 1982.
Murder is No Joke, Holiday House, 1982.
Dead Heat at Long Beach, Holiday House, 1983.
Legacy of Terror, Holiday House, 1984.

OTHER

That's Together (television script), WTTW-TV (Chicago), 1974.
The New Americans (television script), KCET-TV (Los Angeles), 1981.

Also author of several collections of short stories for the General Learning Corporation; author of lesson in television series *Skills Essential to Learning*, Agency for Instructional Television, 1979; author of "Easy to Read" adaptations of classics, all published by Pittman Fearon Publishing, including *Dr. Jekyll and Mr. Hyde, The Time Machine, Frankenstein, The Three Musketeers*, and *The Last of the Mohicans*. Lyricist for *Music*, Silver Burdett, three volumes, 1973-75; also lyricist/librettist for Off-Broadway play *Cities*, 1971, and contributor to *Weigh-in, Way Out*, 1970. Contributor of unattri-

buted pieces to text books. Former contributing editor to *Stereo Review* and *High Fidelity*.

■ Adaptations

New York City Too Far From Tampa Blues was adapted for television by NBC in 1979; *The Dog Days of Arthur Cane* was adapted for television by ABC in 1984.

■ Sidelights

"I wrote my first novel at age forty," Tom Paisley once told *Contemporary Authors (CA)*, "My tardy entry into booklists was attributed to my background. How could a Brooklyn-born Puerto Rican ex-shoeshine boy-turned entertainer ever aspire to become an author?" With more than twenty novels for young adults to his credit under the pseudonym T. Ernesto Bethancourt, an author is precisely what Tom Paisley has become. Always popular with readers, Paisley has earned critical approval for his ability to capture the language, fashions, and fads current with his audience. He consistently assembles casts of characters from diverse backgrounds in an attempt to break down the stereotypes all too frequently encountered in young adult novels. Despite the seriousness of his intentions, Paisley refuses to moralize through his writing, because, he once asserted in *Something About the Author (SATA)*, "preaching implies condescension and condescension is the kiss of death for any adolescent—talk down to a kid and you've lost the kid as an audience."

Tom Paisley was born Thomas E. Passailigue (pronounced Pas-a-laig), on October 2, 1932, in Brooklyn New York. His father, Ernesto Passailigue, a native of the Dominican Republic, was raised in Santurice, Puerto Rico. He and his family immigrated to the United States just prior to the outbreak of World War I. Paisley's mother, Dorothy Charest Passailigue, was of French-Canadian descent, and was originally from Pelham, New York.

The Passailigue family lived in Brooklyn, a borough of New York City. Paisley's father worked as a truck driver until 1942, when his parents decided to move to Tampa, Florida. Although they had friends in the Tampa area the move did not work out as anticipated, and the family never

The Dog Days of Arthur Cane

T. Ernesto Bethancourt

A well-to-do New York teenager awakens to find he has been transformed into a dog in this 1976 novel.

settled in the south. They returned to New York City two years later, and Paisley's father resumed his old job. Years later, Paisley's experiences in Tampa were to provide the material for his first novel, *New York City Too Far from Tampa Blues*.

Throughout his childhood Paisley sought refuge from the mean streets of the city in public libraries. His first impressions of a world outside his own were formed by reading. As an adolescent, Paisley began appearing publicly as a singer and musician. "I think I was ten years old the first time I sang at somebody's bar mitzvah on Bedford Avenue in Brooklyn," Paisley recounted for *SATA*. "I always was a singer." Paisley could not perform however, until he reached the age of eighteen and was legally able to enter the nightclubs and bars that supported the live music scene. In

high school he was a member of the chorus and sang well enough to be chosen for New York City's All City Chorus. He performed with this select group for two years.

Although he entertained ambitions of becoming a writer, Paisley enlisted in the navy immediately after graduating from high school in 1950. The United States entered the Korean War one month after he volunteered. During his three years of service, Paisley trained and worked as an electronics and radar technician. Following his discharge, he became eligible for the "GI Bill," which provided veterans with tuition and enough financial aid for a college education. Paisley returned to New York City and enrolled as a part-time student in the pre-law program at the City College of the City University of New York.

During the day, Paisley held a job as a claims investigator for the insurance corporation Lloyd's of London. "I was a general snoop to see if somebody's claim was legit," Paisley explained to *SATA*. On one occasion, Paisley tracked a claimant who reported being disabled in a gym accident to a club where saw the man dance the Mamba. Amused, he went out to his car, grabbed his guitar and joined in the music, playing and singing for the deceptive claimant. Afterward, the club's owner invited him back to perform on weekends. Soon Paisley was earning more as a weekend musician than he was earning in an entire week as an investigator.

Paisley became a regular performer at folk music venues in and around New York City. He abandoned the name Passailigue, and adopted the more convenient (and slightly psychedelic) Paisley. He played the same clubs as many of the budding stars of folk music, including Bob Dylan, who later became the figurehead of the entire folk movement. Paisley also befriended bluesman Josh White, who taught the aspiring writer and musician to play blues guitar. Paisley made such rapid progress as a student that White invited him to tour with his daughter, a singer, as her accompanist. As Paisley's reputation as a folk entertainer increased, he was given the opportunity to record an album. Unfortunately, the record was never released. While earning his living as a musician, Paisley also began writing professionally. He wrote songs for himself and others and contributed reviews of records and performances to several magazines, including *Stereo Review* and *High Fi-*

delity. Paisley also penned liner-notes and artist press biographies for record companies, including RCA and Columbia Records.

Birth of a New Career

Paisley began work on his first novel without even intending to write a book. Shortly after his daughter was born, he thought it might be important for her to read about his childhood, especially if something should happen to him while she was still quite young. With this in mind, he began an autobiography that he expected his daughter to read when she became a teenager. He was in the habit of working on the autobiography between sets in the clubs where he performed. One night,

In this 1978 work, a high school music critic witnesses a murder at a rock concert and becomes entangled in a web of deceit.

he caught the attention of a patron who asked him if he would let her read his manuscript. Paisley consented, and the patron was so impressed that she introduced him to contacts she had in publishing.

Holiday House quickly agreed to publish the book as fiction under the title, *New York City Too Far from Tampa Blues.* Not surprisingly, the story's protagonist is a young, half-Hispanic musician named Tom, who longs to leave Tampa and return to New York City. His best opportunity for doing so comes when he and his close friend Aurelio form a successful duo, the Griffin Brothers. Critics called attention to the work's depiction of life on the streets and credited Paisley with a highly entertaining style of writing.

Encouraged by the positive reception of *New York City Too Far from Tampa Blues,* Paisley wrote his second novel, *The Dog Days of Arthur Cane.* After teasing an African classmate who claims to have shamanic abilities, privileged Long Island teen Arthur Cane finds himself turned into a dog. Unrecognized by his family, Arthur must fend for himself in New York City. From his dog's-eye point-of-view, Arthur begins to value the comfort and security he took for granted as a human. During the six weeks he spends as a dog, Arthur is renamed "Awful," poisoned, and very nearly executed at the dog pound. So moving is Arthur's escape from his final predicament, asserted *Times Literary Supplement* reviewer Nicholas Tucker, "that it is impossible, by the end, not to feel a little doggish oneself." Melinda Schroeder of *School Library Journal* offered similar praise for *The Dog Days of Arthur Cane,* noting that "events and people (as well as dogs) seem realistic, making this a shaggy dog story with a valid but not dogmatic lesson."

Despite his success as an author, Paisley continued to earn his living as a musician. In 1977, after completing his third and fourth novels, Paisley moved to Southern California. There, he quickly found that live music was not as popular as it had been in New York City. As it became increasingly difficult to make money as a singer, Paisley decided to devote his energy to writing full-time. "If I was going to survive," he told *SATA,* "I had better write more books."

Paisley revived the principal characters from his first novel, Tom and Aurelio, in *T.H.U.M.B.B. (The*

Hippest Underground Marching Band in Brooklyn). This time around, the young musicians are intent on improving their dreadful high school marching band. When the band is mistakenly invited to participate in New York City's St. Patrick's Day parade, Aurelio assembles a bizarre cast of characters to supplement the marchers. T.H.U.M.B.B. is a hit, and for a brief time the boys enjoy national celebrity.

The "Dorris Fein" Mysteries

Between 1980 and 1984, Paisley completed the eight novels that comprise the "Doris Fein" series. Often compared to the Nancy Drew mysteries, the novels feature a teenage sleuth who, in addition to solving crimes, confronts issues of racial and gender discrimination. While the political issues associated with racism are never raised explicitly in Paisley's work, he attempts to explode stereotypes by portraying minorities in positions of leadership, and as everyday people with the same hopes and aspirations as everyone else. Doris Fein is a young, Jewish woman, and her world is populated with characters who, like her, are likely to be judged solely on the basis of appearance.

Readers were introduced to Doris Fein in Paisley's *Dr. Doom: Superstar*, in which she plays a supporting role while her close friend Larry Small solves the mystery surrounding a series of threats received by a pop musician. Doris assumed the role of protagonist herself *In Doris Fein: Superspy.* When she travels to New York City to visit her aunt and uncle, Doris becomes involved in a missing persons case. She solves the riddle of the disappearance with the aid of Detective Carl Suzuki, a Japanese American whose family was interned during World War II.

In *The Quartz Boyar*, an eighteen-year-old Doris is recruited as an agent of the Intelligence Gathering Organization, or I.G.O. She reluctantly accepts her role in the agency, and, as her first assignment, must convey a small figure of a Russian boyar to Paris. The figurine is lost en route, and Doris becomes entangled in a series of events involving spies and counter-spies intent on pursuing her and recovering the strange boyar. "Doris seems very real," asserted Holly Sanhuber in *School Library Journal*, "and her independent, feisty character is revealed through a breezy, irreverent

A holy man from Transylvania, believed by millions to be a new messiah, plots to control the world in this 1979 thriller.

first-person narrative." Janet R. Mura of *Voice of Youth Advocates* characterized the book as a "light, enjoyable murder mystery."

In *Legacy of Terror*, the final novel of the series, Doris travels to Chicago to investigate a man professing to be heir to a fortune Doris has previously inherited. (She is, at this point in the series, a multimillionaire, the former owner of a grand prix race car, the "Red Menace," and a reformed amphetamine addict.) Ashford Miller, an African-American social worker, asserts that he is the illegitimate son of the late Harry Grubb, the white newspaperman who left his fortune to Doris. Despite their competing claims, Doris and Miller work together to find the arsonists responsible for the destruction of Miller's center for dis-

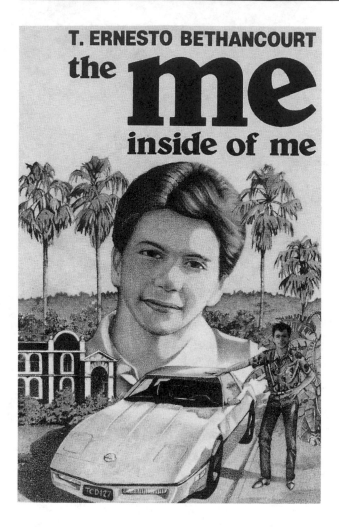

T. ERNESTO BETHANCOURT
the me
inside of me

A seventeen-year-old Mexican American encounters discrimination at a private school in this 1985 novel.

advantaged youth. Ultimately, the pair uncover both a mafia-run real-estate scam and the truth about Grubb's past.

Paisley addressed the issue of racism directly in his work, *The Me Inside of Me*. The story centers on seventeen-year-old Freddie Flores, who receives a million dollar insurance settlement when his entire family is killed in a plane crash. He uses his newfound wealth to enroll at Valverde, a private school where he, as a Mexican American, is victimized by the discrimination of other students. Freddie's only companion is Lenny, a Jewish student who, despite his family's apparent wealth, rejects the conformist values prevalent at Valverde. Freddie ultimately leaves school, and he comes to realize his value as an individual does not depend on the assessment of others. A *Bulletin for*

the Center of Children's Book reviewer called Freddie an "amicable and sensible boy," but regretted that the other characters in the book were not so finely realized. Although Janet Bryan of *School Library Journal* considered *The Me Inside of Me* a strong book, she expressed concern that Freddie's "grief takes a back seat to his adjustment to sudden affluence."

If you enjoy the works of T. Ernesto Bethancourt, you may also want to check out the following books:

Sue Grafton, *I Is for Innocent*, 1992.
Gordon Korman, *Our Man Weston*, 1986.
Peter Nelson, *Deadly Games*, 1992.
Gary Soto, *Pacific Crossing*, 1992.

Paisley's interest as an author are wide-ranging, and among his novels for young adult readers are some works of science fiction. In *Tune In Yesterday*, Paisley takes readers back to pre-World War II New York City through the experiences of Richie Gilroy and Mattie Owen, his time-traveling protagonists. In the book's sequel, *The Tomorrow Connection*, the pair struggle to find their way back to 1976 (the year in which their journey originated), and are given a glimpse of a future that includes fame and fortune for them both.

Paisley often expresses the hope that young readers of his books will have good feelings about reading after encountering one of his books. "You must ask yourself what is the function of young adult literature? What is the function of juvenile literature?" he once wrote in *SATA*. "It is simply to get kids into the idea of reading, to convey that reading is a good thing. You want to establish the reading habit through stimulating the imagination." The function of a writer for young adults, he added, "is to interest the kid in reading and trust that the kid has the intelligence, once they go on to other forms, to make up his or her own mind."

■ Works Cited

Bryan, Janet, review of *The Me Inside of Me*, *School Library Journal*, March, 1986, p. 173.

Review of *The Me Inside of Me, School Library Journal, The Bulletin of the Center for Children's Books,* February, 1988, p. 103.

Mura, Janet R., review of *Doris Fein: The Quartz Boyar, Voice of Youth Advocates,* February, 1981, p. 35.

Paisley, Tom, entry in *Contemporary Authors, New Revision Series,* Volume 15, Gale, 1985, p. 358.

Paisley, Tom, entry in *Something about the Author,* Volume 78, Gale, 1994, pp. 147-53.

Sanhuber, Holly, review of *Doris Fein: The Quartz Boyar, School Library Journal,* April, 1981, p. 137.

Schroeder, Melinda, review of *The Dog Days of Arthur Cane, School Library Journal,* January, 1977, p. 99.

Tucker, Nicholas, "Dog Beneath the Skin," *Times Literary Supplement,* September 29, 1978, p. 1082.

■ For More Information See

BOOKS

Children's Literature Review, Volume 3, Gale, 1978.

PERIODICALS

Horn Book, February, 1979, p. 67; August, 1979, pp. 419-20; August, 1981, p. 429.

Interracial Books for Children, Volume 13, p. 38-39.

Los Angeles Times Book Review, July 1, 1984, p. 6.

School Library Journal, September, 1979, p. 152; April, 1984, p. 121; December, 1984, p.88.

Voice of Youth Advocates, December, 1982, p. 28; April, 1984, p. 28; April, 1985, p. 54.*

—Sketch by Ronie Richele-Garcia Johnson

Kenneth Branagh

■ Personal

Kenneth Charles Branagh, surname pronounced "*bran*-och"; born December 10, 1960, in Belfast, Ireland; son of William (a carpenter) and Frances (a housewife; maiden name, Harper) Branagh; married Emma Thompson (an actress), August, 1989 (divorced, 1995). *Education:* Royal Academy of Dramatic Arts, graduate, 1981. *Religion:* Protestant.

■ Addresses

Agent—Clifford Stevens, STE Representation, 9301 Wilshire Blvd., Suite 312, Beverly Hills, CA 90210; and 888 Seventh Ave., Suite 201, New York, NY 10019.

■ Career

Actor, director, producer, and writer. Member of Royal Shakespeare Theater, 1983-85; Renaissance Theater Company, London, founder, producer, and director, with David Parfitt, 1987—.

■ Awards, Honors

Bancroft Gold Medal, Royal Academy of Dramatic Arts, 1981; Society of West End Theaters (SWET) Award for Most Promising Newcomer, and Plays and Players' Award for Best Newcomer, both 1982, and both for *Another Country; Evening Standard* Award for Best Film, European Award for Best Young Film Maker, European Actor of the Year award, Chicago Film Critics Award, Best Foreign Film, New York Film Critics Circle, Best New Director Award, Academy Award nominations, Best Actor and Best Director, and British Academy of Film and Television Arts (BAFTA) Award for Best Achievement in Direction, all 1989, and all for *Henry V; Evening Standard* Peter Sellers Award for Comedy, 1992, for *Peter's Friends;* Academy Award nomination for Best Short Film, 1992, for *Swan Song;* BAFTA Michael Bacon Award for Outstanding Contribution to the Cinema, 1993; Screen Actors Guild nomination for Best Supporting Actor, 1995, for the role of Iago in *Othello;* Osella d'Oro, Venice Film Festival, 1995, for *In the Bleak Midwinter* (American title, *A Midwinter's Tale*). The television documentary, "Anne Frank Remembered," with narration by Kenneth Branagh, also won many international awards, including an International Emmy for Best Documentary, and an Oscar for Best Achievement in Documentary Features.

■ Film, Stage, and Television Work

STAGE APPEARANCES

(Stage debut) Judd, *Another Country*, London, 1982.

Title role, *Henry V*, Royal Shakespeare Company, Stratford-upon-Avon, 1983.

Laertes, *Hamlet*, Royal Shakespeare Company (RSC), Stratford-upon-Avon, then Barbican Theater Center, London, 1985.

Title role, *Hamlet*, Tivoli Festival, Renaissance Theater Company at Elsinore Castle, Denmark, 1988.

Jimmy Porter, *Look Back in Anger*, Renaissance Theater Company, London, 1989.

Edgar, *King Lear*, Renaissance Theater Company, Mark Taper Forum, Los Angeles, 1990.

A rustic, *A Midsummer Night's Dream*, Renaissance Theater Company, Mark Taper Forum, Los Angeles, 1990.

Title role, *Coriolanus*, Renaissance Theater Company, Chichester, 1992.

Also appeared as St. Francis of Assisi in *St. Francis*, in *Three Sisters*, *The Golden Girls*, and *The Madness*, a one-man show based on Tennyson's poem, *Maud*.

MAJOR TOURS

Toured as Laertes, *Hamlet*, United Kingdom (UK) cities; Benedick, *Much Ado about Nothing*, UK cities; Touchstone, *As You Like It*, UK cities, all 1988.

STAGE WORK

Producer (with David Parfitt), *Hamlet*, Tivoli Festival, Renaissance Theater Company at Elsinore Castle, Denmark, 1988.

Director, *Twelfth Night*, Renaissance Theater Company, 1989.

Director, *A Midsummer Night's Dream*, Renaissance Theater Company, Mark Taper Forum, Los Angeles, 1990.

Director, *King Lear*, Renaissance Theater Company, Mark Taper Forum, Los Angeles, 1990.

Also director of *The Life of Napoleon*, Renaissance Theater Company.

FILM APPEARANCES

(Film debut) Rick, *High Season*, Hemdale, 1987.

James Moon, *A Month in the Country*, Orion Classics, 1987.

Title role, *Henry V*, Renaissance Films/BBC, 1989.

Mike Church/Roman Strauss, *Dead Again*, Paramount, 1991.

Andrew, *Peter's Friends*, Renaissance Films/Samuel Goldwyn Company, 1992.

Major Knoepp (uncredited appearance), *Swing Kids*, Hollywood Picture, 1993.

Benedick, *Much Ado about Nothing*, Renaissance Films/Samuel Goldwyn Company, 1993.

Victor Frankenstein, *Mary Shelley's Frankenstein*, American Zoetrope, 1994.

Iago, *Othello*, Columbia Pictures, 1995.

Title role, *Hamlet*, Castle Rock Films, 1996.

FILM WORK

Director, *Henry V*, Renaissance Films/BBC, 1989.

Director, *Dead Again*, Paramount, 1991.

Director and producer, *Peter's Friends*, Renaissance Films/Samuel Goldwyn Company, 1992.

Director, *Swan Song* (short film), Renaissance Films, 1992.

Director and producer, *Much Ado about Nothing*, Renaissance Films/Samuel Goldwyn Company, 1993.

Director and co-producer, *Mary Shelley's Frankenstein*, American Zoetrope, 1994.

Director and producer, *A Midwinter's Tale* (British title, *In the Bleak Midwinter*), Midwinter Films, 1995.

Director, *Hamlet*, Castle Rock Films, 1996.

TELEVISION APPEARANCES

Thomas Mendip, *The Lady's Not for Burning*, Yorkshire Television, 1987.

Jack, *The Boy in the Bush* (series), PBS, 1988.

Guy Pringle, "The Fortunes of War" (mini-series), *Masterpiece Theater*, PBS, 1988.

Gordon Evans as an adult, *Strange Interlude* (special), PBS, 1988.

Jimmy Porter, *Look Back in Anger*, HBO, 1989.

Title role, "Discovering Hamlet," PBS, 1990.

Donal Davoren, "Shadow of a Gunman," BBC, 1995.

Also appeared in "A Play for Tomorrow: Easter 2016," *The Billy Trilogy* (series), BBC; as Charles Tansley, *To the Lighthouse* (special), 1984; *The Ghosts*, 1985; "Coming Through," 1987; "Thompson" (episodic), 1990. Also was host or narrator on *Life and Adventures of Nicholas Nickleby*, Disney, 1990, "Symphony for the Spire," 1991, "Tales of Gold," BBC, 1992, "The Last Show on Earth,"

Central Independent Television, 1992, "Cinema Europe: The Other Hollywood," 1995, and "Anne Frank Remembered," Disney, 1995.

AUDIO RECORDINGS

Cousin Phyllis, Cover to Cover, 1988.
Last Enemy, ASV Records and Tapes, 1990.
Title role, *Hamlet,* BBC Radio/Bantam Doubleday Dell, 1992.
Anthem for Doomed Youth, Random House Audio Books, 1993.
Romeo, *Romeo and Juliet,* BBC Radio/BDD, 1993.
Cider with Rosie, BBC Radio, 1994.
As I Walked out One Morning/ A Moment of War, BBC Radio, 1994.
Longshot, Harper Audio, 1994.
Edmund, *King Lear,* BBC Radio/BDD, 1994.
Mary Shelley's Frankenstein, Simon & Schuster Audio, 1994.
Captain and the Enemy, Chivers Audio Books, 1995.
Pepys' Diary, Hedder Headline Audiobooks, 1995.

■ Writings

Tell Me Honestly (play), produced by Royal Shakespeare Company, 1985.
Public Enemy (play produced in London, 1987), Faber, 1988.
(Adapter) *Henry V* (film), BBC/Renaissance Films, 1989.
Beginning (autobiography), Chatto & Windus, 1989, Norton, 1990.
(Adapter) *Much Ado about Nothing* (film), Renaissance Films/Samuel Goldwyn Company, 1993.
A Midwinter's Tale (film), Midwinter Films, 1995.

■ Work in Progress

Appearances in a film production of *Pepys' Diary* for the BBC, and *The Gingerbread Man* from an original screenplay by John Grisham.

■ Sidelights

At twenty-eight, Kenneth Branagh seemingly emerged from nowhere to become one of the hottest film properties on either side of the Atlantic. He was, according to Georgina Howell, writing in

Vogue, "the entire force behind the award-winning *Henry V.* He owned the company, he raised the money, he directed it, cast it, adapted it for the screen, and starred in it." But it was not all an easy ride to fame. "My real 'God, what am I doing?' happened four or five days before shooting," Branagh told Michael Billington in *Interview* magazine. Unsure of what was expected of him in his directorial debut, Branagh called for a test and met the crew for the first time, "shaking with fear," as he told Billington. As both actor and director, Branagh had a stand-in to set up his shots as Henry, and this man was seated upon the throne for one of the major speeches of the play. All was ready for the test filming, yet the crew just stood there. "I was looking round and felt things weren't happening as they should and that people were starting to look at me. Then the assistant director whispered in my ear, 'You've got to say "Action,"' and I realized I'd made the classic . . . gaffe on day one."

It was uphill from there on, however, and the final product of *Henry V* not only won Academy Award nominations for Branagh's acting and directing, but also proved that Shakespeare could be a box-office commodity. For Branagh, the real proof of his and the film's popularity came when he was shopping on Beverly Hills' Rodeo Drive shortly after release of the film. A sales person initially ignored him to deal with a television celebrity, Branagh related to Howell in *Vogue,* but when the clerk finally took a look at Branagh, he threw up his hands: "'Oh, my God! Oh, my God! I know you, don't I? You're famous, aren't you? You're the one who played Henry VIII!'" Close enough. Since that initial success with filmed Shakespeare, Branagh has gone on to productions of *Much Ado about Nothing, Othello,* and *Hamlet,* making those Elizabethan plays more accessible to modern audiences while at the same time playing true to the original intent of the texts. Branagh told Dinitia Smith in *New York* magazine that "*Much Ado* means that for a whole generation of kids, some grateful teacher, with a gasp of relief, will be able to say, 'Here are girls with cleavages and boys with tight trousers, class. You will now shut up for an hour and a half and pay attention.'"

But Branagh is more than just a Shakespeare revivalist; he has starred in television and movies, written plays and scripts, founded a theater, and performed on the stage in Europe and the United States. Some say that he is the heir to Sir

This 1989 adaptation of William Shakespeare's *Henry V* earned Branagh Academy Award nominations for Best Actor and Best Director.

Laurence Olivier's theatrical legacy; others that he is the new Orson Welles. He has also taken his knocks, most especially with his 1994 film, *Mary Shelley's Frankenstein*, which was a critical flop, but has come back fighting. His character might best be defined by a comment he made to fellow actor Laurence Fishburne while filming *Othello*. Fishburne, as was quoted by Mark Huisman in an *Advocate* interview with Branagh, was worrying about a particular speech that he could not master, wondering if he should just cut it. Branagh by way of encouragement turned to him and said, "'Look man, I'm a pug Irish kid from Belfast, and I'm not supposed to do this stuff either.'"

Branagh is well trained at doing things from which his background is supposed to disqualify him. Born in Belfast in 1960, he was raised in a lower-middle-class family with grandparents on both sides having worked on the docks. Branagh's father was a joiner and all-round handy man be-

fore the family left violence-riven Ulster in 1969 for Reading, England, forty miles from London. According to Billington, the move was "traumatic and troubling" for Branagh, who was an outcast at school for his Irish accent. "Then your accent changes," Branagh told Billington, "and you feel guilty about this, as if you were betraying your roots." In early adolescence, Branagh, a bit of a social outsider, found solace in books and movies. A set of theater magazines introduced him to the great tradition of the stage in England, especially of Olivier's National Theater. Soon he found a place in school by participating in rugby and soccer, becoming captain of both, "more, I suspect, for my innate sense of drama—I loved shouting theatrically butch [macho] encouragement to 'my lads'—than for any real sporting skill," Branagh wrote in his autobiography, *Beginning*.

Increasingly, however, he found his real passion lay with the theater and movies. As a young boy he was deeply impressed by *The Birdman of Alcatraz*: "No one appeared to be acting," Branagh noted in *Beginning*. The first play he saw was a production of *A Christmas Carol*, and it was "magic" for him, as he recalled in his autobiography. At Reading, he began taking parts in school plays and even wrote a short play for a festival. He was fifteen when he first hitch-hiked to Stratford, pitching his tent and attending as many of the plays of the Royal Shakespeare Company as he could. He was particularly impressed by Derek Jacobi's performance in *Hamlet*. By the age of sixteen, Branagh was set on a career in acting, much to the dismay of his parents. Ironically, however, Branagh was in part inspired to acting by his parents, for he grew up in an oral tradition where "crack" or good conversation was a primary means of entertainment. "They had a natural sense of pace," Branagh told Smith in *New York* magazine. "When to pause, little rhetorical flourishes. They were fireside actors."

Though his school work suffered because of his interest in theater, in 1978 Branagh won an audition to the Royal Academy of Dramatic Art (RADA). Impressed with his technical control, the RADA accepted him, and Branagh won a scholarship from his local country council to help with tuition. At the RADA, Branagh lost his amateur habits of presenting a role and instead let the part play him. He proved an adept student. "We knew straightaway that Ken was first division," fellow actor John Sessions told Howell in *Vogue*. Branagh had early contact with some of his idols: in 1981 he wrote to Sir Laurence Olivier asking for tips on how to play Chekhov's *Three Sisters*—"Have a bash at it and hope for the best," was Olivier's reply, as Branagh recounted in *Beginning*. Also, Sir John Gielgud, then the RADA's president, was impressed by a Branagh rehearsal for *Hamlet*, a role the fledgling actor subsequently performed for the royal family.

Early Successes

The year 1981 proved to be a turning point for Branagh: not only did he win a major role in a BBC production set in Belfast, but he also landed a part in the play *Another Country* and became the recipient of the RADA's Bancroft Gold Medal as the outstanding student of the year. With the airing of the BBC play, *Too Late to Talk to Billy*, Branagh's parents finally realized that their son

was indeed an actor. Other roles followed: the lead in *Francis*, a play about St. Francis of Assisi, and a one-man show, *The Madness*, based on Tennyson's poem *Maud*. Then came a Society of West End Theaters Award for "Best Newcomer" for his role in *Another Country*, and Branagh was on his way. The Royal Shakespeare Company cast him in the title role of *Henry V*, "the most auspicious Stratford debut since Richard Burton's," according to Billington in *Interview*. Preparing for that role, Branagh had an audience with Prince Charles in order to get the feel of royalty for his part. The interview went well, and Prince Charles would later become an important patron for Branagh.

Increasingly, however, Branagh felt disillusioned with his position with the RSC. His play, *Tell Me Honestly*, in part dealt with these frustrations, but he had larger things in mind: starting his own company. His dream was to recreate the old spirit of an actors' theater with its camaraderie intact, and one that would take Shakespeare back to its roots. A fellow actor who had performed with him in *Another Country*, David Parfitt, was also interested in the concept. Money was an obstacle, however. Branagh put himself into the marketplace, acting in movies, including *High Season* and *A Month in the Country*, and in television productions, including an adaptation of the novel, *Fortunes of War*, in which he met his future wife, Emma Thompson. From such work he was able to save $60,000, and with a little help from friends such as Prince Charles and Derek Jacobi, launched the Renaissance Theater Company (RTC). The company's first play, *Public Enemy*, about a Northern Irish youngster who is fixated on Jimmy Cagney, not only starred Branagh but was written by him as well. With the second production, *Twelfth Night*, the company came into its own, and subsequent Shakespeare productions directed by Jacobi and Dame Judith Dench, as well as a production of John Osborne's *Look Back in Anger*, made RTC a respected company not only in London, but also in the United States when they toured there.

Branagh worked as an innovative actor, administrator, director, and front man for RTC, but still found time for other projects, including one long-held dream of making a film version of *Henry V*. Renaissance Films was created to produce the film and Branagh personally helped to raise the money for filming. Assembling a cast of renowned actors

Both Branagh and his former wife Emma Thompson played dual roles in the 1991 thriller *Dead Again*.

including Paul Scofield, Jacobi, and Thompson, Branagh created a movie that was praised by critics and popular at the box-office, a vivid recreation of the 1415 battle of Agincourt in which a vastly out-numbered English army under Henry V defeated the French, making Henry the leading king in Europe. Hal Hinson, writing in the *Washington Post*, noted both Branagh's acting prowess—"brash and flamboyant"—and his directorial skills—"forthright and articulate"—and concluded that Branagh "has made a *Henry V* for his time, and a masterful one." Peter Travers in *Rolling Stone* noted that the "film is more than a promising first try: It's thrilling." Writing in the *New York Times*, Nicholas Wade compared the Branagh film with Olivier's 1944 version and concluded that Branagh had created a "peerless rendition." And Stanley Kauffmann in *New Republic* also made the obvious comparison between Branagh and Olivier, concluding that while Branagh "is not yet near Olivier as a classical actor . . . as director, as ar-

tistic entrepreneur, as sheer charge of filmworld energy, he has won his own Agincourt."

Branagh, however, was not waiting for the reviews. Even during the filming of *Henry V* he was busy late at night writing his autobiography, *Beginning*, in order to help finance new quarters for his RTC. Richard Christiansen, reviewing the book in *Chicago Tribune*, commented that "perhaps because he is so close in time to all the events he describes, Branagh's book has an immediacy not always present in autobiographies." Christiansen went on to describe passages of the books as "quite moving." Meanwhile, Branagh was busy creating his own history. He and Thompson were married in the fall of 1989, a storybook wedding costing upwards of $50,000, fireworks and all.

Branagh's next film project was *Dead Again*, a tip of the hat to movies of the 1940s. Mike Church, a Los Angeles detective, assists a beautiful amnesia victim who is tormented by nightmares. An antiques dealer helps to convince Church that the source of the nightmares is another life experience—the murder of a famous pianist by her composer husband in 1948. Branagh directed the movie and played the dual roles of the detective and composer, while Thompson played dual female roles and Jacobi took the part of the antiques dealer. Kenneth Turan in *Los Angeles Times* called the result a "giddy whirling dervish of a movie," and Vincent Canby in the *New York Times* dubbed the movie a "big, convoluted, entertainingly dizzy romantic mystery melodrama." While filming *Dead Again*, Branagh was also directing his RTC company in performances in Los Angeles; he soon became known for this sort of artistic juggling act, but it was to take its toll.

The 1992 *Peter's Friends*, reminiscent of *The Big Chill*, was lighter fare for Branagh. A group of old college chums gather at the newly inherited country house of Peter and take stock of their years in between. Mostly "sunny and superficial," according to Janet Maslin in the *New York Times*, the movie, directed by Branagh, does strike a grave note when it is revealed Peter has been diagnosed with AIDS. Terrence Rafferty, however, reviewing the movie in the *New Yorker*, found little to like in it: "You cower in your seat," Rafferty wrote, "steeling yourself against the next grisly bit of repartee," and concluded that the movie was inhabited by "arrogant, self-absorbed poseurs." Critics aside, the movie was a box-office success and established Branagh's credentials in Hollywood.

Back to Shakespeare

Branagh returned to filmed Shakespeare with his much-praised adaptation of *Much Ado about Nothing*, a play about love and the battle between the sexes set against a backdrop of misunderstandings,

Branagh directed, co-produced, and starred in the 1994 film, *Mary Shelley's Frankenstein*.

If you enjoy the works of Kenneth Branagh, you may want to check out the following films:

The motion pictures of Japanese director Akira Kurosawa, especially *The Throne of Blood*, 1957, *Kagemusha*, 1980, and *Ran*, 1985.
Sir Laurence Olivier's versions of *Henry V*, 1944, *Hamlet*, 1948, *Richard III*, 1956, and *Othello*, 1965.
Sense and Sensibility (starring Emma Thompson), Columbia, 1995.

mistaken identities, and snappy word play. Caryn James in the *New York Times* noted that Branagh's "is a glorious version of Shakespeare, and it works not because it is Shakespearean but because it is cinematic." Dave Kehr, in the *Chicago Tribune*, described the movie as "sunny and brightly performed," with about half the play removed in the adaptation, while Kenneth Turan in the *Los Angeles Times* called Branagh's adaptation a "rollicking version." Not all the critics praised the production, however. Hal Hinson in the *Washington Post* felt that Branagh did not connect with his material as he had in *Henry V*, noting that Branagh demonstrated "how, in the wrong hands, even Shakespeare can be trivialized and reduced to chatter." Hinson concluded that "we had every reason to expect more from Branagh than Shakespeare dumbed down for the masses."

Branagh's first resounding critical flop was his *Mary Shelley's Frankenstein*, which he not only directed but also starred in as Victor Frankenstein, creator of the legendary monster. The film was big budget with a star-packed cast, but indicative of critical response was that of Janet Maslin in the *New York Times* who felt that Branagh was "in over his head" with the material. "He displays neither the technical finesse to handle a big, visually ambitious film nor the insight to develop a stirring new version of the story," Maslin noted. James Wolcott, writing in the *New Yorker*, called the movie a "frantic, incoherent, pointless mess." Though the film did earn out the money invested in it, making $22 million in the U.S. and $86 million internationally, the critical reception stung Branagh. "I made the film exactly as I wanted and that makes it worse," Branagh told Laurie Werner

in a *Chicago Tribune* interview. "Because you realize that you've put your heart and soul into something that in the end most people thought wasn't very good."

To make matters worse, the Branagh-Thompson marriage floundered, ending in divorce in 1995. Thompson had gone on to make her own film career with starring roles in *Remains of the Day* and *Howard's End*, for which she won an Academy Award. The strains of two separate careers finally were too much. "The end of a marriage is just incredibly sad—deeply, deeply sad," Branagh told Werner.

Work As Therapy

Branagh did not let these personal setbacks stall his career. Taking a hiatus from directing, he performed the role of the villain Iago in the 1995 movie version of *Othello*. "Mr. Branagh's terrific skill as a popularizer is a boon to the new *Othello*," wrote Janet Maslin in a *New York Times* review. Maslin also commented that Branagh has the "rare ability to deliver Shakespearean dialogue as if it were street talk." Meanwhile Branagh was also writing and directing *A Midwinter's Tale*, a comedy about a bumbling theater company trying to mount a production of *Hamlet* in a small village over the Christmas holidays. "My original intent was to make a film about an actor at that moment of crisis where he questions what he's doing and why," Branagh told Terry Lawson in a *Detroit Free Press* interview. Shot in black and white, the movie was something of an antidote to the big production fanfare of his Frankenstein movie, according to James Wolcott in the *New Yorker*. Though Wolcott felt that Branagh's attempt at Woody Allen failed—"the characterizations . . . aren't fresh," he noted—other critics such as Lawson in the *Detroit Free Press* found *A Midwinter's Tale* to be a "warm" comedy. The film won a gold medal at the Venice Film Festival.

In a way, however, *A Midwinter's Tale*—as has been much of Branagh's career to date—was simply a warm-up for his next project, a full-length movie version of *Hamlet* with a cast including Branagh in the title role, Derek Jacobi, Julie Christie, Gerard Depardieu, John Gielgud, Jack Lemmon, Billy Crystal, and Robin Williams. The four-hour film, described by *Time*'s Richard Corliss as "big and pretty, vigorous, thoughtful," was a labor of love for its director, who has performed the role of Hamlet some 300 times onstage. "It's like listening to a great piece of music," Branagh described the play to Werner in his *Chicago Tribune* interview. For Branagh, the play speaks in different ways as one's life experiences change. "One hopes in a slightly deeper way," he added. For Branagh, *Hamlet* is not a story about a man who cannot make up his mind. In fact, Hamlet decides in the first five minutes of the play that he must kill the king. "but he is terrified by the act itself," Branagh told Lawson in the *Detroit Free Press*, "If we get the audience to understand how it feels to be that scared . . . if we can get that right, we'll go on from there." Branagh might just as well have been describing himself and his own high-wire career.

■ Works Cited

Billington, Michael, "Formidable Force," *Interview*, October, 1989, pp. 95, 134, 136.

Branagh, Kenneth, *Beginning*, Norton, 1990.

Canby, Vincent, "Branagh's *Dead Again* Homage to 40's Fiction," *New York Times*, August 23, 1992, pp. C1, C11.

Christiansen, Richard, review of *Beginning*, *Chicago Tribune*, May 20, 1990, p. 5.

Corliss, Richard, "The Whole Dane Thing," *Time*, January 13, 1997.

Hinson, Hal, "The Heart of *Henry V*," *Washington Post*, December 15, 1989, pp. D1, D9.

Hinson, Hal, "Nothing Much about 'Ado'," *Washington Post*, May 21, 1993, p. B7.

Howell, Georgina, "Renaissance Man," *Vogue*, September, 1991, pp. 524-27.

Huisman, Mark, "Prince of Players," *Advocate*, February 20, 1996, pp. 43-49.

James, Caryn, "Why Branagh's Bard Glows on the Screen," *New York Times*, May 16, 1993, p. 17.

Kauffmann, Stanley, movie review of *Henry V*, *New Republic*, December 4, 1989, p. 28.

Kehr, Dave, "Shakespeare by Numbers," *Chicago Tribune*, May 21, 1993, p. C29.

Lawson, Terry, "Branagh Takes a Break behind the Camera," *Detroit Free Press*, February 26, 1996, pp. E1, E3.

Maslin, Janet, "Conflicts and Laughs at English Reunion," *New York Times*, December 25, 1992, p. B4.

Maslin, Janet, "A Brain on Ice, a Dead Toad and Voila," *New York Times*, November 4, 1994, p. C1.

Maslin, Janet, "Fishburne and Branagh Meet Their Fate in Venice," *New York Times*, December 14, 1995, pp. C11, C20.

Rafferty, Terrence, movie review of *Peter's Friends*, *The New Yorker*, February 8, 1993, p. 103.

Smith, Dinitia, "Much Ado about Branagh," *New York*, May 24, 1993, pp. 36-45.

Travers, Peter, video review of *Henry V*, *Rolling Stone*, November 29, 1990, p. 122.

Turan, Kenneth, "Branagh's Lively High-Wire Act," *Los Angeles Times*, August 23, 1991, pp. F1, F6.

Turan, Kenneth, "Star-Powered Lovers in 'Ado'," *Los Angeles Times*, May 14, 1993, pp. F1, F15.

Wade, Nicholas, "Henry V vs. Henry V," *New York Times*, February 6, 1990, p. A28.

Werner, Laurie, "Villainy As Therapy," *Chicago Tribune*, December 24, 1995, section 7, p. 7.

Wolcott, James, movie review of *A Midwinter's Tale*, *The New Yorker*, February 12, 1996, pp. 84-85.

■ For More Information See

BOOKS

Bernard, Jami, *First Films*, Citadel Press, 1993.

Contemporary Theater, Film, and Television, Volume 9, Gale, 1992, pp. 46-7.

Davies, Anthony, and Stanley Wells, editors, *Shakespeare and the Moving Image*, Cambridge University Press, 1994.

Newsmakers: The People behind Today's Headlines, Gale, 1992, pp. 51-56.

Parsons, Keith, and Pamela Mason, *Shakespeare in Performance*, Salamander Books, 1995.

Shuttleworth, Ian, *Ken and Em* (unofficial biography), Headline Book Publishing, 1994.

PERIODICALS

Los Angeles Times Book Review, June 17, 1990, p. 6.

Premiere, September, 1991, p. 74.

Publishers Weekly, March 23, 1990, p. 69.

New York Times, November 13, 1994, section 2, p. 1.

Times Literary Supplement, October 20, 1989, p. 1151.

Wall Street Journal, November 10, 1994, p. A14.

Washington Post, May 21, 1993, p. WW53; November 4, 1994, p. F1; January 28, 1996, p. G1.*

—*Sketch by J. Sydney Jones*

Gwendolyn Brooks

■ Personal

Born June 7, 1917, in Topeka, KS; daughter of David Anderson (a janitor) and Keziah Corinne (a school teacher; maiden name, Wims) Brooks; married Henry Lowington Blakely II, September 17, 1939; children: Henry Lowington III, Nora. *Education:* Graduate of Wilson Junior College (now Kennedy-King College), 1936.

■ Addresses

Home—7428 South Evans Ave., Chicago, IL 60619.

■ Career

Poet and novelist. Publicity director, NAACP Youth Council, Chicago, 1937-38. Taught poetry at numerous colleges and universities, including Columbia College, Elmhurst College, and University of Wisconsin—Madison, 1969; Distinguished Professor of the Arts, City College of the City University of New York, 1971. *Member:* Illinois Arts Council, American Academy of Arts and Letters, National Institute of Arts and Letters, Society of Midland Authors (Chicago).

■ Awards, Honors

Named one of the ten women of the year, *Mademoiselle* magazine, 1945; National Institute of Arts and Letters grant in literature, 1946; National Academy of Arts and Letters award for creative writing, 1946; Guggenheim fellowships, 1946-47; Eunice Tietjens Memorial Prize, *Poetry* magazine, 1949; Pulitzer Prize in poetry, 1950, for *Annie Allen*; Robert F. Ferguson Memorial Award, Friends of Literature, 1964, for *Selected Poems*; Thormod Monsen Literature Award, 1964; Anisfield-Wolf Award, 1968, for *In the Mecca*; named Poet Laureate of Illinois, 1968—; Black Academy of Arts and Letters Award, 1971, for outstanding achievement in letters; Shelley Memorial Award, 1976; Poetry Consultant to the Library of Congress, 1985-86; induction into the National Women's Hall of Fame; winner of the Frost Medal; Lifetime Achievement Award from National Endowment for the Arts, 1989; Jefferson Lecturer, Kennedy Center, 1994; National Medal of Arts award, 1995. Has also received over 70 honorary degrees from universities and colleges, including Columbia College, 1964, Lake Forest College, 1965, and Brown University, 1974. The Gwendolyn Brooks Center for African American Literature, Western Illinois University, was named in her honor, and the Gwendolyn Brooks Junior High School, Harvey, IL, was dedicated in 1981.

■ Writings

POETRY

A Street in Bronzeville (see also below), Harper, 1945.

Annie Allen (see also below), Harper, 1949, Greenwood Press, 1972.

The Bean Eaters (see also below), Harper, 1960.

In the Time of Detachment, In the Time of Cold, Civil War Centennial Commission of Illinois, 1965.

In the Mecca (see also below), Harper, 1968.

For Illinois 1968: A Sesquicentennial Poem, Harper, 1968.

Riot (see also below), Broadside Press, 1969.

Family Pictures (see also below), Broadside Press, 1970.

Aurora, Broadside Press, 1972.

Beckonings, Broadside Press, 1975.

Primer for Blacks, Black Position Press, 1980.

To Disembark, Third World Press, 1981.

Black Love, Brooks Press, 1982.

Mayor Harold Washington [and] *Chicago, The I Will City,* Brooks Press, 1983.

The Near Johannesburg Boy, and Other Poems, David Co., 1987.

Gottschalk and the Grande Tarentelle, David Co., 1988.

Winnie, Third World Press, 1991.

Children Coming Home, David Co., 1991.

Also author of *A Catch of Shy Fish,* 1963.

JUVENILE

Bronzeville Boys and Girls (poems), Harper, 1956.

Aloneness (poems), Broadside Press, 1971.

The Tiger Who Wore White Gloves (verse story), Third World Press, 1974, 1987.

FICTION

Maud Martha (novel; see also below), Harper, 1953, David Co., 1987, Third World Press, 1993.

(Contributor) *Soon One Morning: New Writing by American Negroes, 1940-1962* (contains the short story "The Life of Lincoln West"), edited by Herbert Hill, Knopf, 1963.

(Contributor) *The Best Short Stories by Negro Writers: An Anthology from 1899 to the Present,* edited by Langston Hughes, Little, Brown, 1967.

COLLECTED WORKS

Selected Poems, Harper, 1963.

The World of Gwendolyn Brooks (includes *A Street in Bronzeville, Annie Allen, Maud Martha, The Bean Eaters, In the Mecca*), Harper, 1971.

Blacks (includes *A Street in Bronzeville, Annie Allen, The Bean Eaters, Maud Martha, A Catch of Shy Fish, Riot, In the Mecca,* and most of *Family Pictures*), David Co., 1987.

OTHER

(Author of foreword) *New Negro Poets USA,* edited by Langston Hughes, Indiana University Press, 1964.

(With others) *A Portion of That Field: The Centennial of the Burial of Lincoln,* University of Illinois Press, 1967.

(Editor) *A Broadside Treasury* (poems), Broadside Press, 1971.

(Editor) *Jump Bad: A New Chicago Anthology,* Broadside Press, 1972.

Report from Part One: An Autobiography, Broadside Press, 1972.

(Author of introduction) *The Poetry of Black America: Anthology of the Twentieth Century,* edited by Arnold Adoff, Harper, 1973.

(With Keorapetse Kgositsile, Haki R. Madhubuti, and Dudley Randall) *A Capsule Course in Black Poetry Writing,* Broadside Press, 1975.

Young Poet's Primer (writing manual), Brooks Press, 1981.

Very Young Poets (writing manual), Brooks Press, 1983.

Report from Part Two (autobiography), Third World Press, 1996.

Also author of broadsides *The Wall* and *We Real Cool,* for Broadside Press, *I See Chicago,* 1964, and *The Second Sermon on the Warpland,* Chax Press, 1988. Contributor of poems and articles to periodicals, including *Ebony, McCall's, Nation,* and *Poetry.* Contributor of reviews to *Chicago Sun-Times, Chicago Daily News,* and *New York Herald Tribune.* Brooks has also been recorded on cassette for the American Academy of Poets, 1995. Her papers and letters are collected at Atlanta University, Atlanta, GA. The State University of New York at Buffalo holds the typescript for *Annie Allen.*

■ Work in Progress

A sequel to *Maud Martha.*

■ Sidelights

The first black writer to win the Pulitzer Prize, Gwendolyn Brooks holds, as the critic George E. Kent noted in *Dictionary of Literary Biography*, "a unique position in American letters. Not only has she combined a strong commitment to racial identity and equality with a mastery of poetic techniques, but she has also managed to bridge the gap between the academic poets of her generation in the 1940s and the young black militant writers of the 1960s." Brooks has written poetry for over half a century, beginning in the late 1940s with such popular works as *A Bronzeville Street* and *Annie Allen*, written in folksy ballad form and more formalistic patterns to tell the stories of individuals fighting the twin demons of poverty and racism. As Martha Liebrum noted in the *Houston Post*, Brooks "wrote about being black before black was beautiful."

In the 1960s Brooks embraced more radical themes, influenced by a younger generation of black poets and activists, and in volumes such as *In the Mecca, Riot,* and *Family Pictures* explored racial pride and the possibility of violence to establish equality. Much of her later work has been characterized by a strong political if not polemical stance, though Brooks continues to blend more formal structure and language with contemporary black idiom. Brooks addressed this mid-career shift in the first volume of her autobiography, *Report from Part One*: "I—who have 'gone the gamut' from an almost angry rejection of my dark skin by some of my brainwashed brothers and sisters to a surprised queenhood in the new black sun— am qualified to enter at least the kindergarten of new consciousness now. . . . I have hopes for myself."

Brooks is also notable in that she is one of the few modern poets to put children at the center of much of her creative work. Not only in her adult poems such as *A Street In Bronzeville* and *Annie Allen,* but in volumes specifically written for children such as *Bronzeville Boys and Girls* has Brooks examined the experience of urban youth in mid-century America. She has dissected their aspirations and frustrations in vignettes of individual lives that, in aggregate, "speak for any child of any race," according to Zena Sutherland and May Hill Arbuthnot in *Children and Books*. The poems in *Bronzeville Boys and Girls* "show a rare sensitivity to the child's inner life—the wonder-ments, hurts, and sense of make-believe and play," Sutherland and Arbuthnot concluded. Advice to her own two children, included in her autobiography, could also form a fitting epigraph to Brooks's life and work: "First of all, do not lose faith in yourself. Remember: unhappiness eventually becomes something else—as does everything. . . . Be pleased with the things in life that are called little. The talk of birds. The first light of morning. . . . Mostly keep your head up high. (Sometimes lower it, to cry.). . . . I need not advise you to *remember that you are black*. The society will see to it that you remember. . . . 'Lastly,' little life-lines taped to my closet wall. One—and the chief of them: 'When handed a lemon, make lemonade.'"

Poet in the Making

Brooks has managed to "make lemonade" most of her life. Born in Topeka, Kansas, her parents were descendants of slaves who had migrated west. Her father's father was a runaway slave and soldier in the Civil War. Brooks's own father, David Brooks, was one of twelve children, and the only one of his family to graduate from high school. With hopes of becoming a doctor, he attended Fisk University for one year, then dropped out and married in 1916. Keziah Corinne Wims, Brooks's mother, was a schoolteacher at the time of her marriage, and had trained as a concert pianist. With the birth of her daughter, however, she became a homemaker. David Brooks's professional dreams were likewise sacrificed to the exigencies of earning a living, and, settling in Chicago, he became a janitor for a music company.

Brooks thus grew up in a nurturing and cultured environment (if a spartan one), never realizing the power of race until she began school. There she experienced racism for the first time, and intra-racial prejudice at that. Spurned by other black children because she lacked athletic ability, light skin, and what was considered good-grade hair, Brooks early on turned to writing as a solace. The themes of intra-racial prejudice and rejection would often appear in her mature work. From the age of seven, Brooks was writing poems and was encouraged in the pursuit especially by her mother who told her young daughter that one day she would be a poet. Brooks also read eagerly and widely, taking as early inspiration the works of Wordsworth, Keats, and Longfellow. Her first published poem, "Eventide," appeared in *American Childhood* when Brooks was only thirteen, and by age seventeen she was publishing poems regularly in the *Chicago Defender.*

By the time Brooks graduated from high school she was under the influence of more modern poets, such as Eliot, Pound and Cummings, as well as those of the Harlem Renaissance, such as Langston Hughes and Countee Cullen. Her early poems, while mostly heartfelt adolescent poems of love, already displayed a budding racial consciousness. As Kent noted in *Dictionary of Literary Biography,* "like many adolescents, [Brooks] was seething inwardly and making the most of imaginary pains." Throughout the 1930s and 1940s, Brooks worked to master a variety of poetic forms, encouraged by various teachers and poets, including James Weldon Johnson of the Harlem Renaissance. When Hughes was introduced to her early poems—in Chicago for a reading—he also encouraged Brooks to continue writing. By the late 1930s, Brooks had accumulated some seventy-five published poems as well as scores of others that formed the core of her apprenticeship. She also attended junior college at this time, graduating in 1936, and was then thrust into the working world. She took a job as a maid for a time and then worked as a secretarial assistant to Dr. E. N. French, a spiritual advisor, who was, according to Brooks, a charlatan, exploiting the extreme poverty of the residents of an early prototype of a Chicago 'project,' the Mecca, by selling them "Holy thunderbolts, charms, dusts of different kinds, love potions, heaven knows what all," Brooks wrote in her autobiography. Calling this job the "most horrible four months of my existence," Brooks would later make use of this material in the volume of poems entitled *In the Mecca.*

Poet Emerging

It was a job with the NAACP in 1938, however, which first put her into contact with other young people who were trying to change things for the better and who finally appreciated her for her talents. At an NAACP meeting she met the man who became her husband, Henry Lowington Blakely II. This marriage established Brooks on her own, and also introduced her first-hand to the difficulties of living a kitchenette life in the one-room apartments then available for Chicago blacks. Brooks's son was born in 1940, and the

next year Brooks took part in a poetry workshop led by Inez Cunningham Stark of *Poetry* magazine, where she learned many of the techniques of modern poetry and began the cycle of poems that would become *A Street in Bronzeville.* After winning local prizes for several long poems, Brooks tried publishing a collection through Knopf but was advised by an editor there to concentrate on poems from her own background, which she did, writing nineteen more poems about blacks. The collection was subsequently sent to Harper where an encouraging reading by Richard Wright convinced Brooks to include a longer poem, "The Sundays of Satin Legs Smith." *A Street in Bronzeville* thus appeared in 1945 to enthusiastic critical reception.

The poems of *A Street in Bronzeville* detail the daily lives of the residents of that Chicago district largely occupied by blacks, and are told in "folksy narrative nature," according to Brooks. "I guess that is one way to get poetry in front of people," Brooks noted in her autobiography, "to tell stories. Everyone loves stories." Critics were quick to point out this folksy approach, but also Brooks's "happy ability to vary the manner to suit the matter," as Rolfe Humphries wrote in *New York Times Book Review.* According to Humphries, Brooks appeared equally at home in free verse, sonnets, ballads, or quatrains, and concluded that "we have, in *A Street in Bronzeville,* a good book and a real poet." Amos N. Wilder in *Poetry* echoed these sentiments, concluding that Brooks had displayed a "capacity to marry the special qualities of her racial tradition with the best attainments of our contemporary poetic tradition." And in *Saturday Review of Literature,* Starr Nelson commented that *A Street in Bronzeville* was "a work of art and a poignant social document."

Many of the themes Brooks would explore in the coming years were introduced in this first volume of poems: the frustrations and desperation of life lived on the margin; the alienation of black women; intra-racial as well as interracial prejudice. Exploring the everyday lives of residents of Bronzeville, Brooks was able to present such themes on the individual level, to humanize them. In the poem "The Ballad of Chocolate Mabbie," Brooks looks at the hardships endured by a young woman rejected by other blacks because of her dark skin. Mabbie is jilted by Willie Boone for a light-skinned girl, and the conclusion of the poem reveals new ironies: "It was Mabbie alone by the grammar school gates / Yet chocolate companions had she: / Mabbie on Mabbie with hush in the heart / Mabbie on Mabbie to be."

Some of her longer poems in the collection are ballads, such as "Queen of the Blues" and "Ballad of Pearl May Lee," while others such as "The Sundays of Satin Legs Smith" function as verse stories in which Satin Legs fights against the deadening of life in his own unique way: through flashy clothes and sexual adventures. Brooks describes his outfits as "wonder suits in yellow and in wine / Sarcastic green and zebra-striped cobalt." She details his romantic choices as well— "His lady alters as to leg and eye / Thickness and height, such minor points as these / From Sunday to Sunday." Critics have disagreed, however, as to how optimistic such poems are. For Kent in *Black Women Writers (1950-1980)*, "optimism prevailed" in these early poems of neighborhood and hard lives told with simple syntax

and directness of imagery. In his essay for *Dictionary of Literary Biography*, Kent noted that "the people of the 'kitchenette building' . . . meet limited goals." Brooks describes some of the locals achieving some of these limited goals: "We are things of dry hours and the involuntary plan, / Grayed in, and gray. 'Dream' makes a giddy sound / not strong / Like 'rent,' 'feeding a wife,' 'satisfying a man.'"

For other critics, however, Brooks's tone is more pessimistic. Gary Smith, in a *Melus* overview of Brooks's work, noted that unlike poets of the Harlem Renaissance (many of whom never lived in Harlem), Brooks portrays the "victimization" of black women. Smith also pointed out that, while not completely eschewing the optimistic orientation of the Harlem Renaissance poets, "Brooks rejects outright their romantic prescriptions for the lives of Black women." The very first poem in the collection, "old marrieds," managed to debunk "the prevalent motifs of Harlem Renaissance poetry: its general optimism about the future," according to Smith. That poem ends with less than optimistic lines: "It was quite a time for loving. It was midnight. It was May. / But in the crowding darkness not a word did they say." Critics have also noted that Brooks displayed her ability to blend technical mastery with her homespun stories in this first volume, with the World War II sonnet sequence "Gay Chaps at the Bar," told in Petrarchian and Shakespearean formats.

The Pulitzer Prize and Literary Experiments

Brooks's next book of poems, *Annie Allen*, appeared four years later. The poems gathered in that volume display a continual growth on Brooks's part toward dealing with social issues head on. In between volumes she had been awarded prizes for her poetry and honored with Guggenheim fellowships to help finance her work. She had also begun writing for various newspapers; these activities among others led her to appreciate more fully than ever the position of women in society, and with *Annie Allen* she examined the coming of age of a young black woman. Through the course of several poems, Brooks follows Annie's development from romantic youth to realistic adult. In "Notes from Childhood and Girlhood," readers learn of Annie's parents and some of the ethical lessons she learned growing up. The central part of the volume is the

The World of GWENDOLYN BROOKS

A Street in Bronzeville
Annie Allen   *Maud Martha*
The Bean Eaters   *In the Mecca*

COMPLETE IN ONE VOLUME

This 1971 volume contains four of Brooks's best-known poetry collections as well as her first novel.

long mock-heroic poem "The Anniad," whose title and structure come from Virgil's *Aeneid*. This poem describes the coming of age of "sweet and chocolate" Annie, depicting in realistic terms the situation of black women, and ends with a sonnet-ballad mixture which was Brooks's unique creation. The imagery of this section is, according to Kent, a "mixture of the romantic and the realistic:" "Think of ripe and romp-about / All her harvest buttoned in, / All her ornaments untried; / Waiting for the paladin / Prosperous and ocean-eyed / Who shall rub her secrets out / And behold the hinted bride." A final section, "The Womanhood," is more similar in format to her Bronzeville poems, wherein she details scenes and emotions from everyday life, such as these mixed sentiments of love from a poor mother for her child: "The little lifting helplessness, the queer / Whimper-whine, whose unridiculous / Lost softness softly makes a trap for us."

Critical reception of *Annie Allen* was favorable, though often mixed with reservations about the relative difficulty of the new poems as compared to the Bronzeville ones. J. Saunders Redding, writing in *Saturday Review of Literature*, while noting the pitfalls that obscurity can create in modern poetry, found that *Annie Allen* "is as sure, as emotionally firm, and as esthetically complete as a silver figure by Cellini. . . . [Brooks] is a glory to read." Langston Hughes also reviewed the new book of poems and concluded in *Voices* that "the people and poems in Gwendolyn Brooks' book are alive, reaching, and very much of today." In 1950, Brooks won the Pulitzer Prize for *Annie Allen*, the award's first black recipient. She became something of an institution in Chicago thereafter, widely interviewed and always in demand for public readings. The following year her daughter was born, and the family settled in a new house in Chicago.

In 1953, Brooks published her only novel, *Maud Martha*, the story of a young black woman who leaves behind romantic dreams to enter into the realistic life of a woman and mother. Again, echoing Brooks's own experience, the heroine of this novel suffers prejudice within her own race because of the darkness of her skin. Written in a highly poetic idiom, the book "transcends naturalistic formulas," according to Kent in *Dictionary of Literary Biography*. Maud, as Harry B. Shaw pointed out in his critical study, *Gwendolyn Brooks*, has "doubts about herself and where and how she fits into the world. Maud's concern is not so much that she is inferior but that she is perceived as being ugly." Maud finally takes a stand for her own self-respect, dealing with a racist store clerk. Many of Brooks's standard themes are at play here: standing up to racism, the relativity of beauty, the importance of inner beauty and spirituality. Patricia H. Lattin and Vernon E. Lattin, in a study of the novel in *Critique: Studies in Modern Fiction*, pointed out that Brooks "suggests a positive way of life that can help one maintain one's self respect in the face of the racism and death which surround one. . . . In *Maud Martha*, Brooks has created a female character unique for the time period."

Brooks returned to poetry with her 1956 volume, *Bronzeville Boys and Girls*, a book for young readers told through thirty-four different children. In these short poems Brooks explored childhood disappointment, joy, love, and friendship. In the poem "Otto," for example, she tells of a child who is "prematurely involved in adult problems," according to D. H. Melhem in *Gwendolyn Brooks: Poetry and the Heroic Voice*. Little Otto did not get the Christmas present he was hoping for, and instead of moping, fears for his father's hurt feelings: "My Dad must never know I care / It's hard enough for him to bear." Brooks also explored a child's playfulness with language, as in these lines from "Cynthia in the Snow:" "It SUSHES / It hushes / The loudness in the road. / It flutter-twitters, / And laughs away from me. / It laughs a lovely whiteness / And whitely whirs away, / To be / Some otherwhere, / Still white as milk or shirts / So beautiful it hurts."

The volume was praised by critics for its universality of theme and its rhythmic simplicity. Margaret Sherwood Libby, writing in the *New York Herald Tribune Book Review*, noted that the poems are "universal and will make friends anywhere, among grown-ups or among children from eight to ten." Charlemae Rollins commented in the *Chicago Sunday Tribune Magazine of Books* that "the poems are gay, carefree, and serious—but none is sad. Adults who enjoy reading poetry aloud to children will welcome these for their fresh viewpoint." A later children's book is *The Tiger Who Wore White Gloves*, a children's story in verse. Horace Coleman, writing in *Black Scholar*, noted that "youngsters who have negative feelings about themselves will gain pleasant insights from reading the story or having it read to them."

GWENDOLYN BROOKS

BROADSIDE PRESS $1.00

Brooks's concern for social issues can be seen in this 1971 work about a white man caught in a race riot.

Social Issues to the Forefront

Brooks returned to adult poetry with *The Bean Eaters*, the major theme of which, according to Charles Israel in *Dictionary of Literary Biography*, was "that of the ghetto dwellers' quest for purpose and relief from aimlessness." One poem does not fit this general pattern, however: an elegy for Brooks's father who had died in 1959. "In Honor of David Anderson Brooks, My Father" is a celebration of the man who had been such a rich influence on her life: "A dryness is upon the house / My father loved and tended. / Beyond his firm and sculptured door / his light and lease have ended."

The characters in the other poems in the volume, however, are more familiar. They seek security in a variety of ways reminiscent of Brooks's Bronzeville characters: by identifying with heroes out of movie Westerns, wearing flashy clothes, practicing religion, chasing excesses. One of her most often anthologized poems, "We Real Cool," comes from this collection, and ends with the refrain "We / Sing sin, We / Thin gin. We / Jazz June. We / Die soon." Some critics have pointed out that the poems in *The Bean Eaters* demonstrate further growth away from the purely autobiographical toward increased social awareness. "The Ballad of Rudolph Reed" chronicles the story of a black man who moves his family out of the ghetto to a white suburb with disastrous results. Unfriendly white neighbors gather outside the Reed house one night. When a rock is thrown through the window injuring Rudolph's daughter, Mabel, he runs amok, wounding four of the white men before he is killed. The ending quatrain does not provide solutions, but instead keeps the camera on the tragedy: "Small Mabel whimpered all night long, / For calling herself the cause. / Her oak-eyed mother did no thing / But change the bloody gauze." John W. Parker in a *College Language Association Journal* review of the volume commented that "here is poetry that laughs and cries, sings and shouts." Addison Gayle, Jr., writing in the *New York Times Book Review*, commented that Rudolph Reed represented "the creation of a new folk hero, one who moves beyond the old stereotype, who chooses human life over property values." Many critics have agreed that Brooks's best social poems are contained in *The Bean Eaters.*

Increased social consciousness as well as increasingly politicized verses can also be seen in Brooks's next volume of poetry, *Selected Poems*, some of which were new and some carefully culled from earlier volumes. The social issues of the civil rights movement found a place in such poems as "Riders to the Blood-Red Wrath," a tribute to the Freedom Riders who worked for voter registration in the south. Israel pointed out in *Dictionary of Literary Biography* that "here, for the first time in Brooks's poetry, is the contrast between the 'Old Freedom' of Africa and the slavery and injustice of America." Yet Brooks still saw an America in which blacks and whites could work together for racial harmony: "I / My fellows, and those canny consorts of / Our spread hands in this contretemps-for-love / Ride into wrath, wraith, and menagerie / To fail, to flourish, to wither or to win. / We lurch, distribute, we extend, begin."

Also in the 1960s Brooks began working with the young, teaching poetry workshops at Columbia College in Chicago and at Fisk University. It was at the Second Fisk Writers Conference in April, 1967 where Brooks was inspired with a new sense of mission. The civil rights movement had become subsumed by the black power movement and Brooks came into contact with energetic and emotional younger writers such as LeRoi Jones (Amiri Baraka). Returning to Chicago, Brooks instituted poetry workshops for a street gang, The Blackstone Rangers, among whose members were Don L. Lee (Haki R. Madhubuti).

Toward a New Black Aesthetic

These experiences helped Brooks to finally utilize the material from her early work experience in the Mecca building, which she had tried to fashion into a novel. The long poem "In the Mecca," published in a volume of the same title, is a story within a story written in free verse. While the larger story is a series of ironic character sketches reminiscent of the Bronzeville poems, the connecting story is that of Mrs. Sallie Smith and her search through the dilapidated Mecca apartment building for her little daughter Pepita. Along the way, the denizens of the apartment block are presented, by and large people debased by poverty, with no way out, and who do not even care what has happened to the little girl. Pepita is finally found raped and murdered under the bed of Jamaican Edward: "Beneath his cot / A little woman lies in dust with roaches. / She never went to kindergarten. / She never learned that black is not beloved." Other poems in the book, included under "After Mecca," brought Brooks's social commitment more up to date, one occasioned by a mural of black heroes painted on a slum building, another by the death of Malcolm X: "And in a soft and fundamental hour / a sorcery devout and vertical / beguiled the world. / He opened us— / Who was a key, / Who was a man." Taken as a whole, *In the Mecca* is a paean to racial pride and black militancy, and is "an epic of black humanity," according to Madhubuti as cited in Melhem's *Gwendolyn Brooks: Poetry and the Heroic Voice.*

Since publication of *In the Mecca*, Brooks's career has been highlighted by increased commitment to racial solidarity. It was the last book to be published by her publisher, Harper; Brooks has since published with black-owned firms in Detroit and Chicago. "Her trip to East Africa in 1971 cemented her commitment to both her African heritage and the Third World," noted Israel in *Dictionary of Literary Biography*. She also visited West Africa in 1974. The first part of her autobiography appeared in 1972, *Report from Part One*, which chronicles her growth from a Negro poet to a black poet. Small volumes of poetry also appeared: *Riot, Family Pictures, Beckonings,* and *Primer for Blacks*, some of which were collected in the 1981 work *To Disembark*. In *Riot*, the white protagonist John Cabot comes face to face with black power in the form of a race riot: "Don't let it touch me! the blackness! Lord!" he whispered / to any handy angel in the sky." The central poem of *Family Pictures* is a free-verse ballad, "The Life of Lincoln West," in which Brooks once again explores the theme of beauty versus ugliness. A white man points out little Lincoln as "One of the best samples of the specie." The man goes on ironically to recount the physical qualities: "Black, ugly, and odd. You / can see the savagery. The blunt / blankness. That is the real / thing." But by the end of the poem Lincoln has turned this criticism into an "asset" according to Israel: "He told himself / 'After all, I'm the real thing.' / It comforted him."

Brooks's poetry can be divided into three periods, according to Norris B. Clarke in *A Life Distilled: Gwendolyn Brooks, Her Poetry and Fiction*: "(1) *A Street in Bronzeville* and *Annie Allen*, primarily devoted to craft and exhibit an 'objective and exquisite detachment' from the lives or emotions of individuals; (2) *The Bean Eaters, Selected Poems,* and *In the Mecca*, also devoted to craft, but exhibit a strong awareness of black social concerns; and (3) *Riot, Family Pictures, Aloneness,* and *Beckonings*, less devoted to craft and more concerned about pronounced statements on a black mystique, the necessity of riots (violence), and black unity." It is no surprise that the third category of poems have drawn the most controversy. In a review of *Riot*, L. L. Shapiro, writing in *School Library Journal*, accused Brooks of "celebrating violence," though other critics, such as Addison Gayle, Jr., in *Black Women Writers (1950-1980)*, have defended these poems for their strength and honesty. As Gayle wrote: "It may well be . . . that the function of poetry is not so much to save us from oppression nor from Auschwitz, but to give us the strength to face them, to help us stare down the lynch mob, walk boldly in front of the firing squad."

D. H. Melhem, cited in Kent's *Dictionary of Literary Biography* article, noted that Brooks "assumes the role of prophet in these later poems." In fact Brooks assumed this mantle of prophet and teacher with several writing manuals created specifically with black poets in mind. In her 1975 *A Capsule Course in Black Poetry Writing*, she advised young black writers that "black literature is literature BY blacks, ABOUT blacks, directed TO blacks: ESSENTIAL black literature is the distillation of black life. Black life is different from white life. Different in nuance, different in 'nitty-gritty.' Different *from* birth. Different *at* death." But, characteristically, along with the political message came one of craft, as well: "Try telling the reader a little less. He'll, She'll love you more and will love your poem more, if you allow him to do a little digging. Not *too* much, but *some*." Don L. Lee (Madhubuti), in a survey of Brooks's work in *Black Scholar*, noted that her "post 1967 poetry is fatless." According to Lee, Brooks's early poetry was "written for whites," but her later work moves from "the sayer to the doer. . . . Gwendolyn Brooks is an African poet living and writing in America."

Other critics debate that Brooks can be so easily pigeon-holed. Characteristically, Brooks has simply kept working, writing poetry and collecting honors and awards through the 1980s and into the 1990s. Appointed poetry consultant to the Library of Congress, she has also served as Poet Laureate of Illinois since 1968, endowing literary prizes for young people with her own funds. In 1989, Brooks was the recipient of a lifetime achievement award from the National Endowment for the Arts, and in 1995 won the National Medal of Arts award. Though her later writing has tended more toward the broadside and shorter poems, in 1991 she also published a larger volume, *Winnie*, about that South African leader, the former wife of Nelson Mandela. In 1996 the second part of her autobiography, *Report from Part Two*, was published.

Throughout her career, Brooks has blended a potent brew of both poetry and politics. "I want to write poems that will be non-compromising," she told George Stavros in a *Contemporary Literature* interview. "I don't want to stop a concern with words doing good jobs, which has always been a concern of mine, but I want to write poems that will be meaningful . . . things that will touch them." As Robert F. Kiernan commented in *American Writers Since 1945: A Critical Survey*, Brooks remains "a virtuoso of the lyric and an extraordinary portraitist—probably the finest black poet of the post-Harlem generation." In her startling images, imaginative use of technical craft "in forms as disparate as Italian terza rima and the blues," according to Toni Cade Bambara in the *New York Times Book Review*, and commitment to a cause, Brooks has created a body of work that continues to reach beyond the narrow confines of race or gender. As Norris Clarke noted, "Regardless of how one chooses to classify Brooks's poetry . . . her corpus remains an undeniable statement about the condition humane."

■ Works Cited

Bambara, Toni Cade, review of *Report from Part One*, *New York Times Book Review*, January 7, 1973, pp. 1, 10.

Brooks, Gwendolyn, *A Street in Bronzeville*, Harper, 1945.

Brooks, Gwendolyn, *Annie Allen*, Harper, 1949.

Brooks, Gwendolyn, *Bronzeville Boys and Girls*, Harper, 1956.

Brooks, Gwendolyn, *The Bean Eaters*, Harper, 1960.

Brooks, Gwendolyn, *Selected Poems*, Harper, 1963.

Brooks, Gwendolyn, *In the Mecca*, Harper, 1968.

Brooks, Gwendolyn, *Riot*, Broadside Press, 1969.

Brooks, Gwendolyn, *Family Pictures*, Broadside Press, 1970.

Brooks, Gwendolyn, *Report from Part One*, Broadside Press, 1972.

Brooks, Gwendolyn (with others), *A Capsule Course in Black Poetry Writing*, Broadside Press, 1975.

Clarke, Norris B., "Gwendolyn Brooks and a Black Aesthetic," *A Life Distilled: Gwendolyn Brooks, Her Poetry and Fiction*, edited by Maria K. Mootry and Gary Smith, University of Illinois Press, 1987, pp. 81-99.

Coleman, Horace, review of *The Tiger Who Wore White Gloves, Black Scholar*, March-April, 1981, p. 92.

Gayle, Addison, Jr., review of *The World of Gwendolyn Brooks, New York Times Book Review*, January 2, 1972, pp. 4, 20.

Gayle, Addison, Jr., "Gwendolyn Brooks," *Black Women Writers (1950-1980): A Critical Evaluation*, edited by Mari Evans, Anchor Books, 1984.

Hughes, Langston, "Name, Race, and Gift in Common," *Voices*, Winter, 1950, pp. 54-6.

Humphries, Rolfe, "Bronzeville," *New York Times Book Review*, November 4, 1945, p. 14.

Israel, Charles, "Gwendolyn Brooks," *Dictionary of Literary Biography*, Volume 5: *American Poets Since World War II*, Gale, 1980, pp. 100-6.

Kent, George E., "Gwendolyn Brooks' Poetic Realism: A Developmental Survey," *Black Women Writers (1950-1980): A Critical Evaluation*, edited by Mari Evans, Anchor Books, 1984, pp. 88-105.

Kent, George E., "Gwendolyn Brooks," *Dictionary of Literary Biography*, Volume 76: *Afro-American Writers, 1940-1955*, Gale, 1988, pp. 11-24.

Kiernan, Robert F., *American Writing Since 1945: A Critical Study*, Ungar, 1983.

Lattin, Patricia H., and Vernon E. Lattin, "Dual Vision in Gwendolyn Brooks's 'Maud Martha'," *Critique: Studies in Modern Fiction*, Summer, 1984, pp. 180-88.

Lee, Don L., "The Achievement of Gwendolyn Brooks," *Black Scholar*, Summer, 1972, pp. 32-41.

Libby, Margaret Sherwood, review of *Bronzeville Boys and Girls, New York Herald Tribune Book Review*, November 18, 1956, p. 2.

Liebrum, Martha, *Houston Post*, February 11, 1974.

Melhem, D. H., *Gwendolyn Brooks: Poetry and the Heroic Voice*, University Press of Kentucky, 1987.

Nelson, Starr, review of *A Street in Bronzeville, Saturday Review of Literature*, January 19, 1946.

Parker, John W., "Saga of the Bronzeville Community," *College Language Association Journal*, September, 1960, pp. 59-61.

Redding, J. Saunders, "Cellini-Like Lyrics," *Saturday Review of Literature*, September 17, 1949, pp. 23-27.

Rollins, Charlemae, review of *Bronzeville Boys and Girls, Chicago Sunday Tribune Magazine of Books*, November 11, 1956, p. 20.

Shapiro, L. L., review of *Riot, School Library Journal*, August, 1982, p. 124.

Shaw, Harry B., *Gwendolyn Brooks*, Twayne, 1980.

Smith, Gary, "Gwendolyn Brooks's 'A Street in Bronzeville', the Harlem Renaissance and the Mythologies of Black Women," *Melus*, Fall, 1983, pp. 33-46.

Stavros, George, "An Interview with Gwendolyn Brooks," *Contemporary Literature*, Winter, 1970, pp. 1-20.

Sutherland, Zena, and May Hill Arbuthnot, "The Range of Poets for Children: 'Bronzeville Boys and Girls'," *Children and Books*, Scott, Foresman, 1986, p. 318.

Wilder, Amos N., "Sketches from Life," *Poetry*, December, 1945, pp. 164-66.

■ For More Information See

BOOKS

Berry, S. L., *Gwendolyn Brooks*, Creative Education, 1993.

Black Literature Criticism, Volume 1, Gale, 1989.

Children's Literature Review, Volume 27, Gale, 1992, pp. 44-56.

Contemporary Authors, New Revision Series, Volume 27, Gale, 1989, pp. 68-73.

Contemporary Literary Criticism, Gale, Volume 1, 1973, Volume 2, 1974, Volume 4, 1976, Volume 15, 1980, Volume 49, 1988.

Kent, George E., *Gwendolyn Brooks: A Life*, University Press of Kentucky, 1988.

Madhubuti, Haki R., *Say That the River Turns: The Impact of Gwendolyn Brooks*, Third World Press, 1987.

Miller, R. Baxter, *Langston Hughes and Gwendolyn Brooks: A Reference Guide*, Hall, 1978.

Miller, R. Baxter, *Black American Poets between Worlds, 1940-1960*, University of Tennessee Press, 1986.

Poetry Criticism, Volume 7, Gale, 1990, pp. 51-109.

Tate, Claudia, *Black Women Writers at Work*, Continuum, 1983.

Wright, Stephen Caldwell, editor, *On Gwendolyn Brooks: Reliant Contemplation*, University of Michigan Press, 1996.

PERIODICALS

Atlantic Monthly, September, 1960.

Best Sellers, April 1, 1973, p. 9.

Booklist, February 1, 1987, p. 847.

Black World, August, 1970; January, 1971; July, 1971; September, 1971; October, 1971; January, 1972; March, 1973; June, 1973; December, 1975.

College Language Association Journal, December, 1962, pp. 90-97; December, 1963, pp. 114-25; September, 1973, pp. 16-20; September, 1977, pp. 19-40.

Ebony, July, 1968.

Essence, April, 1971; September, 1984.

Jet, June 26, 1989.

Kenyon Review, Winter, 1995, p. 136.

Library Journal, November 15, 1971, p. 3916; February 15, 1972, p. 672; September 1, 1972, p. 2759; November 1, 1981, p. 2142.

Los Angeles Times Book Review, September 2, 1984.

Negro American Literature Forum, Summer, 1974, pp. 199-207.

New Yorker, September 22, 1945; December 17, 1949; October 10, 1953; December 3, 1979.

New York Times Book Review, October 23, 1960; October 6, 1963; March 2, 1969; June 4, 1972, p. 29; December 3, 1972, p. 84; June 10, 1973; December 2, 1973; June 8, 1980, p. 41; September 32, 1984; July 5, 1987.

Obsidian, spring, 1978, pp. 19-31.

Poetry, March, 1964.

Studies in Black Literature, spring, 1977, pp. 1-3.

Washington Post Book World, November 3, 1968; November 11, 1973.*

—Sketch by J. Sydney Jones

John Donovan

Personal

Born in 1928, in Lynn, MA; died of cancer, April 29, 1992, in Manhattan, NY. *Education:* Graduated from William and Mary College; University of Virginia, J.D.

Career

Writer. Children's Book Council, New York City, president, 1967-92; International Board on Books for Young People (IBBY), executive director of U.S. National Section, 1967-87, treasurer, 1986-90, chairman of Congress Programme Committee, 1990. Writer-in-residence, University of Michigan Residential College, 1983. Worked as an English teacher, as a lawyer for the Library of Congress, as an examiner in the U.S. Copyright Office, and was affiliated with St. Martin's Press.

Awards, Honors

Children's Book of the Year citation, Child Study Association of America, honor list citation, *Horn* *Book*, Children's Spring Book Festival, honor book citation, *Book World*, and Newbery Medal nomination, 1969, all for *I'll Get There. It Better Be Worth the Trip;* best book citation, *School Library Journal*, Outstanding Book of the Year citation, *New York Times*, both 1971, and National Book Award finalist, Children's Books category, 1972, all for *Wild in the World;* Children's Book of the Year citation, Child Study Association of America, 1976, for *Family;* Children's Reading Roundtable of Chicago award, 1983; Jella Lepman Medal, International Board on Books for Young People, 1991, for IBBY program development.

Writings

JUVENILE FICTION

The Little Orange Book (picture book), illustrated by Mauro Caputo, Morrow, 1961.
I'll Get There. It Better Be Worth the Trip (novel), Harper, 1969, Macdonald, 1970.
Wild in the World (novel), Harper, 1971.
Remove Protective Coating a Little at a Time (novel), Harper, 1973.
Good Old James (picture book), illustrated by James Stevenson, Harper, 1974.
Family: A Novel, Harper, 1976.
Bittersweet Temptation, Zebra Books, 1979.
(Translator) Henri Bernardin De Saint-Pierre, *Paul and Virginia*, Dufour, 1983.

FOR ADULTS

Riverside Drive (two plays, *Damn You, Scarlett O'
Hara* and *All My Pretty Little Ones*), produced
in New York, 1964.
The Businessman's International Travel Guide, Stein
and Day, 1971.
(Editor) *U.S. & Soviet Policy in the Middle East,*
Facts on File, 1972.
Business Re-Engineering with Technology, Prentice
Hall, 1994.

I'll Get There. It Better Be Worth the Trip has been
translated into Spanish and published as *Espero
Que El Viaje Valga La Pena; Riverside Drive* was
translated into various languages. Also author of
the introduction for *Children's Books: Awards &
Prizes* (revised edition), Children's Book Council,
Inc., 1993. Contributor of articles to *Publishers
Weekly, Wilson Library Bulletin, Horn Book,* and
School Library Journal.

■ Adaptations

The film rights for *I'll Get There. It Better Be Worth
the Trip,* were sold in 1973.

■ Sidelights

"I guess I kiss Altschuler and he kisses me," explains the protagonist of John Donovan's first
novel. "It just happens. And when it stops we sit
up and turn away from each other." As the narrator voicing these lines is a teenage boy, *I'll Get
There. It Better Be Worth The Trip* incited controversy in 1969. Some critics asserted that a book
which seemed to contain a homosexual episode
was not suitable for children. Others applauded
Donovan's bold treatment of adolescent sexual
experimentation and his willingness to discuss
tough subjects like death, divorce, and alcoholism.
The writer continued to address these subjects and
to compose what Jean F. Mercier of *Publishers
Weekly* called "astonishingly innovative novels"
dealing with "things which matter." By 1973, as
John Rowe Townsend of the *New York Times Book
Review* noted, Donovan had earned a reputation
as a "taboo-buster."

John Donovan was born in Lynn, Massachusetts,
and educated in Virginia, where he earned an
undergraduate degree from William and Mary

College and a law degree from the University of
Virginia. As a young adult, he worked as an English teacher, a lawyer for the Library of Congress,
and an examiner in the U.S. Copyright Office.
Donovan launched his career in the publishing
world in the 1960s. His first book, *The Little Orange Book,* was published in 1961, and Donovan
began work as the Executive Director of the
Children's Book Council in 1967. From that time
until his death in 1992, Donovan worked as both
a children's book writer and an expert on
children's book publishing. He advocated the publication of a wide variety of children's books and
suggested, as he did in *Publishers Weekly* in 1970,
that publishers work with educators to bring new
books into the classroom.

I'll Get There. It Better Be Worth the Trip, published
in 1969, was Donovan's first novel for young
people. As the *Washington Post Book World*'s Alice
Hungerford observed, this novel "portrays . . . a
few months' flow" of thirteen-year-old Davy's "experience" with "natural realism." The story is told
by Davy in the first person, in a realistic style
and language (including mild expletives) that
many critics compared to those of J. D. Salinger's
The Catcher in the Rye. The novel begins as Davy's
family is returning home from his grandmother's
funeral. Davy had lived with his grandmother
since his parents' divorce when he was just a little
boy, and her death is very difficult for him. Davy
insists on taking Fred, the black dachshund dog
his grandmother had given him on his eighth
birthday, to live with him in his mother's small
New York apartment.

Davy is not very happy in New York. His alcoholic mother either smothers him with love or
lectures him about what a burden he is to her.
Although Davy enjoys the company of his stepmother, Stephanie, Davy's visits with his father
make him uncomfortable. Davy does, however, get
along well at his private school. His exploits in
drama and baseball make him popular, and he
makes one good friend, Altschuler. Altschuler and
Davy have much in common. When they meet,
Davy has taken the classroom seat of Altschuler's
best friend, Larry, who has left the school because
he is dying from a blood disease. Eventually,
Larry dies, and Altschuler, like Davy, experiences
the grief death brings. Altschuler's parents are also
divorced, and like Davy, Altschuler lives with his
mother. Together, Davy and Altschuler explore the
city.

The boys' relationship takes an unexpected turn one day when they are playing with Fred in Davy's apartment. After rolling on the floor with the dog, they pause, look at each other, and begin to kiss. Neither boy understands the kiss. "'What was that all about?'" Davy asks Altschuler. He tells himself, "a couple of guys like Altschuler and me don't have to worry about being queer or anything like that. Hell, no." Later, Davy and Altschuler continue their sexual exploration by "making out." Davy is confused, and asks, "There's nothing wrong with Altschuler and me, is there? I know it's not like making out with a girl. It's just something that happened. It's not dirty, or anything like that. It's all right, isn't it?"

Davy's mother becomes suspicious about the boys' relationship and asks his father to have a talk

I'll Get There. It Better Be Worth The Trip.

a novel by John Donovan

A thirteen-year-old boy's homosexual encounter with his best friend leads to self-awareness and maturity in this controversial 1969 novel.

with Davy while she takes Fred out for a walk. Davy's father's assurance that sexual exploration is normal is forgotten when Fred is hit by a car and killed. Thinking that Fred's death is punishment for his sexual encounters with Altschuler, Davy avoids his friend. After Davy and Altschuler discuss their relationship and Fred's death, as Mary L. Nolan of *ALAN Review* explained, Davy "realizes that the kiss is not indicative of homosexuality, not a threat to his masculinity."

I'll Get There. It Better Be Worth The Trip, recalled one critic in the *Times Literary Supplement*, "made a mild sensation in the United States." Some critics asserted that the novel was unsuitable for young adults. Martha Bacon of *Atlantic Monthly* argued that the "novel celebrates the child's homosexual encounter" and "might arouse in the unconcerned unnecessary interest or alarm or both." Others, like Nolan, suggested that the theme of the "novel is of friendship not homosexuality" and that *I'll Get There. It Better Be Worth the Trip* may be used to "reassure adolescents that they are not" homosexual "because of their desires to demonstrate love" to someone of the same sex. John Weston of the *New York Times Book Review* similarly argued that Donovan's message was that "homosexuality is to some degree a natural occurrence among close friends old enough for sexual desires but without sexual outlets." Writing in 1977, David Rees worried about the potential of *I'll Get There. It Better Be Worth the Trip* to aggravate the fears of young homosexuals and to reinforce heterosexual "prejudice" against homosexuals.

Some critics de-emphasized the controversial episode in *I'll Get There. It Better Be Worth the Trip*, or praised its other features. Lavinia Russ of *Publishers Weekly* asserted that the "incident with homosexual ingredients," is just another moment in a "perceptive, funny, touching story." Paul Heins of *Horn Book* especially appreciated Davy's "mercilessly honest" understanding of the adults in his life, and he enjoyed the "lifelike and unforgettable canine portrait" of Davy's dog, Fred.

Isolation, Alienation, and Unlikely Friendships

When readers are introduced to the Gridleys and their farm on Rattlesnake Mountain in New Hampshire in *Wild in the World* (1971), all but three of the original thirteen family members have

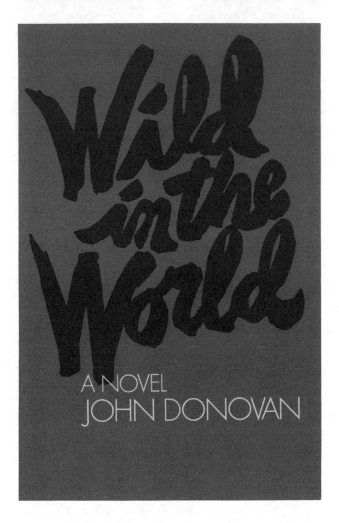

John Gridley, the last surviving member of his family, befriends a stray wolf-dog in this 1971 work.

died from rattlesnake bites, fevers, and self-inflicted wounds. It is not long before two more family members die in accidents, and young John Gridley is left completely alone. Without mourning the passage of his family, or caring about anyone, or feeling much of anything, John continues with his farm work and fends for himself. He rarely sees his neighbors, and when he does, he doesn't say much to them.

John's indifferent isolation is disturbed when a wolf, or a dog, wanders onto the Gridley property. John gradually befriends the creature, and before long, man and dog begin to depend on each other and care for each other. John names the dog "Son," and fights to save its life when it is bitten by a rattlesnake. It is John, in the end, who gets sick and dies of pneumonia. When the

neighbors find his body, they conclude that the dog killed him, and force the dog off the property. Yet Son is determined to come back home to the farm. He curls up to sleep in the spot where John died.

Like *I'll Get There. It Better Be Worth the Trip*, Donovan's second novel, *Wild in the World*, inspired debates about whether or not the book's subject matter was suitable for children. At issue this time was Donovan's treatment of death. June Jordan, writing in the *New York Times Book Review*, described *Wild in the World* as "a horror story told in monotone" that would not help kids who "turn to a book . . . to find reassurance there." *Horn Book* critic Paul Heins commented that *Wild in the World* may "appeal" to a young reader inclined to become a "congenital pessimist."

Another *New York Times Book Review* critic, Barbara Wersba, claimed that *Wild in the World* was "one of the most moving books ever written for children." She asserted that the novel's attempt to "explore the nature of love—and the nature of man's isolation—is very close to being noble." A *Publishers Weekly* critic described *Wild in the World* as a "[h]auntingly beautiful novel of life and death" and friendship, and a *Booklist* reviewer asserted that the work may "impress" some readers with the "deep but unsentimentalized" relationship it portrays. John W. Conner of *English Journal* suggested that teachers and students would have "exciting hours exploring the social manifestations and psychological motives inherent" in the novel. *Wild in the World* was selected as a 1972 National Book Award finalist.

In the opinion of *New York Times Book Review* critic John Rowe Townsend, *Remove Protective Coating a Little at a Time* (1973) is similar to Donovan's first two novels because it demonstrates the idea that every human lives in isolation: "Donovan seems concerned with a special state of isolation that is often felt by young people in our time." Harry Knight, just fourteen years old, is beginning to explore his sexuality by masturbating and attempting to make out with a girl at camp. Although Harry lives with both his parents, Bud and Toots, he cannot communicate with them. Bud is busy working, and Toots is depressed; their marriage, begun when Toots became pregnant with Harry, is deteriorating. Lacking parental guidance and support, Harry gains satisfaction from his friendship with Amelia, a seventy-two-year-old woman who lives in a condemned building. Harry's brief opportunity to communicate frankly with another person ends when Amelia's building is to be torn down and she disappears.

Some reviewers questioned the treatment of sexual issues in *Remove Protective Coating a Little at a Time*. Sister M. Constance Melvin, I.H.M., writing in *Best Sellers*, did not appreciate the novel's "overloading with sex." Paul Heins of *Horn Book* argued that, while some sexual references were included in what could be termed a "naturalistic" manner, others seemed "sensational." *New York Times Book Review* critic Townsend was concerned that, although the book "is hardly at all about sex," it "will give some people wrong impressions" about Donovan's message and work.

Although *Good Old James* (1974) is a picture book with illustrations provided by James Stevenson, an artist and writer for the *New Yorker,* it also takes up the themes of isolation, alienation, and friendship. The book begins when James decides to retire. At first, he enjoys his freedom from work, but gradually, he becomes lonely and bored. He sells his home and travels, but he isn't satisfied. James tries to return to his past, but he finds that younger people have taken his place in his old house and at his old job.

James takes up residence in a hotel room which is occupied by a fly. Although James attempts to set the annoying fly free at first, he begins to admire it and to talk to it. He even provides it with food and water. "James named the fly Gwen and grew deeply attached to it," explains the narrator at the book's end. Louise Armstrong of the *New York Times Book Review* characterized the book as "spare" and "charming" and suggested that adults and children share it. A *Booklist* critic thought readers may ponder the "social and emotional implications" of the story and appreciated the way Donovan allows the reader to interpret the book's ending "as either bitter or sweet."

An Ape's Perspective in *Family*

The story in *Family* (1976) is narrated by an ape. Sasha, a laboratory ape, explains ape language, knowledge, and feelings as he attempts "to share . . . a personal experience." Sasha explains how he was born in captivity and how he served as a subject in many experiments before he was sent

Four laboratory apes escape from captivity and establish a new home in the wilderness in this 1976 novel.

to a laboratory at a university in the eastern part of the United States. There, he met other laboratory apes and a number of "naturals," or apes born in the wild. Sasha began to suspect that the experiment to be conducted at this lab was not one of the more common ones involving language and communication. Sasha believed that, instead, the professors and graduate students were going to dissemble the twenty-three apes to reconstruct a perfect ape with their parts.

Sasha and three other apes, Dylys, a female born in captivity, Moses, a huge, powerful, and silent "natural," and Lollipop, a young female born in captivity, escaped from the laboratory. In one frightening night, they traveled through the trees surrounding the university and made their way up into the mountains overlooking it. By the time

If you enjoy the works of John Donovan, you may also want to check out the following books and films:

Lynda Barry, *The Good Times Are Killing Me,* 1988.
Francesca Lia Block, *Weetzie Bat,* 1989.
M. E. Kerr, *Night Kites,* 1988.
My Life as a Dog, a Swedish film directed by Lasse Hallstroem, 1985.

the apes found a place to live, in some trees near a cave and a pool, they had suffered enough together to know each other intimately. Even Moses, who had kept away from the other apes at the laboratory, began to show his feelings for the other three apes. Sasha felt as if Moses and Dylys were his brother and sister, and the four apes began to live as a family. Moses instructed Sasha, Dylys, and Lollipop on survival in the wild, taught them the series of sounds that apes use in the wild to communicate, and told them the legends and folktales apes use to explain the world and their place in it. When Dylys became "ripe," Moses became her partner, and the four apes happily awaited the birth of their child.

It was during this time that the apes saw their first human since they had been in the wilderness. The human was gentle and unafraid, and they named him Man. Man made friends with the apes, played with them, brought them food to eat and store, and slept beneath their tree-top nests. He became a beloved member of the ape family. One day, as winter approached, Man left the apes. Later, Lollipop heard a human voice that she mistook for Man's. Before the adult apes could stop her, she bolted from their cave and was killed by deer hunters. Moses, who had followed Lollipop out of the cave, was also killed. Grieving, Sasha and Dylys realized that they could not survive in the wild and decided to return to the university with the hope that "Man is not lost."

Some critics of *Family,* like *Bulletin of the Center for Children's Books'* Zena Sutherland, applauded Donovan's convincing portrayal of the feelings and thoughts of apes. Ruth M. Stein of *Language Arts* noted that the book takes up the theme of the "interdependence of all living things." According to Virginia Haviland of *Horn Book, Family* is a

"singular work—as are all of this author's creations—a story that an intelligent, reflective young person will find provocative and haunting."

Although John Donovan did not publish many more young adult books after *Family,* he continued to write and to contribute to children's literature until he died of cancer in 1992. In 1983, with funds from a National Endowment for the Arts grant, Donovan worked as a writer-in-residence at the University of Michigan Residential College. At a talk in February of that year in Ann Arbor, Donovan explained trends in the children's book publishing industry from his perspective as the President of the Children's Book Council. He offered advice about publishing, and observed that "it helps to be young" and to "have a lot of ambition" when seeking a publisher. Yet Donovan stressed that potential publication is not the only reason to write. According to Donovan, one should also "express one's self for one's self and nobody else." Donovan also emphasized the importance of keeping a journal. "Please, if you're writing a journal—keep with it . . . your successors, hundreds of years from now, will value your words far more than any publisher or any reader might today."

■ Works Cited

Armstrong, Louise, review of *Good Old James, New York Times Book Review,* May 4, 1975, p. 40.

Bacon, Martha, review of *I'll Get There. It Better Be Worth the Trip, Atlantic Monthly,* December, 1969, p. 150.

Conner, John W., review of *Wild in the World, English Journal,* January, 1972, p. 138.

Donovan, John, *I'll Get There. It Better Be Worth the Trip.* Harper & Row, 1969.

Donovan, John, "Observations about Children's Book Week," *Publishers Weekly,* November 9, 1970, pp. 31-33.

Donovan, John, *Good Old James,* Harper & Row, 1975.

Donovan, John, *Family,* Harper & Row, 1976.

Donovan, John, "Children's Book Publishing Today," video recording of a lecture in the "Booked for Lunch" series, Ann Arbor Public Library, Ann Arbor, MI, February 8, 1983.

Review of *Good Old James, Booklist,* May 1, 1975, p. 912.

Haviland, Virginia, review of *Family, Horn Book,* August, 1976, p. 404.

Heins, Paul, review of *I'll Get There. It Better Be Worth the Trip*, Horn Book, August, 1969, pp. 415-16.

Heins, Paul, review of *Wild in the World*, Horn Book, February, 1972, p. 57.

Heins, Paul, review of *Remove Protective Coating a Little at a Time*, Horn Book, February, 1974, p. 54.

Hungerford, Alice, review of *I'll Get There. It Better Be Worth the Trip*, Washington Post Book World, May 4, 1969, p. 5.

Review of *I'll Get There. It Better Be Worth the Trip*, Times Literary Supplement, July 2, 1970, p. 712.

Jordan, June, review of *Wild in the World*, New York Times Book Review, September 12, 1971, p. 8.

Melvin, Sister M. Constance, I.H.M., review of *Remove Protective Coating a Little at a Time*, Best Sellers, October 15, 1973.

Mercier, Jean F., review of *Family*, Publishers Weekly, April 26, 1976, p. 60.

Nolan, Mary L., review of *I'll Get There. It Better Be Worth the Trip*, ALAN Review, Spring, 1982, pp. 4, 6, 13.

Rees, David, review of *I'll Get There. It Better Be Worth the Trip*, Children's Literature in Education, Summer, 1977, p. 86.

Russ, Lavinia, review of *I'll Get There. It Better Be Worth The Trip*, Publishers Weekly, March 17, 1969, p. 57.

Stein, Ruth M., review of *Family*, Language Arts, May, 1977, p. 582.

Sutherland, Zena, review of *Family*, Bulletin of the Center for Children's Books, July/August, 1976, p. 173.

Townsend, John Rowe, review of *Remove Protective Coating a Little at a Time*, New York Times Book Review, November 4, 1973, pp. 34, 36.

Wersba, Barbara, review of *Wild in the World*, New York Times Book Review, September 12, 1971, p. 8.

Weston, John, review of *I'll Get There. It Better Be Worth The Trip*, New York Times Book Review, May 4, 1969, part II, pp. 8, 10.

Review of *Wild in the World*, Booklist, November 1, 1971, p. 240.

Review of *Wild in the World*, Publishers Weekly, August 2, 1971, p. 64.

■ For More Information See

PERIODICALS

Booklist, April 1, 1976, p. 1112.
Bulletin of the Center for Children's Books, June, 1969, p. 156.
Commonweal, May 23, 1969, p. 300.
Kirkus Reviews, April 1, 1975, p. 373.
Library Journal, May 15, 1974, p. 1481.
School Library Journal, September, 1976, p. 131.
Variety, January 31, 1973.*

—Sketch by David Johnson

Michael Dorris

■ Personal

Born January 30, 1945, in Louisville, KY; son of Jim and Mary Besy (Burkhardt) Dorris; married Louise Erdrich (a writer) in 1981; children: Reynold Abel (died in 1991), Jeffrey Sava, Madeline Hannah, Persia Andromeda, Pallas Antigone, Aza Marion. *Education:* Georgetown University, B.A. (cum laude), 1967; Yale University, M. Phil., 1970.

■ Addresses

Home—Erdrich/Dorris, Box 70, Cornish Flat, NH 03746. *Agent*—Charles Rembar, Rembar and Curtis, 19 West 44th Street, New York, NY 10036.

■ Career

Writer. University of Redlands, Johnston College, Redlands, CA, assistant professor, 1970; Franconia College, Franconia, NH, assistant professor, 1971-72; Dartmouth College, Hanover, NH, instructor, 1972-76, assistant professor, 1976-79, associate pro-

fessor, 1979, professor of anthropology, 1979-88, adjunct professor, 1989—, chair of Native American Studies Department, 1979—, chair of Master of Arts in Liberal Studies program, 1982-85. University of New Hampshire, visiting assistant professor, 1973-74; University of Auckland, New Zealand, visiting senior lecturer, 1980. Director of urban bus program, summers, 1967, 1968, and 1969. Society for Applied Anthropology, fellow, 1977—; Save the Children Foundation, board member, 1992—; U.S. Advisory Committee on Infant Mortality, member, 1992—. Consultant to National Endowment for the Humanities, 1976—, and to television stations, including Los Angeles Educational Television, 1976, and Toledo Public Broadcast Center, 1978. Has appeared on many radio and television broadcasts. *Member:* PEN, Authors Guild, Writers Guild, Modern Language Association of America (delegate assembly and member of minority commission, 1974-77), American Anthropological Association, American Association for the Advancement of Science (opportunities in science commission, 1974-77), National Indian Education Association, National Congress of American Indians, National Support Committee (Native American Rights Fund), Research Society on Alcoholism, National Organization for Fetal Alcohol Syndrome, Phi Beta Kappa, Alpha Sigma Nu.

■ Awards, Honors

Woodrow Wilson fellow, 1967 and 1980; fellowships from the National Institute of Mental Health,

1970 and 1971, John Simon Guggenheim Memorial Foundation, 1978, Rockefeller Foundation, 1985, National Endowment for the Arts, 1989, and Dartmouth College, 1992; Outstanding Academic Book of 1984-85 citation, *Choice*, for *A Guide to Research on North American Indians*; Indians Achievement Award, 1985; best book citation, American Library Association (ALA), 1988, for *A Yellow Raft in Blue Water*; PEN Syndicated Fiction Award, 1988, for "Name Games"; honorary degree, Georgetown University, 1989; National Book Critics Circle Award for general nonfiction and Governor's Writing Award, State of Washington, both 1989, and Christopher Award, Heartland Prize, and Outstanding Academic Book, *Choice*, all 1990, all for *The Broken Cord: A Family's Ongoing Struggle with Fetal Alcohol Syndrome*; Best Audio of 1990 of Author Reading His or Her Own Work citation, *Audio World*, for the audiocassette version of *The Broken Cord: A Family's Ongoing Struggle with Fetal Alcohol Syndrome*; Medal of Outstanding Leadership and Achievement, Dartmouth College, 1991; Sarah Josepha Hale Literary Award, 1991; Scott Newman Award, 1992, and Gabriel Award for National Entertainment Program, ARC Media Award, Christopher Award, Writers Guild of America award, and Media Award, American Psychology Association, all for the television film of *The Broken Cord: A Family's Ongoing Struggle with Fetal Alcohol Syndrome*; Montgomery Fellow, Dartmouth College, 1992; International Pathfinder Award, World Conference on the Family, 1992; Award for Excellence, Center for Anthropology and Journalism, 1992, for essays on Zimbabwe; Scott O'Dell Award for Historical Fiction, American Library Association, 1992, for *Morning Girl*; Citation for Excellence, Overseas Press Club, for "House of Stone"; *Morning Girl* was named to best or notable book lists by *Publishers Weekly*, *Horn Book*, *School Library Journal*, *Booklist*, and *New York Times Book Review*.

■ **Writings**

NOVELS

A Yellow Raft in Blue Water, Holt, 1987.
(With Louise Erdrich) *The Crown of Columbus*, HarperCollins, 1991.
Morning Girl , Hyperion, 1992, translated as *Tainos*, Santillana Publishing Company, 1996.
Guests, Hyperion, 1994.
Sees Behind Trees, Hyperion, 1996.

Cloud Chamber, Simon & Schuster, 1997.

OTHER

Native Americans: Five Hundred Years After, Crowell, 1975.
(Contributor) *Racism in the Textbook*, Council on Interracial Books for Children, 1976.
(With Arlene B. Hirschfelder and Mary Gloyne Byler) *Guide to Research on North American Indians*, American Library Association, 1983.
The Broken Cord: A Family's Ongoing Struggle with Fetal Alcohol Syndrome, Harper, 1989.
(With Louise Erdrich) *Route Two and Back*, Lord John Press, 1991.
Rooms in the House of Stone, Milkweed Editions, 1993.
Working Men (stories), Holt, 1993.
(Contributor) Leslie M. Silko, *A Circle of Nations: Voices and Visions of American Indians*, Beyond Words Publishing, 1993.
(Contributor) Ruth Coughlin, *Grieving: A Love Story*, Random House, 1993.
(Contributor) Laura W. Wittstock, *Ininatig's Gift of Sugar: Traditional Native Sugarmaking*, Lerner Group, 1993.
Kinaalda: A Navajo Girl Grows Up, Lerner Group, 1993.
Paper Trail: Collected Essays, 1967-1992, HarperCollins, 1995.

■ **Adaptations**

The Broken Cord: A Family's Ongoing Struggle with Fetal Alcohol Syndrome was produced for television by Universal and ABC-TV, 1992; *A Yellow Raft in Blue Water* and *The Broken Cord: A Family's Ongoing Struggle with Fetal Alcohol Syndrome* were released on audiocassette by HarperAudio in 1990; *The Crown of Columbus* was released on audiocassette by HarperAudio in 1991.

■ **Sidelights**

The word interdisciplinary seems to have been invented just for Michael Dorris: his writing embraces both fiction and nonfiction, the themes are personal and political, and his concerns are for the individual and the group, particularly the Native American community. Dorris is part Modoc on his father's side, an inheritance he has explored by co-authoring a North American Indian research guide, founding the Native American Studies Department at Dartmouth College, and doing research on Fetal Alcohol Syndrome (FAS)—the abnormalities in children that result from ingestion of alcohol during pregnancy which causes brain cell damage in the fetus. Because alcohol abuse rates on Native American reservations tend to be higher than the national average, FAS poses a significant threat to some Native Americans. Dorris has also written juvenile fiction with Native American characters and situations that reflect Native American life. Resisting easy categorization, Dorris forces his readers to actively address their own assumptions about Native Americans and about America itself.

Born in 1945 in Louisville, Kentucky, Dorris lost his father during World War II. His mother raised him and looked after his grandmother, all of them supported by his aunt who worked for the city. He spent some of his childhood on a reservation in eastern Montana, but lived most of the time in Louisville. He earned a bachelor's degree with honors in English and classics at Georgetown University in 1967. From 1967 to 1968 he studied in the Department of History of the Theatre and in the Department of Anthropology at Yale University, culminating in a master's degree in philosophy in 1970.

In addition to other academic appointments, Dorris taught at Dartmouth College, where he established the Native Studies Department in 1979. He continues to serve as chairman of the department. His first major contribution to scholarly literature was his collaboration with Arlene B. Hirschfelder and Mary Gloyne Byler on the *Guide to Research on North American Indians*, which appeared in 1975.

Dorris met writer Louise Erdrich when she was an undergraduate at Dartmouth. They were married several years later, though Dorris got a head start on family life by adopting three children as a bachelor. About his decision to take on fatherhood as a bachelor, Dorris said in the *Los Angeles Times* that "I had known many Native American youngsters who had lost their parents and who faced a bleak future. I thought I could offer them something because of my heritage." The couple subsequently had three more children, all girls.

Aside from their domestic partnership, Dorris and Erdrich also became professional partners. Although they each have separate and well-estab-

A novel by
Michael Dorris

This 1987 work, Dorris's first novel, tells the story of three generations of Indian women who live on a Montana Indian reservation.

lished reputations as writers, no discussion of the work of either writer can exclude discussion of the other. Their professional lives are closely linked, their work often collaborative even if not always credited precisely that way. As Vince Passaro noted in his profile of Dorris and Erdrich in the *New York Times Magazine*, "The impression they have promoted is that they are attempting to make themselves, by mutual consent, into one voice, one vision, one language. Theirs is an art, as well as a life, directed toward synthesis and unity."

Dorris's first novel, *A Yellow Raft in Blue Water*, appeared in 1987. Although he collaborated with Erdrich on several short stories for women's magazines (Milou North being their joint authorial pseudonym), Dorris had not written fiction on his own for some fifteen years. A story he published in his college newspaper came in for heavy criticism and made him reluctant to continue with fiction. *Yellow Raft* brings together three separate narratives—Rayona, the half black, half Native American teenager; Christine, her mother; and Ida, Rayona's grandmother. In her review in the *New York Times*, Michiko Kakutani praised Dorris's "delicate orchestration of tiny emotional details" to portray "remarkable psychological density." Although Charles R. Larson also found much to praise, his review in the Chicago *Tribune Books* section noted that the "stunning" opening section is followed by narratives that "scarcely advance what has already been hinted in Rayona's unified tale." Still, he pointed out that Dorris managed to communicate the generational disparities among his three women "effortlessly." *Voice of Youth Advocates* reviewer Cathi Edgerton deemed the novel "remarkable, seamlessly crafted" and found that "Dorris fascinates us with the enigma of American Indian culture in its odd balance of patriotism and Red Power, ravaged by the inroads of Western ways." Writing in the *Los Angeles Times Book Review*, Penelope Moffet echoed the criticism of other reviewers who noted that the women characters were far better realized than the men. But she admitted to being hooked by Dorris's "energetic, understated and seductive" style and congratulated the writer for his "elegant weaving" of the three stories.

The Personal Becomes Political

Among the children Dorris adopted initially, the eldest, Adam (an alias used in the *Broken Cord: A Family's Ongoing Struggle With Fetal Alcohol Syndrome*), showed early and persistent learning difficulties. Dorris had adopted him around 1969, one of the first single men approved as an adoptive father in South Dakota. The three-year-old Sioux boy had already fallen prey to abuse and neglect earlier in his life.

His son's lingering developmental problems, such as mental retardation and attention deficit, coupled with severe seizures and skeletal abnormalities, prompted Dorris to investigate further into the boy's history. He determined that his son's mother had died of alcohol poisoning. Adam's symptoms matched those of Fetal Alcohol Syndrome (FAS)—first officially named in 1968, the year his son was

born—whose debilitating effects no amount of attention, love, and care on Dorris's part could completely reverse.

Bolstered by a grant from the Rockefeller Foundation, Dorris spent a year in Minnesota researching the affliction, whose effects are not genetic; alcohol is the only culprit. Studies from all over the world showed the same results, the same developmental problems. In 1984, Dorris signed a contract to write an academic book on the subject. But in the first thirty pages of his narrative, he noticed two distinct stories emerging—the research itself and the difficulties Dorris and his family faced. Drawing from his experiences in writing *A Yellow Raft in Blue Water*, which he was composing at the same time, he saw that the FAS book would have to incorporate both stories. In an interview with Dulcy Brainard of *Publishers Weekly*, Dorris said he knew it had to avoid being "so pedantic or preachy or academic that nobody would read it."

The Broken Cord managed to convey massive information on this little-understood affliction, while also portraying an adoptive father's efforts to come to terms with his son's true prospects, quite different from those he had envisioned for him. Part memoir, part confession (Dorris was honest about his frustrations and consequent fury), the book also had a larger aim: to warn people of this easily avoidable calamity. As Dorris told Brainard, the *Broken Cord* was "written for a lot of reasons, one of them political: it is a book that hopes to effect change."

Critics were unstinting with their praise. Typical of the responses was the review by Josh Greenfeld in the *Washington Post Book World* who deemed the *Broken Cord* "both an anthropological detective story and an impassioned warning that no thinking would-be parent can ignore." Although Greenfeld found that Dorris occasionally "fumbles in juggling all his roles" as a writer, he emphasized the importance of Dorris's urgent message: "Alcohol and babies do not mix." Carl A. Hammerschlag, writing in the *Los Angeles Times Book Review*, described *The Broken Cord* as "written like a prayer from the heart of someone strong enough to share his pain." In the *New York Times Book Review*, Patricia Guthrie noted that "the alarming statistics and consequences of fetal alcohol syndrome are skillfully interwoven with the human story of one of its victims in *The Broken*

Cord. [It] should be required reading for all medical professionals and social workers, and especially for pregnant women, and women who contemplate pregnancy, who may be tempted to drink." A critic in *Publishers Weekly* pointed out that "in graceful, unencumbered prose, Dorris . . . bares the frustration of day-to-day living with Adam, admits his rage at his own impotence to make his son's life fuller and eloquently describes moments of pride, hope and—always—love." Among its many honors, *The Broken Cord* was awarded the National Book Critics Circle Award for general nonfiction. Dorris adapted the story for a television movie in 1992.

Expanding on their already cooperative role as each other's first readers and editors, Dorris and Erdrich collaborated fully on a 1991 novel titled

Dorris chronicles his adopted son's battle with Fetal Alcohol Syndrome in this 1989 work.

The Crown of Columbus. The idea for the book had been gestating for about ten years, from the time when the two writers read the translation of Bartolomé Las Casas's sixteenth-century edition of Christopher Columbus's lost diary.

Two perspectives inform the narrative—that of Roger Williams and his on-again, off-again lover Vivian Twostar, both of whom are on staff at Dartmouth College and both of whom are working on material about Columbus. Vivian Twostar is part Navajo, with a live-in grandmother, a troublesome teenage son, and a new baby girl (fathered by Roger) to contend with. Roger Williams is a stodgy, New England Protestant poet, at work on a heroic celebration of Columbus. Their quest for information about Columbus, including missing pages from his diary, takes them to the Bahamas, where they have a series of life-threatening adventures. Uncovering incontrovertible evidence of the havoc wreaked by Columbus's exploits on the Native American people, Vivian and Roger decide to compensate for these wrongs by altering their own relationship to reflect a different power hierarchy.

Critics had mixed responses to the Dorris-Erdrich collaboration, often finding *The Crown of Columbus* less satisfying than the writers' previous works. *Time*'s John Elson noted that "curiously, the talent pooling has spawned a novel with as much spontaneity as if it had been plotted by a computer." But in the *New York Times Book Review* Robert Houston praised the "moments of genuine humor and compassion, of real insight and sound satire." Ann Fisher, in *Library Journal*, also found the effort successful, particularly the two protagonists' relationship which she pronounced "funny, vivid, and life-affirming." *Times Literary Supplement* contributor Michael Kerrigan found that this "shamelessly improbable adventure yarn" made for "a grown-up voyage of discovery."

Addressing a New Audience: Children

Dorris made his debut as a children's writer with *Morning Girl* in 1992. Using alternating brother and sister narrators—Morning Girl and Star Boy— it is the chronicle of two young members of the Taino (Bahamian) tribe, who were among the indigenous peoples encountered by Columbus. Prompted by Columbus's quick and quite dismissive description of the Tainos as "a people poor in everything," Dorris imagined the meeting from another angle: that of the young girl who happened upon the long boat filled with strangers. Drawing on his training as an anthropologist, the writer used information about the day-to-day life of the tribe. The children's personal joys and losses in their family are blended with the unchanging dilemmas of self-discovery and understanding that face young people of every era. The book won the Scott O'Dell Award for Historical Fiction and garnered high praise from reviewers. *Bloomsbury Review*'s Chick Flynn enjoyed "the sheer joy of Morning Girl's voice and Dorris's unique and powerful way of sharing her way of life in 1492 with a young audience." A *Publishers Weekly* contributor advised that "with its spare, compelling prose, Dorris's singularly involving work should be read by both children and adults for many generations to come." Writing in the *New York Times Book Review*, Alice McDermott found the "graceful and engaging narrative" of *Morning Girl* "a warm story full of real characters and situations, told in marvelous language that makes it a pleasure to read out loud." Putting the story in a larger context, Suzanne Curley wrote in the *Los Angeles Times Book Review* that "this sad, lovely and timely tale gives us an alternative view of America's 'discovery'."

Dorris's second book for younger readers was *Guests*. The narrator, a Native American boy named Moss, is poised between childhood and adulthood. Set in what appears to be seventeenth-century North America, the story revolves around Moss's distress at his community's decision to include strangers in the annual harvest fest. These guests (probably Pilgrims) do not understand the language or customs of Moss's people and seem to appropriate the celebration as their own. Unhappy and frustrated, Moss sets off for the surrounding forest. Along the way, he meets Trouble, a young girl who shares many of his feelings, and encounters a porcupine who helps him to face some important aspects of himself. *Horn Book*'s Nancy Vasilakis deemed *Guests* "a short and powerful survival *cum* coming-of-age tale" and praised Moss's language for "sometimes coming close to poetry." In the *New York Times Book Review*, Linda Perkins noted that "like the storytellers in Moss's family, Mr. Dorris weaves important moral themes—identity, responsibility, generosity—into his tale" and noted that "Mr. Dorris writes lyrically of nature . . . his images are vivid." In *Bulletin of the Center for Children's Books*, Susan Dove

Lempke stated that "possibly the finest feature of *Guests* is that although the strangers are clearly the Pilgrims, making this historical fiction, the writing is so immediate that one is barely aware the story is taking place over three hundred years ago."

Dorris used the pre-Colonial setting for his next novel, *Sees Behind Trees,* as well. Walnut, the young narrator, is smart and determined but hampered in his desire to be a good hunter by his near-sightedness. In charge of his training, his mother suggests that he learn to look with his ears, an accomplishment that not only earns him his name, but allows him to accompany Gray Fire, a respected elder of the tribe, on a pilgrimage. The narrative focusses on this journey and offers Sees Behind Trees the opportunity to see strangers (people not of the tribe) for the first time and to prove his manhood by finding his way back to the village on his own. Though the setting and particulars are historically remote, the difficulties Walnut encounters—finding his place in his community and in the world at large—are perennials. A critic in *Publishers Weekly* pronounced the novel "beautifully crafted" and "both sharply and lyrically observed, fraught with emotion" that shows itself to be a "thrilling read." Writing in the *School Library Journal,* Luann Toth noted that "Dorris takes on some meaty existential issues here; he does so with grace, bighearted empathy, and always, with crystal-clear vision."

Adult Fiction Revisited

Dorris published two collections of shorter writing during this time. A collection of short stories, titled *Working Men,* was published in 1993, and *Paper Trail: Collected Essays, 1967-1992,* a collection of essays spanning twenty-five years, came out in 1995. *Working Men* met with mixed critical response. Writing in the *New York Times Book Review,* Tony Eprile said that the fourteen stories in the collection "demonstrate his skilled and subtle storytelling, roving imagination and embracing humanism." He praised Dorris for "delivering up a wide range of personalities, economic and ethnic backgrounds and historical periods," but found "a sameness of narrative tone to these stories." Ultimately, Eprile determined, "the flaws are easily eclipsed by the overall strength of this sensitive and beautifully observed book." Among the essays in *Paper Trail* is an examination of the

If you enjoy the works of Michael Dorris, you may want to check out the following books and films:

Louise Erdrich, *The Beet Queen*, 1986.

Three autobiographical journals by Josh Greenfeld: *A Child Called Noah: A Family Journey* (1972), *A Place for Noah* (1979), and *A Client Called Noah* (1987), which describe life with an autistic child.

Scott O'Dell, *Thunder Rolling in the Mountains*, 1992.

James Welch, *The Indian Lawyer*, 1990.

Dances with Wolves, Orion, 1990.

author's difficulties with reading the Laura Ingalls Wilder "Little House" series to his daughters, given its implicit assumptions about Native Americans.

After years of writing for younger readers, Dorris returned to adult fiction in 1997 with *Cloud Chamber*. Rayona, last heard from in *A Yellow Raft in Blue Water*, reappears in this saga of five generations descended from an Irish firebrand named Rose Mannion. The story, which takes place in the aftermath of Rose's decision to abandon Ireland for Kentucky, chronicles the family's struggles, particularly the competition between Rose and her equally controlling daughter-in-law Bridie. One of Bridie's daughters, Marcella, is mother to Elgin, who will eventually father Rayona. Elgin, who is part black, keeps the existence of his Indian wife and Rayona secret from his Caucasian family. It is up to Rayona to unify this history, to plait the various strands of the family into one braid. A *Publishers Weekly* reviewer gave Dorris high marks for his "evocative prose" and his "moving and persuasive image of reconciliation for which America still yearns."

Though his work nearly always includes Native American characters, Dorris casts a much wider net than mere ethnicity. As he noted in the *North Dakota Quarterly*, "Native American literature is about as descriptive a term as non-Native American literature. If by definition non-Native American literature is about and by people who are not Native Americans, fine; except that doesn't tell you a great deal. I think what [Louise Erdrich, my wife] and I do is either within the tradition of a particular tribe or reservation or it is within the context of American literature."

Dorris's concerns have a timeless, classic quality: rather than settling for easy moralizing, he personalizes the universal, showing how all people struggle with questions of identity, the transition from childhood to adulthood, the acceptance of responsibility and liability. His language verges on the poetic, drawing on sharp imagery, expressing complex ideas with simplicity and clarity. By challenging the standard categories of historical truth and by using the anthropologist's techniques in the service of social commentary and literature, Dorris makes demands not only on himself but his readers as well—demands they are happy to meet.

■ Works Cited

Brainard, Dulcy, "Michael Dorris," *Publishers Weekly*, August 4, 1989, pp. 73-74.

Review of *The Broken Cord: A Family's Ongoing Struggle with Fetal Alcohol Syndrome, Publishers Weekly*, June 2, 1989.

Review of *Cloud Chamber, Publishers Weekly*, November 11, 1996, p. 55.

Curley, Suzanne, *Los Angeles Times Book Review*, September 27, 1992, p. 12.

Dorris, Michael, article in *North Dakota Quarterly*, Winter, 1987, pp. 196-218.

Edgerton, Cathi, *Voice of Youth Advocates*, August-September, 1987, p. 119.

Elson, John, "1+1<2," *Time*, April 29, 1991, p. 76.

Eprile, Tony, "We Are What We Do," *New York Times Book Review*, October 17, 1993, p. 12.

Fisher, Ann, *Library Journal*, March 15, 1991, p. 114.

Flynn, Chick, *Bloomsbury Review*, October 29, 1992, p. 23.

Greenfeld, Josh, "Wounded Before Birth," *Washington Post Book World*, July 23, 1989, pp. 1, 11.

Guthrie, Patricia, *New York Times*, July 30, 1989.

Hammerschlag, Carl A., "Substance Abuse as Child Abuse," *Los Angeles Times Book Review*, July 30, 1989, p. 1, 11.

Houston, Robert, review of *The Crown of Columbus, New York Times Book Review*, April 28, 1991, p. 10.

Kakutani, Michiko, "Multiple Perspectives," *New York Times*, May 9, 1987, p. 17.

Kerrigan, Michael, "Seeking an America of the Heart," *Times Literary Supplement*, July 19, 1991, p. 21.

Larson, Charles R., *Tribune Books* (Chicago), May 10, 1987, p. 6.

Lempke, Susan Dove, *Bulletin of the Center for Children's Books*, November, 1994, p. 86.

Los Angeles Times, July 24, 1989.

McDermott, Alice, *New York Times*, November 8, 1992, p. 33.

Moffet, Penelope, *Los Angeles Times Book Review*, June 21, 1987, p. 2.

Review of *Morning Girl*, *Publishers Weekly*, August 10, 1992, p. 71.

Passaro, Vince, "Tales from a Literary Marriage," *New York Times Magazine*, April 21, 1991, pp. 35-43, 76.

Perkins, Linda, review of *Guests*, *New York Times Book Review*, January 29, 1995, p. 20.

Review of *Sees Behind Trees*, *Publishers Weekly*, October 7, 1996, p. 76.

Toth, Luann, *School Library Journal*, October, 1996, p. 120.

Vasilakis, Nancy, *Horn Book Magazine*, January, 1995, p. 58.

■ For More Information See

BOOKS

Berger, Laura Standley, *Twentieth Century Young Adult Writers*, 1st Edition, St. James Press, 1994.

Bestsellers, Issue 1, Gale, 1991.

Contemporary Authors, Volume 102, Gale, 1981.

Contemporary Authors, New Revision Series, Volume 19, Gale, 1987.

Kamp, Jim, editor, *Reference Guide to American Literature*, 3rd Edition, St. James Press, 1994.

Notable Native Americans, Gale, 1995.

Seventh Book of Junior Authors and Illustrators, edited by Sally Holmes Holtze, H. W. Wilson, 1996.

Twentieth-Century Western Writers, St. James Press, 1991, pp. 190-91.

PERIODICALS

Booklist, June 1 and 15, 1993, pp. 1820-22.

Bulletin of the Center for Children's Books, January, 1997, p. 168.

Commonweal, December 7, 1990, p. 728.

Horn Book, November-December, 1995, p. 698.

Los Angeles Times Book Review, May 12, 1991, p. 3.

Nation, October 21, 1991, p. 488.

New Republic, January 6, 1992, p. 30.

New Statesmen and Society, September 7, 1990, p. 44; July 26, 1991, p. 35.

New York Times Book Review, June 7, 1987, p. 7; July 30, 1989, p. 1.

Publishers Weekly, November 15, 1996, p. 87.

School Library Journal, October, 1992, p. 116.

Times Literary Supplement, March 11, 1988, p. 276; August 24, 1990, p. 893.

Tribune Books (Chicago), July 23, 1989, p. 1; April 28, 1991, p. 5.*

—Sketch by C. M. Ratner

Anne Fine

■ Personal

Born December 7, 1947, in Leicester, England; daughter of Brian (a chief scientific experimental officer) and Mary Laker; married Kit Fine (a university professor), 1968; children: two daughters. *Education:* University of Warwick, Coventry, B.A. in history and politics (with honors), 1968.

■ Addresses

Home—Barnard Castle, County Durham, England. *Agent*—Murray Pollinger, 4 Garrick St., London WC2E 9BH, England.

■ Career

Cardinal Wiseman Girls' Secondary School, Coventry, England, English teacher 1968-70; Oxford Committee for Famine Relief (OXFAM), Oxford, England, assistant information officer, 1970-71; Saughton Jail, Edinburgh, Scotland, teacher, 1971-72; freelance writer, 1973—. Volunteer for Amnesty International.

■ Awards, Honors

Guardian/Kestral Award nominations, 1978, for *The Summer-House Loon,* for *The Granny Project,* 1983, and 1987, for *Madame Doubtfire;* Scottish Arts Council Book Award, 1986, for *The Killjoy;* Observer Prize for Teenage Fiction nomination, 1987, for *Madame Doubtfire;* Smarties (6-8) Award, 1989, for *Bill's New Frock;* Guardian Award for Children's Fiction, 1989, and Carnegie Medal, 1990, both for *Goggle-Eyes; Publishing News's* Children's Author of the Year, British Book Awards, 1990; American Library Association Notable Book, *School Library Journal* Best Book of the Year and International Reading Association Young Adult Choice citations, 1991, for *My War with Goggle-Eyes;* Carnegie Medal, 1992, and Whitbread Children's Novel award, 1993, both for *Flour Babies;* Whitbread Children's Book of the Year, 1996, for *The Tulip Touch.*

■ Writings

YOUNG ADULT FICTION

The Summer-House Loon, Methuen, 1978, Crowell, 1979.
The Other, Darker Ned, Methuen, 1979.
The Stone Menagerie, Methuen, 1980.
Round behind the Ice-House, Methuen, 1981.
The Granny Project (also see below), Farrar, Straus, 1983.

Madame Doubtfire, Hamish Hamilton, 1987, published as *Alias Madame Doubtfire*, Little, Brown, 1988.

My War with Goggle-Eyes, Little, Brown, 1989 (published in England as *Goggle-Eyes*, Hamish Hamilton, 1989).

The Book of the Banshee, Hamish Hamilton, 1991, Little, Brown, 1992.

Flour Babies, Hamish Hamilton, 1992, Little, Brown, 1994.

Step by Wicked Step, Hamish Hamilton, 1996, Little, Brown, 1996.

The Tulip Touch, Hamish Hamilton, 1996.

YOUNG ADULT DRAMA

The Granny Project, adaptation of her novel of the same title, Collins, 1986.

CHILDREN'S FICTION

Scaredy-Cat, illustrated by Vanessa Julian-Ottie, Heinemann, 1985.

Anneli the Art Hater, Methuen, 1986.

Crummy Mummy and Me, illustrated by David Higham, Deutsch, 1988.

A Pack of Liars, Hamish Hamilton, 1988.

Bill's New Frock, illustrated by Philippe Dupasquier, Methuen, 1989.

Stranger Danger?, illustrated by Jean Baylis, Hamish Hamilton, 1989.

A Sudden Puff of Glittering Smoke (also see below), illustrated by Adriano Gon, Piccadilly, 1989.

The Country Pancake, illustrated by Philippe Dupasquier, Methuen, 1990.

Only a Show, illustrated by Valerie Littlewood, Hamish Hamilton, 1990.

A Sudden Swirl of Icy Wind (also see below), illustrated by David Higham, Piccadilly, 1990.

The Angel of Nitshill Road, illustrated by K. Aldous, Methuen, 1991.

Design-a-Pram, Heinemann, 1991.

Poor Monty (picture book), illustrated by Clara Vulliamy, Methuen, 1991, Clarion, 1992.

A Sudden Glow of Gold (also see below), Piccadilly, 1991.

The Worst Child I Ever Had, illustrated by Clara Vulliamy, Hamish Hamilton, 1991.

Same Old Story Every Year, Hamish Hamilton, 1992.

The Chicken Gave It to Me, illustrated by Cynthia Fisher, Methuen, 1992, Little, Brown, 1993.

The Genie Trilogy (includes *A Sudden Puff of Glittering Smoke*, *A Sudden Swirl of Icy Wind*, and *A Sudden Glow of Gold*), Mammoth, 1992.

The Diary of a Killer Cat, illustrated by Steve Cox, Puffin, 1996.

Countdown, illustrated by D. Higham, Heinemann, 1996.

How to Write Really Badly, illustrated by Philippe Dupasquier, Methuen, 1996.

Care for Henry, illustrated by Paul Howard, Walker, 1997.

FOR ADULTS

The Killjoy (novel), Bantam, 1986, Mysterious Press, 1987.

The Captain's Court Case (radio play), 1987.

Taking the Devil's Advice (novel), Penguin, 1990.

Facing Three Ways: Woodfield Lecture VXI, Woodfield, 1993.

In Cold Domain, Viking, 1994.

Also author of radio play, *The Captain's Court Case*, 1987; contributor of short stories to periodicals.

■ Adaptations

Goggle-Eyes was made into a serial shown on British television; *Alias Madame Doubtfire* was made into a motion picture by Twentieth Century-Fox, *Mrs. Doubtfire*, 1993, starring Robin Williams, Sally Field, and Pierce Brosnan; *Goggle-Eyes* was produced on cassette by Chivers Sound & Vision, 1992.

■ Sidelights

"A vast apparition towered over her on the doorstep. It wore a loose salmon pink coat, beneath which hung boldly patterned skirts that hid all but a few inches of dark green rubber boots. Its head was swathed in a bulging turban held together with numerous safety pins and a glittery turquoise brooch. Coils of feathery scarf floated around its neck, and tucked under its arm was an enormous imitation crocodile handbag."

This colorful description of the divorced dad who dresses as a housekeeper in order to see more of his children comes from Anne Fine's popular young adult novel, *Alias Madame Doubtfire*, made into Twentieth Century-Fox's 1993 movie hit, *Mrs. Doubtfire*. While Fine wasn't involved in the making of the film, it sparked more interest in her work than any of the many awards she has won throughout her long career. A noted British author of novels for adults and children as well as for teenagers, Fine entered the young adult field in 1978 with *The Summer-House Loon*. Like *Alias Madame Doubtfire*, *The Summer-House Loon*, Fine's first published novel, deals with the humorous side of family relationships gone awry and growing up in the ensuing turmoil. Humor and social issues, such as divorce, single parenthood, and social activism, are a constant in Fine's fiction. "Growing through to full autonomy is, for anyone, a long and doggy business; for some, more sabotaged than others by their nature or upbringing," Fine told *Twentieth-Century Children's Writers*, "it can seem impossible. I try to show that the battle through the chaos and confusions is worthwhile and can, at times, be seen as very funny."

While Fine is noted for the humorous scenes that punctuate her novels, the circumstances surrounding the writing of *The Summer-House Loon* were far from funny. "Clinically depressed, and kept from the library by a snowstorm, I waited till the baby fell asleep," she recalls in her *Something About the Author Autobiography Series* essay, "then snatched up a pencil and began to write. It came out fast and easily. . . . When I look back at the bleak miserable creature who sat down to write it, I can hardly believe that she was me." Originally turned down by two publishers, Fine eventually entered the manuscript in a contest run by the *Guardian* newspaper. It tied for third place, but thanks to contacts made through the competition, Fine's manuscript was sold to Methuen and became her first published book. She has steadily produced critically acclaimed fiction for more than fifteen years, collecting a number of literary prizes including two Carnegie Medals and *Publishing News*'s Children's Writer of the Year.

The Summer-House Loon is the story of teenage Ione Muffet, the only child of a widowed blind professor of history. One day, while day-dreaming in the summer-house in her garden, Ione meets Ned Hump, one of her father's top students. Ned is lovesick for Caroline Hope, Professor Muffet's secretary. Ione does her best to help Ned convince Caroline to marry him through various stratagems. Her interference reaches a comedic climax in a scene in which all four become drunk: the professor and Ned with a bottle of whiskey as the elder man tries to convince the younger that his theories about the Early Sardinian Trade Routes are wrong, and Ione and Caroline with cooking sherry as they discuss what marriage

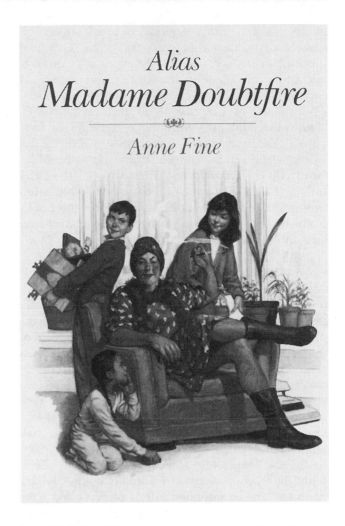

The Hilliard children's new babysitter, who calls herself Madame Doubtfire, bears a suspicious resemblance to their father in this humorous 1988 work.

should be like. It all takes place in only twenty-four hours, but during that time, according to Kate M. Flanagan in *Horn Book*, Ione's views on "life, love and human relationships are forever changed." Fine continued the story of Ione, her father, and the now married Ned and Caroline in her next novel, *The Other, Darker Ned*.

Both Marcus Crouch in *Junior Bookshelf* and Peter Hollindale in the *Times Literary Supplement* found *The Summer-House Loon* to be an accurate portrait of the bittersweet uncertainties of growing up. "Here is a book with deep understanding, wisdom, and compassion," wrote Crouch. "It tosses the reader between laughter and tears with expert dexterity." Calling the book "inventive and very funny," Hollingdale nevertheless discovered in the novel "a fine emotional delicacy which sensitively captures, among all the comic upheaval, the passionate solitude of adolescence." Considering both *The Summer-House Loon* and its sequel, *Growing Point*'s Margery Fisher commented, "Fine's lively sense of the ridiculous and her talent for composing dialogue with the real sound of individual voices are seen at their best in [these] two exhilarating and pointed domestic comedies." Similarly, in *Junior Bookshelf*, E. Colwell feels that in *The Other, Darker Ned* Fine excels in creating true-to-life individuals. "The strength of the book," Colwell writes, "lies in its highly original characters and their reactions to each other."

Continuing her interest in social concerns, Fines deals with homelessness and mental illness in her next novel, *The Stone Menagerie*. The book is the story of Ally, a teenage boy who accompanies his parents on weekly visits to a mental institution to see his aunt who is withdrawn and unresponsive. One day, looking out the window of the hospital, he happens to see a man and a woman among a group of large stone cages, once used to house wild animals, now overgrown with brambles. Curious, he arranges to meet the pair, whom he learns are named Flora and Riley. Eventually, he brings his aunt to talk to them. Being with the couple seems to enliven both Ally and his aunt. The uninhibited antics of Flora and Riley echo the activities of the student and the secretary from Fine's first two novels, according to Julie Blaisdale in *School Librarian*. "Their wayward crazy magic works on Ally," she notes, "in the same way as Ned and Caroline fascinate Ione; and he watches transfixed as they live out their fantasies, secluded in fairy-tale fashion by brambles and thorns." While Colwell, writing in *Junior Bookshelf*, thought the novel too "bizarre" to be appealing to teens and D. Atkinson in *School Librarian* dubbed the book an "uneasy mixture of realism and whimsy," *Growing Point*'s Margery Fisher applauded Fine as "one of the sharpest and humorous observers of the human condition writing for the young."

Fisher also lauded Fine's next novel, *Round behind the Ice-House*, especially delighting in how the novelist "builds up a narrative which compels attention for every word and phrase." The novel explores the relationship between Tom and Cass, a pair of twins, and how their responses to each other change as they move into adolescence. Whereas before the twins used to pull pranks on

their farm's handyman, now Cass seems to want to be alone with him. Tom also notices his own feelings towards the handy man's daughter changing as well. Comparing Fine's *The Stone Menagerie* to this novel, Blaisdale notes, "In contrast with the fairy-tale beauty of the stone menagerie, the ice-house acts as a damp, brick repository for some of Tom and Cass's oldest and darkest secrets." Probably Fine's most serious book, *Round behind the Ice-House* caused *Junior Bookshelf* reviewer R. Baines to complain about too much "misery" in the novel and hope that Fine could "make her next book jollier." However, in the *Times Literary Supplement* Nicholas Tucker pointed to the "passages of genuine power and feeling" and cautioned those who might want to give up on the book that "there are distinct rewards here for readers who persevere with this occasionally disjointed and highly emotional narrative."

Fine's next novel, *The Granny Project*, was indeed "jollier" while at the same time dealing with the serious subjects of aging and dying. The "granny" of the title is Mrs. Harris, grandmother to Ivan, Sophie, Tanya, and Nicholas. The children are at odds with their parents, Henry Harris and Natasha Dolgorova, because they have discovered that their mom and dad are planning on putting the elderly Mrs. Harris into a nursing home. The four concoct a plan of their own, deciding to write a school project on what is going on in their family. The parents, upset at their children for defying their authority, decide to leave the entire care of the grandmother in the hands of their children, so they will see first hand how much work is involved in seeing after all of her needs. Just as a compromise plan is about to be set into place, the grandmother dies. Calling the novel "mordantly funny [and], ruthlessly honest," Nancy C. Hammond in *Horn Book* also admires the novel's "finely drawn characters." However, both Zena Sutherland in *Bulletin of the Center for Children's Books* and C. Nordhielm Wooldridge in *School Library Journal* found the characterizations flawed. "Especially weak," noted Sutherland, "is the depiction of the mother and father." "Her characters . . .," claimed Wooldridge, "come across as mere two-dimensional bundles of idiosyncrasies."

Divorce Made Funny

Whatever problems with characterizations Fine might have had, any and all were soon forgotten in the wake of the general acclaim afforded her 1987 hit *Madame Doubtfire* (published the following year in the United States as *Alias Madame Doubtfire*). Like *The Granny Project*, the book deals with the problems of parents trying to bring up their children during an emotionally stressful time. In this instance, however, the parents are divorced, and the book focuses on what happens to children caught between clashing ex-spouses. It all begins when Daniel Hilliard's former wife, Miranda, starts bringing their three children late to scheduled visits with their father and picking them up early. Infuriated with her plan to hire a housekeeper to help with the housework and watch the children after school, he decides to answer her help-wanted ad, arriving at his interview in disguise. While two of the three children recognize their father immediately, Miranda finds

Kitty's troublesome relationship with her mother's new boyfriend forms the backdrop of this 1989 novel.

herself dumbfounded by this huge, turbaned woman who seems to have a magical way with her offspring and makes a delightful cup of tea. Madame Doubtfire gets the job. All goes well until the day Miranda comes home early from work. Daniel, who is supposed to be helping out as Madame Doubtfire, is there in her front room posing nude for the neighbor's art class. On top of that, because of a strike at school, her children are gaping through the windows at the whole scene from the garden. A tremendous fight ensues, but Daniel uses the opportunity to tell his ex-wife that she had driven him to desperate measures and they decide together on an amicable solution.

Although *Madame Doubtfire* was nominated for both England's *Guardian* award and the *Observer*'s Prize for Teenage Fiction, Chris Powling theorized in the *Times Educational Supplement* that it was only because the book was "sublimely, creasingly, *funny*" that Fine didn't win, since book awards usually seem to go to authors of more serious works. But, while "novels about divorce for children are rarely funny," according to Roger Sutton in the *Bulletin of the Children's Center for Books*, "here's one that will have readers laughing from the first page." In *Booklist* Ilene Cooper praised Fine's ability to create so many vivid characters that each contribute to the success of the story. "By showing the charade from everyone's point of view," she wrote, "Fine lets readers gain insight into the complex cocoon of the family unit. Moreover, all the characters grow in elaborate and real ways." Margery Fisher welcomed the book's focus on a more significant subject than that usually discussed in young adult literature. In *Growing Point* she noted, "Readers of the teenage novel, weary of perfunctory blue-prints of reality, should be thankful to Anne Fine for giving them such nourishing food for thought within an entertaining piece of fiction." Concluding his *New York Times Book Review* critique of the book, Mark Geller observed: "*Madame Doubtfire* is sweet and amusing. I can't imagine anyone not enjoying it."

The effect of divorce on children is also the topic of Fine's next young adult novel, *My War with Goggle-Eyes*. As the book begins, Helen Johnston arrives at school feeling very down. Within minutes, she runs, crying, out of her classroom. Miss Lupey, her teacher, sends her classmate Kitty Killin to look after her. Soon, Kitty catches up with Helen—hiding amid the coats and scarves in the school's coatroom—and quickly figures out that

Helen's problem is that she can't stand her divorced mother's new boyfriend. Kitty had the same problem in the past when her mother began seeing Gerald Faulkner. As the girls move into a lost-property closet for more privacy, Kitty settles in to tell the story of Gerald, whom she calls Goggle-Eyes because of the way he stares at her mother's legs, and his relationship with Kitty's Mom, her younger sister, Judith, and, of course, Kitty herself. After many humorous clashes between Kitty and the boyfriend, the girl's hatred of Gerald comes to a head when he accompanies the family to an anti-nuclear demonstration. When Kitty's mom gets arrested, Gerald volunteers to take care of the girls until she is released from jail. Kitty grows to accept him as she realizes that although his ideas are different than hers, they often hold some truth.

Winner of both the *Guardian* award for children's literature and the Carnegie Medal in England, *My War with Goggle-Eyes* also received recognition from the American Library Association, the *School Library Journal*, and the International Reading Association. Critical approval focused on Fine's ability to capture the humorous side of family relationships while providing thoughtful insights on contemporary social issues. "The book offers wonderful, unique characterizations, thought-provoking ideas, and a fine depiction of the way people change," Ilene Cooper remarked in *Booklist*, "even when they don't want to." "Fine's gentle anti-nuclear subplot never overshadows the main theme of acceptance and tolerance in relationships," observed Susan Schuller in *School Library Journal*. "Her characters are . . . people with a wide range of feelings and reactions; the dialogue is especially expressive and full of feeling." In the *School Librarian* Julie Blaisdale wrote: "This is an excellent novel, told with sensitivity and humor, which also manages to make a strong case for nuclear disarmament." Several reviewers compared the humor and subject matter of *My War with Goggle-Eyes* to that found in Fine's previous novel. "As in this book's excellent predecessor, *Alias Madame Doubtfire*," noted Nancy Vasilakis, for instance, in *Horn Book*, "Fine aims deadly accurate darts at modern relationships."

In *The Book of the Banshee* Fine turns from a family pulled apart by divorce and its aftermath to a family whose life is being made unbearable by the suddenly demanding nature of their teenage daughter, Estelle. After reading the fictional account of William Scott Saffery's World War I adventures, Will Flowers, Estelle's younger brother, decides that since his home is like a war zone, he, like Saffery, should write an account of what is going on around him. He notes: "Our house is a battleground, too, in its own way. That's what Mum says, at least. She claims that since Estelle turned into a shrieking banshee over night, our house has been hell on earth." Their house is in such a state of confusion that Will's parents usually can't come up with lunch money for him, so he makes stale-carrot lunches to take to school with him. Will's mom often comes in through the

The students in a classroom of underachievers are assigned to take care of their "babies"—actually six-pound sacks of flour—in this work, winner of the 1992 Carnegie Medal.

window instead of the front door to avoid a confrontation with Estelle, who waits for her in the front room. The breaking point comes when Will arrives home late one evening and finds his little sister, Muffy, up past her bedtime and unfed, while his mother is out at a school meeting and his father and Estelle are arguing about whether or not she can go to a party. Will loses his temper and tells his parents and sister that he is tired of Muffy and him being neglected and demands peace in his home. His outburst seems to stun his parents into taking more control of their household. After a hysterical family fight including flying spice jars, family life soon returns to normal.

A *Publishers Weekly* critic saw *The Book of the Banshee* as a typical Fine offering, noting, "As usual, Fine . . . uses humor to blend impeccable characterization with real-life problems." Like reviewers of previous Fine novels, Hanna B. Zeiger found much to praise in the book. "The author's deft handling of characters and relationships is again apparent," Zeiger wrote in *Horn Book*, "and her mastery of the comedy inherent in family life will bring many a laugh to the reader." In *School Library Journal* Connie Tyrrell Burns claimed the book "has some of the funniest fight scenes in YA literature," while further observing that it was also "a well-crafted work with layers of meaning and serious themes richly interwoven with the more comic ones." In his *Bulletin of the Center for Children's Books* review Robert Strong also felt the fight scenes merited special mention. "Estelle's adolescent angst and injuries are perfect material for Fine, who, when it comes to family fights," he commented, "always has the best seat in the house."

"A Life Sentence"

The idea for Fine's next novel came when she read a magazine article about a group of students who were given sacks of flour to look after as if they were babies. The purpose of the assignment was to teach the children about the pressures of parenthood. This is exactly what happens in Fine's novel, *Flour Babies*. The six-pound sacks of flour are given to the boys in Room 8 at St. Boniface School, the room containing the troublemakers and the underachievers. Not only are they told that they can't leave their "babies" unattended and they must keep them clean and dry, but the boys also learn that as part of their assignment they

If you enjoy the works of Anne Fine, you may want to check out the following books and films:

Norma Klein, *Mom, the Wolfman, and Me,* 1972.
Jean Little, *Hey World, Here I Am!,* 1989.
Barbara Park, *My Mother Got Married (and Other Disasters),* 1989.
Kramer vs. Kramer, Columbia, 1979.

must "keep a Baby Book, and write in it daily." While some of the boys find the experiment foolish, Simon Martin seems quite taken with his flour baby. He talks to her and keeps her safe during his soccer practice. He finds himself wondering how his father could have left him when he was just a baby and comes to a new appreciation for his mother. "Being a parent," he thinks, "was pretty well a life sentence. Why, if instead of going off to the hospital to have a baby all those years ago, his mother had stabbed someone to death with a bread knife, she'd be out of jail by now." Some of Simon's and the other boys' "Baby Book" entries make up part of the text of the novel.

Flour Babies won England's highest literary award, the Carnegie Medal, as well as more enthusiastic praise from critics. A *Publishers Weekly* reviewer wrote, "[Fine] takes a down-to-earth scenario and, like her protagonist, turns it into an extraordinary adventure in living and learning." As usual, critics especially enjoyed Fine's ability to find humor in everyday situations. "[Fine's] keen powers of observation of human nature," noted Ellen Fader in *Horn Book*, "combined with her sharp sense of humor, pay off in a novel that is full of hilarious one-liners and situations that result in farcical misunderstandings." In *Voice of Youth Advocates* Myra Feldman commented, "YAs will enjoy the antics of the Room 8 boys and the interplay between them and the school faculty." In *Bulletin of the Center for Children's Books* Deborah Stevenson highlighted Fine's portrait of Simon Martin, noting "his endearingly goofy character makes him an appealing focus."

In a more recent work, *Step by Wicked Step*, Fine looks at the effects of divorce and remarriage. While spending the night in a ghostly mansion during a class trip, five teens stumble across the nineteenth-century diary that describes a young man's troublesome relationship with his stepfather. The students gradually reveal how divorce has altered the events of their own lives, and, according to a contributor in *Horn Book*, their stories are "powerful and intensely moving tales of children struggling with change and shifting family conditions." Jamie S. Hansen, writing in *Voice of Youth Advocates*, found Fine's resolution particularly effective, stating that the author's "ending is sensitive without being preachy and rings as true as her dialogue."

While Fine continues producing young adult novels, as well as juvenile books and novels for adults, at a tremendous rate, in *Something About the Author Autobiography Series*, she describes her life as "quiet." "I spend my life walking my dog, reading, and sitting working," she explains. "I still work in pencil. I use an eraser and a pencil sharpener. I'll write a whole chapter this way, writing, erasing, writing again, over and over until I'm sure it's right. Then I'll type it up, and start to alter it again. A book for older children will take me about a year, and though each time I swear that at the end of this one I'll buy a word processor, I never have." According to Jean Richardson in *Publishers Weekly*, readers will be happy to know that, so far, for Fine "there is no shortage of ideas and commissions for more children's books." Undoubtedly, Fine will stay in the forefront of literature for the young because, as Richardson concludes, "like all the best children's authors, Anne Fine is writing for herself, for the child who fell under the spell of books, who identified passionately with her favorite characters and wanted to know what happened next."

■ Works Cited

Baines, R., review of *Round behind the Ice-House, Junior Bookshelf*, April, 1982, pp. 71-72.

Blaisdale, Julie, review of *Goggle-Eyes, School Librarian*, August, 1989, p. 113.

Blaisdale, Julie, "In Touch with the Child: The Novels of Anne Fine," *School Librarian*, November, 1991, pp. 135-36.

Review of *The Book of the Banshee, Publishers Weekly*, November 22, 1991, p. 58.

Burns, Connie Tyrrell, review of *The Book of the Banshee, School Library Journal*, December, 1991, pp. 135-36.

Colwell, E., review of *The Other, Darker Ned, Junior Bookshelf*, October, 1979, p. 277.

Colwell, E., review of *The Stone Menagerie, Junior Bookshelf*, October, 1980, p. 245-46.

Cooper, Ilene, "Focus: Alias Madame Doubtfire, by Anne Fine," *Booklist*, May 15, 1988, p. 1611.

Cooper, Ilene, review of *My War with Goggle-Eyes, Booklist*, April 15, 1989, p. 1465.

Crouch, Marcus, review of *Summer-House Loon, Junior Bookshelf*, August, 1978, pp. 202-03.

Feldman, Myra, review of *Flour Babies, Voice of Youth Advocates*, June, 1994, p. 82.

Fine, Anne, *The Book of the Banshee*, Little, Brown, 1992.

Fine, Anne, *Alias Madame Doubtfire*, Bantam, 1993.

Fine, Anne, essay in *Something About the Author Autobiographical Series*, Volume 15, Gale, 1993, pp. 141-55.

Fine, Anne, *Flour Babies*, Little, Brown, 1994.

Fisher, Margery, review of *The Stone Menagerie, Growing Point*, September, 1980, p. 3756.

Fisher, Margery, review of *Round behind the Ice-House, Growing Point*, January, 1982, p. 4010.

Fisher, Margery, review of *Madame Doubtfire, Growing Point*, September, 1987, p. 4858.

Fisher, Margery, review of *The Summer-House Loon* and *The Other, Darker Ned, Growing Point*, May, 1990, pp. 5343-45.

Flanagan, Kate, review of *The Summer-House Loon, Horn Book*, August, 1979, p. 422.

Review of *Flour Babies, Publishers Weekly*, March 21, 1994, p. 73.

Geller, Mark, review of *Alias Madame Doubtfire, New York Times Book Review*, May 1, 1988, p. 34.

Hammond, Nancy C., review of *The Granny Project*, October, 1983, p. 573.

Hansen, Jamie S., review of *Step by Wicked Step, Voice of Youth Advocates*, August, 1996, p. 156.

Hollindale, Peter, "Teenage Tensions," *Times Literary Supplement*, July 7, 1978, p. 767.

Powling, Chris, "Relative Values," *Times Educational Supplement*, June 3, 1988, p. 49.

Richardson, Jean, "Having a Fine Year," *Publishers Weekly*, November 22, 1993, pp. 29-30.

Schuller, Susan, review of *My War with Goggle-Eyes, School Library Journal*, May, 1989, p. 104.

Review of *Step by Wicked Step, Horn Book*, July/August, 1996, p. 463.

Stevenson, Deborah, review of *Flour Babies, Bulletin of the Center for Children's Books*, pp. 317-18.

Strong, Robert, review of *The Book of the Banshee, Bulletin of the Center for Children's Books*, February, 1992, p. 154.

Sutherland, Zena, review of *The Granny Project*, *Bulletin of the Center for Children's Books*, October, 1983, p. 25.

Sutton, Roger, review of *Alias Madame Doubtfire*, *Bulletin of the Center for Children's Books*, April, 1988, p. 155.

Tucker, Nicholas, "Confrontations," *Times Literary Supplement*, November 20, 1981, p. 1355.

Twentieth-Century Children's Writers, 4th edition, St. James Press, 1995, pp. 343-44.

Vasilakis, Nancy, review of *My War with Goggle-Eyes*, *Horn Book*, July/August, 1989, p. 482.

Wooldridge, C. Nordhielm, review of *The Granny Project*, *School Library Journal*, October, 1983, p. 157.

Zeiger, Hanna B., review of *The Book of the Banshee*, *Horn Book*, March/April, 1992, p. 209.

■ For More Information See

BOOKS

Children's Literature Review, Volume 25, Gale, 1991.

Contemporary Authors, New Revision Series, Volume 38, Gale, 1993.

Something about the Author, Gale, Volume 29, 1982, Volume 72, 1993.

PERIODICALS

Books for Keeps, March, 1996, pp. 20-21; July, 1996, p. 12; September, 1996, p. 33; January, 1997.

Bulletin of the Center for Children's Books, May, 1989, p. 222.

Carousel, spring, 1996, pp. 20-21.

Magpies, March, 1996, pp. 4-5.

New York Times Book Review, May 22, 1994, p. 23.

Observer, May 4, 1986, p. 23.

Publishers Weekly, March 24, 1989, p. 72.

School Librarian, December, 1980, p. 393.

School Library Journal, May, 1979, p. 60.

Spectator, July 4, 1987, pp. 34-36.

Times Literary Supplement, June 22, 1990, p. 674.

Wilson Library Bulletin, February, 1990, pp. 84-85.*

—Sketch by Marian C. Gonsior

Brian Jacques

■ Personal

Surname is pronounced "Jakes"; born June 15, 1939, in Liverpool, England; son of James (a truck driver) and Ellen Jacques; married; wife's name, Liz (a former school teacher); children: David, Marc. *Education:* Attended St. John's School, Liverpool, England. *Politics:* "Humanitarian/socialist." *Religion:* Roman Catholic. *Hobbies and other interests:* Opera, walking his dog, crossword puzzles.

■ Addresses

Home—Liverpool, England. *Office*—BBC-Radio Merseyside, 55 Paradise St., Liverpool L1 3BP, England.

■ Career

Worked in numerous occupations, including seaman, 1954-57, railway fireman, 1957-60, longshoreman, 1960-65, long-distance truck driver, 1965-75, docks representative, 1975-80, as well as logger, bus driver, boxer, policeman, postmaster, stand-up comic, and member of folk singer group, The Liverpool Fisherman; freelance radio broadcaster, 1980—. Radio broadcasts for BBC-Radio Merseyside include the music programs "Jakestown" and "Saturday with Brian Jacques"; six half-hour programs for junior schools, "Schools Quiz"; ten half-hour programs on cinematic knowledge, "Flixquiz"; and documentaries "We All Went Down the Docks," "Gangland Anthology," "The Eternal Christmas," "Centenary of Liverpool," "An Eyefool of Easter," "A Lifetime Habit," and "The Hollywood Musicals," a six-part series; contributor to the "Alan Jackson" show; broadcaster for BBC-Radio and BBC-Radio 2; member of BBC Northwest Television Advisory Council. Presents humorous lectures at schools and universities. Patron of Royal Wavertree School for the Blind.

■ Awards, Honors

National Light Entertainment Award for Radio from Sony Company, 1982, for BBC-Radio Merseyside's "Jakestown"; Rediffusion Award for Best Light Entertainment Program on Local Radio, 1982, and Commendation, 1983; Parents' Choice Honor Book for Literature, 1987, for *Redwall*; *Booklist* Editor's Choice, 1987, for *Redwall*; Children's Book of the Year Award from Lancashire County (England) Library, 1988, for *Redwall*, and also for *Mossflower* and *Salamandastron*; Western Australian Young Readers' Award, for *Redwall*, *Mossflower*, and *Mattimeo*; Carnegie Medal nominations, for *Redwall*, *Mossflower*, *Mattimeo*, and *Salamandastron*; *Redwall* was also selected as an American Library Association Best Book for Young Adults, and a *School Library Journal* Best Book.

■ Writings

"REDWALL" SERIES

Redwall, illustrated by Gary Chalk, Hutchinson, 1986, Philomel, 1987.

Mossflower, illustrated by Gary Chalk, Hutchinson, 1988, Philomel, 1988.

Mattimeo, illustrated by Gary Chalk, Hutchinson, 1989, Philomel, 1990.

The Redwall Trilogy (contains *Redwall*, *Mossflower*, and *Mattimeo*), three volumes, Red Fox, 1991.

Mariel of Redwall, illustrated by Gary Chalk, Hutchinson, 1991, Philomel, 1991.

Salamandastron, illustrated by Gary Chalk, Hutchinson, 1992, Philomel, 1992.

Martin the Warrior, illustrated by Gary Chalk, Hutchinson, 1993, Philomel, 1993.

The Bellmaker, illustrated by Allan Curless, Hutchinson, 1994, Philomel, 1995.

Outcast of Redwall, illustrated by Allan Curless, Hutchinson, 1995, Philomel, 1995.

The Great Redwall Feast (rhymes excerpted from previously published material), illustrated by Christopher Denise, Philomel, 1995.

Pearls of Lutra, Hutchinson, 1996.

OTHER

Seven Strange and Ghostly Tales, Philomel, 1991.

Also author of numerous documentaries and plays for television, radio, and the stage; stage plays include *Brown Bitter*, *Wet Nellies*, and *Scouse*, all performed in Liverpool, England, at the Everyman Theatre. Columnist for *Catholic Pictorial*.

■ Adaptations

Jacques narrated the cassette recording of *Seven Strange and Ghostly Tales*, Listening Library, 1996; *Redwall* and *Mossflower* have been released on audio cassette, Recorded Books, 1996.

■ Sidelights

Once planned by their author to be only a trilogy—and, before that, not intended for publication at all—the "Redwall" books by English radio personality Brian Jacques have blossomed into a nine-novel phenomenon with a growing fandom on both sides of the Atlantic. And there is currently no end in sight to the saga of Redwall Abbey and the continuing stories of its resident gentlebeasts. These fantasy novels feature a broad cast of anthropomorphized animals who follow the author's successful good-versus-evil formula that appeals to young and old readers alike. Jacques' heroes and heroines (mice, moles, hares, badgers, otters, squirrels, hawks, and the like) can be counted on to be brave, true, and kind, while the villains (rats, foxes, ferrets, snakes, weasels, and stoats) are always appropriately wicked, violent, and depraved and are dutifully defeated by the end of each novel, much to the reader's satisfaction. But if it had not been for one of Jacques' former teachers, the Redwall series might never have seen print.

Jacques did not become a published author until he was in his late forties. Before then, he had worked a long list of jobs, until he finally settled on a steady career in radio. Jacques' parents were Irish Catholic immigrants to Liverpool, England, whose son grew up in humble but loving surroundings at home and around the ocean docks. Fortunately for the young Jacques, his father, a truck driver, had a healthy appreciation for literature, which he passed along to his son. Through him, Jacques learned to love books by such authors as Sir Arthur Conan Doyle, Robert Louis Stevenson, and Edgar Rice Burroughs.

Jacques composed his first tale for an assignment at St. John's School when he was ten years old, but he was immediately discouraged by his teacher, who felt that his story about a crocodile and the bird who cleaned its teeth was too good for a child to have written. The teacher called the young Jacques a liar when the boy insisted that he had, indeed, authored the story. Though the event was a disquieting experience, it brought Jacques to the realization that he had some talent. Another of his teachers, Austin Thomas, was a less severe task master and encouraged Jacques to read Greek literature and poetry. Higher education was not the destiny for most children growing up among Liverpool's lower classes, however, and the young Jacques left school at the age of fifteen. What followed was a string of jobs in just about every occupation imaginable, from longshoreman and logger, to policeman and postmaster, to stand-up comic and folk singer for a group called The Liverpool Fisherman.

By the time he was in his early forties, Jacques had found his niche as an entertainer. He began a career as a radio personality, playwright, poet, and storyteller, and he now has a successful weekly radio show called "Jakestown," a program featuring selections from Jacques' favorite operas that airs Sundays on BBC Radio Merseyside. Jacques enjoys performing and giving humorous lectures before children and adults, and he explains that this was how the story of Redwall first came into being. "I did not write my first novel, *Redwall,* with publication in mind," he once commented. "It was mainly written as a story for [the Royal Wavertree School for the Blind in Liverpool,] where I am a patron. Luckily it was picked up by a reputable author and sent to Hutchinson." That author was one of his former English teachers, Alan Durband, who sent out the manuscript without Jacques' knowledge. And so the Redwall series was born.

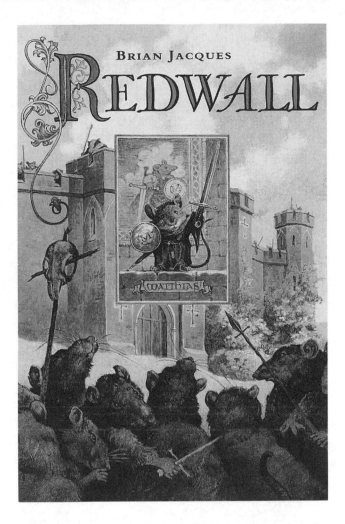

This 1986 fantasy introduces the gentlebeasts of Redwall Abbey and their nemesis, Cluny, the one-eyed rat.

Redwall

The first book in the series opens at peaceful Redwall Abbey, where a young mouse named Matthias is living as a novice among the abbots and laycreatures in a medieval-like setting. Life at the abbey involves a lot of work, but the mice and other creatures enjoy a prosperous, comfortable existence, which Jacques describes in detail near the story's beginning with a long description of a splendid and sumptuous feast. But trouble is afoot in the form of an evil rat named Cluny the Scourge, who, with his barbarous horde of followers, spends his time wreaking havoc upon the countryside. His path leads him eventually to Redwall Abbey, clearly a plum of prosperity fit for plunder. Upon hearing of Cluny's imminent approach, the Redwallers at first consider fleeing their abbey, but Matthias convinces them to stay and defend themselves.

Matthias has stumbled upon a mysterious riddle written long ago by Martin the Warrior, the legendary mouse who founded the abbey, and he hopes that by solving the riddle he will be able to locate Martin's legendary sword and defeat Cluny's army. After successfully deciphering the puzzle, Matthias learns that he is actually Martin's descendant and he figures out that the sword has been taken by the warlike sparrows who live in the abbey's tower. Risking his life, Martin manages to retrieve the sword. Meanwhile, Cluny has besieged Redwall but is at a disadvantage against the well-fortified, well-supplied abbey. He devises several plans of attack that are defeated one by one, but finally manages, through trickery, to enter the abbey and take the gentlebeasts prisoner. But the fight is not over yet, and Martin leads

A Prequel to REDWALL

MOSSFLOWER

BRIAN JACQUES

This 1988 work, a prequel to *Redwall*, follows the adventures of the brave mouse Martin and his sidekick, the mousethief Gonff, as they attempt to thwart the evil plans of the clever wildcat queen, Tsarmina.

an attack that ends in a final lethal confrontation between the young hero and Cluny.

With *Redwall* Jacques created a flavorful recipe with all the right ingredients of admirable heroes and contemptible villains in classic battles between good and evil. Inevitably, comparisons have been drawn between *Redwall* and other English books with anthropomorphized animal characters like Richard Adams' *Watership Down* and Kenneth Grahame's *The Wind in the Willows*, though about the only common feature of these books is that they include animal protagonists exhibiting human-like behavior to greater or lesser degrees. Some critics have even argued that Jacques' characters are more animal than human, despite the

fact that they wear clothes, construct buildings, and sail ships. Jane Inglis, writing in *Books for Your Children*, felt that the author's "creatures are true first and foremost to their animal natures." Noting the comparison with *Watership Down*, Margery Fisher perceptively noted in her *Growing Point* assessment of *Redwall* that for "all the similarities of idiom, alert sophisticated narrative and neat humanisation, *Redwall* has an intriguing and unusual flavour of its own." Looking deeper into the nature of the first book in the series, *School Library Journal* critic Susan M. Harding observed that *Redwall* is more than merely a classic story of good versus evil; it is also a study of the *nature* of the two sides of this coin. Jacques, Harding explained, does not create characters who are merely "personifications of attributes," for the heroes do have flaws, and even the reprehensible Cluny has his admirable points. The "rich cast of characters, the detailed accounts of medieval warfare, and Jacques' ability to tell a good story *and* make readers think" all make the author's first novel a worthwhile book, Harding concluded.

A History of Redwall Abbey

Jacques followed *Redwall* with the stories of *Mossflower* and *Mattimeo*, which take place before and after events in *Redwall*, respectively. For readers to go through the series chronologically according to the events Jacques describes in them, they would have to read the books in the following order: *Martin the Warrior* (1993), *Mossflower* (1988), *Outcast of Redwall* (1995), *Mariel of Redwall* (1991), *The Bellmaker* (1994), *Salamandastron* (1992), *Redwall* (1986), *Mattimeo* (1989), and *Pearls of Lutra* (1996). Although each story can stand easily on its own—and there is no telling which part of his ongoing saga Jacques will delve into next—readers might find taking this approach to the series a rewarding one.

The story of Redwall actually begins before the abbey is built. In *Martin the Warrior*, a mouse named Martin has been enslaved by the sinister stoat Badrang, who tortures the poor mouse and forces him to work long hours without rest. One day, Martin can take no more and attacks one of Badrang's captains. It takes six of the stoat's soldiers to bring Martin down. Tying the upstart mouse to a pole atop a hill, Badrang sentences Martin to death by leaving him exposed to the local birds as prey. Martin would surely have died had not a mouse named Rose and her friend Grumm the mole come to his rescue. After saving him, Rose asks Martin whether he has seen her brother, who was also imprisoned by Badrang. Martin now has a mission: enlisting the help of other brave animals, he plans an attack against Badrang to defeat the stoat and free all his slaves.

In *Mossflower* Martin once again finds himself in dire circumstances. Having wandered into Mossflower Country, he is taken prisoner by the wildcat Verdauga, King of Kotir, and ruler over Mossflower woods. Martin then becomes a point of dispute between the aging and sickly Verdauga's two potential heirs: his son, Gingivere, and his daughter, Tsarmina. Gingivere is sympathetic to Martin, who insists that he was not aware he was trespassing on their land. But the more willful and ruthless Tsarmina, in a bid for power, manages to have her brother thrown in prison and poisons her father the king. Having assumed the throne, Tsarmina throws Martin into the dungeon, where the mouse meets a thief named Gonff. With the help of Gonff's talent for getting out of tight fixes, Martin escapes. Not one to forget an injustice, Martin gathers together an army that leads to Tsarmina's downfall. With the tyrant wildcat defeated, Martin founds Redwall Abbey in the heart of Mossflower and begins a new order whose members are sworn to be kind to their fellow creatures and offer aid to those in need.

Outcast of Redwall moves away from Martin to focus on new characters and includes a somewhat more complex plot, though the story begins again with a protagonist being held prisoner by an evil carnivore. But, instead of a mouse, this time the hero is a badger named Sunflash, the son of Bella of Brockhall and heir to the badgers' mountain stronghold of Salamandastron. Swartt Sixclaw, a ferret who leads a band of outlaws, has captured Sunflash, but the badger escapes with the help of his friend Skarlath the hawk. Attacking Swartt with a stick, Sunflash cripples the ferret's hand, after which Swartt swears revenge. Sunflash and Skarlath raise troops of their own and begin skirmishing with the ferrets. Swartt follows his enemies to Redwall Abbey and lays siege to it. During the battle, his own infant son is left in the confusion, and one of the abbey mice, Byrony, adopts it. But Veil, as the ferret is later named, is predestined by his blood to become wicked, and, despite the kindness of the Redwall creatures, he unsuccessfully tries to poison the Abbey Friar.

Fleeing the abbey, he goes off in pursuit of the father who abandoned him. Meanwhile, Sunflash is having dreams of Salamandastron, a place he does not remember for his childhood has been wasted as Swartt's prisoner. Taking a band of warrior hares and other beasts with him, he departs on a journey to his true mountain home, and so, at Salamandastron, events come to a head in a final battle.

Mariel of Redwall and *The Bellmaker*, the two books following *Outcast of Redwall* chronologically, fea-

In this thriller, first published in 1989, Matthias, the great warrior mouse, must hunt down a crafty fox who has kidnapped his son Mattimeo and the other mousechildren of Redwall Abbey.

ture the brave mouse Mariel and tell something of the history of the great bell that hangs in the abbey tower. *Mariel of Redwall* opens as the story of a young mouse who has been washed ashore from the sea and has lost her memory. Attacked by seagulls, she defends herself with a rope she finds and so, unable to remember her true name, calls herself Storm Gullwhacker. Managing to find her way to safety at Redwall Abbey, she is befriended there by a young mouse named Dandin. The Redwallers take good care of her and invite her to one of their many feasts. During the dinner, however, one of the mice sings an ancient rhyme that sparks some of Mariel's memories. Suddenly she recalls that she was thrown off a ship by Gabool the Wild, the wicked king of the searats. Now knowing what she must do, Mariel, with Dandin (who has Martin the Warrior's sword) and other friends, sets out to seek her revenge and rescue her father. *The Bellmaker* reunites Mariel and Dandin, this time in a mission to defeat Foxwolf Urgan Nagru, who has usurped the throne of Southsward from good Gael Squir-relking. Joining forces with the woodland creatures still loyal to the king, the mice set about their dangerous task. Meanwhile, at the abbey, Mariel's father has visions that his daughter is in danger and sends out additional Redwallers to help.

As was the case in *Outcast of Redwall, Salamandastron* again combines characters and plotlines involving both Redwallers and the badger lords. Mara, a badger who is Lord Urthstripe's adopted daughter, and her hare friend Pikkle Ffolger become friends with Klitch and Goffa, a weasel and his ferret companion. The friendship leads to trouble, however, for Klitch, unbeknownst to Mara and Pikkle, is the son of Ferahgo the Assassin, who is planning to lay siege to Salamandastron. At Redwall the resident mice have made a similar error by befriending Dingeye and Thura, two stoats who are Ferahgo's followers. The stoats murder the abbey's records keeper and flee Redwall after stealing the sword of Martin the Warrior; Samkin the squirrel and Arula the mole set off in pursuit of the stoats. A third plotline involves Thrugg the otter and Dumble the dormouse, who are on a quest to find the Flowers of Icetor that are the only cure for the Dryditch Fever plaguing Redwall.

Mattimeo and *Pearls of Lutra,* involving the descendants of Matthias, follow the events in *Redwall.*

Mattimeo, the son of Matthias (who now serves as the abbey's protector), and the other children of Redwall are kidnapped after one of the abbey feasts by the fox Slagar the Cruel, who tricks the Redwallers by posing as a harmless magician. Matthias rounds up a band of warriors and pursues Slagar across a forbidding desert to the fox's slave kingdom. Matthias has to use all his wits and courage to save his son from his wicked captor. In *Pearls of Lutra* the hero is Martin, son of Mattimeo, son of Matthias, the descendant of Martin the Warrior. Martin's quest is to find the Pearls of Lutra, which were lost after a band of

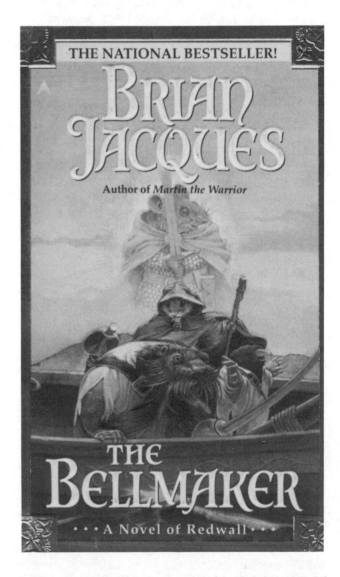

Joseph the Bellmaker dreams that his daughter, Mariel the Warriormaid, is in grave danger from Foxwolf Urgan Nagru in this novel, first published in 1994.

searats slaughtered the otter Lutra and his tribe. The pearls are needed as ransom for the Abbess of Redwall, whom the searats have taken prisoner. But there is one factor in this plan that neither the searats nor Martin are aware of: Lutra's daughter Grath Longfletch is still alive and out for revenge.

Criticism of *Redwall*

Though settings vary and characters are legion in Jacques' series, all of the Redwall books conform, more or less, to a formula that has proved immensely successful and has gained the author a loyal following. *Voice of Youth Advocates* contributor Katharine L. Kan summarized the basic plotline as: "goodbeast sanctuary threatened by nogoodnik vermin and/or natural disaster, young untested heroes to the rescue." While such a device can be reassuring to readers, who always know what to expect when they pick up a Redwall book, it also has a downside, as Ruth S. Vose pointed out in her *School Library Journal* review of *Mossflower*: "Suspense does not arise from the situation itself," she remarked, "for the end is never really in doubt." Marcus Crouch, also writing about *Mossflower* in *Junior Bookshelf*, felt that, although Jacques demonstrates narrative skill in the way he weaves different subplots together, the author goes into too much unnecessary detail, his style is filled with "narrative cliches," and the characters "are mostly stereotypes."

One of the more common complaints about Jacques' stories concerns the author's delight in describing sumptuous Redwall feasts in great detail and at great length. Not a story is told without at least one of these festive soirees of fish, vegetables, fruit, fresh breads, and luscious desserts. The Redwallers' "love of food . . . makes for a persistent and slightly repetitious theme in all the books," commented Katherine Bouton in the *New York Times Book Review*. More emphatically, Kan lamented, "*Why* do English authors spend so much time describing meals in such excruciating detail?" But "the repasts are not the only part of the story that go on too long," wrote one *Publishers Weekly* contributor in a review of *Outcast of Redwall*, who complained that the qualities of each character is fixed by his or her species: the hares are all upper class, foppish but brave warriors; the moles are all rural types who speak in a difficult-to-interpret dialect; the children

If you enjoy the works of Brian Jacques, you may want to check out the following books and films:

Richard Adams, *Watership Down*, 1974.
Clare Bell, *Clan Ground*, 1984.
Kenneth Grahame, *The Wind in the Willows*, 1908.
Andre Norton, *The Mark of the Cat*, 1992.
Ladyhawke, Twentieth Century-Fox, 1985.
The NeverEnding Story, Neue Constantin Film, 1984.

(or "dibbuns") are all rascally mischief-makers; the hawks all speak with Scottish accents; the sparrows are all primitive barbarians who speak a sort of pidgin English, and so on.

Nevertheless, there is also much to enjoy about the Redwall series, as Jacques' fans are well aware. While admitting that the stories are "formulaic," Bouton asserted that they are also "wonderfully imaginative in their variety of plot and character." Jacques approaches his subject not with a heavy hand in an attempt to suggest some epic struggle, but rather finds plenty of opportunity for levity. As Andy Sawyer remarked in his *School Librarian* review of *Outcast of Redwall*, not only is there much jollity in the regular feasts in which the gentlebeasts partake, but there are also plenty of "hearty japes, slapstick humour and swashbuckling action [that is] pitched perfectly at the intended readership." Much of the humor comes from the antics of the mischievous dibbuns, but also from Jacques' satirical jibes at English upper crust military types who in his books take the form of hares. A sterling example of this is Basil Stag Hare, who appears in several of the stories. Basil, whose primary concern is for filling his stomach, has a way of showing up at every Redwall feast. A veteran fighter, he can always be counted upon in a battle, and, in a classically droll British manner, he remains undisturbed by violence (the sight of a stoat who has met a grisly end engenders concern only in that it might put him off his supper). His love for his Hon Rosie, a brutish female hare with an appallingly loud laugh, also adds humor to the character. A satiric air is lent even to the villains, as *School Librarian* critic Peter Andrews observed: "Evil as they may be, none of the villains can be taken seriously because most are of the pantomime variety."

Another feature of Jacques' books that critics have admired is his complete lack of chauvinism: there are just as many brave and daring heroines in the series as there are heroes; likewise, the villains are often vixens or female wildcats who are just as treacherous as their male counterparts. "The author must be commended for creating a world of equal-opportunity adventuring," commented one *Publishers Weekly* reviewer. "For once," Carolyn Cushman wrote in her *Locus* assessment of *Mariel of Redwall*, "it's not just the boys who get to hear the spirit of Martin the Warrior—the ladies really get their chance this outing. Having a valiant female protagonist is a nice touch."

Of course, there is also the swashbuckling action, which Jacques adds in liberal doses, that make the series, simply put, a good read. But there is something else in the books that many readers find appealing: the satisfaction of a story about good fighting evil in which both can be easily distinguished and the victor is always in the right. While some critics might see this as a drawback, others have perceived its benefits. Selma Lanes, writing in the *New York Times Book Review*, found the world of Redwall "a credible and ingratiating place, one to which many young readers will doubtless cheerfully return." "Jacques," Sawyer concluded, "is writing for an audience who want—even need—clearly identifiable labels for their moral signposts."

This distinction between good and evil, right and wrong, is carried out deliberately by Jacques, who once remarked: "In writing children's books, I feel that a 'good yarn' is essential, keeping in mind a strong moral sense of values for children." While the popularity of this approach remains unflagging, the author will likely continue to spend the warmer months in Liverpool sitting in his garden with his terrier, Baby Mac, and using his old mechanical typewriter to write more stories about Redwall and Salamandastron, brave mice and barbarous searats.

■ Works Cited

Andrews, Peter, review of *Redwall, School Librarian*, November, 1994, p. 151.

Review of *The Bellmaker, Publishers Weekly*, February 20, 1995, p. 206.

Bouton, Katherine, review of *Martin the Warrior, New York Times Book Review*, February 27, 1994, p. 24.

Crouch, Marcus, review of *Mossflower, Junior Bookshelf*, December, 1988, pp. 304-305.

Cushman, Carolyn, review of *Mariel of Redwall, Locus*, March, 1992, p. 64.

Fisher, Margery, review of *Redwall, Growing Point*, March, 1987, pp. 4756-7.

Harding, Susan M., review of *Redwall, School Library Journal*, August, 1987, p. 96.

Inglis, Jane, review of *Redwall, Books for Your Children*, spring, 1988, p. 31.

Kan, Katharine L., review of *Salamandastron, Voice of Youth Advocates*, June, 1993, p. 102.

Lanes, Selma, review of *Redwall, New York Times Book Review*, August 23, 1987, p. 27.

Review of *Outcast of Redwall, Publishers Weekly*, January 15, 1996, pp. 462-63.

Sawyer, Andy, review of *Outcast of Redwall, School Librarian*, February, 1996.

Vose, Ruth S., review of *Mossflower, School Library Journal*, November, 1988, pp. 125-26.

■ For More Information See

BOOKS

Twentieth-Century Young Adult Authors, 1st edition, edited by Laura Standley Berger, St. James Press, 1994.

PERIODICALS

Booklist, March 1, 1994, p. 1262; April 1, 1995, p. 1391.

Bulletin of the Center for Children's Books, August, 1987, p. 211; January, 1994, p. 157; March, 1996, pp. 30-31.

Growing Point, January, 1992, pp. 5630-4.

Horn Book, January-February, 1988, p. 71; March-April, 1989, p. 217; May-June, 1992, p. 340; September-October, 1994, p. 611; May-June, 1995, p. 349.

Kirkus Reviews, November 1, 1988, p. 1605; February 1, 1994, p. 144; January 1, 1997, p. 59.

Kliatt, July, 1996, p. 20.

New York Times Book Review, August 23, 1987.

Publishers Weekly, April 13, 1990, p. 66; August 19, 1996.

School Library Journal, December, 1991, p. 116; March, 1993, p. 198; August, 1995, p. 142.

Voice of Youth Advocates, February, 1989, p. 294; June, 1992, pp. 109-10.

Washington Post Book World, November 6, 1988.

Wilson Library Bulletin, September, 1993, p. 102; May, 1994, p. 83; June, 1995, p. 97.*

—Sketch by Janet L. Hile

Mike Judge

■ Personal

Born c. 1963, in Quayaquil, Ecuador; son of an archaeology professor and a school librarian; married Frances Morocco, 1989; children: Julia, and another daughter. *Education:* University of California at San Diego, degree in physics, 1985; attended graduate school. *Hobbies and other interests:* Classical piano.

■ Addresses

Home—New York.

■ Career

Physics teaching assistant at the University of California at San Diego; worked at two jobs as an electronics engineer in California until 1987; played bass in various bands in Texas; creator of television series *Beavis and Butt-head,* supplying voices for several characters and contributing to the animation and the writing, 1993—; creator (with Greg Daniels) of television series *King of the*

Hill, Fox, 1997—. The voices of Beavis and Butt-head appeared in the movie *Airheads,* Twentieth Century-Fox, 1995.

■ Writings

"Frog Baseball," *Liquid Television,* MTV, 1993.
(With others) *Beavis and Butt-head* (television series), MTV, 1993—.
(With others) *Beavis and Butt-head's Ensucklopedia,* MTV/Pocket Books, 1994.
(With Joe Stillman; and director) *Beavis and Butt-head Do America* (movie), Paramount, 1996.
(With Greg Daniels) *King of the Hill* (television series), Fox, 1997—.

Also coauthor of *This Book Sucks,* with Sam Johnson and Chris Marcil. Recorded the CD *The Beavis and Butt-head Experience* (includes Cher duet of "I Got You Babe"), released by Geffen. Episodes of *Beavis and Butt-head* have been collected on the videotapes *Work Sucks, There Goes the Neighborhood,* and *Final Judgment.*

■ Adaptations

The characters of Beavis and Butt-head have been adapted into video games for Sega and SNES and into a screen saver for Windows. Merchandise includes buttons, posters, trading cards, comic books, calendars, T-shirts, and other merchandise.

■ **Sidelights**

"Beavis and Butt-head are not role models. They're not even human. They're cartoons. Some of the things they do would cause a person to get hurt, expelled, arrested, possibly deported. To put it another way: Don't try this at home." As this disclaimer fades from the screen, the adventures of *Beavis and Butt-head* continue for another half hour. These adventures mainly consist of the show's young heroes sitting on a couch while watching and critiquing music videos, with occasional outings into the generic Suburbia around them. Hanging out at the local Burger World, trying to score with trailer chicks only to be thwarted at the last minute by a tornado, attempting to buy jock straps and ending up with eye patches, rotating inside a dryer just to make themselves dizzy, playing frog baseball, and visiting a prison with their underachiever class from Highland High are among the pair's many exploits.

Mike Judge, the creator and voices of Beavis and Butt-head, never expected his characters to become the stars of MTV's most popular show, earning ratings twice as high as any other program on the channel. "Judge is everything his work isn't—calm, thoughtful and self-deprecating," observes Kevin Cook in *Playboy*. "He works hard but never forgets how Warholian his story is—Texas egghead musician hatches cartoon craze."

Judge's animated twosome have caused quite a media stir, primarily for their gross behavior. "Explosions and flatulence are part of Beavis and Butt-head's universe," describes Jim Sullivan in the *Ann Arbor News*. "They don't study at school; they snicker at their teacher. They get their butts caught in drain pipes. They think constantly of scoring—but never do, never will. They live for heavy metal, Beavis in his Metallica T-shirt, Butt-head in his AC/DC T-shirt. Indeed, Beavis and Butt-head are not proper role models." Of the two delinquents, Butt-head is the leader and instigator, seemingly more intelligent than his partner in crime. He has beady little eyes, very tall brown hair, his mouth consists mostly of gums and braces, and he can often be heard saying, "Huh huh huh huh huh huh." Beavis, with his blond pompadour, reptile-like eyes, and an obsession with fire, is the more psychotic of the two and will basically do whatever Butt-head wants; his most recognizable saying is "Heh heh hmm hmm heh heh." A couple of moronic teenagers whose

world is divided into things that are "cool" and things that "suck," Beavis and Butt-head cannot be reached or corrected by anyone.

"Beavis and Butt-head are America's Inner Teenager," writes Charles M. Young in *Rolling Stone*, adding that they, "two thunderously stupid and excruciatingly ugly pubescent males who live somewhere in the Southwest, do rotten stuff all the time. They are cruel to animals. They vandalize their neighbors. They torture their teachers. Their libidos rage unchecked, except by the uniform unwillingness of the female sex to associate with them. And they are the biggest phenomenon on MTV since the heyday of Michael Jackson."

The Makings of a Sick Cartoonist

Judge's beginnings and schooling gave no indication that he would one day be the creator of such a controversial and successful animated series. The second of three children, he was born in Quayaquil, Ecuador, where his father was working as an organizer for the Cooperative League of the United States. Most of his childhood was spent in Albuquerque, New Mexico, though, where the family moved when Judge's father accepted a position teaching archaeology at the University of New Mexico. Judge was a relatively normal child, and his mother is quick to reassure Young that "no, he was certainly nothing like Beavis and Butt-head as a child."

After excelling in grade school, Judge faltered a bit in the public junior high school he attended but got back on the honor roll while attending a Catholic high school. "Junior high and the early part of high school were the worst years of my life," reveals Judge in an interview with Chip Brown for the *Ann Arbor News*. "I was a skinny kid who got pushed around a lot." Although he experienced some problems at school, Judge was like many other students (and Beavis and Butt-head) when it came to experimenting with scientific elements, including fire. "I built an X-ray machine when I was a kid," he tells Cook. "I used a Tesla coil—it looked like the stuff in old Frankenstein movies. I'd sit with my hand in it, watching the green glow. Maybe all that radiation helped create Beavis and Butt-head—some kind of mutation." Junior high also brought a mutation of Judge's early artwork. "I was a serious, fanatical animal lover when I was a kid," remembers Judge in his interview with Young. "Used to draw really pretty pictures of deer and things like that. When I started drawing cartoons in the sixth grade or so, it went in the other direction. I drew really sick cartoons. I'd go through phases where I'd try to learn to draw better, and it would always turn into a sick joke. I have this urge to deface my own art."

Despite his interests in art, comedy, and music, Judge decided to major in physics when he left high school to attend the University of California at San Diego. In essence, his practical side won out; he thought he would always be able to find a job as an engineer and could make some money while he tried to do what he really wanted. After graduating in 1985 with a degree in physics, Judge worked for a military contractor in California until he became bored and decided to give a musical career another shot. Leaving for Texas, Judge played bass in a couple of blues-rock bands before the constant travel became too much for him. This led Judge to the decision to attend graduate school, with the idea of teaching at a community college when he was done. While working as a teaching assistant he met his future wife, Francesca Morocco, who was one of his students; the couple married in 1989 and have since had two daughters.

Junior High Metalheads

The late 1980s saw Judge returning to his interest in art; he began drawing cartoons at home during his spare time. Among his first characters were Milton, an office worker who threatens to burn down his building if his boss moves his desk again, and Inbred Jed, a young man who gives a public service announcement against inbreeding. Judge created the earliest illustrations of Beavis and Butt-head after attending a Dallas animation festival; he drew upon memories of a boy he knew in junior high school. During the summer of 1990 Judge attempted to draw the boy he remembered, and although the end product didn't look much like him, Judge was amused with the drawing when he came back to it a week later. Thus, Butt-head was born.

"The guy I tried to draw, he had that laugh: 'Huh-huh, huh-huh-huh,'" Judge describes in his *Rolling Stone* interview. "I looked in the mirror to see what my face did when I laughed like that,

If you enjoy the works of Mike Judge, you may also want to check out the work of the following animators:

Bill Griffith, creator of "Zippy the Pinhead."
Matt Groening, best known for the hit television series, *The Simpsons*.
John Kricfalusi, creator of "Ren and Stimpy."

and I thought the face would be funnier if it was this other guy I knew in junior high, who had since got braces to correct the problem. And he had a really awful haircut. Actually, *my* hair is really unmanageable, so I may have gotten Butt-head's hair from myself." The character of Beavis soon followed: "There were probably four or five guys who inspired Beavis, just a little Bic-flipping pyro kid," continues Judge. "I've noticed that 13-year-old metalheads haven't changed very much over the years. . . . It's just this funny, awkward moment in life when you want to be supermacho and show everyone you're not a kid anymore. You wear serious, badass death-rock T-shirts but you've got to put rubber bands on your braces."

Now that Judge had drawn his two new characters he needed to name them. Beavis was actually the last name of a kid in his neighborhood; Judge just liked the sound of it. Butt-head, on the other hand, was not such an easy pick. "When I did the first B&B cartoon, I'd drawn them before I named them, I was just thinking, *What am I going to name these guys?* I almost didn't name Butt-head 'Butt-head,'" explains Judge in an interview with John Kricfalusi for *Wild Cartoon Kingdom.* "I came real close to calling him something else. I can't remember what it was, but I put the storyboard down and came back to it like two weeks later and saw that I had written 'Butt-head' next to the picture, and it kind of made me laugh and I thought, *Well, might as well go for every laugh you can get.*"

And laughs are just what Judge got when he used his two newly named characters in the animated short "Frog Baseball," which features Beavis and Butt-head blowing up a locust with a firecracker and playing baseball with a live frog. A week after the short appeared in "Spike and Mike's Sick and Twisted Festival of Animation," it was picked up by Colossal Pictures for MTV's *Liquid Television* series in 1993. Shortly after that, Beavis and Butt-head appeared again, this time at a monster truck rally during which a truck crashes into some portable outhouses, prompting Sterculius, the Roman god of feces, to appear and drop a giant turd on the stadium. Based on these two episodes, MTV picked up *Beavis and Butt-head* as a regular series, putting together an assembly line in May of that same year to create sixty-five episodes.

Success Sparks Controversy

Since 1993, *Beavis and Butt-head* has become one of MTV's most popular and most controversial shows, running every weeknight in half-hour blocks, which usually consist of two fifteen-minute episodes. Critics who understand the inherent satire in the show give Judge and MTV rave reviews for being able to make fun of the very network on which the show appears. James Gardner, writing in the *National Review*, suggests that those who tune in to *Beavis and Butt-head* do not agree with the message of violence and stupidity, but instead "they respond intuitively to its irony, to its attack not on liberal ideals so much as on the posturings of many who claim to uphold these ideals and who, in the very act of posturing, often betray them. It is for this irony that I, together with millions of other Americans, like Beavis and Butt-head." *New Yorker* reviewer James Wolcott also praises the satirical aspects of the show: "The more you watch Beavis and Butt-head, the more you're struck by how apt, beautifully timed, and effortlessly funny their backtalk is." He goes on to conclude that "their effect is so contagious that regular rock videos seem incomplete without the yellow 'Beavis and Butt-head' sticker on the corner of the screen."

While Judge was the major creative force behind *Beavis and Butt-head* when it first started, his role in the production of the show has changed as the number of episodes increased. Although he drew most of the animation in the first couple of seasons, he has since had to hand this off to an animation studio that can handle the volume. Basically, Judge supervises the production of *Beavis and Butt-head*, acts as the creative force behind the writing, and continues to supply the majority of the voices in the show; he even wrote the show's theme song and plays all the instruments in it.

Most importantly, Judge remains very involved in his creations. "A lot of planning goes into making Beavis and Butt-head completely lame and stupid," he maintains in his *Playboy* interview. "I write memos to the animators about the way Butt-head's top lip should curl when he says, 'This sucks.'" Providing the voices for Beavis and Butt-head also keeps Judge connected to his characters. "I do personalize them," he continues in *Playboy*. "I used to put their pictures in the studio and stare at them when I did their voices, but now I just shut my eyes and go to their world. It looks like my dreams. I dream in cartoons. Once I had a scary feeling, thinking, God, these guys are a bigger part of my mind than I am."

Critics of *Beavis and Butt-head* would find this even scarier, as Judge has come under fire because of the show's content. Over the course of the first two seasons, Beavis was obsessed with fire and explosions, both of which were definitely "cool." But when an Ohio woman blamed the show for her son setting fire to their trailer home and killing his younger sister, all such references were removed from past episodes and were barred from future ones. Other incidents have since been blamed on the troublesome teens, a phenomenon which Judge sees as undeserved. "It saddens and amazes me," states Judge in an interview with Jon Katz for *Rolling Stone*. "To link the program to a tragedy like that with absolutely no evidence—it's just unbelievable." Such accusations imply that Beavis and Butt-head have become role models for today's youth, another theory that Judge quickly discounts. "I'm always surprised when people think Beavis and Butt-head have hypnotized the youth of America, because I've never met a kid who doesn't get it, who doesn't see what losers they are," he points out to Cook. Katz similarly writes: "The most striking thing about the furor over the program . . . is that critics don't seem to get that it's supposed to be funny. It gives kids an opportunity to laugh at themselves and us. Grown-ups don't get that this program is unique and valuable precisely because it brilliantly lampoons the qualities it is accused of propagating—stupidity, sexism, the simple-minded, macho rites of adolescence."

The King of Animation

Grown-ups, however, may better relate to Judge's new animated series, *King of the Hill*. Premiering on the Fox network in January of 1997, the show features Hank Hill, a well-meaning but rather dim husband and father living in Texas with his wife and son. The animation is as flat and rough as that found in *Beavis and Butt-head*, and plot lines deal with everyday life, including Little League games, neighborhood activities, and working on the car. Pointing out that *King of the Hill* is "funny and intelligent," *Entertainment Weekly* reviewer Ken Tucker goes on to add: "Very quickly, these vividly written, barely stick figures come to life as three-dimensional humans confronting existence with deadpan glares." Unlike the main audience of *Beavis and Butt-head*, Tucker concludes that "it's adults who'll appreciate *King*."

Judge's new series follows closely on the heels of the release of his first full-length animated film— *Beavis and Butt-head Do America*. Premiering in December of 1996, the film finds the heros of MTV without their most prized possession—their television. As Beavis and Butt-head set out to a seedy motel in an effort to replace their stolen TV, they are mistakenly taken for hit men by a drunk who wants them to "do" his wife. Thinking that they're going to get "lucky," they accept the offer and set out for Las Vegas to do the deed. The wife turns out to be an arms dealer, however, and she sews a dangerous chemical weapons device (smaller than a computer disk) into Beavis's pants, telling the two boys to meet her in Washington, D.C. Beavis and Butt-head wreak havoc as they hurtle across America, stopping at the Hoover Dam, the Grand Canyon, Yellowstone National Park, and finally the White House, where Butt-head attempts to pick up Chelsea Clinton.

"The good news is, *Beavis and Butt-head Do America* doesn't suck," states Joe Leydon in *Variety*. "The bad news is, it doesn't rule either. This gleefully junky Christmas present for arrested adolescents of all ages has some genuinely amusing moments of dumb and dumber silliness." Owen Gleiberman, writing in *Entertainment Weekly*, similarly states that the movie "has its share of chuckles, yet this is one case where more turns out to be less." *New York Times* reviewer Stephen Holden, however, asserts that "*Beavis and Butt-head Do America* has the same double vision as the MTV series from which it is spun. It views the world simultaneously through the porcine eyes of its characters and through the cooler perspective of their creator and cartoon voice, Mike Judge." Judge himself believes that the movie stays true

to the characters of Beavis and Butt-head found in the series. "I mean, you can't make a movie where the guys are fighting for their lives, because they don't really think like that, you know," he states in an interview with Terry Lawson for the *Detroit Free Press*. "They need simple, reasonable, juvenile motivations. Scoring. Getting their television back. The real stuff that makes life worth living."

And so Judge's creations continue to sit on the couch, enjoying the simple life of watching rock videos. Cook, though, sees more in the future of Beavis and Butt-head—and their creator. "Now Judge must somehow top himself," he concludes. "He must point Beavis and Butt-head toward midadolscence. I think he'll succeed because he has that rare artistic gift—a perfect memory of junior high." Judge will also succeed because he consistently challenges his critics. "As far as dumbing down America, Judge is adamant against his critics," writes Brown. "Are you going to say that you shouldn't do a show about real life?" asks Judge in his interview with Brown. "Should TV be showing all straight-A students and people with good jobs? *The Cosby Show* was like a doctor, a lawyer and kids who go to Princeton. After a while, you start feeling inadequate."

■ Works Cited

Brown, Chip, "Beavis Creator No Butt-head? Cool," *Ann Arbor News*, April 7, 1996, p. C3.

Cook, Kevin, "20 Questions: Mike Judge," *Playboy*, January, 1997, pp. 168-70.

Gardner, James, "Leave It to Beavis," *National Review*, May 2, 1994, pp. 60-62.

Gleiberman, Owen, "Butt Seriously," *Entertainment Weekly*, December 20, 1996, pp. 54, 56.

Holden, Stephen, "*Beavis and Butt-head Do America*: Hormones Coursing O'er the Land," *New York Times*, December 20, 1996.

Judge, Mike, *Beavis and Butt-head* animated series, MTV, 1993—.

Judge, Mike, in an interview with John Kricfalusi, *Wild Cartoon Kingdom*, Number 3, 1994.

Katz, Jon, "Animated Arguments," *Rolling Stone*, March 24, 1994, p. 45.

Lawson, Terry, "Crude Boys Come to the Big Screen," *Detroit Free Press*, December 17, 1996, pp. C1, C6.

Leydon, Joe, review of *Beavis and Butt-head Do America*, *Variety*, December 13, 1996.

Sullivan, Jim, "Beavis' Creator Has Last Heh-heh," *Ann Arbor News*, December 30, 1996, p. B4.

Tucker, Ken, "Fine 'Tooning," *Entertainment Weekly*, January 17, 1997, p. 52.

Wolcott, James, "Everyone's a Critic," *New Yorker*, February 28, 1994, pp. 96-98.

Young, Charles M., "The Voice of a New Generation," *Rolling Stone*, August 19, 1993, pp. 43-50, 87.

■ **For More Information See**

PERIODICALS

Chicago Tribune, December 20, 1996.

Entertainment Weekly, September 24, 1993, pp. 42-44.

People, October 4, 1993, pp. 146-47.

Rolling Stone, March 24, 1994, pp. 38-40, 42.

San Francisco Chronicle, December 20, 1996, p. C3.*

—Sketch by Susan Reicha

R. R. Knudson

■ Personal

Real name, Rozanne Knudson; surname is pronounced with a silent "k"; born June 1, 1932, in Washington, DC; daughter of James K. (a lawyer and statesman) and Ruth (Ellsworth) Knudson. *Education*: Brigham Young University, B.A., 1954; University of Georgia, M.A., 1958; Stanford University, Ph.D., 1967. *Religion*: Mormon. *Hobbies and other interests*: Playing baseball, basketball, hockey, tennis, golf, squash, skiing, skin diving, amateur bird-watching.

■ Addresses

Home—73 The Boulevard, Sea Cliff, NY 11579.

■ Career

English teacher in various public high schools in Florida, 1957-60; Purdue University, West Lafayette, IN, assistant professor of English, 1965-67; Hicksville Schools, Long Island, NY, supervisor of English, 1967-70; York College of the City University of New York, Jamaica, NY, assistant professor, 1970-71; full-time writer, 1972—. University of Lethbridge, Lethbridge, Alberta, instructor in English, summer, 1969; Kean College, writer in residence, 1986. Fellow at MacDowell Colony, Virginia Center for the Creative Arts, Ragdale, Dorland Mountain Colony, Hambridge Center, Villa Montalvo, and Cummington Community of the Arts. Executor, The Literary Estate of May Swenson. Speaker at conferences.

■ Awards, Honors

Dorothy Canfield Fisher Book Award nomination, 1978, for *Zanbanger*; Maud Lovelace Book Award nomination, 1979, for *Zanboomer*.

■ Writings

JUVENILE; UNDER NAME R. R. KNUDSON

(With J. A. Wilson and others) *Books for You* (nonfiction), Washington Square Press, 1971.
Zanballer, Delacorte, 1972.
Jesus Song, illustrated by Joel Shick, Delacorte, 1973.
You Are the Rain, Delacorte, 1974.
Fox Running, illustrated by Ilse Koehn, Harper, 1975.
Zanbanger, Harper, 1977.
Zanboomer, Harper, 1978.

(With Franco Columbu) *Weight Training for Young Athletes* (nonfiction), Contemporary Books, 1979.

Rinehart Lifts, Farrar, Straus, 1980.

Just Another Love Story, Farrar, Straus, 1982.

Muscles! (nonfiction), illustrated by Carole Gallagher, Avon, 1983.

Speed, illustrated by Linda Eber, Dutton, 1983.

Zan Hagen's Marathon, Farrar, Straus, 1984.

Babe Didrikson: Athlete of the Century (nonfiction), illustrated by Ted Lewin, Viking Kestrel, 1985.

Frankenstein's 10K, illustrated by Judy Glasser, Viking Kestrel, 1986.

Martina Navratilova: Tennis Power (nonfiction), illustrated by George Angelini, Viking Kestrel, 1987.

Rinehart Shouts, Farrar, Straus, 1987.

Julie Brown: Racing against the World (nonfiction), illustrated by J. Brian Pinckney, Viking Kestrel, 1988.

(Compiler with May Swenson) *American Sports Poems,* Orchard Books/F. Watts, 1988.

The Wonderful Pen of May Swenson (nonfiction), Macmillan, 1993.

NONFICTION FOR ADULTS; UNDER NAME R. R. KNUDSON

(With Franco Columbu and Anita Columbu) *Starbodies: The Women's Weight Training Book,* Elsevier-Dutton, 1978.

Punch!, illustrated by Carole Gallagher, Avon, 1983.

Punch It!, Simon & Schuster, 1984.

(With Lynda Huey) *The Waterpower Workout,* illustrated by Glenn S. Capers, New American Library, 1986.

(With Pat Connolly) *Coaching Evelyn,* Harper, 1990.

OTHER

(Under name Rozanne Knudson; with Arnold Lazarus) *Selected Objectives for the English Language Arts: Grades 7-12,* Houghton, 1967.

(With P. K. Ebert; under name R. R. Knudson) *Sports Poetry,* Dell, 1971.

(Compiler) May Swenson, *May Out West,* Utah State University Press, 1996.

(With Suzanne Bigelow) *May Swenson: A Poet's Life in Photos,* Utah State University Press, 1996.

Contributor to *The Scribner's Anthology for Young People,* Scribner, 1976. Contributor to periodicals, including *American Library, English Journal, Teacher's College Record, Phi Delta Kappan,* and *School Library Journal.* Coeditor, *Quartet,* 1966-68.

Knudson's papers and manuscripts are collected in the Kerlan Collection, University of Minnesota.

■ Sidelights

In an era when women's sports were virtually nonexistent, Rozanne Knudson blazed new trails by participating in male-dominated sports like football and basketball. She turned her then-considered roguish interests into many young adult books about strong female athletes. The classic novels *Zanballer* and *Zanbanger* feature a semi-autobiographical character with the author's own nickname, Zan. Knudson has done extensive research in many sports that has helped her write authoritatively on these subjects. In addition to her novels, Knudson has written biographies on Martina Navratilova and marathoner Julie Brown and has published two books of sports poems.

The young Knudson spent most of her childhood in Washington, D.C. She admits that her early memories may have been greatly influenced by the extensive baby books that were maintained by her mother. Her childhood was a very happy one; her mother recalled that for the first twelve weeks of her life she never cried. In *Something about the Author Autobiography Series* (*SAAS*), Knudson stated that "childhood photos show me smiling all the time. I had fun coasting in a wagon, riding a pony, aiming my popgun at targets. 'Zan likes boys' things—cowboy suits, toy trains, tin soldiers, trucks, skates, toy airplanes. She'd rather play outdoors than in. At age five her sole desire is for a policeman's suit. She's always perfectly happy with books—looking through them for hours at a time,' Mom wrote to accompany the photos." Her early interest in what were considered traditional "boys things" was a sign of her budding interest in sports. During the decades of Knudson's youth, girls were not expected to be interested in sports.

Knudson's interest in reading came at an early age. She noted in her autobiographical essay that "before I knew how to read I would memorize stories and poems my parents read aloud. When alone I'd turn pages and recite the words, pretending to be reading. I also memorized the songs my mom and dad sang to me at bedtime. . . . Words to these songs were the first poems I memorized." These skills were to come in handy as she once kept her family entertained for a trip from Washington, D.C., to Texas by singing her arsenal of thirty-one songs at the tender age of two.

Crazy for Sports

When Knudson went to school, her natural abilities at sports quickly shone. She wrote in *SAAS* that she was "the only girl who played baseball at recess. Team captains quickly chose me, for I could throw, catch, and hit better than most boys. These skills seemed to have been natural, born of good eyesight, foot speed, agility, fearlessness, and a strong wish to excel." Knudson also excelled in her schoolwork, although her true passion was out there on the playground. She added in her essay that "I became a fiend for practice. I'd go home and throw a baseball against our house for hours, aiming at spots I'd marked on a brick wall."

Knudson also enjoyed going to junior high school because the classes, and sports teams, were more structured. She did well on all her school projects and competed in a league where her team won every game in her three years at that school. Still, she felt socially like an outcast, but made friends by putting her fellow students' names in her gossip column for the school newspaper. Her parents decided that for Knudson's high school years she needed to be at a private school for the extra challenge; however, it turned out to be a difficult experience for her. She felt out of place among her wealthy classmates and developed what she termed in her *SAAS* essay "a reputation for being difficult and unladylike. Nor was I valued as an athlete," Knudson added. "My vigorous play was wasted on a team that didn't care if it won or not." Knudson developed many of her writing skills while at that school, even though she was asked to leave before her senior year. She finished off her senior year at a public high school with the company of some of her junior high school friends.

After high school, Knudson went off to Brigham Young University in Provo, Utah, a Mormon school that was approved of by her Mormon parents. She majored in English and had a good time with her literature classes. She also wrote a column for the college paper called "Zannerisms," where she extolled the local gossip. She wasn't a very serious student though, and when it came time to graduate, she decided that teaching would

be a good field for her. After graduation, she went to the University of Georgia on a scholarship to learn more teaching skills. In this program, she learned to be a disciplined writer—a skill she had not achieved previously.

After obtaining her master's degree, she drove down to Key West, Florida, to look for a teaching job. The principal there hired her on the spot. "He handed me a roll book for my 180 students and pointed to the book room," she recalled in *SAAS*. "Unluckily for me, the veteran teachers of English had cleaned off the shelves. My bookless students had to bring newspapers and magazines from home and buy paperbacks to read in class. In this way we built up the lending library that caused my downfall. I was called a 'dirty' teacher because some of my students read the 'dirty' book they'd brought, [J. D. Salinger's] *Catcher in the Rye.* Their parents were up in arms. On the last day of school I was warned not to come back in the fall to teach. The principal also told me I'd been his best teacher because I'd kept the kids quiet. He was right about quiet. They were reading."

Disappointed, but not discouraged, Knudson headed to another school in Miami, Florida, to try teaching again. During her tenure in the public schools, she found that she had a talent teaching even the most reluctant readers. However, she felt that she wanted more concrete ideas on how to become a better teacher. So she saved her money and headed to Stanford University to earn her Ph.D. While there, she told *SAAS*, she found that "no two professors agreed on the right stuff to teach, the right way to teach it. We argued endlessly. I had the time of my life." During this time she read widely in Stanford's library and studied with, among others, the novelist Wallace Stegner, whom Knudson credits with teaching her how to write fiction. "His lectures made writing seem simple," Knudson concluded.

Novel Inspiration

Knudson received her Ph.D. and decided to have a go at teaching at Purdue University in Indiana, but she found the cold weather and the academic atmosphere didn't suit her. "I had exactly one friend there to help me poke fun at the dull professors around campus," she quipped in her autobiographical essay. "My friend was May Swenson, the poet. She'd come from New York to teach poetry writing." Her friendship with Swenson was to have an indelible influence on her life. After the two became fast friends, they decided to move in together in a house at Sea Cliff on Long Island Sound. They lived together until Swenson's death many years later. In New York, Knudson began teaching again, but this was interrupted when an editor at Dell Publishing Company asked her to try writing a book about a girl athlete.

It was a serendipitous moment for Knudson. Not only would this give her a chance to take a break from teaching, but it would put together her writing skills and interest in sports. She quickly decided to write about a young woman with her own nickname, Zan, who wants to play football. "The story tumbled out of me in thirty days. I

Wanting to see some blue birds nesting on some islands in the Potomac River, Arthur Rinehart must overcome his fear of water in this 1987 story.

stole the plot from my own life in junior high, where I'd organized a girls' football team in rebellion against the dance lessons in our gym class. . . . The bad guys are blends of real people, including the coach of the boys' team at Swanson. He'd watched me throwing a football and exclaimed, 'If only you were a boy.' He wanted me for his backfield yet he was too conventional and wimpy to put me there. Nor did he let his precious boys play against us girls."

Zanballer debuted in 1972 with rave reviews for the book's humor, quick pacing, and well-targeted satire. Knudson revived the characters of *Zanballer* several times, for such works as *Zanbanger*—in which Zan Hagen, with the help of her friend Arthur Rinehart, wins the opportunity to play basketball on the boys' varsity team—and *Zanboomer*, in which Zan hurts her shoulder playing baseball and Rinehart helps lift her spirits by getting her involved in running races. In a review of *Zanboomer*, a *Wilson Library Bulletin* contributor declared, "Knudson has always had originality and energy, but her work is now beginning to show sureness and flow."

After her great success with *Zanballer*, Knudson had dreams of quitting teaching forever and cranking out novel after novel. She wrote in *SAAS* that "it was so much fun writing my letter of resignation! Now I wouldn't have to wear my hated school clothes anymore—my 'disguises,' I called them. Impulsively I gave away all of my dresses, skirts, shoes with heels; my raincoat and bulky winter-coat. I carried my panty hose to the beach, spread them on the foam, and watched waves take them to China. In cutoff Levi's and bare feet I went to my desk, sharpened pencils, and wrote a sentence."

Unfortunately, Knudson fell victim to a bout of writer's block. She had accepted an advance to write a story about the "Jesus people" of the early 1970s—youths who claimed to have a love for humanity and were able to perform miracles. Once she overcame her block and started writing, she was horrified by the result. In her essay in *SAAS*, she called the book "a mess. I couldn't hold a steady point of view. I believed in the Jesus people on one page. Turn that page and I made fun of every character who had faith. I pushed my story's pace along at breakneck speed. I did it for laughs. When I tried to get serious I couldn't do it." Despite her doubts about the qual-

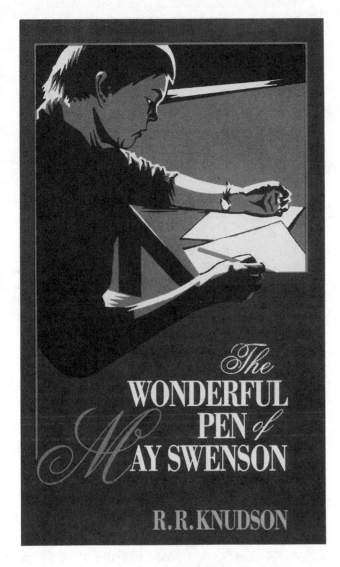

The
**WONDERFUL
PEN** *of*
***M*AY SWENSON**

R. R. KNUDSON

Knudson's personal biography of poet May Swenson, which includes personal letters, diaries, previously unpublished poems and photographs, offers readers a detailed account of the writer and her work.

ity of the book, there was favorable critical response to *Jesus Song* (1973). A reviewer for *Bulletin of the Center for Children's Books* called the work "a raucous, rollicking story," and a contributor to *Kirkus Reviews* dubbed it "joyously hyperkinetic."

Sticks to Sports

After *Jesus Song* was published, Knudson regretted it. But it taught her a valuable lesson: Stick to writing what you know. "In the years to come I ignored my editors when they suggested subjects," she confessed in her autobiographical es-

say. "I didn't try to get rich quick by writing their problem novels of drug addiction, gang warfare, or fatal diseases. I stuck with the subjects I knew and loved. I used themes I deeply believed in. My main characters sprang from my heart."

Money was tight after Knudson began to rely only on her income from writing books. She gave up many of her expensive habits, such as golfing, and instead sailed on other people's boats and hiked for fun. While sailing from New York to Bermuda, she began formulating a sea story. While that story was never to come to fruition, she went on to write an exciting adventure story about a group of women kayaking in the Everglades. *You Are the Rain* (1974), was based loosely on the trips Knudson and Swenson had taken in the Everglades, except in the novel, the protagonists are younger.

The novel's title was taken from a line in one of Swenson's poems. The plot of the book was described by the author in *SAAS* as "a young poet named June [is] in a group of athletic girls who are paddling kayaks in the Everglades. June is afraid of the deep water but she's not afraid to speak up for herself when a rowdy girl, Crash Adams, tries to bully her. None of them know there's a hurricane swirling toward them. They continue racing each other and laughing at June. They encounter poisonous trees, rattlesnakes, and eventually get separated from each other and lost. During the eye of the storm, Crash is bitten by a deadly coral snake. Only a miracle can save her."

But June is able to keep Crash alive by reading her poems. "Well, why not?" questioned Knudson in *SAAS*. "I was the author, wasn't I? I could end my story any way I wanted. Playing around at my desk with those snakes . . . had been more exciting than being in the Everglades myself." She proudly took it to her publisher with the admonition "Take it or leave it," she related in *SAAS*. It was published to mixed reviews. A critic in *Kirkus Reviews* noted Knudson's "heavy-handed caricature," while Jean Mercier of *Publishers Weekly* characterized the book's finale as "slightly overheated but still convincing."

Knudson gained confidence by writing a book where she was in charge of the concept from beginning to end. This gave her enough energy to start research for the book *Fox Running* (1975), featuring a Mescalero Apache woman who is discovered by a track coach and trained for the Olympics. In the end, she is triumphant and wins two gold medals. While some reviewers complained about the ending of the book, most appreciated Knudson's authentic rendering of training and competing for the Olympics.

Lifting and Curling

The next sport that caught Knudson's eye was weight lifting. She discovered it almost by accident: She was wintering in Los Angeles and working on her running when she saw an advertisement in a campus newspaper about a body builder who was looking for a woman sportswriter to help him write a book about weight lifting for women. Knudson contacted the man, a former Mr. Olympia named Franco Columbu, who became her writing companion. "For once I wasn't lonely at my typewriter," wrote Knudson in *SAAS.* "When we finished *Starbodies* I talked Franco into helping with another book, *Weight Training for Young Athletes.* After that I wrote *Muscles,* a book for much younger athletes."

After finishing these three books on weight lifting, Knudson realized that she had done just about as much as she could for this sport. However, she was forever changed by her exposure to the sport, and it did have an affect on her future work. She wrote in *SAAS* that "the comfy gyms full of clinking iron, loud rock music, and cheerful partners became second homes for me. I put these feelings into a novel, *Rinehart Lifts,* and then into another novel, *Just Another Love Story."*

The novel *Just Another Love Story* (1982) is about Dusty Blaisdale, a teen so upset by his recent breakup with his girlfriend that he drives his car off a pier in grief. Luckily for Dusty, a group of bodybuilders are on the beach that day, and they save him from his attempted suicide. Impressed by their physiques, Dusty begins a weight lifting program himself, mainly to win back his girlfriend. Sidney Offit, writing in the *New York Times Book Review,* claimed that "the style of this novel is neither sufficiently lyrical nor bittersweet to evoke empathetic identification with the characters," but Gerry Larson of the *School Library Journal* concluded: "The story's strength lies not in its love story but in its insights into the psyche, training, language and brotherhood of bodybuilders."

If you enjoy the works of R. R. Knudson, you may want to check out the following books and films:

Chris Crutcher, *Athletic Shorts: Six Short Stories,* 1991.
Nancy Rue, *The Janis Project,* 1988.
Jerry Spinelli, *There's a Girl in My Hammerlock,* 1991.
Prefontaine, Hollywood Pictures, 1997.

Knudson's real life love of running inspired many of her works. In *Zan Hagen's Marathon* (1984), Knudson brings back her autobiographical main character as a young woman determined to win the women's marathon in the Olympics, an event that did not exist for women at the time Knudson wrote the book. The work was widely praised; a reviewer in *Bulletin of the Center for Children's Books* called Knudson's depiction of long-distance running "vivid and convincing." Though Candace Lyle Hogan, in her *New York Times Book Review* assessment, felt that some of Knudson's dialogue sounded "old-fashioned," she also remarked that "Knudson's athletic detail is a pleasure, and it's authentic." The book also features Katherine Switzer, the first woman to register for and run in the Boston Marathon.

Julie Brown, a champion runner who won many races and then mysteriously lost the 1984 Olympic marathon, was an athlete that caught Knudson's eye. She decided to write her biography, but, when she interviewed Brown, she found herself awestruck. Brown broke down in the interview and revealed some things about her life that she begged Knudson not to put in the biography. Knudson agreed but later regretted her decision. Reviewing *Julie Brown: Racing against the World* in *Bulletin of the Center for Children's Books,* Betsy Hearne noted Knudson's difficulties with her subject, stating that "one wants to know more about the heart of this 'running machine.'"

Profiles Famous Female Athletes

Knudson wrote two other biographies of famous female sports figures. *Babe Didrikson: Athlete of the Century* covers the breadth of the outstanding athlete's career, from her track and field victories at the Olympics in the 1930s to her second career as a professional golfer in the 1940s and 1950s. Although Knudson's writing style was at times faulted, reviewers praised her choice of subject and her spirited approach. A *School Library Journal* reviewer commented on the "gusto and enthusiasm" with which the book is written. In *Martina Navratilova: Tennis Power,* Knudson provides an overview of the career of a woman widely considered the best female tennis player in history. A number of critics applauded the work, although some observed that certain controversial aspects of the tennis star's life were glossed over or omitted entirely. A writer in *Bulletin of the Center for Children's Books* commented, "This gives a better-than-usual feel for what it took an athlete to get to the top."

In 1988, Knudson published a book that was a labor of love. *American Sports Poems* was finished with the help of her longtime companion, Swenson. "My best collaborator on a book was May Swenson," Knudson told *SAAS,* "and I didn't have to drive or fly away from Sea Cliff to reach her. We sifted through my files stuffed with sports poems and selected 158 of them for our book." Reviewers praised the selection for the wide variety of sports covered, as well as the large number of poets, both famous and obscure, whose works were included in the volume. *Bulletin for the Center for Children's Books* contributor Roger Sutton called attention to *American Sports Poems* as "a terrific read-aloud alternative to rainy day health and hygiene movies" for gym teachers.

Swenson died in 1989, leaving the rights to her literary estate to Knudson. After that, Knudson found herself quite busy with the many requests for reprints of Swenson's work, and she wrote a biography of the poet, *The Wonderful Pen of May Swenson,* in 1993. Pat Katka, writing in *School Library Journal,* called the book "an insightful look at a writer and her craft."

Knudson had many reasons for pursuing a career in writing. In *SAAS* she wrote that in looking back on her youth "I find one reason I became a writer—to get attention." Then, later, she concluded that "At first I did it for money. Then for fun, tough fun. Then for something harder than tough, to discover what I had down deep to say and to find out more about myself." With her depictions of women who have broken the gender barrier in sports, she has encouraged future

generations of young women to take the same risks necessary for the love of their sports.

■ Works Cited

Review of *Babe Didrikson: Athlete of the Century, School Library Journal,* May, 1985, p. 112.

Hearne, Betsy, review of *Julie Brown: Racing against the World, Bulletin of the Center for Children's Books,* October, 1988, pp. 43-44.

Hogan, Candace Lyle, review of *Zan Hagen's Marathon, New York Times Book Review,* August 5, 1984.

Review of *Jesus Song, Bulletin of the Center for Children's Books,* September, 1973, p. 10.

Review of *Jesus Song, Kirkus Reviews,* May 1, 1973, p. 521.

Katka, Pat, review of *The Wonderful Pen of May Swenson, School Library Journal,* January, 1994, p. 124.

Knudson, Rozanne, essay in *Something about the Author Autobiography Series,* Volume 18, Gale, 1994.

Larson, Gerry, review of *Just Another Love Story, School Library Journal,* April, 1983, p. 125.

Review of *Martina Navratilova: Tennis Power, Bulletin of the Center for Children's Books,* April, 1986.

Mercier, Jean, review of *You Are the Rain, Publishers Weekly,* January 21, 1974, p. 85.

Offit, Sidney, review of *Just Another Love Story, New York Times Book Review,* May 1, 1985, p. 30.

Sutton, Roger, review of *American Sports Poems, Bulletin of the Center for Children's Books,* September, 1988, p. 12.

Review of *You Are the Rain, Kirkus Reviews,* March 15, 1974, p. 308.

Review of *Zanboomer, Wilson Library Journal,* October, 1978.

Review of *Zan Hagen's Marathon, Bulletin of the Center for Children's Books,* November, 1984.

■ For More Information See

BOOKS

Contemporary Authors, New Revision Series, Volume 35, Gale, 1991.

PERIODICALS

Chicago Tribune Book World, April 13, 1986.
English Journal, February, 1989, p. 84.

Horn Book, February, 1976.
Voice of Youth Advocates, October, 1983, p. 204; August, 1985, p. 198; October, 1988, p. 197.*

—Sketch by Nancy Rampson

Maya Lin

Personal

Born October 5, 1959, in Athens, OH; daughter of Henry Huan (dean of the Ohio University art school and a ceramic artist) and Julia Chang (an Ohio University professor of English and Asian literature and poet) Lin. *Education:* Yale University, B.A., 1981, M.Arch., 1986; attended Harvard University Graduate School of Design, 1983.

Addresses

Office—Sculptor, Architect, c/o Sidney Janis Gallery, 110 W. 57th St., New York, NY 10019.

Career

Cooper-Lecky Partnership, design consultant, 1981-82; Peter Forbes & Associates, Boston, MA, architectural designer, 1983, New York City office, design associate, 1986-87; Batey & Mack, architectural designer, 1984; Fumihiko Maki & Associates, Tokyo, Japan, architect apprentice, 1985; Maya Lin Studio, founder and principal, 1987—. Artist in residence, Wexner Center for the Visual Arts, Ohio State University, Columbus, OH. *Member:* Energy Foundation, Presidio Council.

■ Awards, Honors

Winner, Vietnam Veterans Memorial Design Competition, Vietnam Veterans Memorial Fund, 1981; Henry Bacon Memorial Award, American Institute of Architects, 1984; Honorary Doctor of Fine Arts degree, Yale University, 1986; National Endowment for the Arts grant, 1988; named to the Commission on the Future of the Smithsonian, 1994; Honorary Doctor of Arts degree, Harvard University, 1996.

■ Works

(Designer) Vietnam Veteran's War Memorial, Washington, DC, 1981.

(Designer) Southern Poverty Law Center Civil Rights Memorial, Montgomery, AL, 1988.

(Co-designer with Henry Arnold) "TOPO" (topiary park), Charlotte Coliseum, Charlotte, NC, 1991.

(Designer) "Ground Swell" (landscape installation), Wexner Center for the Visual Arts, Ohio State University, Columbus, OH, 1993.

(Designer) "The Women's Table" (sculpture), Yale University, New Haven, CT, 1993.

(Co-designer, with David Hotson) Museum for African Art, New York City, 1993.

(Designer) "Eclipsed Time" (clock), Pennsylvania Station, New York City, 1994.
(Designer) "Wave Field" (landscape sculpture), University of Michigan, Ann Arbor, MI, 1995.

■ Exhibitions

Jane Voorhees Zimmerli Art Museum, Rutgers State University, New Brunswick, NJ, 1985.
"60's-80's Sculpture Parallels," Sidney Janis Gallery, New York City, 1988.
Group exhibition, Rosa Esman Gallery, New York City, 1990.
"Maya Lin: Public/Private" (retrospective), organized by Sarah J. Miles, Wexner Center for the Visual Arts, Ohio State University, Columbus, OH, 1993.

Also designer of private residences in Williamstown, MA, and Santa Monica, CA.

■ Work in Progress

Sculptures for the headquarters of the Rockefeller Foundation, the Manhattan Federal Courthouse, and the Cleveland Public Library; designing a recycling plant in the South Bronx, NY; designing a private residence in Connecticut.

■ Sidelights

Sculptor and architect Maya Lin is best known as the designer of the Vietnam Veterans Memorial, in Washington, D.C. Conceived as a place for personal reflection and healing, the v-shaped incision in the landscape was harshly criticized by some who favored a figurative monument. Today, the memorial is the most popular in Washington, and is visited by more than a million visitors annually. Inscribed with the names of the 58,000 servicemen killed or missing in Vietnam, the memorial has indeed become what Lin anticipated: a sanctuary for both grief and reconciliation. Although made wary of celebrity by the controversy that surrounded her throughout the construction and unveiling of the memorial, Lin regularly produces works at the public scale. In addition to her uncommon sensitivity to site and social context, critics routinely call attention to Lin's ability to erode the boundaries that have traditionally existed between architecture and sculpture.

Maya Lin was born on October 5, 1959, in the small college town of Athens, Ohio. Her parents, Julia Chang Lin and Henry Huan Lin, immigrated to the United States from China in 1940. Both were esteemed members of the faculty at Ohio University, and they provided Maya with an environment that stimulated both her imagination and her intellectual curiosity. Maya's father was dean of the Ohio University art school and a well-known ceramic artist with his own studio, where Maya explored her creativity through the earthen materials of his craft. Julia Lin was a poet and professor of Asian and English literature, and she imbued her daughter with a love of reading.

During her school years Maya demonstrated a facility for mathematics and art. She was an above average student, and in high school took college level courses to challenge herself. It was during these studies that she was exposed to the existentialist writings of Albert Camus and Jean Paul Sartre. Existentialist philosophy, in combination with the reading of poetry encouraged by her mother, exerted a strong influence in Lin's later memorial designs. When she wasn't studying, Lin spent her free time reading, or indulging her love of nature with a walk in the woods.

Sculpture or Architecture?

After graduating from high school as co-valedictorian of her class, Lin entered Yale University in New Haven, Connecticut. There she realized her irresistible affinity for both architecture and sculpture. Despite teachers who encouraged her to pursue one discipline or the other, she found it impossible to chose between the two. Although her field of concentration was officially architecture, she was often in the art school where she took classes in sculpture.

Lin spent 1979, her junior year at Yale, abroad and made a point of visiting cemeteries throughout Europe. When she returned to Yale the following year, she enrolled in a funerary architecture design studio. As a requirement for the class, she entered the nationwide Vietnam Veterans Memorial design competition. In November of 1980, Lin visited the proposed site for the memorial, the Mall in Washington, D.C. While photographing the Mall (a grassy promenade around which many commemorative monuments are arranged), she was moved by its near emptiness. Any memorial located there, Lin concluded, must be experienced through the simultaneous acts of moving and viewing. To accomplish this, she employed two low, black granite walls, which converge at one end of the site. The walls are set into the earth, opening a space below ground. In the statement she submitted with her competition entry, Lin explained that visitors would proceed along one wall toward the narrow end of this space, and then turn and follow the other wall out. She intended this pattern of movement to be analogous to the experience of loss. Visitors see both the sky and their images mirrored in the highly polished surface of the granite, engraved with the names of roughly sixty thousand dead and missing veterans from the Vietnam War.

Vietnam Veterans Memorial

Lin's scheme was selected from 1,420 entries (the largest design competition in the history of the United States) and was revealed to the public in the spring of 1981. Public reaction was a mix of surprise and disappointment. Lin was still a twenty-one-year-old student, remarkably young to receive such a distinguished commission, and her design differed radically from heroic monuments of the past. The judges' decision invited contention. Protests against the memorial were organized by veterans groups who found the design too abstract. Coverage in the media and comments by fellow artists continued to fuel the debate over the appropriateness of the design. As emotions reached the boiling point, Maya herself was victimized by racist and sexist slurs. As she told Jim Sexton in *USA Weekend*, "All I could think about at the time was: [All this anger] is not about the art. This is about the country coming to terms with something."

Eventually, without Lin's input, a compromise was reached. A bronze monument composed of three servicemen supporting an American flag was to be added to the site, approximately 120 feet from the entrance to her memorial. The memorial committee never notified Lin of their decision; she heard it in a television news broadcast.

In the fall of 1982, Lin graduated cum laude from Yale and began graduate studies in architecture at Harvard University. Lin attempted to resume the inconspicuous life of a student. The opening of the Vietnam Veterans Memorial, however, was scheduled for that November. Although she was the principal designer and had overseen the construction, Lin's name was not mentioned during the dedication ceremonies. Frustrated and disillusioned, she found herself unable to focus on her classes and withdrew from Harvard's Graduate School of Design. She spent most of 1983 working in the Boston architecture office of Peter Forbes & Associates.

Despite the negative criticism associated with the memorial, both critics and visitors immediately responded to its power. "Lin's Vietnam Memorial has become a place of pilgrimage and healing, functioning as a spiritual sanctuary," asserted Judith E. Stein in *Art in America*. Lin told Sexton, "I designed it so that a child a hundred years from now will still be able to go to that piece and have a sober understanding about a high price of the war. I was there one day—I don't go there that often—and a noisy, noisy group of schoolchildren gets off a bus, goes in. Teacher says nothing. They hit the beginning. Silence. No one said anything. No adults said anything; they just knew. I felt so good right then."

Beyond the Wall

In the fall of 1983, Maya returned to Yale to resume the education she had abandoned at Harvard. She studied with architect Frank Gehry, known for his sculptural approach to architecture, and sculptor Richard Serra, whose large public works have often stirred controversy. Before completing graduate school, Lin also held an internship in Tokyo, Japan, with internationally renowned architect Fumihiko Maki. After receiving her masters degree in architecture in the spring of 1986, Lin worked in Peter Forbes's New York office, where she held the position of design associate.

In 1987 Lin founded her own studio in New York City. Projects from this early period of independent work include "Aligning Reeds," an installation of aluminum rods in a Connecticut stream bed, and "TOPO," grounds designed in collaboration with landscape architect Henry Arnold. "TOPO" occupies the median between incoming and outgoing traffic at the entrance to the Charlotte Coliseum in North Carolina. Topiary shrubs on the site are pruned to maintain precise spherical forms.

A sanctuary for both grief and reconciliation, the Vietnam Memorial is visited by more than one million visitors annually.

In the winter of 1987, Maya received a request from the Southern Poverty Law Center of Montgomery, Alabama, to design a memorial to those who died advancing the Civil Rights Movement. Although she was initially reluctant to design another memorial, she later embraced the opportunity. Lin researched the movement and its era for several months before visiting the site with representatives from the center. She found inspiration in a phrase from the Old Testament, which civil rights leader Dr. Martin Luther King, Jr. had quoted in his pivotal "I Have a Dream" speech of 1963. "We will not be satisfied," Dr. King proclaimed, "until 'justice rolls down like water and righteousness like a mighty stream.'"

In Lin's memorial for the Southern Poverty Law Center, those words are etched into a curving granite wall, in front of which rests a horizontal granite disk, twelve feet in diameter. A catalogue of the major events in the Civil Rights Movement, and names of activists murdered because of the roles they played, are inscribed on the upper surface of the disk. Water flows over the disk, at a barely perceptible rate, from a small hole in its center. "I realized that I wanted to create a time line," Lin told William Zinsser of *Smithsonian*, "a chronological listing of the movement's major events and its individual deaths, which together would show how people's lives influence history and made things better."

The Women's Table

Lin spent the early part of the 1990s designing a private residence in Williamstown, Massachusetts, and renovating a New York loft for a new Museum for African Art. Critics praised Lin's bold use of color as a backdrop for non-western art in the latter design. In 1992 Lin received a commission from Yale to design a monument commemorating women at the university. For this, Maya produced "The Women's Table," a three-foot-high elliptical table made of green granite, washed by a thin film of water. The table is engraved, in spiraling fashion, with the number of women students enrolled at Yale each year, beginning in 1701, with the college's founding, and concluding in 1993 with installation of the table. The majority of numbers are zeroes, depicting women's exclusion from the university until well into the nineteenth century.

In 1993, the Wexner Center for the Visual Arts at Ohio State University invited Maya to become an artist in residence. She accepted, and the center mounted a retrospective exhibit of her work titled, "Maya Lin: Public/Private." In an attempt to demonstrate Lin's range as an artist, the exhibit featured drawings and models of her memorials and architectural commissions, as well as several smaller-scale pieces executed in a variety of materials, including lead and wax.

At the Wexner Center Lin produced "Ground Swell," a permanent installation within the building. The center, which was designed by architect Peter Eisenman, is a restless collage of form and space. Surrounded by this demonstrative architecture, Lin sought relatively quiet areas for her installation. "Ground Swell" occupies areas of the building that were never intended to be seen, including a rooftop. Lin executed three versions of "Ground Swell," requiring a total of forty-three tons of shattered safety glass. Two of the installations were formed by spilling the glass, which had been lifted by a crane under Lin's direction, selectively over the chosen sites. Handled this way, the glittering glass forms small mounds, like sand poured from a pail. The third installation was raked into shape. Shortly after its completion, a vandal splashed red paint on the third "Ground Swell," requiring its removal and replacement.

Lin returned to her studio in 1994 and designed "Eclipsed Time," a fourteen-foot-long clock for the Long Island Railroad Terminal at New York City's Pennsylvania Station. Like a sundial, the piece measures time by casting a shadow across a graduated scale on the ceiling.

Wave Field

In October of 1995 Lin's "Wave Field" was dedicated at the University of Michigan's François-Xavier Bagnoud aerospace engineering building.

If you enjoy the artistry of Maya Lin, you may want to check out the works of the following artists:

Alexander Calder, a proponent of kinetic art—sculpture that incorporates moving parts into its design.

Isamu Noguchi, a sculptor and landscape designer who advocated bringing sculpture out of the museum and into public places.

I. M. Pei, architect and designer of the Louvre pyramid in Paris, France.

Bagnoud, a former student at the university, lost his life in 1986 while piloting a rescue effort in the deserts of West Africa. In his memory, his family provided funds for a building to be named after him, and invited Lin to create a permanent installation on the grounds.

The resulting work took more than two years to complete. While conducting background research for the project, Lin obtained an obscure work on fluid dynamics which contained an image of a stable, three-dimensional waveform. Excited by its beauty, Lin began a series of models exploring the form, culminating in the construction of "Wave Field." The project is composed entirely of soil and grass sculpted into the undulating waveform Lin found so compelling. "The 'Wave Field' is a clear expression of the Maya Lin's consistent fascination—artistic and scientific—with earth and water, geology, topography, landscape, light, fluidity, and transformation," wrote Tresna Lim in *Dimensions*. "In the 'Wave Field' liquid becomes solid—the nature of motion is inverted," she concluded. In a press release issued by the Francois-Xavier Bagnoud foundation, Lin said, "The 'Wave Field' is very special because it expresses my desire to completely integrate a work with its site. It reveals the connectedness of art to landscape, and landscape as art."

In 1995 Lin was also the subject of a documentary film, *Maya Lin: A Strong Clear Vision*, directed by Freida Lee Mock. The Academy Award-winning film emphasized Lin's courage and perseverance in the face of severe criticism of her early work. *San Francisco Examiner* film critic Barbara Shulgasser observed that Lin's "continued growth as an artist and as a human being are the real subject of this film." Gary Susman of the *Boston Phoenix* was somewhat more critical of the film, asserting that "for all the movie's nobility of purpose, and for the compelling nature of the artist's story, *Maya Lin* lacks focus and is often frustratingly vague."

Lin continues to accept large commissions, and is currently at work on installations for the Rockefeller Foundation and the new Federal Courthouse in Manhattan, New York. She frequently exhibits her smaller works in galleries in New York City. In the spring of 1996, Harvard University president presented Lin with an Honorary Doctor of Fine Arts degree. Expressing what many feel about her work, Harvard president Neil Rudenstine lauded Maya Lin as "[a]n artist of resourcefulness and grace: poignant in remembrance of a nation's anguish, eloquent in synthesis of sculpture and design."

■ Works Cited

"Honoris Causa" (Neil Rudenstine's characterizations of honorary degree recipients), *Harvard Magazine*, July-August, 1996, p. 76.

Lim, Tresna, "Making Waves: Maya Lin's 'Wave Field,'" *Dimensions*, Journal of the College of Art and Architecture at the University of Michigan, Volume 10, 1996, pp. 4-8.

Shulgasser, Barbara, *San Francisco Examiner*, November 10, 1995.

Sexton, Jim, "Making Art That Heals," *USA Weekend*, November 1-3, 1996, pp. 4-5.

Stein, Judith E., "Space and Place," *Art in America*, December, 1994, pp. 67-71, 117.

Susman, Gary, "Freida Lee Mock's Not So Clear Look at Maya Lin," *Boston Phoenix*, November 10-17, 1995.

"The 'Wave Field,' Maya Lin's Latest Lanscape Sculpture," press release from Francois-Xavier Bagnoud foundation, October 6, 1995.

Zinsser, William, "I Realized Her Tears Were Becoming Part of the Memorial," *Smithsonian*, September, 1991, pp. 32-43.

■ For More Information See

BOOKS

Ergas, G. Aimee, *Artists: From Michelangelo to Maya Lin* (two volumes), UXL, 1995.

Notable Asian Americans, Gale, 1995.

PERIODICALS

Architectural Record, February, 1990, pp. 186-87.

Art in America, April, 1983, pp. 120-27.

Art News, January, 1983, p. 11.

House & Garden, March, 1990, p. 214.

McCall's, June, 1988.

Ms., September-October, 1990, pp. 20-23.

Newsweek, October 25, 1982, p. 30; January 20, 1986, p. 6.

People, March 8, 1982, pp. 38-39; November 20, 1989, pp. 78-80.

Seventeen, June, 1990, p. 40.

Time, November 6, 1989, pp. 90-94.

Vogue, February, 1993, p. 61; April, 1995, pp. 364-74.*

—Sketch by David P. Johnson

John Marsden

Christopher Award, 1989, ALA Notable Book, 1989, all for *So Much to Tell You . . .* ; Writers' Fellowship, Australia Council, 1993; Australian Muticultural Children's Book Award and New South Wales Talking Book Award, both for *Tomorrow, When the War Began*; New South Wales Talking Book Award, for *The Dead of the Night*.

■ Personal

Born September 27, 1950, in Melbourne, Victoria, Australia; son of Eustace Cullen Hudson (a banker) and Jeanne Lawler (a homemaker; maiden name, Ray) Marsden. *Education:* Mitchell College, diploma in teaching, 1978; University of New England, B.A., 1981. *Politics:* "!!!"

■ Addresses

Home—Box 139, Newstead, Victoria 3462, Australia.

■ Career

Geelong Grammar School, Geelong, Victoria, Australia, English teacher, 1982-90; writer, 1991—; worked as primary school teacher, c. 1995—. Worked at various jobs, including truck driver, hospital worker, and delivery person, c. 1968-77.

■ Awards, Honors

Children's Book of the Year award (Australia), 1988, Premier's Award (Victoria), 1988, Young Adult Book Award (New South Wales), 1988,

■ Writings

So Much to Tell You . . . , Walter McVitty, 1988, Little, Brown, 1989.
The Journey, Pan Australia, 1988.
The Great Gatenby, Pan Australia, 1989.
Staying Alive in Year 5, Pan Australia, 1989.
Out of Time, Pan Australia, 1990.
Letters from the Inside, Pan Australia, 1991, Houghton Mifflin, 1994.
Take My Word for It, Pan Australia, 1992.
Looking for Trouble, Pan Australia, 1993.
Cool School, Pan Australia, 1995.

Also author of *Creep Street*, 1996; *Checkers*, 1996; and *Norton's Hut*, illustrated by Peter Gouldthorpe, 1996.

"TOMORROW, WHEN THE WAR BEGAN" SERIES

Tomorrow, When the War Began, Pan Australia, 1993, Houghton Mifflin, 1995.
The Dead of Night, Pan Australia, 1994, Houghton Mifflin, 1997.
The Third Day, the Frost, Pan Australia, 1995, published as *The Killing Frost*, Macmillan, 1995.

Darkness, Be My Friend, Pan Australia, 1996.

OTHER

Everything I Know about Writing (nonfiction), Heinemann Australia, 1993.
So Much to Tell You: The Play, Walter McVitty, 1994.

Also editor of *This I Believe* (essays), 1996, and *For Weddings and a Funeral* (poetry), 1996.

■ **Sidelights**

"I'd have to say that when I finished school I didn't have much understanding of life," John Marsden admitted in an autobiographical essay in *Something about the Author Autobiography Series* (*SAAS*). Marsden, the well-known author of books about adolescents, spent many years after finishing school drifting from job to job and seeking his true vocation. Despite his disillusionment with school, he eventually became a teacher and gradually built his understanding of the language, morality, and character of his teenage students. This experience, coupled with Marsden's ability to craft the English language, has resulted in several well-received young adult novels.

Marsden grew up in Australia. In his autobiographical essay, he debunked some of the myths of his native land: "Growing up in Australia wasn't a matter of kangaroos, surfboards, and the wild outback. Not for me, anyway. My childhood was spent in the quiet country towns in the green southern states of Victoria and Tasmania. It was peaceful, secure, and often very boring." Marsden's father managed a bank, a job he maintained for forty-eight years. This had a marked yet contrary effect on the young Marsden. He related to *SAAS:* "Perhaps one of the things I've done in my adult life is to react against that kind of commitment. At the latest count I've had thirty-two different jobs."

Growing up in small Australian towns during the 1950s gave Marsden experiences that were quite different from children in urban America during the same era. In his village, ice was still delivered to people for their iceboxes, cooking was mainly done on stoves powered by fuel, and no one he knew owned a television set. "I first saw television when I was ten years old. In our small Tasmanian town an electrical shop brought

WINNER OF AUSTRALIA'S
1988 BOOK OF THE YEAR AWARD
John Marsden
So Much To Tell You

She could never talk again. Not after what happened....

"Unique and affecting."
Booklist

FAWCETT JUNIPER
0-449-70374-6

In this emotionally charged story, fourteen-year-old Marina slowly begins to reach out to others after experiencing a traumatic incident that leaves her mute.

in a TV and put it in their window, for the wedding of Princess Margaret. On the great day the whole town gathered in front of the shop and the set was switched on. All we saw was 'snow'—grey and white static, with a few figures vaguely visible through the murk," Marsden recalled.

Marsden was too infatuated with written literature to care if his family had a television. "I read and read and read," he commented to *SAAS*. "When I ran out of books for boys I read the girls' books. . . . Some days, I'd borrow three titles (the maximum allowed) from the town library, read them, and get them back to the library by five o'clock, in time to exchange them for three more before the library shut. I'd become a speed reader without really trying!" Marsden also found another pastime that was to help him with his later writing. "My favourite game was to draw a town layout on the driveway with chalk and use little model cars to bring the town to life. Perhaps that's how I first became used to creating and living in imaginary worlds."

Marsden became such a bookhound that by the time he was in grade three, he had memorized *The Children of Cherry Tree Farm.* His teacher would use him when she wanted to take a break. "She'd have me stand up in front of the class and recite the next chapter to the other kids . . . from memory. She'd go off to the staff room and leave me there. I loved it! Maybe that's where I got my first taste of the power of storytelling."

That school year was also a difficult one for Marsden. His teacher would fly into rages and yell at the children. She believed in corporal punishment and would cane the children for the slightest disobedience. Each Friday the teacher would give the class a ten-question quiz; if a student failed to answer at least seven questions correctly, he was beaten. "Recently I met up with a girl who'd been in that class with me. As she talked about those Friday tests she started to tremble with the memories. At the age of forty-four she was still haunted by her grade three days," Marsden related in *SAAS.* It was a unsettling year for Marsden, but it made him look unsentimentally at things in the past. "When people talk about the good old days," he observed, "I think they're being a bit simplistic. Like everything, there was good and bad in those times."

When he moved to the next grade, he was rewarded in several ways. First, his teacher was much more nurturing. And second, she saw in him the seeds of a writer and let him edit the school paper. "This was my first taste of publication," he told *SAAS.* "It was a heady experience. Seeing my name in print, having people—even adults—reacting to and commenting on what I'd written was powerful stuff."

When Marsden was ten, the family moved to the large city of Sydney. Having mainly grown up in country towns, Marsden was fascinated with his new experience. "I thought Sydney was huge and

exotic, and wildly exciting," Marsden commented in *SAAS.* "I spent my first week collecting bus tickets, to the amusement of the staff in the hotel where we stayed. Riding on the escalators was as good as Disneyland."

His parents enrolled him at The King's School, a prestigious private school that was run like a military establishment. There was very little Marsden liked about the place, from the stuffy uniforms to the military drills they were required to perform. He also felt out of touch with happenings in the world. "The rest of the Western world was embarking on a decade of drugs, free love, and the Beatles, but at King's boys continued to salute their teachers, drill with rifles for hours every week, and stand to attention when speaking to prefects." Marsden spent his time in somewhat subversive activities: he wrote short books that were stolen from famous mystery novels, distributed his underground newspaper about new rock bands, and read books under his desk during class.

At the time, Marsden found that there was very little literature written for adolescents. But he was amazed by his first reading of J. D. Salinger's *Catcher in the Rye,* a classic coming-of-age story that was—and still is—controversial. The book "had me gasping for breath," Marsden commented in *SAAS.* "I'd never dreamt you were allowed to write like that. . . . For the first time I was reading a genuine contemporary teenage voice. If I've had any success at capturing teenage voices on paper, it's because of what I learnt at the age of fifteen from J. D. Salinger."

School had very little settling influence on Marsden; he continued being a rebel despite the conservative atmosphere. "I began to question everything: religion, education, law, parenting. All the institutions and customs that I'd been taught to accept unquestioningly," he related to *SAAS.* Little surprise that when Marsden graduated from King's he had not received any military awards or promotions. He did, however, win some academic prizes, including one for an essay on poets of World War I.

Merry-go-round of Jobs

After graduating, Marsden intended to go on to study at the University of Sydney, but he lost interest and soon dropped out. It was working that interested him, and he tried his hand at many exotic jobs. He told *SAAS* that some of his employment included "collecting blood, looking after a mortuary at nights, working in a side-show, being a night clerk in the casualty department of Sydney Hospital, and guarding Australia's oldest house from vandals." His interest never lasted very long. "Once I mastered a job I got bored with it and started restlessly looking for the next challenge. Maybe that was a reaction to the boredom of my early life and the tedium of most of my years in schools."

Marsden continued to write and submitted a novel to a publisher that was rejected. He drifted from

John Marsden

Set in Australia, this first volume of a four-book series introduces Ellie and her six companions who, upon returning from a camping trip, find their town has been invaded by soldiers.

job to job, yet somehow succeeded in finishing the first year of a law school course. However, he went into a deep depression and ended up in a psychiatric institution. It was there that he met a fourteen-year-old girl who would not speak to anyone. He wondered what had caused her to do this, and on her last day at the institution he did get to talk to her. She became the inspiration for his later novel about a mute girl titled *So Much to Tell You. . . .*

At the age of twenty-seven, bored with his latest promotion to a desk job at a delivery company, he saw a newspaper advertisement about teaching classes and decided to apply. "I'd always had a vague idea that I might enjoy [teaching], but then I'd had the same vague ideas about other jobs and they hadn't worked out. . . . From the very first day, however, I knew I'd found my vocation." Marsden soon had a position teaching at Geelong Grammar School, a very famous Australian school. After several years of teaching, Marsden was encouraged by someone to do more writing. It was the impetus he needed to start working on his first novel.

During a school holiday, Marsden told *SAAS* that "I sat down and started to write. I made two decisions that turned out to be critical. One was to use the diary format, the other was to aim it at teenage readers. These two decisions seemed to free me to write more fluently than before. I worked in an intensity of emotion, a state that I often slip into when writing." On the very last day of his vacation, Marsden finished the book. He sent it off to a variety of publishers but received only negative responses. Luckily, a chance meeting with a bookseller helped Marsden get the manuscript to a new publisher that snapped it up. *So Much to Tell You . . .* focuses on a mute girl who is sent to a special boarding school rather than a psychiatric hospital. She has been tragically scarred in an accident. The reader gets to know her through her diary entries, where her secrets are gradually revealed: her father scarred her with acid that was meant to injure her mother and now he is in jail. One of the girl's teachers is able to break into her silent world, and at the end of the novel, there is the hope that she will begin coming out of her isolation. The book soon became an Australian best-seller. "A good proportion of the first print run was bought by my students, who were smart enough to know how to improve their grades in English," Marsden joked.

Reviews for the book were mostly positive. Jo Goodman, writing in *Magpies*, declared that the book was "a riveting first novel which grips the reader from the start," and added that "I found the observation and the characters authentic, the suspense gripping, and the slow and subtle revelation of the truth both painful and illuminating." Libby K. White related in *School Library Journal* that "Marsden is a master storyteller." I. V. Hansen, commenting in *Children's Literature in Education*, claimed that the novel offers "a moving story, tragic, simple, generous, tender. It is the kind of novel that seems to come from nowhere, yet we know it has been with us all the time."

The Inner Life of Adolescents

In *The Journey*, Marsden built a fable around adolescent coming-of-age rituals. In this tale, a society sends its adolescents on a journey of self-discovery; the youths return with seven stories of experience and enlightenment. The local council then judges whether the stories are suitable enough for the youths to pass into adulthood. Margot Nelmes commented in *Reading Time* that "this is a rare book, fortifying to the spirit, gripping, and worthy of reading more than once." Marsden turned to lighter works with the publication of *The Great Gatenby* and *Staying Alive in Year 5*. *The Great Gatenby* is about the popular but reckless Erle Gatenby, who causes trouble wherever he goes. *Staying Alive in Year 5* concerns a schoolteacher, Mr. Merlin, who makes the classroom as magical as his namesake. Halina Nowicka in *Reading Time* termed *Staying Alive* "a really good, humorous story. . . ."

A 1991 work, *Letters from the Inside*, evoked some controversy. The novel centers around two girls, Mandy and Tracy, who have become pen pals. After a few exchanges of letters, Tracy reveals that she is actually serving time in a maximum security prison. Despite this information, their friendship grows. Mandy admits that her brother is quite violent, and the end of the novel suggests that Mandy might have been attacked by him. In *Reading Time*, Ashley Freeman called *Letters from the Inside* a "compelling story, which totally involves the reader." Other critics were shocked that Marsden handled the subject of domestic violence with such little sentimentality. Elizabeth Gleick contended in the *New York Times Book Review* that the book "might be faulted for one reason and

one reason alone: it offers not the palest glimmer of hope."

"One of my childhood fantasies had been of a world without adults, a world in which the adults had magically disappeared and the kids were left to run the place," Marsden wrote in *SAAS*. Out of this fantasy came a series of novels that centered around an invasion of Australia. The first novel in the series, *Tomorrow, When the War Began*, is about a group of teenagers, led by the intrepid Ellie, who go on a camping trip in the bush. On their return they realize that everyone in their town has been captured, and they must fend on their own. Quickly, the group organizes to resist the invaders, blowing up a lawn mower to kill one soldier. *The Dead of the Night* and *The Third Day, The Frost* furthered the story of the teenagers as the war in their country continued.

Writing these books became an obsession for Marsden. "I realised that when I was halfway through [the first novel] that one book would not be enough to tell the story. The scenario was just too big for one volume. . . . As I wrote the second book, . . . I began to realise that two wouldn't be enough either. With some reluctance I came to the conclusion that there would have to be a third one," Marsden related in *SAAS*. After finishing *The Dead of the Night*, Marsden tried to turn to other projects, but couldn't, because the characters were still in his head. "Finally, sulkily, I admitted to myself that there was only one thing I wanted to do, and that was to return to the world of Ellie and her friends," he wrote in *SAAS*. Even after this "trilogy" was complete, Marsden wasn't satisfied. He has also finished a fourth book in the series, titled *Darkness, Be My Friend*. "I imagine I'll always be writing, all my life, because there is something within me that needs to tell stories," Marsden related to *SAAS*. Paradoxi-

If you enjoy the works of John Marsden, you may also want to check out the following books and films:

Mitzi Dale, *Round the Bend*, 1991.
Barthe DeClements, *Breaking Out*, 1991.
Carolyn Meyer, *Killing the Kudu*, 1990.
Margaret Rostkowski, *After the Dancing Days*, 1991.
Red Dawn, MGM, 1984.

cally, Marsden returned to teaching school after taking several years off to write full-time. "The other passion of my life is the preservation of life," Marsden commented in *SAAS*. "The older I get, the more disturbed I get by the wanton destruction of other creatures by humans. . . . I hope I continue to improve in my treatment of my fellow creatures, be they animal or vegetable."

■ Works Cited

Freeman, Ashley, review of *Letters from the Inside*, *Reading Time*, Volume 35, number 4, 1991, p. 32.

Gleick, Elizabeth, review of *Letters from the Inside*, *New York Times Book Review*, November 13, 1994, p. 29.

Goodman, Jo, review of *So Much to Tell You . . .* , *Magpies*, March, 1988, p. 30.

Hansen, I. V., "In Context: Some Recent Australian Writing for Adolescents," *Children's Literature in Education*, September, 1989, pp. 151-63.

Marsden, John, autobiographical essay in *Something about the Author Autobiography Series*, Volume 21, Gale, 1996, pp. 169-85.

Nelmes, Margot, review of *The Journey*, *Reading Time*, Volume 33, number 2, 1989, p. 28.

Nowicka, Halina, review of *Staying Alive*, *Reading Time*, Volume 33, number 4, 1989, p. 24.

White, Libby K., review of *So Much to Tell You . . .* , *School Library Journal*, May, 1989, p. 127.

■ For More Information See

BOOKS

Contemporary Authors, Volume 135, Gale, 1992, p. 292.

Contemporary Literary Review, Volume 34, Gale, 1995, pp. 140-51.

Something About the Author, Volume 66, Gale, 1991, pp. 161-62.

Twentieth-Century Young Adult Writers, 1st edition, edited by Laura Standley Berger, St. James, 1994, pp. 423-24.

PERIODICALS

Booklist, July, 1989, pp. 1904-5; October 15, 1994, p. 420; April 15, 1995, p. 1493.

Bulletin of the Center for Children's Books, April, 1989, p. 201.

Carousel, summer, 1996.

Emergency Librarian, March-April, 1992, p. 22.

Horn Book Magazine, September-October, 1989, p. 630; September, 1995, pp. 634-39.

Journal of Reading, March, 1991, p. 496.

Junior Bookshelf, June, 1996, pp. 128-29.

Kirkus Reviews, May 15, 1989, p. 766.

Listener, December 7, 1989, pp. 28-29.

Magpies, April, 1989, pp. 20-22; September, 1990, pp. 5-9.

Pandemonium, Volume 1, issue 1, March, 1996.

Publishers Weekly, March 24, 1989, pp. 73-74.

Quill and Quire, January, 1990, p. 18.

Reading Time, Volume 32, number 3, 1988, p. 56; Volume 33, number 4, 1989, pp. 4-6, 24; Volume 34, number 4, 1990, p. 31; Volume 37, number 2, 1993, pp. 34-35; Volume 37, number 1, 1994, pp. 36-37.

School Library Journal, May 15, 1989, p. 127.

Voice of Youth Advocates, February, 1990, p. 345; December, 1994, p. 276; August, 1995, p. 162.*

—Sketch by Nancy Rampson

William Mayne

■ Personal

Full name William James Carter Mayne; also writes under the pseudonyms Martin Cobalt and Charles Molin, and the joint pseudonym Dynely James; born March 16, 1928, in Kingston upon Hull, Yorkshire, England; son of William (a physician) and Dorothy (Fea) Mayne. *Education:* Attended Cathedral Choir School, Canterbury, England, 1937-42. *Religion:* Church of England. *Avocational interests:* Vintage cars, composing music, building onto his Yorkshire cottage.

■ Addresses

Agent—David Higham Associates Ltd., 5-8 Lower John St., Golden Square, London W1R 4HA, England.

■ Career

Writer. Deakin University, Geelong, Victoria, Australia, lecturer, 1976, 1977; Rolle College, Exmouth, Devon, England, fellow in creative writing, 1979-80.

■ Awards, Honors

Carnegie Medal, British Library Association, 1957, for *A Grass Rope; Boston Globe-Horn Book* honor award, 1989, for *Gideon Ahoy!;* Phoenix award honor, 1991, for *A Game of Dark.*

■ Writings

FOR YOUNG ADULTS

Follow the Footprints, illustrated by Shirley Hughes, Oxford University Press, 1953.

The World Upside Down, illustrated by Shirley Hughes, Oxford University Press, 1954.

A Swarm in May, illustrated by C. Walter Hodges, Oxford University Press, 1955, Bobbs-Merrill, 1957.

The Member of the Marsh, illustrated by Lynton Lamb, Oxford University Press, 1956.

Choristers' Cake, illustrated by Shirley Hughes, Oxford University Press, 1956, Bobbs-Merrill, 1958, reprinted with illustrations by C. Walter Hodges, Jade, 1990.

The Blue Boat, illustrated by Geraldine Spence, Oxford University Press, 1957, Dutton, 1960.

A Grass Rope, illustrated by Lynton Lamb, Oxford University Press, 1957, Dutton, 1962.

The Long Night, illustrated by D. J. Watkins-Pitchford, Basil Blackwell, 1957.

Underground Alley, illustrated by Marcia Lane Foster, Oxford University Press, 1958, Dutton, 1961.

(With R. D. Caesar under joint pseudonym Dynely James) *The Gobbling Billy,* Dutton, 1958.

The Thumbstick, illustrated by Tessa Theobald, Oxford University Press, 1959.

Thirteen O'Clock, illustrated by D. J. Watkins-Pitchford, Basil Blackwell, 1959.

The Rolling Season, illustrated by Christopher Brooker, Oxford University Press, 1960.

Cathedral Wednesday, illustrated by C. Walter Hodges, Oxford University Press, 1960.

The Fishing Party, illustrated by Christopher Brooker, Hamish Hamilton, 1960.

Summer Visitors, illustrated by William Stobbs, Oxford University Press, 1961.

The Changeling, illustrated by Victor Adams, Oxford University Press, 1961, Dutton, 1963.

The Glass Ball, illustrated by Janet Duchesne, Hamish Hamilton, 1961, Dutton, 1962.

The Last Bus, illustrated by Margery Gill, Hamish Hamilton, 1962.

The Twelve Dancers, illustrated by Lynton Lamb, Hamish Hamilton, 1962.

The Man from the North Pole, illustrated by Prudence Seward, Hamish Hamilton, 1963.

On the Stepping Stones, illustrated by Prudence Seward, Hamish Hamilton, 1963.

Words and Music, illustrated by Lynton Lamb, Hamish Hamilton, 1963.

Plot Night, illustrated by Janet Duchesne, Hamish Hamilton, 1963, Dutton, 1968.

A Parcel of Trees, illustrated by Margery Gill, Penguin, 1963.

Water Boatman, illustrated by Anne Linton, Hamish Hamilton, 1964.

Whistling Rufus, illustrated by Raymond Briggs, Hamish Hamilton, 1964, Dutton, 1965.

Sand, illustrated by Margery Gill, Hamish Hamilton, 1964.

A Day without Wind, illustrated by Margery Gill, Dutton, 1964.

The Big Wheel and the Little Wheel, illustrated by Janet Duchesne, Hamish Hamilton, 1965.

Pig in the Middle, illustrated by Mary Russon, Hamish Hamilton, 1965, Dutton, 1966.

Earthfasts, Hamish Hamilton, 1966, Dutton, 1967.

Rooftops, illustrated by Mary Russon, Hamish Hamilton, 1966.

The Old Zion, illustrated by Margery Gill, Hamish Hamilton, 1966, Dutton, 1967.

The Battlefield, illustrated by Mary Russon, Dutton, 1967.

The Big Egg, illustrated by Margery Gill, Hamish Hamilton, 1967.

The Toffee Join, illustrated by Shirley Hughes, Hamish Hamilton, 1968.

Over the Hills and Far Away, Hamish Hamilton, 1968, published as *The Hill Road,* Dutton, 1969.

The Yellow Aeroplane, illustrated by Trevor Stubley, Dutton, 1968.

The House on Fairmont, illustrated Fritz Wegner, Dutton, 1968.

Ravensgill, Dutton, 1970.

Royal Harry, Hamish Hamilton, 1971, Dutton, 1972.

A Game of Dark, Dutton, 1971.

The Incline, Dutton, 1972.

Skiffy, illustrated by Nicholas Fisk, Hamish Hamilton, 1972.

(Under pseudonym Martin Cobalt) *The Swallows,* Heinemann, 1972, published as *Pool of Swallows,* Nelson, 1974.

The Jersey Shore, Dutton, 1973.

A Year and a Day, illustrated by Krystyna Turska, Dutton, 1976.

Party Pants, illustrated by William Stobbs, Knight, 1977.

It, Hamish Hamilton, 1977.

Max's Dream, Hamish Hamilton, 1977, Greenwillow Books, 1978.

While the Bells Ring, illustrated by Janet Rawlins, Hamish Hamilton, 1979.

Salt River Times, illustrated by Elizabeth Honey, Greenwillow Books, 1980.

The Mouse and the Egg, illustrated by Krystyna Turska, Greenwillow, 1981.

The Patchwork Cat, illustrated by Nicola Bayley, Knopf, 1981.

Winter Quarters, J. Cape, 1982.

Skiffy and the Twin Planets, Hamish Hamilton, 1982.

All the King's Men, J. Cape, 1982, Delacorte, 1988.

The Mouldy, illustrated by Nicola Bayley, Random House, 1983.

Underground Creatures, Hamish Hamilton, 1983.

A Small Pudding for Wee Gowrie, illustrated by Martin Cottam, Macmillan, 1983.

Drift, J. Cape, 1985, Delacorte, 1986.

Kelpie, J. Cape, 1987.

Tiger's Railway, illustrated by Juan Wijngaard, Walker, 1987.

The Blemyahs, illustrated by Juan Wijngaard, Walker, 1987.

Gideon Ahoy!, Viking Kestrel, 1987, Delacorte, 1989.

The Farm That Ran Out of Names, J. Cape, 1989.

Antar and the Eagles, Doubleday, 1990.

Low Tide, Delacorte, 1992.

Cuddy, Cape, 1994.

Cradlefasts (sequel to *Earthfasts*), Hodder & Stoughton, 1995.

FOR CHILDREN

No More School, illustrated by Peter Warner, Hamish Hamilton, 1965.

(Under pseudonym Charles Molin) *Dormouse Tales* (five books), illustrated by Leslie Wood, Hamish Hamilton, 1966.

Robin's Real Engine, illustrated by Mary Dinsdale, Hamish Hamilton, 1972.

The Yellow Book of Hob Stories, illustrated by Patrick Benson, Philomel Books, 1984.

The Blue Book of Hob Stories, illustrated by Patrick Benson, Putnam, 1984.

The Green Book of Hob Stories, illustrated by Patrick Benson, Putnam, 1984.

The Red Book of Hob Stories, illustrated by Patrick Benson, Putnam, 1984.

The Book of Hob Stories (contains *The Yellow Book of Hob Stories, The Blue Book of Hob Stories, The Green Book of Hob Stories,* and *The Red Book of Hob Stories*), illustrated by Patrick Benson, Walker, 1984, Philomel, 1984.

Netta Next, illustrated by Krystyna Turska, Hamish Hamilton, 1990.

The Second-hand Horse and Other Stories, Heinemann, 1990.

Rings on Her Fingers, illustrated by Thelma Lambert, Hamish Hamilton, 1991.

And Never Again, illustrated by Kate Aldous, Hamish Hamilton, 1992.

The Egg Timer, illustrated by Anthony Lewis, Heinemann, 1993.

Bells on Her Toes, illustrated by Maureen Bradley, 1994.

Hob and the Goblins, illustrated by Norman Messenger, Dorling Kindersley, 1994.

Pandora, illustrated by Dietlind Blech, Knopf, 1995.

Fairy Tales of London, illustrated by Peter Melnyczuk, Hodder & Stoughton, 1995.

Lady Muck, illustrated by Jonathon Heale, Houghton Mifflin, 1996.

"ANIMAL LIBRARY" SERIES; FOR CHILDREN

Come, Come to My Corner, Prentice-Hall, 1986.
Corble, Prentice-Hall, 1986.
Tibber, Prentice-Hall, 1986.
Barnabas Walks, Prentice-Hall, 1986.
Lamb Shenkin, Prentice-Hall, 1987.
A House in Town, Prentice-Hall, 1987.
Leapfrog, Prentice-Hall, 1987.
Mousewing, Prentice-Hall, 1987.

OTHER

(Contributor) *Over the Horizon; or, Around the World in Fifteen Stories* (for children), Duell, Sloan & Pearce, 1960.

(Editor with Eleanor Farjeon) *The Hamish Hamilton Book of Kings,* illustrated by Victor Ambrus, Hamish Hamilton, 1964, published as *A Cavalcade of Kings,* Walck, 1965.

(Editor with Eleanor Farjeon) *A Cavalcade of Queens,* illustrated by Victor Ambrus, Walck, 1965, published in England as *The Hamish Hamilton Book of Queens,* Hamish Hamilton, 1965.

(Compiler) *The Hamish Hamilton Book of Heroes,* illustrated by Krystyna Turska, Hamish Hamilton, 1967, published as *William Mayne's Book of Heroes,* Dutton, 1968.

(Under pseudonym Charles Molin) *Ghosts, Spooks, Spectres,* Hamish Hamilton, 1967, David White, 1968.

(Compiler) *The Hamish Hamilton Book of Giants,* Hamish Hamilton, 1968, published as *William Mayne's Book of Giants,* Dutton, 1969.

(Editor) *Ghosts,* Thomas Nelson, 1971.

(Editor) *Supernatural Stories,* illustrated by Martin Salisbury, Kingfisher, 1995.

Also composer of incidental music for Alan Garner's play, *Holly from the Bongs,* 1965. Contributor to periodicals.

■ Sidelights

It has been a repeated theme of critics of William Mayne's novels that, while his writing is excellent, it is too difficult for most young readers and will never find a large audience with them. Some critics have even wondered whether the author's works should be considered children's literature in the first place. Mayne doesn't debate this point. When asked in a *Children's Literature in Education* article why he writes for children, Mayne replied, "I don't. I write for myself, but myself of long ago." Mayne also does not apologize for the difficulty of his writing: "I'm only concerned with the [child] who is an avid reader already because what I've done is written something down. That's up to him, or somebody, to read it." For those who are up to the challenge, however, Mayne's books offer many rewards. As one *Junior Bookshelf* contributor put it, Mayne "writes joyously and unashamedly . . . for those who may be expected to enjoy fine style, original and provocative ideas and rich characters."

Though he has written for children—most notably his Hob stories—Mayne is best known as a novelist for young adults. His books often contain elements of fantasy (*A Game of Dark, It*), involve some type of treasure hunt (*Follow the Footprints, A Grass Rope*, and many others), or are about time travel (*Earthfasts, The Hill Road*), but Mayne is by no means limited to these subjects, having also written historical novels (*Drift*) and books that focus on family relationships (*Gideon Ahoy!*). What makes all these stories distinctly his is the author's love of language and his demand that the reader expend some effort in order to discover the meaning behind his words. He is also noted for his willingness to experiment with plots, characters, and narrative style. Mayne's "refusal to use stock situations and stereotyped characters is part of his excellence," according to one *Times Literary Supplement* writer. "He can be intricate and, indeed, downright obscure, but he is incapable of being commonplace."

Train Ticket to Authorship

Mayne's fascination with words was what inspired him to choose his career. One day in 1936, while he was riding a bus, his life changed when he read his ticket and something wonderful happened. "I had two thoughts, there and then," Mayne wrote in his *Something about the Author Autobiography Series* (*SAAS*) entry, "and with those two thoughts my whole life came into a sensible shape. My first new thought . . . making sense of everything, was that someone had *written* the words 'Issued subject to' and so on; . . . in time I shall be able to do the same thing; it shall be my career. And the second part of the thought was that some other skilled person had taken those words and in some way turned them into print, not once, but many times. . . . Life must be simple after that, I knew. There could be nothing more to worry about: I would write down the things that I thought, and have them printed."

A year later, Mayne began attending Cathedral Choir School in Canterbury as a boarder student. The school was in a monastery that had been closed since 1537—four hundred years earlier—and the history of the place imbued every aspect of life there. "What came to me more than the

singing was the great continuity of the place, how it had endured and endured," Mayne reflected. He and the other boys spent many hours exploring "every inch of the building and everything that was written there." "Eventually," the author later wrote, "I left that school, as a natural consequence of losing my treble voice: there was no shock involved. . . . I was sure . . . that I had had enough schooling and there was no more to learn. In that I am right, and cannot see that the inculcation of facts confers worthiness on mentor or scholar."

At that time in his life, Mayne had two careers toward which he aspired: "to be an errand boy [which] was not socially possible then," or to be a writer, although writers "don't qualify for being useful." Mayne chose the latter, a difficult path to follow, but one that has proved successful for him. Mayne's first two books, *Follow the Footprints* and *The World Upside Down*, are both treasure hunt stories that received positive reviews. Although the plots of these stories are not highly original, critics noted the well-drawn characters. "The author understands children and he has drawn parents with hearts as young as their offspring's," observed Betty Brazier in a *School Librarian and School Library Review* article on *The World Upside Down*.

Choir School and *A Grass Rope*

Mayne was off to a good start, but he received even more attention with the first of his choir school books, *A Swarm in May*. For this book Mayne drew directly from his experiences at Cathedral Choir School to create a sense of place that was just as alive and vibrant as the real thing. The story here is a simple but unusual one: the youngest member of the boys' choir must sing a solo in front of the bishop, a traditional ceremony which assures him that there will be enough candles for the year. But although the story is not complicated, there is much in the writing to merit a full-length book. *Signal* contributor Charles Sarland explained: "First and foremost . . . , [Mayne] is concerned to show exactly what it feels like to be a small boy in a choir school. He does this by detailing the physical environment from precisely the point of view of such a small boy." But what is unusual in the book is how Mayne deliberately slows the pace of the story to draw the reader's attention toward a study of character. "In other words," said Sarland, "the wordplay alienates the reader from the drama of the narrative and draws his attention instead to the formal linguistic elements that serve to unite Mayne's delineation of character." While this approach might be a drawback in terms of creating narrative tension, it is a stylistic tour de force. "With *A Swarm in May*," asserted Marcus Crouch in his book *Treasure Seekers and Borrowers: Children's Books in Britain 1900-1960*, "it became apparent that a major novelist had arrived." Other books in the choir school series include *Choristers' Cake* (1956), *Cathedral Wednesday* (1960), and *Words and Music* (1963). Together, as Edward Blishen observed in *The Use of English*, these books "form a loving tribute to a special way of young life."

Besides his choir school books, the best known of Mayne's early works is also the one which won him the 1957 Carnegie Medal, *A Grass Rope*. The central plot device in this book is again the treasure hunt—a common one for Mayne. A group of children go in search of the silver collars that were supposedly lost when a pack of hounds disappeared in the Yorkshire dales during the time of the Crusades. Although the plot is grounded in reality, the palette is colored by fantasy as it is seen through the eyes of a young girl, Mary, who believes in fairies and unicorns (the title refers to the grass rope she weaves to catch a unicorn). It is her unerring faith in her beliefs that guides the searchers in the right direction. At the conclusion of the tale, the children find the legendary collars, but Mary and some of the others prefer to believe in the ancient story rather than the practical solution divined by Mary's father.

As is typical with Mayne, the story is fairly uncomplicated. What makes it special, several critics have maintained, is the author's skill in depicting childhood through the eyes of Mary. "In his studies of children," Helen Stubbs commented about *A Grass Rope* in *In Review: Canadian Books for Children*, "he is able to express for us their essential thought-workings, projected as they are, from imaginative conception into real adventure." Again with this book, as with many others by Mayne, critics wondered whether it was suitable for children. "It is difficult to read," wrote one *Junior Bookshelf* contributor, "with the twin obstacles of dialect and uninhibited vocabulary. It depends on subtleties of writing and observation. It is, nevertheless, completely in tune with childhood. It is written from the child's point of view, not from that of an adult thinking about children."

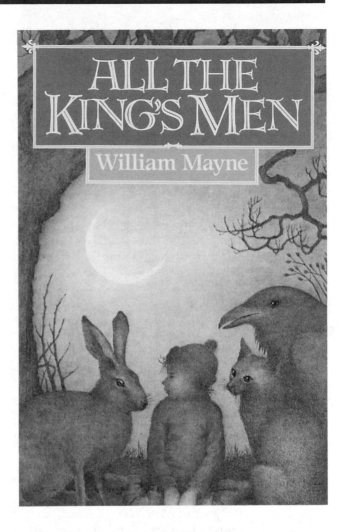

Filled with magic and wonder, this 1982 work presents a world where only a child with courage can outsmart the powerful fairies.

Mayne's Use of Language

One of the difficulties in *A Grass Rope* that is typical of Mayne is his use of dialogue. Mayne depends on conversations between his characters to set his scenes, rather than using direct physical descriptions (though with a few select words, he still manages to effectively evoke the mood of a place). His characters speak in a simple yet elliptical manner that forces the reader to work to interpret the meanings that exist between their words. In his *British Children's Books in the Twentieth Century*, Frank Eyre wrote that Mayne's "stories are introduced, developed and concluded with talk. . . . [If] you have the kind of visual rather than intellectual imagination that demands constant description to keep you 'on scene' you are likely to miss the essential point of his books—and may even lose your way in them." Mayne employs, as one *Times Literary Supplement* writer observed, "a cunning technique of maintaining the thread of thought behind the words of the different speakers" in his stories. In other words, his characters tend to speak obliquely, such as in this exchange found in *Earthfasts:*

"It must be water," said David. "It's water rocking a stone about, or a boulder or something, and then it's going to break out here and be another spring. At least, it won't be another spring, because there isn't one in this field, even though it's called High Keld. This must be the High Keld itself, and it dried up and went. Now it's coming back."

"Oh well," said Keith. "I'd rather have badgers."

"Of course," said David. "Of course."

As the author put it in *Children's Literature in Education,* "I only think . . . [my dialogue is] any good if it says exactly the opposite of what I meant, because I think that might be more natural." But this obliqueness, some critics have observed, applies not only to Mayne's use of dialogue, but also to his approach in probing the emotions of his characters. In *A Sense of Story: Essays on Contemporary Writers for Children,* author John Rowe Townsend wrote: "I am inclined to feel that Mayne as a writer has a characteristic which deprives his work of a substantial and vital element. This, I think, is a tendency to shy away from the passions. . . . Mayne is aware of the passions, most notably so in *Ravensgill,* but even there he appears to define deep feeling by drawing round its edges rather than plunging in." Later, Townsend added, "I suspect that it is a lack of robustness and of red corpuscle in Mayne's work which often causes it to make a less satisfying impact than that of writers who are more crude in their perceptions and far less gifted artistically."

Mayne's ability to recreate a child's view of the world has also been a point of much discussion among critics of his work. Some believe that his books are too difficult for young readers to understand, while at the same time recognizing that his works poignantly express the experience of being a child as seen through young eyes. The author, who once said that he develops his plot first and adds characters second, explained in *Children's Literature in Education* that he is not so much writing for children as he is "looking at things now and showing them to myself when I was young." The approach has proved effective, according to a number of critics. In the *Times Literary Supplement* review of *Ravensgill,* for example, a critic declared that "Mayne's greatest gift is his ability to inhabit the moment-to-moment consciousness of the young." Stubbs called Mayne's writings "studies of children, [in which] he is able to express for us their essential thought-workings, projected as they are, from imaginative conception into real adventure."

From the late 1950s through the mid-1960s, Mayne continued to write stories and often, as with *The*

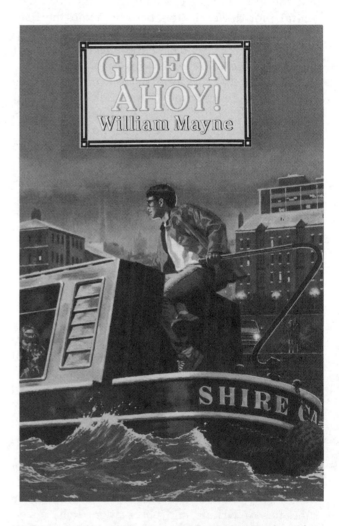

In this *Boston Globe-Horn Book* Honor Book, a family is brought closer together after Gideon, a deaf and brain-damaged teenage boy, gets into an accident.

Twelve Dancers and *The Thumbstick,* used the treasure hunt as his basis for plotting. Townsend noted a change in direction with the novels *Sand* and *Pig in the Middle,* stories "about the everyday lives of boys and young adolescents." These are tales about children coming together for a huge undertaking: in *Sand* a group of boys set about to uncover the buried bones of what they think might be a prehistoric animal; in *Pig in the Middle* another band tries to turn an old barge into a seaworthy vessel they can sail away in. Although these books have drawn praise from reviewers, Townsend felt that they seemed strained, as if Mayne wasn't entirely comfortable with his subject. In *Children's Literature in Education,* Mayne himself admitted there were times he finished a book just because he didn't want it "lying about unfinished."

Earthfasts and the Importance of Time

In 1966, however, Mayne published a work that would earn him wide acclaim: *Earthfasts.* In this "extraordinarily fine book" according to Townend, "[Mayne] at last . . . surpassed his early work." As with *A Grass Rope,* Mayne used local legends of the Dales district of England for background to his tale. Two hundred years ago, a drummer boy named Nellie Jack John went on a quest to find King Arthur's treasure somewhere in a cave beneath Garebridge Castle. He is discovered by two modern boys, David Wix and Keith Heseltine, when he emerges from the cave, carrying with him a candle that burns an unnatural, cold flame. The flame possesses unusual powers, and David is drawn irresistibly to it. The world around them begins to change inexplicably as magical creatures that have slept for ages begin to stir, including giants, a bogart, a wild boar, and stone figures that have been frozen in time since the days of King Arthur. But David's experiments with the candle prove dangerous, for the flame is a part of Time that has gone out of joint, and in acquiring a sort of second sight he is pulled out of his present world into another era. Only then does Keith gain the maturity and insight to realize that he must return the candle to King Arthur's table in order to restore the natural order.

Because of its strong theme of time affecting the present, *Earthfasts* has won praise from critics. Declaring that *Earthfasts* is "much grander and stronger than anything Mayne has done before,"

*Growing Point'*s Margery Fisher predicted that for "many people it will be a landmark in the progress of children's literature." A *Junior Bookshelf* contributor supported this conclusion, asserting that *Earthfasts* "is a book in a thousand; William Mayne at his very considerable best." While *Earthfasts* is clearly a fantasy, it is not of the simple good versus evil variety, but rather possesses a more frightening theme about the dangers of altering the order of Time and the fabric of reality. As Eleanor Cameron stated in her *The Green and Burning Tree: On the Writing and Enjoyment of Children's Books,* "one is almost inclined to say to oneself that this is not fantasy at all but the story of a psychic phenomenon in which the whole countryside has been caught up."

In 1995, almost thirty years after the publication of *Earthfasts,* Mayne wrote the sequel *Cradlefasts,* which brings David and Keith together again. In this story, David is having trouble dealing with the death of his mother and infant sister. As with *Earthfasts,* there is mystery in this story, but it is a tale quite different from its predecessor. Marcus Crouch pointed out in his *Junior Bookshelf* review that Mayne "no longer plays with words and ideas." Crouch added that the novel is "beautifully written, with characters three-dimensional in their consistency and waywardness." *Cradlefasts* deals with the emotional side of life and death—something Townsend had felt was lacking in the author's earlier work—with sensitivity and a touch of humor. Crouch called it Mayne's "finest book."

Mayne's interest in writing about the relationship between time and place continued with *Over the Hill and Far Away,* published in the United States as *The Hill Road.* With this book, the author juxtaposed modern Britain with the Britain of the Dark Ages just after the Roman occupation and allowed the characters to interact. In a less direct but no less potent way, the effects of the past are also felt in Mayne's *Ravensgill.* The story is a murder mystery of sorts in which Bob and Judith, two cousins whose families in the Yorkshire moors have been enemies since an apparent murder some forty-six years earlier, set out to solve the crime and put an end to the two families' differences. For years people have suspected that the late husband of Bob's grandmother was guilty of the crime, but Bob and Judith manage to clear his name in the end. Although there are some flaws in the story—one *Times Literary Supplement* critic noted that Bob's fortuitous discovery of a secret tunnel demonstrates "the bare bones of the outline structure" and that the conclusion falls back on "contrived coincidence"—Mayne's characterizations were highly praised, especially his complex depiction of Bob's grandmother, a woman who can be lovable, mysterious, spirited, and stubborn. The character of Grandma, declared Townsend, "is one that I would once have thought outside [Mayne's] range."

Psychological Symbolism in Fantasy

The tensions that exist within families is once more explored in *A Game of Dark,* in which Mayne mixes fantasy and reality to study the relationship between a boy named Donald Jackson and his parents. Donald's mother is a remote figure who is so disinterested in her son that she often calls him by his last name. His father, a minister, is also not close to his son. Because his father is dying, Donald feels particularly guilty about his inability to feel love for him. Donald retreats from his troubles by journeying into a fantasy world in which he must face a dragon that is besieging a town. He is told that he must defeat the creature honorably, but Donald is only able to kill the monster through deception and is thus rejected by his fantasy world as well. Yet, by defeating the beast, Donald is able to return home, face his father's death, and come to terms with their relationship. Russell Hoban, writing in *The Thorny Paradise: Writers on Writing for Children,* noted the symbolic meanings behind Donald's fantasy world: "Needing to be a man, Donald drifts into a world where he is needed as a man. He rescues a girl who is reminiscent of his dead sister."

The usual criticism—a mantra by this time—of the novel being too difficult for children was heaped on *A Game of Dark.* In addition to this, however, some reviewers accused Mayne of working out his personal hangups through the book. "Reviewers . . . have gone chasing phallic symbols and Zeus/ Cronos patterns," remarked Brian Alderson in *Children's Book Review,* "and have neglected what is emotionally and technically one of the book's triumphs: Donald's ambivalent relationship with his Other World and the absolute reality of that place as a paradigm of his home world." What may be more important, however, is Mayne's continued development toward presenting characters who are more human and less emotionally remote from the reader. *Horn Book* contributor Paul Heins noted that, although the characters remain a bit "stand-offish," Mayne has allowed himself "more human involvement . . . than in some earlier" books.

Books Outside of England

Never one to remain satisfied with past accomplishments, Mayne changed focus again with his 1973 work, *The Jersey Shore.* Not only does he set most of the story in America, rather than the England with which he is so familiar, but the novel shifts decidedly from the child's viewpoint to the adult's. Beginning in the 1930s, the narrative tells of young Arthur's trip to the New Jersey shore with his mother to visit with his grandfather and aunt. His grandfather—who does most of the talking here—tells Arthur all about the side of the family that lived in the village of Osney in East Anglia, including the story of his one true love, whom he was never able to marry. One of these ancestors was a man who survived a shipwreck and came to the English shore draped in chains. Interestingly, there is an important point of the story that differs between the English and American editions of the book: in the English edition, the text makes it plain that the mysterious man with the chains was a slave from Africa, and that Arthur, being his descendant, is therefore black; the American edition, however, never makes this clear, and the reader is left to wonder what this man's significance is to the story. It is an important omission, since it explains why Arthur's grandfather never married his true love. Ten years after Arthur leaves the Jersey shore, he becomes a tail gunner in the Air Force during World War II. Arthur has the chance to visit the village of his ancestors and reflect upon his grandfather's stories. He "goes there to find what the old man lost," explained a *Times Literary Supplement* reviewer, "to mend what was broken, to break the chain hanging on the wall."

"Technically," continued the reviewer later, "[*The Jersey Shore*] ranks with the best that [Mayne] has done. By giving most of the narrative to the old man he avoids all but a dash of the whimsical chit-chat that is the most dispensable part of his writing." Mayne's interest in the effects of the past upon the present are again seen in this story, and it is the stories Arthur's grandfather tells about his ancestors that give "the book its energy," ac-

In this riveting 1989 work, Antar is kidnapped by an eagle and soon finds out that he has been selected by the Great Eagle to complete a special mission.

cording to Alderson. But, the critic adds, with this novel "it seems . . . that William Mayne has crossed 'the misty edge' and written a book where the complexity of experience requires more than childish resources for its appreciation." Still, a number of reviewers felt *The Jersey Shore* was a masterful accomplishment. A group of *Junior Bookshelf* critics, for example, praised how the whole story is formed of "tantalizing details," making it "a deeply satisfying book for that rare bird, the sensitive, adolescent reader."

One of the complaints against *The Jersey Shore*, however, was the way in which Mayne made his American characters speak. For example, Alderson notes that Arthur talks in a manner more "too akin to [a] . . . young gentleman." Similarly, in a

more recent book, *Drift*, which is set in the Canadian North sometime during the nineteenth century, critics had problems with what they considered Mayne's awkwardness portraying non-English characters. In this survival story, a young boy named Rafe is kidnapped by two Indian women after journeying out into the wilderness with an Indian girl named Tawena. The Indians "are made to communicate in a demeaning pidgin . . . that has no resonance beyond the comic strip," according to *Times Literary Supplement* contributor Neil Philip. Later the critic added, "The dialogue is rudimentary and bare of nuance; the weight of meaning rests on narrative passages which are already overloaded in their attempt to evoke an unfamiliar landscape and to keep moving an unconvincing story." Certainly not all reviewers felt the tale was a failure, however. *Junior Bookshelf* writer Marcus Crouch, for example, said that as "a study of triumph over the harshest of conditions, and above all as an examination in depth of two people [Rafe and the girl Tawena] under stress, it is wonderfully successful."

The Child's Perspective—Once Again

Mayne did not abandon his interest in the child's perspective after *The Jersey Shore*, however, and novels like *Max's Dream* and *It* reaffirm the author's belief in "the magical rightness and sincerity of children's ideas of the world round them," as Margery Fisher put it in a *Growing Point* review of *Max's Dream*. Like *The Jersey Shore*, *Max's Dream* is a reminiscence: an elderly woman named Katy tells of how she met an unusual boy while working as a servant during the 1890s. Max, a sickly orphan child who remains upstairs in the house the thirteen-year-old Katy works in, has a dream of an island, a house filled with riches, and the strange, silent girl who lives there. The story describes Katy's efforts to unravel the meaning of Max's dream and its effects upon him. *It* is a kind of horror story in which a girl named Alice receives a ring with which she can wield a supernatural power. The "It" of the story is a demon who brings her nine other rings; however, if Alice uses the power of those rings, the demon will be able to control her. Alice, however, proves she is stronger than It and resists the demon's temptation. The basic theme of the tale, as Dominic Hibberd explained it in the *Times Literary Supplement*, is that "adolescent feelings that are not controlled can become socially destructive."

Mayne's next critically acclaimed book was 1987's *Gideon Ahoy!* In this work, the author went back to what some consider his greatest strengths—the depiction of family interrelationships and skilful use of language—and continued to improve upon his past accomplishments. The title character of *Gideon Ahoy!* is Gideon Catterell, a teenage boy who is deaf and mentally handicapped, both conditions having been caused by a childhood illness. When given the opportunity to work on a canal boat during the summer tourist season, Gideon is ecstatic and has a wonderful time with his new job. But when autumn arrives, he can't comprehend why he has to stop working. He becomes upset and runs away. His family finds him again, but an accident almost leads to his death. "The possibility of losing Gideon draws [his] unique family even closer together and taps the depth of their family solidarity," reported Marlene M. Kuhl in *Voice of Youth Advocates.*

One way Mayne illustrates the closeness of the Catterell family is in how they are able to communicate with Gideon, who is only capable of uttering words like "Hyagh" and "Gaboo." Eva, his twelve-year-old sister who serves as the story's narrator, is able to understand Gideon's meaning perfectly, as if he were merely speaking a foreign language in which she and her family were also fluent. The descriptive passages between the dialogue have also been highly praised. *Washington Post Book World* contributor Elizabeth Ward said that the language in the book "comes close to poetry in its intensity, its compression and its quality of profound utterance." Calling *Gideon Ahoy!* an insightful book, *Bulletin of the Center for Children's Books* critic Betsy Hearne praised Mayne for continuing to be "an experimenter, one of the few who will take a chance on unusual techniques of crafting fiction for the young."

Mayne Steps into the '90s

Entering his fifth decade as a published author, Mayne proved again that he could come up with fresh and surprisingly original new stories. *Antar and the Eagles,* published in 1990, concerns a boy named Antar who is kidnapped by eagles who believe he is the only person capable of finding the egg that contains their next great leader. To rescue the egg, the eagles teach Antar how to fly, but while doing so treat him very harshly. Antar doesn't mind too much, however, because he re-

---

If you enjoy the works of William Mayne, you may want to check out the following books and films:

Bill Brittain, *Wings,* 1992.
Sylvia Cassedy, *M. E. and Morton,* 1987.
Louise Cooper, *The Sleep of Stone,* 1991.
Legend, Universal, 1985.

---

alizes the eagles are simply acting like eagles, and he knows they have given him a great gift by showing him he could do things he never thought himself capable of before. Ward, writing in a *Washington Post Book World* article in which she compared Antar to Rudyard Kipling's Mowgli, commented, "Without a single moralizing word, Mayne plunges little Antar, and us all, into a school of the imagination that is so different it shocks. But for the child who is ready for it, this book may provide a rare and exhilarating experience." "I don't know if children will take to this wise, strange, uncompromising, yet warm book," concluded Penelope Farmer in the *Times Educational Supplement,* "but I hope so."

With *Low Tide,* Mayne once again set a story outside his native England: this time it is nineteenth-century New Zealand. Charlie, his sister Elizabeth, and their Maori friend Wiremu are swept away by a tidal wave into the hinterlands of New Zealand, where the legendary wild man, the Koroua, is supposed to live. They meet the Koroua, who indeed seems wild and dangerous, but he is not like the creature of the legend. Several things are strange about his behavior, and he soon proves to be the children's savior, teaching them how to survive in the wild and return home. The wild man turns out not to be the Koroua at all (he's a German sailor who has been shipwrecked), but the children's perception of him as such lends mystery and humor to the tale.

Though there are certain commonalities in each of Mayne's works, including most especially his uncompromising use of language, he has managed to make all of his novels and stories unique creations. Perhaps one reason for their differences, as Mayne mischievously suggests in *Children's Literature in Education,* is that "I always forget between books how it's done. I don't know at all. I don't even know how it's done when I do it." Mayne also likes to challenge himself by always tackling a story that is new and difficult. As he proclaimed in *SAAS*, "If each book did not seem impossible it would not be worth attempting; and of course each one has a different impossibility. But who has conquered Everest that went up in the chairlift hugging a hot-water bottle?" The debate remains, however, whether these difficult books—accomplishments both for the author and the reader to wade through—are for children, adults, or both. In an article in *Signal*, Peter Hunt described how he tested this question on a group of adult readers, who would not otherwise pick up a book by Mayne, by asking them to read some of his work. The group agreed they enjoyed the stories very much, which proved they were appropriate for adults, but what about for children? Hunt doesn't answer this question directly, and perhaps it is actually a moot point. He is an author for all ages. As Hunt concluded, "Mayne is a major writer, who should be recognized as such. . . . In his style, Mayne is an original, one of the few true stylists of the twentieth century."

■ Works Cited

Alderson, Brian, "On the Littoral: William Mayne's 'The Jersey Shore,'" *Children's Book Review,* October, 1973, pp. 133-35.

Blishen, Edward, "Writers for Children, 2: William Mayne," *The Use of English*, autumn, 1978, pp. 99-103.

Brazier, Betty, review of *The World Upside Down*, *School Librarian and School Library Review*, July, 1955, p. 361.

Cameron, Eleanor, *The Green and Burning Tree: On the Writing and Enjoyment of Children's Books*, Atlantic/Little, Brown, 1969, pp. 3-136.

Crouch, Marcus, *Treasure Seekers and Borrowers: Children's Books in Britain 1900-1960*, The Library Association, 1962, pp. 112-38.

Crouch, Marcus, review of *Drift, Junior Bookshelf*, August, 1985, pp. 187-88.

Crouch, Marcus, review of *Cradlefasts, Junior Bookshelf*, February, 1996, pp. 38-39.

Review of *Earthfasts, Junior Bookshelf*, December, 1966, p. 386.

Eyre, Frank, *British Children's Books in the Twentieth Century*, Dutton, 1973.

Farmer, Penelope, review of *Antar and the Eagles*, *Times Educational Supplement*, October 27, 1989, p. 25.

Fisher, Margery, review of *Earthfasts, Growing Point*, July, 1965, pp. 769-70.

Fisher, Margery, review of *Max's Dream, Growing Point*, November, 1977.

Review of *A Grass Rope, Junior Bookshelf*, December, 1957, pp. 318-19.

Hearne, Betsy, review of *Gideon Ahoy!, Bulletin of the Center for Children's Books*, February, 1989, pp. 151, 153.

Heins, Paul, review of *A Game of Dark, Horn Book*, February, 1972.

Hibberd, Dominic, review of *It, Times Literary Supplement*, April 7, 1978, p. 376.

Hoban, Russell, "Thoughts on Being and Writing," in *The Thorny Paradise: Writers on Writing for Children*, edited by Edward Blishen, Kestrel Books, 1975, pp. 65-76.

Hunt, Peter, "The Mayne Game: An Experiment in Response," *Signal*, January, 1979, pp. 9-25.

Review of *The Jersey Shore, Junior Bookshelf*, August, 1973.

Review of *The Jersey Shore*, "Old Man's Tale," *Times Literary Supplement*, June 15, 1973, p. 674.

Kuhl, Marlene M., review of *Gideon Ahoy!, Voice of Youth Advocates*, June, 1989, p. 104.

Mayne, William, *Earthfasts*, Hamish Hamilton, 1966.

Mayne, William, "A Discussion with William Mayne," *Children's Literature in Education*, July, 1970, pp. 48-55.

Mayne, William, *Something about the Author Autobiography Series*, Volume 11, Gale, 1991.

Review of *The Member for the Marsh, Junior Bookshelf*, July, 1956, p. 144.

Philip, Neil, "Cracking the Code," *Times Literary Supplement*, March 29, 1985.

Review of *Ravensgill*, "Yorkshire Family Quarrel," *Times Literary Supplement*, July 2, 1970, p. 713.

Sarland, Charles, "Chorister Quartet," *Signal*, September, 1976, pp. 107-13.

Stubbs, Helen, "William Mayne's Country of the Mind," *In Review: Canadian Books for Children*, winter, 1972, pp. 5-14.

Townsend, John Rowe, *A Sense of Story: Essays on Contemporary Writers for Children*, J. B. Lippincott, 1971, pp. 130-42.

Ward, Elizabeth, review of *Gideon Ahoy!, Washington Post Book World*, February 12, 1989, p. 9.

Ward, Elizabeth, review of *Antar and the Eagles*, *Washington Post Book World*, February 11, 1990, p. 6.

"William Mayne: Writer Disordinary," *Times Literary Supplement*, November 24, 1966, p. 1080.

■ For More Information See

BOOKS

Cadogan, Mary, and Patricia Craig, *You're a Brick, Angela! A New Look at Girls' Fiction from 1839-1975*, Victor Gollancz, 1976, pp. 355-72.

Chambers, Aidan, *Booktalk: Occasional Writing on Literature and Children*, Bodley Head, 1985, pp. 34-58.

Children's Literature Review, Volume 25, Gale, 1991, pp. 137-74.

Contemporary Literary Criticism, Volume 12, Gale, 1980, pp. 386-407.

Fisher, Margery, *Intent Upon Reading: A Critical Appraisal of Modern Fiction for Children*, Brockhampton Press, 1961, pp. 270-96.

Fisher, Margery, *The Bright Face of Danger*, Horn Book, 1986, pp. 318-44.

Fisher, Margery, *Classics for Children & Young People*, Thimble Press, 1986, pp. 47-48.

Inglis, Fred, *The Promise of Happiness: Value and Meaning in Children's Fiction*, Cambridge University Press, 1981, pp. 213-31.

Landsberg, Michele, *Reading for the Love of It: Best Books for Young Readers*, Prentice Hall, 1987, pp. 9-34.

Meigs, Cornelia, editor, *A Critical History of Children's Literature*, Macmillan, 1969, pp. 567-600.

Stott, Jon C. *Children's Literature from A to Z: A Guide for Parents and Teachers*, McGraw Hill, 1984, pp. 183-84.

Waggoner, Diana, *The Hills of Faraway: A Guide to Fantasy*, Atheneum, 1978, pp. 125-302.

PERIODICALS

Books and Bookmen, November, 1976.

Books for Keeps, March, 1996, p. 12, 13.

Bulletin of the Center for Children's Books, June, 1986, pp. 190-91; March, 1993, pp. 220-21.

Chicago Tribune Book World, May 11, 1969.

Children's Literature, Volume 21, 1993, pp. 101-17.

Children's Literature in Education, November, 1972, pp. 7-23; March, 1973, pp. 50-63; May, 1973, pp. 37-38.

Five Owls, June, 1971; July-August, 1990, p. 109.

Growing Point, October, 1966, pp. 546-47; January, 1978.

Horn Book, August, 1957, pp. 307-308; December, 1973; July/August, 1990, p. 456; September-October, 1993, pp. 600-601.

Junior Bookshelf, July, 1953, p. 121; November, 1954, p. 247; December, 1956, pp. 341-42; July, 1957, pp. 143-44; July, 1959, pp. 152-53; October, 1959, pp. 185-89; December, 1960, p. 370; July, 1963, p. 156; December, 1963; April, 1968; February, 1978; August, 1993, pp. 154-55.

Junior Libraries, October, 1957.

Kirkus Reviews, September 1, 1972.

Listener, November 16, 1967.

New Statesman, November 6, 1970, pp. 608, 610.

New York Herald Tribune Book Review, April 3, 1960, p. 9.

New York Review of Books, February 18, 1988, pp. 11-13.

New York Times Book Review, September 24, 1961, p. 40; November 28, 1965; October, 1971, p. 8; May 2, 1976; September 24, 1989, p. 26.

Publishers Weekly, January 27, 1997, p. 106.

School Librarian, March, 1969; September, 1970; September, 1971, pp. 262, 265; March, 1972, pp. 63-64; September, 1972, pp. 259-60; March, 1984, pp. 5-12.

School Librarian and School Library Review, March, 1956, p. 69; July, 1964, pp. 206-207; March, 1965; March, 1968.

School Library Journal, April, 1969; August, 1986, p. 104; June, 1990, pp. 124-25; March, 1993, pp. 198, 200.

Signals, May, 1977.

Times Educational Supplement, June 8, 1990, p. B9.

Times Literary Supplement, May 11, 1956, p. vii; November 23, 1956, p. vii; November 15, 1957; November 21, 1958, p. viii; November 25, 1960, p. xii; December 9, 1965; December 2, 1977.

Voice of Youth Advocates, June, 1986, p. 81; February, 1991, p. 365; April, 1993, pp. 43-44.

Washington Post Book World, November 5, 1972; July 10, 1988, p. 11.*

—Sketch by Janet L. Hile

Jim Murphy

■ Personal

Born September 25, 1947, in Newark, NJ; son of James K. (a certified public accountant) and Helen Irene (a bookkeeper and artist; maiden name, Grosso) Murphy; married Elaine A. Kelso (a company president), December 12, 1970. *Education:* Rutgers University, B.A., 1970; graduate study, Radcliffe College, 1970.

■ Addresses

Home and office—138 Wildwood Ave., Upper Montclair, NJ 07043.

■ Career

Seabury Press, Inc. (later Clarion Books), juvenile department, New York City, 1970-77, began as editorial secretary, became managing editor; freelance author and editor, 1977—. *Member:* Asian Night Six Club (founding member).

■ Awards, Honors

Children's Choice, International Reading Association, 1979, for *Weird and Wacky Inventions;* Society of Children's Book Writers and Illustrators Golden Kite Award for nonfiction, and American Library Association (ALA) Best Books for Young Adults citation, both for *The Boys' War: Confederate and Union Soldiers Talk about the Civil War;* ALA Notable Children's Book citation, 1982, for *Death Run;* Society of Children's Book Writers and Illustrators Golden Kite Award for nonfiction, 1992, and ALA Best Books for Young Adults citation, both for *The Long Road to Gettysburg;* ALA Notable Children's Book citation, ALA Best Books for Young Adults citation, *School Library Journal* Best Book of the Year citation, *Booklist* Editor's Choice citation, and National Council of Teachers of English (NTCE) Orbis Pictus Award, all for *Across America on an Emigrant Train;* ALA Notable Children's Book citation, ALA Best Book for Young Adults citation, *Boston Globe/Horn Book* Award Honor Book, *Bulletin of the Center for Children's Books* Blue Ribbon Book, *Publishers Weekly* Best Book of the Year, *School Library Journal* Best Book of the Year, Notable Children's Trade Book in the Field of Social Studies, *Booklist* Editor's Choice citation, NCTE Orbus Pictus Award, 1996, and Newbery Honor Book citation, 1996, all for *The Great Fire.*

■ Writings

JUVENILE FICTION

Rat's Christmas Party, illustrated by Dick Gackenbach, Prentice-Hall, 1979.
Harold Thinks Big, illustrated by Susanna Natti, Crown, 1980.

Death Run, Clarion Books, 1982.

The Last Dinosaur, illustrated by Mark Alan Weatherby, Scholastic, 1988.

The Call of the Wolves, illustrated by Mark Alan Weatherby, Scholastic, 1989.

Backyard Bear, illustrated by Jeffrey Greene, Scholastic, 1992.

Dinosaur for a Day, illustrated by Mark Alan Weatherby, Scholastic, 1992.

Night Terrors, Scholastic, 1993.

JUVENILE NONFICTION

Weird and Wacky Inventions, Crown, 1978.

Two Hundred Years of Bicycles, Harper, 1983.

The Indy 500, Clarion Books, 1983.

Baseball's All-Time All-Stars, Clarion Books, 1984.

Tractors: From Yesterday's Steam Wagons to Today's Turbo-Charged Giants, Lippincott, 1984.

The Custom Car Book, Clarion Books, 1985.

Guess Again: More Weird and Wacky Inventions, Four Winds Press, 1985.

Napoleon Lajoie: Modern Baseball's First Superstar, Society for American Baseball Research, 1988.

Custom Car: A Nuts-and-Bolts Guide to Creating One, Clarion Books, 1989.

The Boys' War: Confederate and Union Soldiers Talk about the Civil War, Clarion Books, 1990.

The Long Road to Gettysburg, Clarion Books, 1992.

Across America on an Emigrant Train, Clarion Books, 1993.

Into the Deep Forest with Henry David Thoreau, illustrated by Kate Kiesler, Clarion Books, 1995.

The Great Fire, Scholastic, Inc., 1995.

A Young Patriot: The American Revolution as Experienced by One Boy, Clarion Books, 1995.

Also contributor of articles to *Cricket.*

■ Sidelights

"It was Sunday and an unusually warm evening for October eighth, so Daniel 'Peg Leg' Sullivan left his stifling little house in the West Side of Chicago and went to visit neighbors. One of his stops was at the shingled cottage of Patrick and Catherine O'Leary. The one-legged Sullivan remembered getting to the O'Learys' house at around eight o'clock, but left after only a few minutes because the O'Leary family was already in bed. . . ."

It was about 8:45 PM, author Jim Murphy continues in *The Great Fire,* his account of the Great Chicago Fire of 1871, when Sullivan first spotted trouble—"a single tongue of flame shooting out the side of the O'Learys' barn."

"Sullivan didn't hesitate a second. 'FIRE! FIRE! FIRE!' he shouted as loudly as he could. . . . The sound of music and merrymaking stopped abruptly, replaced by the shout of 'FIRE!' It would be a warning cry heard thousands of times during the next thirty-one hours."

These passages from *The Great Fire* illustrate some of Murphy's strengths as a writer: his attention to detail, exacting research, and ability to make history come to life. The author's works span both the fiction and nonfiction genres, ranging from technical and historical to zoological and ecological. He has won recognition for his ability to present information in a clear, unambiguous, and entertaining fashion. "I thoroughly enjoy my work," Murphy once told *Something about the Author (SATA).* "The nonfiction projects let me research subjects that I'm really interested in; they provide an opportunity to tell kids some unusual bits of information. The fiction lets me get out some of the thoughts and opinions that rattle around in my head."

Murphy harbored few writing ambitions while he was growing up. "I was raised in Kearny, New Jersey," Murphy reminisced to *SATA,* "a nice enough suburban town, made up largely of Scots, Irish, and Italians. My friends and I did all the normal things—played baseball and football endlessly, explored abandoned factories, walked the railroad tracks to the vast Jersey Meadowlands, and, in general, cooked up as much mischief as we could. And since Kearny was close to both Newark and New York City, we would often hop a bus or train to these cities. We loved wandering through those places, so much different than our comfortable, tree-lined streets, watching the people and eating strange and usually greasy foods."

The Advantages of a Well-Rounded Education

"Oddly enough, I wasn't a very big reader back then," Murphy admitted to *SATA.* "In fact, I hardly cracked a book willingly until a high school teacher announced that we could absolutely, positively NOT read Hemingway's *A Farewell to Arms.* I promptly read it, and every other book I

This illustration of an 1885 flying machine is just one example of the strange contraptions included in Murphy's *Guess Again: More Weird and Wacky Inventions.*

could get a hold of that I felt would shock my teacher. I also began writing, mostly poetry, but with an occasional story or play tossed in there."

"Now this doesn't mean that I abandoned physical activity completely," Murphy continued. "I ran track while in school and was part of national championship teams for the 440 and mile relays. I was also ranked somewhere in the top ten of high school sprinters. In addition, I had a series of strange jobs, including repairing boilers, tarring roofs, putting up chain link fences, operating a

mold injection machine, and doing maintenance for two apartment buildings. The highlight, however, was a stint as a tin knocker on several New York City construction jobs.

"It wasn't too long after this that I landed an editorial job in the juvenile department (later named Clarion Books) of Seabury Press. I stayed there seven years, going from editorial secretary to managing editor. It was during this time that I realized that many of my earlier experiences could be of value in my writing."

Murphy began his writing career with a book that reflected his mechanical experience. *Weird and Wacky Inventions* and its sequel *Guess Again: More Weird and Wacky Inventions* set a pattern for several of Murphy's early nonfiction books. Both works employ a multiple-choice quiz format which invites readers to guess a use for an unusual invention. Contraptions featured include a coffin with an escape hatch for people who have a fear of being buried alive, training pants for dogs who aren't housebroken, and a hammock for use on trains. Each is accompanied by a drawing based on an original patent diagram and an invitation for the reader to guess its use before being presented with the solution. Although the major focus of both books is the many strange contraptions that have passed through the U.S. Patent Office, Murphy also includes information on inventions that have helped shape American history. As critic Marrgaret M. Hagel states in *School Library Journal*, "the act of invention to fulfill a need is an important ingredient of the American spirit." The books are rounded out with essays on the inventing and patent process.

Several of Murphy's other works also examine mechanical devices. *Tractors: From Yesterday's Steam Wagons to Today's Turbo-Charged Giants* presents the history of this useful farm machine. Lee Bock in *School Library Journal* remarks that, although other children's tractor books are worthwhile, "none, however, carries the same detailed and readable historical information" as found in Murphy's book. *Custom Car: A Nuts-and-Bolts Guide to Creating One* tells how the author bought a junk car and, with the help of mechanic Tom Walsh, rebuilt the engine and replaced damaged interior and exterior parts. The book features step-by-step procedures for car repairs, including illustrations, explanations and advice, sources for buying parts, and ideas onwhere to find further information. "They encourage installing good used parts and accessories," declares Ann G. Brouse in the *School Library Journal*, "rather than always buying brand new." Although reviewers caution readers that *Custom Car* is not the only source that will be needed to attempt this type of project on their own, they praise the volume for its enthusiasm and accessibility.

Two Hundred Years of Bicycles also looks at the history of mechanical devices. In this book, Murphy traces the story of how bicycles changed from late eighteenth-century "celeriferes" to modern racers and dirt bikes. He also looks at the ways that human powered vehicles (HPVs) may become important in the future. "Murphy's book focuses solely and comprehensively on the history of the bicycle, unlike others which include safety tips and information on how parts work," writes *School Library Journal* contributor Connie Tyrrell. "Murphy's is a fine addition to the growing body of literature about bicycling." *The Indy 500* is an examination of auto racing's most famous event, again from a historical perspective. When the race began in 1911, the winning vehicle's average speed was just under seventy-five miles per hour—a speed readily reached by most automobiles today. The 1983 Indy 500 winner averaged 162 miles per hour. Murphy looks at the race and tries to understand what has attracted people to it for so many years. Robert Unsworth, writing in the *School Library Journal*, calls the book "a sure winner."

Murphy has also tried his hand at fiction. *Death Run* tells of how four high school age boys—Brian,

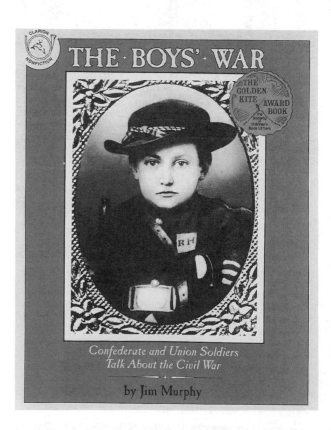

In this award-winning work, Murphy discusses both the thrilling and horrific experiences of boys, mostly between the ages of twelve and sixteen, who fought in the Civil War.

Roger, Sticks, and Al—are accidentally involved in the death of another young man on a local suburban basketball court. Originally, public opinion has it that the death is from natural causes, but the boys, fearing that someone will accuse them, panic and flee. Detective Sergeant Wheeler recognizes their flight as a sign of guilty consciences, and he begins his own investigation into the death after the case has been officially closed. "Justice prevails," declares Drew Stevenson in the *School Library Journal*, "in an ending that is painfully realistic." *Night Terrors* is a selection of five stories told by an old grave digger. They range from mummies coming to life to contemporary werewolf and vampire tales. "Murphy has a knack for evocative descriptions," opines *Booklist* contributor Stephanie Zvirin, while Margaret Mary Ptacek states in *Voice of Youth Advocates*, "This is your better than average horror collection."

Several of Murphy's books for younger readers mix fact and fiction to tell about animal life from the point of view of the animals. *Dinosaur for a Day* dramatizes the life of a vegetarian hypsilophodon and her eight babies as they search for food. *The Last Dinosaur* combines a number of facts about dinosaur life and the factors that probably contributed to their extinction. The story features a small herd of triceratops and their encounters with a tyrannosaurus rex, with mammals who prey on the triceratops' eggs, and finally with a forest fire that destroys their last remaining nest. Murphy also acknowledges the effects that an asteroid collision, new diseases, and temperature changes may have had on late dinosaur populations. "The scenario certainly renders the end of the Age of Dinosaurs more immediate than many non-fiction accounts," declares a *Bulletin of the Center for Children's Books* reviewer.

The Call of the Wolves tells how one wolf, separated from his pack during a hunt for caribou, faces the dangers posed by illegal hunters, other packs of wolves, and sled dogs. Deborah Abbott in her *Booklist* review comments that the "taut story line, [and] compelling illustrations" increases the readers' interest in the account. Betsy Hearne concludes in *Bulletin of the Center for Children's Books* that "the style is straightforward and the dramatically textured paintings . . . are so dynamic, this can be read by independent readers older than the picture book listeners for whom it's intended."

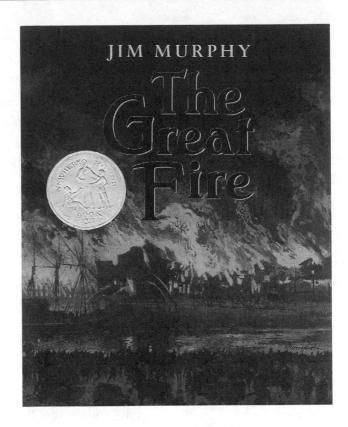

Continuing his work in historical nonfiction, Murphy examines the origin and aftermath of the fire of 1871, which left the city of Chicago in ruins and 100,000 people homeless.

Young Men in the Civil War

It is for his historical books for young readers that Murphy has received the greatest critical acclaim. He draws on primary sources written by participants in the events he narrates and works by later historians in order to understand the background of the incidents as well as their significance. The first of Murphy's historical nonfiction books was the Golden Kite Award-winning *The Boys' War: Confederate and Union Soldiers Talk about the Civil War*. Like filmmaker Ken Burns's epic PBS documentary *The Civil War*, the author uses photographs and reports to tell how the young soldiers adjusted to the demands made on them by the bloodiest war in American history. One of the factors Murphy emphasizes is how many of the soldiers on both sides were under sixteen when they enlisted. "After the war," Murphy writes in the introduction to *The Boys' War*, "an army statistician did manage to do a study of several battalions, matching names with birth certificates when possible. From this he estimated that between 10 and 20 percent of all soldiers were underage when they signed up." The eyewitness accounts of soldiers age twelve to sixteen bring to life the battles, living conditions, and psychological impact of combat on the youths who participated.

While many reviewers found the book grim, Murphy was praised for bringing home the reality of war for young adult readers. David A. Lindsey, reviewing *The Boys' War* for *School Library Journal*, observes that the boys' accounts "bring to life, as no other versions can, the Civil War and all of its glories and horrors." "It is startling to learn of the large number of very young soldiers whose lives were given to the war," Margaret A. Bush states in *Horn Book*, and she concludes, "This well-researched and readable account provides fresh insight into the human cost of a pivotal event in United States history." A *Newsweek* contributor calls it "a gut-turning but commendable chance for young people to hear from others their own age what war is all about."

Murphy's second book for young adults on the Civil War, *The Long Road to Gettysburg*, focuses on two young men—Lieutenant John Dooley, a Confederate soldier, age nineteen, and Corporal Thomas Galway, a Union soldier, age seventeen—who were present at one of the war's most pivotal battles. This personalized view of the fight is augmented with maps, photographs, and the text of Abraham Lincoln's "Gettysburg Address." "By focusing on these two ordinary soldiers," writes Elizabeth M. Reardon in *School Library Journal*, "readers get a new perspective on this decisive and bloody battle." Anita Silvey, reviewing *The Long Road to Gettysburg* for *Horn Book*, remarks, "Jim Murphy uses all of his fine skills as an information writer . . . to frame a well-crafted account of a single battle in the war." A *Publishers Weekly* reviewer declares that Murphy "conveys all of the tension, tedium and excitement of the battlefield."

Murphy moved from military to social history with the award-winning *Across America on an Immigrant Train*, the story of Scottish writer Robert Louis Stevenson's 1879 journey from his native land to Monterey, California. Stevenson kept a journal of the trip, and Murphy draws on it and on other contemporary sources to provide a picture of mid-nineteenth century America's westward movement. Murphy tells how the trains

---

If you enjoy the works of Jim Murphy, you may want to check out the following books:

The nonfiction works of Brent Ashabranner, including *Always to Remember: The Story of the Vietnam Veterans Memorial*, 1988.

The historical fiction of Howard Fast, including *Seven Days in June*, 1994.

Nat Hentoff's nonfiction works, including *The First Freedom: The Tumultuous History of Free Speech in America*, 1980.

Julius Lester's *To Be a Slave*, 1968.

---

brought to the west immigrants from France, Sweden, and Germany fleeing war in Europe, as well as African Americans trying to escape racism in the South. He explains how the trains disrupted the lives of the Native Americans of the Great Plains and the effect the railroad had on the lives of its workers. "Murphy has woven meticulously researched, absorbing accounts of the building of the railroad and its effect on the territory it crossed," explains Diane S. Marton in *School Library Journal*. A later book for younger readers, *Into the Deep Forest with Henry David Thoreau*, uses Thoreau's journals of a trip into the Maine woods in the 1850s to emphasize the environmental impact of nineteenth-century industrialization.

Myth and Reality

Murphy's Newbery Award-nominated *The Great Fire* combines the techniques the author used in his studies of the Civil War and of immigrants. The book looks at a great event—the fire that burned most of Chicago, Illinois, between October 8th and October 10th, 1871. Murphy carefully traces the beginnings of the fire and its progress on detailed maps, explaining how a variety of factors, including the stubbornness of local officials, contributed to the spread of the blaze. He introduces the individual stories of people whose lives were directly affected by the fire, including reporter Joseph E. Chamberlin of the *Chicago Evening Post*, Horace White, editor in chief of the *Chicago Tribune*, and Claire Innes, a girl of twelve whose family had only recently moved to Chicago. "Through the eyes of all these people," Murphy writes in his introduction to *The Great Fire*, "you will see the fire from many distinct vantage points, and feel a wide range of emotions as the hot breath of the fire draws nearer and nearer."

But Murphy also takes pains to put the fire into perspective. He sees the tragedy of the Great Fire not exclusively in terms of lives lost, but in the way it reveals an America divided against itself. Rich residents, many of whom lost their homes, were quick to blame the city's poor immigrant population for the fire. Contemporary Chicago newspapers quickly accused Catherine and Patrick O'Leary, in whose barn the blaze started, as responsible. Murphy points out that there were many more factors: the high proportion of the city's buildings made of wood, the dry weather and heavy breeze, and the lack of organization of the city's fire brigades. One result of rich people's prejudice was that poor residents were forced into slums or out of the city altogether. "These tensions and animosities would brew and simmer for many decades," Murphy writes, "and eventually they would result in urban unrest on a grand scale in the twentieth century."

Critics praised Murphy's narrative technique and careful selection of material in *The Great Fire*. A *Publishers Weekly* critic called the work "engrossing," and Frances Bradburn, writing in *Booklist*, noted that the graphics, including maps, engravings, and archival photographs, "add fuel to the author's dramatic text, a riveting narrative that combines the details of the fire itself" with first-person accounts and newspaper clippings.

In his award-winning books of historical nonfiction, Murphy makes the past accessible through painstaking research and clear, expressive writing. That his works continue to garner him award after award, and praise from reviewers and readers alike, is a tribute to his success.

■ Works Cited

Abbott, Deborah, review of *The Call of the Wolves*, *Booklist*, January 1, 1990, p. 919.

Bock, Lee, review of *Tractors: From Yesterday's Steam Wagons to Today's Turbo-Charged Giants*, *School Library Journal*, November, 1984, p. 127.

Review of *The Boys' War: Confederate and Union Soldiers Talk about the Civil War*, *Newsweek*, December 3, 1990, p. 66.

Bradburn, Frances, review of *The Great Fire*, *Booklist*, June 1 and 15, 1995, p. 1757.

Brouse, Ann G., review of *Custom Car: A Nuts-and-Bolts Guide to Creating One*, *School Library Journal*, July, 1989, p. 96.

Bush, Margaret A., review of *The Boys' War: Confederate and Union Soldiers Talk about the Civil War*, *Horn Book*, January, 1991.

Review of *The Great Fire*, *Publishers Weekly*, May 8, 1995, p. 297.

Hagel, Margaret M., review of *Guess Again: More Weird & Wacky Inventions*, *School Library Journal*, October, 1986, p. 180.

Hearne, Betsy, review of *The Call of the Wolves*, *Bulletin of the Center for Children's Books*, September, 1989, p. 13.

Review of *The Last Dinosaur*, *Bulletin of the Center for Children's Books*, June, 1988, p. 213.

Lindsey, David A., review of *The Boys' War: Confederate and Union Soldiers Talk about the Civil War*, *School Library Journal*, January, 1991, p. 120.

Review of *The Long Road to Gettysburg*, *Publishers Weekly*, April 20, 1992, p. 58.

Marton, Diane S., review of *Across America on an Immigrant Train*, *School Library Journal*, December, 1993, pp. 129-30.

Murphy, Jim, *The Boys' War: Confederate and Union Soldiers Talk about the Civil War*, Clarion Books, 1990.

Murphy, Jim, comments in *Something about the Author*, Volume 77, Gale, 1993, pp. 139-42.

Murphy, Jim, *The Great Fire*, Scholastic, Inc., 1995.

Ptacek, Margaret Mary, review of *Night Terrors*, *Voice of Youth Advocates*, December, 1993, p. 312.

Reardon, Elizabeth M., review of *The Long Road to Gettysburg*, *School Library Journal*, June, 1992, p. 146.

Silvey, Anita, review of *The Long Road to Gettysburg*, *Horn Book*, July, 1992, pp. 469-70.

Stevenson, Drew, review of *Death Run*, *School Library Journal*, May, 1982, p. 85.

Tyrrell, Connie, review of *Two Hundred Years of Bicycles*, *School Library Journal*, April, 1983, p. 116.

Unsworth, Robert, review of *The Indy 500*, *School Library Journal*, December, 1983, p. 87.

Zvirin, Stephanie, review of *Night Terrors*, *Booklist*, October 1, 1993, p. 332.

■ For More Information See

PERIODICALS

Booklist, July, 1986, p. 1615; May 1, 1988, p. 1527; October 15, 1992, p. 435.

Bulletin of the Center for Children's Books, September, 1983; July/August, 1984; January, 1991, p. 126; January, 1994, p. 164; June, 1996, p. 347.

Horn Book, August, 1982, p. 415; April, 1994, pp. 220-21.

Junior Bookshelf, December, 1980, p. 295.

Kirkus Reviews, April 1, 1989, pp. 551-52; May 1, 1992, p. 614; December 1, 1993, p. 1527.

Publishers Weekly, June 27, 1986, p. 97; August 22, 1986, p. 36; April 29, 1988, p. 75; September 27, 1991, p. 59.

School Library Journal, November, 1984, pp. 127, 135; September, 1988, p. 184; December, 1989, pp. 86-87; October, 1992, p. 107; September, 1993, p. 252.

Voice of Youth Advocates, October, 1982, p. 45; April, 1991, p. 60.

Wilson Library Journal, September, 1990, p. 4.*

—Sketch by Kenneth R. Shepherd

Georgia O'Keeffe

■ Personal

Born November 15, 1887, in Sun Prairie, WI; died from complications of old age, March 6, 1986, in Santa Fe, NM; daughter of Francis (a farmer) and Ida (Totto) O'Keeffe; married Alfred Stieglitz (a photographer and art exhibitor), December 11, 1924 (died July 13, 1946). *Education:* Studied under John Vanderpoel, Art Institute of Chicago, 1905-06; William Merrit Chase, F. Luis Mora, and Kenyon Cox, Art Students League (New York City), 1907-08; Alon Bement, University of Virginia, 1912; and Bement and Arthur Dow, Columbia University, 1914-16. *Hobbies and other interests:* Gardening, the southwest.

■ Career

Artist. Worked as a freelance commercial artist in Chicago, including illustrator for advertising firms, 1908-10; Amarillo, TX, public schools, art instructor, 1912-13; West Texas State Normal College (now West Texas State University), Canyon, head of art department, 1916-18; full-time artist, 1918—. Instructor in art at University of Virginia,

1913-16, and Columbia College, Columbia, SC, 1915-16. *Exhibitions:* Works exhibited internationally and represented in permanent collections, including Metropolitan Museum of Art, Museum of Modern Art, Whitney Museum of American Art, and Art Institute of Chicago. One-woman retrospectives include Art Institute of Chicago, 1943, Museum of Modern Art, 1946, Worcester Museum of Art, 1960, Whitney Museum of American Art, 1970, and Metropolitan Museum of Art, 1989. *Member:* American Academy of Arts and Letters, American Academy of Arts and Sciences, American Watercolor Society (honorary member), National Institute of Arts and Letters.

■ Awards, Honors

Chase Still Life Award, 1907-08; medal from American Academy of Arts and Letters, 1962; creative arts award, Brandeis University, 1963; Wisconsin Governor's Award for Creativity in the Arts, 1966; distinguished service citation in the arts, Wisconsin Academy of Sciences, Arts and Letters, 1969; Benjamin Franklin fellow, Royal Society for the Encouragement of Arts Manufactures and Commerce (London), 1969; gold medal, National Institute of Arts and Letters, 1970; M. Cary Thomas Prize, Bryn Mawr College, 1971; National Association of Schools of Art citation, 1971, for contributions to the visual arts; Edward MacDowell Medal, MacDowell Colony, 1972; gold medal, Skowhagen School of Painting and Sculpture, 1973; first annual New Mexico Governor's

Award, 1974; Presidential Medal of Freedom, 1977; National Medal of Arts, 1985; honorary degrees from universities, including College of William and Mary, 1938, University of Wisconsin, 1942, Mount Holyoke College, 1952, University of New Mexico, 1964, School of Art Institute of Chicago, 1967, Brown University and Columbia University, both 1971, Minneapolis College of Art and Design, 1972, Harvard University, 1973, and College of Santa Fe, 1977.

■ Writings

The Work of Georgia O'Keeffe: A Portfolio of Twelve Paintings, introduction by James W. Lane, Knight Publishers, 1937.
Drawings, introduction by Lloyd Goodrich, Atlantis Editions (New York City), 1968.
Some Memories of Drawings, Atlantis Editions, 1974.
Georgia O'Keeffe (autobiography), Viking (New York City), 1976.
(Author of introduction) Alfred Stieglitz, *Georgia O'Keeffe: A Portrait by Alfred Stieglitz*, Viking, 1978.
Georgia O'Keeffe: One Hundred Flowers, edited by Nicholas Callaway, Knopf (New York City), 1987.
Lovingly, Georgia: The Complete Correspondence of Georgia O'Keeffe and Anita Pollitzer, edited by Clive Giboire, Simon & Schuster (New York City), 1990.
Georgia O'Keeffe: Paintings, Random House (New York City), 1994.

O'Keeffe's work has been represented in numerous exhibition catalogues. Collections of O'Keeffe's letters are housed at Yale University, New Haven, CT (closed to the public until 2011).

■ Adaptations

A television documentary of O'Keeffe's life was directed by Perry Miller Adato, PBS, 1977. O'Keeffe has been the subject of numerous educational films and several motion pictures.

■ Sidelights

From her roots in rural Wisconsin, painter Georgia O'Keeffe rose within an art world dominated by what she called "the men" to become the best-known female artist in the United States. A reflection of O'Keeffe's strong, independent spirit, the label of "female artist" was one that she herself disagreed with throughout her life; defiant of both social and artistic conventions, she preferred to think of herself as, simply, an "Artist," producing works that could hold their own in comparison with those of her male colleagues. While classified by critics as everything from "surreal" to "precisionist" or "romantic," O'Keeffe's paintings were done in a deliberately original and independent style intended, the artist later said, to "satisfy no one but myself." Despite her continuous battles with critics who insistently tried to pigeon-hole her work into one or another school of painting, O'Keeffe thrilled both art critics and art lovers and enjoyed huge amounts of praise, a reputation for quality, and top dollar for the paintings that she sold, even during her lifetime. "Somehow, what I painted happened to fit into the emotional life of my time," O'Keeffe once told *New Yorker* contributor Calvin Tompkins of her ability to connect with the public conscience of the nation. Indeed, O'Keeffe's lasting legacy has been a body of work that reflects the nature of Americans to look at the world around them in a fresh light.

O'Keeffe was born November 15, 1887, in the rural community of Sun Prairie, Wisconsin. Because Wisconsin winters are so harsh, the young Georgia was kept inside, away from the bitter cold, for the first half year of her life. Blessed with an amazing memory, she recalled even as an adult the rush of excitement she experienced upon first being brought outside into the warm spring sunlight. The power of light to transform objects found its way into many of O'Keeffe's later works of art.

One of seven children born to Francis O'Keeffe, a farmer of Irish descent, and his wife, Ida, a woman of aristocratic Eastern European heritage, Georgia was raised within a large extended family that included grandparents, aunts, and uncles. Despite the constant hubbub caused by friends and family that surrounded her during childhood, O'Keeffe tended towards being a loner; while she could be sociable and even fun to be with, she also often rejected the company of others, preferring to go to a quiet corner of the house or yard and read or draw.

Ida O'Keeffe, although living the life of a farmer's wife—which revolved around practical, necessary matters like cooking, doing laundry and mending, and keeping house—wanted her children to benefit from the exposure to culture that she had acquired during her more affluent childhood. Reading aloud to her family everything from classic works of literature such as the *Thousand and One Arabian Nights* to imaginative tales from the Wild West, Ida also encouraged her daughters to take art lessons. An amateur artist herself, she sacrificed in order to send each of the O'Keeffe girls to an art tutor, despite the fact that the family's financial circumstances grew increasingly strained during Georgia's childhood. Left to her own devices, however, young Georgia's tendency was to draw totally from her imagination—palm trees and ocean coastlines and other exotic things that she had never actually seen around her home in the northern Midwest.

At the age of thirteen, O'Keeffe attended Madison, Wisconsin's Sacred Heart Convent School, where her art education included drawing still-lifes from actual objects, a task that forced the young artist to develop her powers of observation. For that is what O'Keeffe already was: an artist. Despite the limited opportunities available to women at the turn of the twentieth century, she knew she wanted more from life than the traditional—and expected—roles of wife and mother could offer. She had decided early on that she would become an artist; by age ten she had already confided her plans to a playmate. That decision having been made, O'Keeffe pursued it with single-minded determination for the rest of her life.

When O'Keeffe and her family moved to Virginia in 1903, she kept up with her art studies, attending Chatham Episcopal Institute, a private school near Lynchburg. Because attending private school left her without the chance to meet other teens her own age, O'Keeffe remained a loner. In the milder, mid-Atlantic climate, she became interested in objects from nature and disappeared for hours, following trails winding through the Virginia countryside in solitary pursuit of wildflowers, rocks, and other subjects for her drawings.

Makes First Trip to New York City

After graduating from Chatham in 1905, O'Keeffe moved to Chicago for a year in order to study at that city's Art Institute. There, under teachers like artist John Vanderpoel, she was taught the artistic traditions of the European masters, whose dark, static style was revered and copied by most artists of the period. There also she began drawing from live models and studying human anatomy. A hard-working pupil who followed the instructions of her teachers despite her personal dislike of the heavy European style, O'Keeffe became one of the top students at the Art Institute.

A bout of typhoid fever prevented O'Keeffe from returning to Chicago the following year; instead she remained at home, though not without her drawing materials. In 1907 the twenty-year-old artist moved to New York City, attending classes at the famous Art Students League while modeling for other art classes to help pay her way. Her instructor here was William Merritt Chase, a respected artist who taught O'Keeffe to paint rapidly using quick, short brush strokes. Through constant practice—Chase demanded a new painting from his students every day—O'Keeffe mastered the traditional European portrait painting techniques being taught. She even won a top prize for a still-life composition at the Art Students League. But she remained frustrated that she had not yet discovered her true "calling" as an artist. "[A] lot of people had done this kind of thing before I came along," she later wrote in her self-titled autobiography, adding that "I didn't think I could do it any better."

Another frustration that O'Keeffe was probably experiencing during this period was less an inner dissatisfaction with her own performance than an outer one. Because she was a woman she was not taken seriously as an artist, either by her teachers or her fellow students. Despite the fact that women made up more than half of the student body at the Art Students League, it was assumed that those who did not find husbands, marry, and begin to raise families immediately after graduation would become art teachers. Even with the natural talent and proficiency that kept O'Keeffe at the top of her class, she was never given any sort of personal guidance towards making her living as an exhibiting artist.

Unfortunately, due to the O'Keeffe family's increasingly difficult financial circumstances—caused by her father's failed business dealings and her mother's long and ultimately fatal battle with tuberculosis—the free and easy life of a student would no longer be possible for Georgia. Forced

The artist standing next to *Life and Death*, in which she combined two of her famous images, a flower and a sun-bleached cow skull.

to end her studies at the Art Students League, O'Keeffe moved her aunt's home to Chicago in 1908 and found work as a commercial illustrator, drawing lace and embroidery designs for advertising companies. She also designed the little Dutch girl, a logo that is still used on cans of Dutch Cleanser today. O'Keeffe worked in Chicago for the next two years, before leaving the Midwest altogether to teach art, first at Chatham Episcopal Institute, and then in the state of Texas.

Continually frustrated by her perceived lack of progress and hating commercial art, O'Keeffe was all but ready to set aside her dreams of being a painter by 1910. Fortunately, it was while attending a class at the University of Virginia in the summer of 1912 that her desire to paint and draw was reawakened. Studying art with Alon Bement, a regular faculty member at Columbia University in New York City and a disciple of noted teacher Arthur Wesley Dow, O'Keeffe was struck with her instructor's overriding design tenet: "to fill space in a beautiful way." She realized that she didn't have to copy the traditional or current European painting styles that she had been taught. And she didn't have to continue to use her teachers' methods, except as she chose to. With a new sense of her own potential as a painter, O'Keeffe left New York to begin her new job as a high school art instructor in Amarillo, Texas. She filled her spare hours by painting the southwestern landscape she loved in a way completely her own.

From 1912 to 1913 O'Keeffe continued to teach in Amarillo's public schools; her summers found her close to her family, teaching art to summer-school students at the University of Virginia. It was while teaching in Virginia during the summer of 1913 that a fellow instructor introduced her to the works of Russian artist Wassily Kandinsky. Kandinsky's colorful, abstract images caused O'Keeffe to look at her own art through different eyes. She realized again the importance of breaking away from the style of the European school. This meant unlearning much of what had been taught to her during her studies in Chicago.

Inspired by Kandinsky's work, including his book, *On the Spiritual in Art*, O'Keeffe resolved to begin to use her art to express her personal, non-European vision; packing up her canvases and her belongings, she returned to New York City, where Bement had invited her to work as his graduate assistant. There, from 1914 to 1915, she enrolled in classes with Dow at Columbia University. Once again energized by the creative bustle of the city, O'Keeffe, like many other young avant-garde, or experimental, painters, began to frequent the 291 Gallery located on Fifth Avenue in downtown Manhattan. Co-founded by pioneering photographers Alfred Stieglitz and Edward Steichen in 1907, the gallery—with Stieglitz now at its helm—had become a mecca for artists like the radical Dadaists, who used the gallery as a meeting place and a space for holding regular exhibitions of new works.

In the fall of 1915, with money running low, O'Keeffe was forced to return to teaching. This time she worked at Columbia College, a small Methodist institution in Columbia, South Carolina. Again removed from the artistic mainstream of New York, O'Keeffe started to once again question her work as an artist. Recalling her reaction to the works of Kandinsky, she left painting with heavy oils and began to use simpler tools—charcoal and paper—as a way of more loosely shaping her inner feelings in a visual manner. The pictures that resulted were unlike anything that was being done; and the abstract direction her emotions appeared to be taking alarmed O'Keeffe, who feared she was losing her artistic ability. Once again, she started to think about stopping her painting altogether.

During the long months she spent teaching down in South Carolina, O'Keeffe corresponded almost every week with Anita Pollitzer. Pollitzer, a former schoolmate at the Art Students League, an officer in the National Women's Party, and an ardent feminist, was the perfect person to keep O'Keeffe's confidence from crumbling. Through their letters, later published as *Lovingly, Georgia: The Complete Correspondence of Georgia O'Keeffe and Anita Pollitzer*, it was obvious that the relationship between the two students was a supportive one: depressed and often lonely due to her isolation from the energy of the New York City art world, O'Keeffe was able express her frustrations at her works-in-progress. Pollitzer, living in Manhattan during a period of great intellectual and artistic activity, could keep her friend informed of trends in the art world, sending books, art supplies, and news of cultural events she attended. At the beginning of 1916, O'Keeffe rolled up some of the abstract drawings she done in charcoal—work that she later described as a creative breakthrough, "essentially a woman's feeling"—and mailed them to her friend; Pollitzer was so impressed that, despite O'Keeffe's request not to show them to another soul, she took the drawings to Stieglitz. The gallery-owner was impressed with the work, which, as Pollitzer wrote to O'Keeffe, he described as "the purest, finest, sincerest things that have entered 291 in a long while."

Begins Relationship with Stieglitz

Holding a liberal feminist viewpoint compared to most of the other leaders of the art world, Stieglitz hung O'Keeffe's drawings in his next show. Without her knowledge, the twenty-nine-year-old schoolteacher became an overnight celebrity among Manhattan's avant-garde art community. Managing to appease the angry young artist, who had returned to New York City to enroll in a summer class at Columbia only to find her works on exhibit without her permission, the persuasive Stieglitz eventually convinced O'Keeffe to quit teaching and devote her full attention to artistic pursuits. With his financial support—and eventually as his mistress—she left her current job as head of the art department of West Texas State Normal College after only two years and returned to New York City. Joining Stieglitz in 1919 and warmly welcomed into the inner circle of New York-based artists and photographers, O'Keeffe gained increasing fame as, one after another, one-woman exhibits of her work were launched at his galleries 291, Intimate Gallery, and An American Place. Interested primarily in O'Keeffe as an accomplished artist producing work as good as that of any man, Stieglitz also found himself falling in love with this aloof, independent woman. Despite an age difference of twenty-three years, the two married on December 11, 1924.

While Pollitzer continued to be instrumental in aiding O'Keeffe throughout her early career, the relationship between the two friends reached a sad impasse several decades later. In 1955 Pollitzer began to write, with O'Keeffe's approval, a biography of her artistic friend. But when it was completed, after two years of copious research, the uncompromising O'Keeffe refused to allow the book's publication. Her last letter to the stunned Pollitzer—"It is a very sentimental way you like to imagine me. It reads as if . . . we didn't understand one another at all"—ended their friendship. Despite the artist's objection, Pollitzer's biography, entitled *A Woman on Paper: Georgia*

O'Keeffe, would eventually be published in 1990, fifteen years after its author's death.

Critics Read Much into Her Works

O'Keeffe's early, abstract works in charcoal astonished critics when they were first exhibited at 291 in the spring of 1916. In fact, because of their absolute originality when compared to her later work in oils, these drawings have caused some critics to think less of the many series of paintings that would follow. While O'Keeffe decided to abandon her abstract style in the early 1920s—a woman who disliked being disagreed with, she became increasingly irritated by the widely differing critical interpretations being attached to her drawings—many biographers have since claimed that O'Keeffe herself considered works like *Evening Star III* (1917) to be among her most accomplished. By abandoning this early, abstract style, it is felt, she left her artistic potential untapped. "Surely it is her early work, made when she was still influenced by the principles that imbued 291, by its insistence on independence, its commitment to personal expression, and its faith in its revolutionary promise, that is today the most strikingly provocative," noted Edward Abrahams, discussing the many books and exhibits that appeared in 1989 (the hundred-year anniversary of the artist's birth) in *New Republic.* "These are the abstract watercolors and charcoals, which, unlike most of O'Keeffe's better known art, still retain their expressive power. They are the works about which Stieglitz wrote in 1916 that '291 had never before seen woman express herself so frankly on paper.'"

As her relationship with Stieglitz matured, O'Keeffe spent time with him both in New York City and at his family's summer home on Lake George in upstate New York. Even before they were married, she became the subject of many of the noted photographer's famous studies. Stieglitz shot over three hundred pictures of the serious, dark haired painter, many from his Lake George home. Working in their New York apartment, O'Keeffe used oils to depict the skyscrapers, clouds, and buildings that shaped the city skyline, and from their summer home she painted country vistas, gathering the shells, rocks, and flowers that later became characteristic themes in her work. Some of the more notable paintings of this period include *Lake George by Moonlight*, done in 1924, and *The Shelton with Sunspots*, a render-

Calla Lillies (1930), oil on board, 15 1/2 x 12 inches, exemplifies O'Keeffe's work with flowers.

ing of the Lexington Avenue apartment building where she and Stieglitz lived, worked in oils in 1926.

Begins Flower Paintings

After the 1920s O'Keeffe's work became increasingly objective, or realistic, in nature. Gradually the impressionistic watercolors, with their feminine, almost musical quality, and the unconventional cityscapes were replaced by more clearly drawn objects. O'Keeffe especially became noted for her oversized flower paintings, which display her talent for amplifying the inner design and purpose of ordinary objects. Producing the first of her flower paintings as early as 1919, the artist arranged greatly enlarged and vibrantly colored stylized flower blossoms decoratively on the picture plane. She often did several versions of the same subject, experimenting with changes in light, position, and color. Notable among these works are *Oriental Poppies*, completed in 1928, and her famous *Jack-in-the-Pulpit* series, done during 1930. According to Calvin Tompkins in the *New Yorker*, "to many people, the swelling forms and mysterious dark voids [of the flowers] bore unmistakably sexual overtones, and any number of critics in discussing them made heavy use of Freud." In her typical response to any sort of critical interpretation of her work, O'Keeffe vehemently rejected such inferences to sexuality, simply stating that she painted the flower image large so that people would "be surprised into taking time to look at it" and see, as the artist did, its wonderful color, shape, and texture. In the same way, the shells, rocks, and landscapes she also painted express, as she wrote in her autobiography, "what is to me the wideness and wonder of the world as I live it." While some critics took issue with O'Keeffe's later work for its stylized, posterlike quality, others applauded these more "objective" works. "Her [flower] work is charged with the mysterious," Ralph Pomeroy later remarked in *Contemporary Artists*. "In her hands, flowers, looked at so closely and presented so out of natural scale, become worlds threatening to engulf us in sensual floods of shape and color as though we are bees about to become drunk on nectar."

By the end of the twenties O'Keeffe began to feel that her creativity was beginning to end; she decided to take a summer trip to Taos, New Mexico, at the invitation of good friends Rebecca Strand and Mabel Dodge Luhan. Although she had visited the area before and had been impressed by the southwest's dramatic diversity ever since teaching in Texas, it was during this trip in 1929 that O'Keeffe was first awakened to the austere beauty of the southwestern landscape and inspired to make it part of her creative work. While she travelled extensively around the United States, Mexico, and the rest of the world for the next three decades, the sunlight, sun-dried adobe walls, and desert plants common to the dry, arid Southwest climate continued to be a magnet for her artistry. In the mid-1930s O'Keeffe established a second home in Taos, away from both New York City and Stieglitz, with whom she had become semi-estranged over the years due to the marital infidelities of both. While occasionally returning to the East Coast to visit her husband, O'Keeffe's hours spent hiking through the areas mountain and desert terrain were among her most joyous. As this joy was transferred onto the canvas, more and more people became saw the beauty of the desert through O'Keeffe's eyes. Eventually such notable nature artists as photographers Eliot Porter and Ansel Adams came to New Mexico to travel the desertscape alongside O'Keeffe.

On one hike near Taos, taken after the area had experienced a prolonged drought, O'Keeffe was unable to find the flowers that were her usual subjects. Instead, her eyes were drawn to the brilliant, sun-bleached bones that lay scattered among the cacti and low-lying brush. In the bleached desert bones of animals, where critics saw death and allusions to crucifixion, O'Keeffe saw beauty: "The bones," she later explained in her autobiography, "seem to cut sharply to the center of something that is keenly alive on the desert even tho' it is vast and empty and untouchable—and knows no kindness with all its beauty." One of her most famous paintings of this period, *Cow's Skull: Red, White, and Blue*, painted in 1931, incorporated these bones. In the composition, the deathly white skull of a bull is positioned starkly on a rectangle of blue over a gray-white background; framed by a band of red running down both side edges, O'Keeffe's painting combines truly American elements.

Moves Permanently to the Southwest

After Stieglitz died in 1946 at the age of eighty-two, O'Keeffe returned to live in the Southwest.

She made her permanent home in Abiquiu, New Mexico, in 1949. From there she often travelled to visit Ghost Ranch, a remote vacation resort located several miles northwest of Espanola, New Mexico. The earthen colors—ocher, tan, and red—reflected from the New Mexico landscape to the huge canvasses she painted, both in Abiquiu and at Ghost Ranch. The simplicity of the region's landscape and its vast scale—with huge cliffs and large expanses of space—were also reflected in her work, which often utilized simple geometric shapes and large contrasts between light and shadow. Always based on something seen in the landscape, O'Keeffe's paintings (and watercolors, used in those instances when "I never had the time for oils") render form in an austere manner, eliminating details, reducing subjects to their essential components, strongly modelled and luminously colored.

"She turns sun-bleached skulls into icons for some unknown cult," Pomeroy comments on works of this period, which include *Blue River*, from 1935, and *Pelvis with Moon*, painted in 1943. "Hills heave and spread like bodies, high-altitude clouds could be ice floes in a thin blue sea. The architecture of the adobe is shown so pure in line as to vie with Mies or Mondrian." Hilton Kramer discusses O'Keeffe's work in the *New York Times Book Review* by noting that, "Like a good deal of American painting, O'Keeffe's take an essentially romantic view. . . . In contrast to earlier romantic styles, however, her own impulse has been to simplify and essentialize the forms . . . to reduce them to a few spare elements of color and light organized within a firm structure of drawing, and then to amplify what remains with a sort of ascetic grandeur. . . . The result is an art at once sensuous and detached—an art of organic forms and earthly light transformed into cool structures of exquisite color in which we may still discern the shape and texture and atmosphere of the observable world."

Published "Artistic" Life Story

From 1947 to 1949 O'Keeffe occasionally left her home in Taos to work on retrospective exhibitions from the Stieglitz estate for display in Manhattan's Museum of Modern Art; she also directed artistic installations of her late husband's life work for the Art Institute of Chicago. Although afraid of flying at first, the elderly artist gradually became

If you enjoy the work of Georgia O'Keefe, you may want to check out the work of the following artists:

The photography of Alfred Stieglitz, O'Keeffe's husband who often used her as a model.
The paintings of Russian artist Wassily Kandinsky, considered the father of abstract art.
The black-and-white photography of Ansel Adams, who visited O'Keeffe in New Mexico.

fascinated by the view above the clouds and painted several pictures, such as the *Sky above Clouds* series, painted between 1963 and 1965. These pictures seemed, at first glance, to be abstract paintings, until the viewer suddenly sees the outlines of meandering riverbeds, the geometric patterning of cultivated farmland, and the traceries of roadways, all of which serve as a backdrop for drifting clouds. As the years went by, O'Keeffe grew confident enough of the advances in air travel to attempt a world tour, which took her to Peru, Greece, and Paris among other places.

Juan Hamilton, a young potter, entered O'Keeffe's life in 1973. Out of work and looking for a job, he started as a handyman of sorts; he remained by the otherwise reclusive artist's side until her death years later, kindling in her an interest in sculpture which grew after her eyesight failed and she could no longer paint. While some biographers have hinted that a love relationship developed between the elderly painter and the young potter (he would inherit the bulk of her estate—as well as twenty-four of her paintings—which the I.R.S. valued at over $70 million), it was Hamilton who encouraged O'Keeffe to write her autobiography, *Georgia O'Keeffe* (1976), which was illustrated with photographs of her paintings. The artist was also prompted to set forth the facts of her life because she was tired of the misinformed interpretations critics were making about her paintings. "No one else can know how my paintings happen," she said in the book's opening passage. Eschewing the usual biographical data, the autobiography is a personal commentary on O'Keeffe's work, revealing her *artistic* rather than personal life. "Where I was born and where and how I lived is unimportant," she explains in the book's introduction.

"It is what I have done with where I have been that should be of interest."

Georgia O'Keeffe, which sold over 300,000 copies, was praised by many reviewers, not only for its fascinating manner of revealing one artist's way of seeing the world, but because of its illustrations. A *Washington Post Book World* critic found *Georgia O'Keeffe* "a wonderful book that is really worth what it costs, not only for the beautiful reproductions of Georgia O'Keeffe's paintings, but for the remarkable text she has written to explain herself as an artist; how many of these paintings came to be, and what they mean to her." "It's rare to have such commentary from an artist," he added, "but the lucidity, the exactness, the spare eloquence, the fine honesty of the writer give it the quality of a classic." Kramer, too, hailed *Georgia O'Keeffe* as a "beautiful book" describing a career "that embraces not one or another phase of [the] history [of U.S. modern art], but virtually the whole of it." "Naturally, we are eager to have more than she has given us," Kramer added, "but what she has given us is extraordinary. . . . Both the writing and the plates have the effect of renewing our appreciation of a very remarkable artist."

Interest in O'Keeffe's life and work rose sharply during the 1970s, a result not only of the publication of her autobiography but also of the women's movement then underway. Feminists hailed her as an icon—independent, self-sufficient, successful in a male-dominated culture; responding to the changing mood of a nation, President Gerald Ford awarded O'Keeffe the Medal of Freedom in 1977. O'Keeffe, it should be remembered, had adamantly resisted any attempts to label her a "woman artist"—in fact, she prohibited the publisher of the 1976 work entitled *Women Artists: 1550-1950* from reproducing any of her flower pictures in their volume. It is ironic, therefore, that it was as a woman artist that she was ultimately revered. In the decades since this reflowering of interest in her work occurred, O'Keeffe's canvasses have been eagerly hunted by collectors willing to pay a high price for an original painting; her flower paintings, in particular, have found their way to stationary, calendars, wall graphics, and other consumer goods; her image as a wrinkled, self-sufficient, lone woman standing amid the sunbaked landscape of New Mexico prefaces almost all accounts of her life and work, from biographies to museum catalogues of her paintings.

In 1983 O'Keeffe was honored by President Ronald Reagan as the first recipient of the National Medal of the Arts. While some critics have suggested that the artist's public persona was as carefully crafted by O'Keeffe as her paintings in an effort to continue her fame as an artist even into old age, with her death in 1986, she became part of the mythos of the twentieth century. O'Keeffe died in Santa Fe; her ashes were scattered over the sunbaked hills of her beloved New Mexico.

■ Works Cited

Abrahams, Edward, "The Image Maker," *New Republic*, January 30, 1989, pp. 41-45.

Review of *Georgia O'Keeffe*, *Washington Post Book World*, December 5, 1976.

Kramer, Hilton, review of *Georgia O'Keeffe*, *New York Times Book Review*, December 12, 1976.

O'Keeffe, Georgia, *Georgia O'Keeffe*, Viking, 1976.

Pomeroy, Ralph, essay in *Contemporary Artists*, St. James Press, 1996, pp. 859-60.

Tompkins, Calvin, interview with Georgia O'Keeffe in *New Yorker*, May 4, 1974.

■ For More Information See

BOOKS

Buckley, Christopher, *Blossoms and Bones: On the Life and Work of Georgia O'Keeffe*, Vanderbilt University Press (Nashville), 1988.

Castro, Jan Garden, *The Art and Life of Georgia O'Keeffe*, Crown (New York City), 1985.

Cowart, Jack, and Juan Hamilton, *Georgia O'Keeffe: Art and Letters*, National Gallery of Art (Washington, DC), 1987.

Eisler, Benita, *O'Keeffe and Stieglitz: An American Romance*, Doubleday, 1991.

Eldredge, Charles C., *Georgia O'Keeffe*, Abrams (New York City), 1991.

Eldredge, Charles C., *Georgia O'Keeffe: American and Modern*, Yale University Press (New Haven, CT), 1993.

Gherman, Beverly, *Georgia O'Keeffe: The Wideness and Wonder of Her World*, Atheneum (New York City), 1986.

Hoffman, Katherine, *An Enduring Spirit: The Art of Georgia O'Keeffe*, Scarecrow Press (Metuchen, NJ), 1984.

Hogrefe, Jeffrey, *O'Keeffe: The Life of an American Legend*, Bantam (New York City), 1992.

Lisle, Laurie, *Portrait of an Artist: A Biography of Georgia O'Keeffe*, University of New Mexico (Albuquerque), 1986.

Merrill, Christopher, and Ellen Bradbury, editors, *From the Faraway Nearby: Georgia O'Keeffe as Icon*, Addison-Wesley (Reading, MA), 1992.

Messinger, Lisa Mitz, *Georgia O'Keeffe*, Thames & Hudson (New York City), 1988.

Munro, Eleanor, *Originals: American Women Artists*, Simon & Schuster, 1982.

O'Keeffe, Georgia, interview with Katherine Kuh, in *The Artist's Voice: Talks with Seventeen Artists*, [New York City], 1962.

Patten, Christine Taylor, and Alvaro Cardona-Hine, *Miss O'Keeffe*, University of New Mexico Press (Albuquerque), 1992.

Peters, Sarah Whitaker, *Becoming O'Keeffe: The Early Years*, Abbeville Press (New York City), 1991.

Robinson, Roxana, *Georgia O'Keeffe*, Harper (New York City), 1989.

PERIODICALS

Art News, March, 1993, p. 59.
Nation, December 18, 1976.

Newsweek, November 22, 1976; October 30, 1977; January 8, 1979.
New Yorker, August 28, 1978.
People, February 12, 1979.
Reader's Digest, May, 1979.
Saturday Review, November 27, 1976; January 22, 1977.
Time, July 19, 1976; December 13, 1976; November 28, 1977.
Village Voice, December 13, 1976.
Vogue, November, 1977.
Washington Post Book World, May 11, 1980.

■ Obituaries

PERIODICALS

Chicago Tribune, March 8, 1986.
Los Angeles Times, March 7, 1986; March 10, 1986.
New York Times, March 7, 1986.
Time, March 17, 1986.
Times (London), March 10, 1986.
Washington Post, March 7, 1986.*

—*Sketch by Pamela L. Shelton*

Uri Orlev

in German concentration camp during World War II. *Military service:* Israeli Army, 1949-51. *Member:* Hebrew Writers Association.

■ Personal

Name originally Jerzy Henryk Orlowski; given name changed to Uri, 1945, surname changed to Orlev, 1958; born February 24, 1931, in Warsaw, Poland; son of Maksymilian (a physician) and Zofia (Rozencwaig) Orlowski; immigrated to Palestine (now Israel), 1945; married Erella Navin, 1956 (divorced, 1962); married Ya'ara Shalev (a dance therapist) November 19, 1964; *children:* Li (daughter; first marriage), Daniella, Itamar (son), Michael (second marriage).

■ Addresses

Home—Yemin Moshe, 4 Ha-berakhah, Jerusalem, Israel.

■ Career

Member of Kibbutz in Lower Galilee, Israel, 1950-62; writer, 1962—. Prisoner in Geto Warsaw and

■ Awards, Honors

Awards from Israeli Broadcast Authorities, 1966, for "The Great Game," 1970, for "Dancing Lesson," and 1975, for "The Beast of Darkness," and Television Prize, 1979, for youth program *Who Will Ring First?*; prize from Youth Alia, 1966, for *The Last Summer Vacation*; Prime Minister Prize (Israel), 1972, and 1989, for body of work; Ze-ev Prize from Israel Ministry of Education and Culture, 1977, and International Board on Books for Young People (IBBY) Honor List (Israel), 1979, both for *The Beast of Darkness*; Haifa University Prize for Young Readers, 1981; IBBY Honor List (Israel), 1982, *Horn Book* Books of 1984 honor list citation and American Library Association (ALA) Notable Book of the Year, both 1984, Sydney Taylor Book award, Association of Jewish Libraries, Mildred L. Batchelder Award, ALA, Edgar Allan Poe award runner-up, Mystery Writers of America, and Jane Addams Children's Book award Honor Book, Jane Adams Peace Association, all 1985, Silver Pencil Prize (Holland) for best book translated to Dutch, 1986, Honor award, Ministry of Youth, Family, Women and Health of the Federal Republic of Germany and West Berlin, 1987, and first recipient of Janusz Korczak International Literary Prize (Poland), 1990, all for *The Island on Bird Street;*

Television Prize, Broadcast Authorities for television script, 1990; Mildred L. Batchelder Award, ALA, 1992, for *The Man from the Other Side;* 1995 Honor Award, Jane Addams Peace Association and Women's International League for Peace and Freedom; Notable Children's Books citation, *Booklist,* and Mildred L. Batchelder Award, ALA, both 1996, both for *The Lady with the Hat;* Hans Christian Andersen Award, IBBY, 1996, for body of work.

■ Writings

IN ENGLISH TRANSLATION; FICTION

Hayale-oferet (adult novel), Sifriat Paolim, 1956, reprinted, Keter (Jerusalem), 1989, translation from the original Hebrew by Hillel Halkin published as *The Lead Soldiers,* P. Owen, 1979, Taplinger, 1980.

ha-I bi-Rehov ha-tsiporim, Keter, 1981, translation from the original Hebrew by Hillel Halkin published as *The Island on Bird Street,* Houghton, 1984.

Ish min ha-tsad ha-aher, Keter, 1988, translation from the original Hebrew by Hillel Halkin published as *The Man from the Other Side,* Houghton, 1991.

Lidyah, malkat Erets Yisra'el (based on the life of the Israeli poet Arianna Haran), Keter, 1991, translation from the original Hebrew by Hillel Halkin published as *Lydia, Queen of Palestine,* Houghton, 1993.

Hagueret Im Hamigbaat, Keter, 1990, translation from the original Hebrew by Hillel Halkin published as *The Lady with the Hat,* Houghton, 1995.

IN HEBREW; JUVENILE FICTION

The Beast of Darkness (also see below), Am Oved (Tel Aviv), 1976.

The Big-Little Girl, Keter, 1977.

The Driving-Mad Girls, Keter, 1977.

Noon Thoughts, Sifriat-Poalim (Tel Aviv), 1978.

It's Hard to Be a Lion, Am Oved, 1979.

The Lion Shirt, Givatayim, Massada, 1979.

Siamina, Am Oved, 1979.

The Good Luck Passy, Am Oved, 1980.

Granny Knits, Givatayim, Massada, 1980.

Mr. Meyer, Let Us Sing, Givatayim, Massada, 1980.

Wings Turn (short stories), Givatayim, Massada, 1981.

Big Brother, Keter, 1983.

The Dragon's Crown (science-fiction novel), Keter, 1985.

Journey to Age Four, Am Oved, 1985.

Shampoo on Tuesdays, Keter, 1986.

The Wrong Side of the Bed, Keter, 1986.

IN HEBREW; FOR ADULTS

Til Tomorrow (novel), Am Oved, 1958.

The Last Summer Vacation (short stories), Daga, 1966.

IN HEBREW; SCRIPTS

"The Great Game" (juvenile), Israel Broadcasting Authority, 1966.

"Dancing Lesson," Israel Broadcasting Authority, 1970.

"The Beast of Darkness" (juvenile), Israel Broadcasting Authority, 1975.

"Who Will Ring First" (juvenile), Israel Broadcasting Authority, 1979.

TRANSLATOR FROM POLISH TO HEBREW

Henryk Sienkiewicz, *In the Desert and Jungle,* Y. Marcus (Paris), 1970.

The Stories of Bruno Schulz, Schocken, 1979.

Janusz Korczak, *King Matthew I,* Keter, 1979.

Stanislaw Lem, *Eden,* Massada, 1980.

Stanislaw Lem, *Pirx the Pilot,* Schocken, 1981.

Stanislaw Lem, *The Invincible,* Schocken, 1981.

Janusz Korczak, *The Little Jack's Bankruptcy,* Hakibutz Hameuchad, 1985.

Kornel Makuszinski, *The Devil of the Junior Year,* Zmora-Bitan, 1990.

■ Sidelights

"Uri Orlev's life and works are a testimony to the indomitable spirit of childhood," writes Meena Khorana in her *Bookbird* article celebrating the Polish-born Israeli author's 1996 Hans Christian Anderson Award, the most prestigious of all international prizes given to an author for young people. Although Orlev writes in Hebrew, translations of his works, which include three adult novels and more than a dozen novels for children and young adults, have garnered him an admiring audience worldwide. The handful of his books available in English translation have won him numerous prizes, including three Mildred L. Batchelder awards for best foreign language book translated into English. When granting the Hans Christian Anderson Award, the prize jury commended Orlev's work, in a statement quoted by Khorana. "Whether his stories are set in the Warsaw Ghetto or his new country Israel," they observed, "he never loses the view of the child he was. His stories have integrity and humour, while his characters learn a loving, accepting attitude towards others—the lesson of how to accept being different in an alien world."

The alien world of which Orlev writes so eloquently in his novels is a nightmare realm of childhood memories of war-torn Poland. When Nazi leader Adolf Hitler became chancellor of Germany in 1933, the author was a toddler living in Warsaw, as yet unaware of his Jewish identity. In the years that followed, the true horror of Hitler's anti-Jewish policies became evident even to children as Jews living in Germany and then other countries occupied by the German army were forced to endure a multitude of injustices, including losing their jobs or their businesses because of their heritage. In 1939 Hitler's troops invaded Poland, marking the beginning of World War II and the onset of severe persecution of Polish Jews.

Orlev's family, like Jewish families throughout Poland, was forced to leave their home and move into a wall-enclosed section of the city, called the ghetto. There, the living accommodations were crowded, with food rationed and unemployment widespread. In an effort to eliminate the European Jewish population, the Germans soon built concentration camps, some with facilities for gassing inmates, and began mass deportations of the Jews out of the ghettos and into the camps. By the war's end, millions of Jews and other persons considered detrimental to German society had been killed in the camps and elsewhere. Although a child, Orlev was spared none of the brutality of the war; his mother was murdered by the Nazis and he and his brother and the aunt who cared for them spent nearly two years in a concentration camp at Bergen-Belsen, Germany.

The horrors of the war would ultimately give Orlev material for future writing projects, but his talent as a storyteller grew out of the awful, surreal existence of his childhood. When the realities of what was going on around him became too much for the boy, his imagination provided a refuge from the uncertainty of daily existence. In his *Something about the Author Autobiography Series* essay, Orlev describes how his imagination created a buffer between his feelings and reality as he and his relatives fled a burning building during the bombing of Warsaw. "Every now and then," he recalls, "we stopped to stare at the unbelievable sight of the large city burning in the quiet night, the flames lighting the lower half of the sky. It dawned on me that I was now living in a book myself." Being a character in a book somehow made the unbearable easier to bear. In a similar example, Orlev excuses himself for referring to episodes in his life that happened during the war as "adventures." "I talk about adventures," Orlev explains, "because that's how it seemed to me: I thought of myself as the hero of a thriller who had to survive until the happy ending on the book's last page, no matter who else was killed in it, because he was the main character."

Luckily for Orlev, fate provided the dreamed-of happy ending. Orlev's wartime experiences concluded in April 1945 when the U.S. Army rescued him, his brother, and his aunt from a train on which they had been placed at Bergen-Belsen by their German captors. Orlev and his relatives were among only 350 survivors of the 3000 Jews brought to the camp from Warsaw. After the war, with their mother dead and their father captured on the Russian front while serving in the Polish Army, Orlev and his brother were sent to Palestine with a group of other Jewish children whose relatives hoped for a better life there for their offspring. Both boys completed their education at a kibbutz, or farming collective, in their new home, and, after the State of Israel was created by a United Nations mandate in 1948, fulfilled their required service in the Israeli army. While Orlev's brother chose then to move to the United States, the author decided to stay in Israel. There he attempted to again write the poetry that he had begun to produce during the war, but, as he comments in *Twentieth-Century Young Adult Writers*, "When I tried to write poetry, I found that I was no longer able to. So I began to write stories, and later, books for adults. Not until I was forty-five did I write my first book for young people, *The Beast of Darkness*."

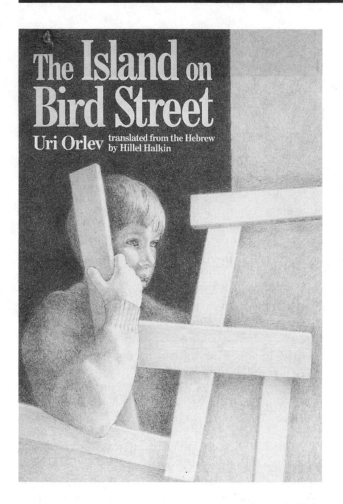

In this 1984 work, an eleven-year-old boy struggles to survive in a bombed-out Jewish ghetto during World War II.

The Horrors of War

While Orlev has become best known for his books for young people, his first novel as well as his first work translated into English, *The Lead Soldiers,* was aimed at adults. The story covered in the book is very close to being an autobiography. The protagonists are two Jewish boys, Yurik and his younger brother Kazik, who live in Warsaw during World War II. After their mother dies, the boys are cared for by their aunt. Eventually, the threesome end up in the concentration camp at Bergen-Belsen but survive the war and are saved from their German captors by members of the U.S. Army. Critics found the description of the war through the eyes of the children especially powerful. In the *New York Times Book Review* Leslie Epstein expresses his admiration for the novel, while presenting the belief that Orlev "used [the book] to teach himself his craft." The constant dialogue between the brothers, according to Epstein, "are the very tissue of the novel, and they secure for it, I think, a place in the gallery of holocaust literature only a little below that reserved for the finest portraits of children." In *New Statesman and Society* Victoria Neumark asserts: "*The Lead Soldiers* touches one of the most poignant stories of the Holocaust, the story of the butterflies children drew on the walls before they went into the gas chambers, keeping faith with their imaginary worlds in the optimism of a Stoic who can't see beyond the moment." A *Publishers Weekly* reviewer called the novel "an unforgettable story that makes its mark as literature."

Orlev's next novel to be translated into English is the acclaimed *The Island on Bird Street.* Like *The Lead Soldiers,* it too is autobiographical, but to a lesser degree. The story takes place in a Jewish ghetto, but not necessarily the Warsaw ghetto, during World War II. It follows the activities of eleven-year-old Alex, who is awaiting the return of his father from a labor camp. Alex must somehow manage to survive by himself in a bombed-out building on Bird Street, a street filled with vacant buildings. In the author's introduction to the novel, Orlev explains how Alex's hideaway is in many ways similar to the island on which Daniel Defoe's fictional hero Robinson Crusoe found himself. "[Alex] must survive by himself for many months," Orlev comments, "taking what he needs from other houses the way Robinson Crusoe took what he needed from the wrecks of other ships that were washed up on the beach. The difference is that Alex can't grow his own food, that he has to hide, and that he has no spring to get water from." Orlev also notes that while Alex has no man Friday to keep him company, he does enjoy the companionship of his pet mouse, who even helps to find him food. "And, yes," Orlev adds, "one more thing: Alex has hope."

The optimism that Neumark found in Orlev's *The Lead Soldiers* plays a major role in this novel as well. "The power of the book comes through Alex's unwavering hope," maintains Gary D. Schmidt in *Twentieth-Century Young Adult Novelists,* "his sense that he will do whatever it takes to survive and wait for his father." In his *Christian Science Monitor* review of the book, Randy Shipp also mentions "the thread of hope that runs throughout the book," making it stand out from other similar war stories. Orlev's ability to blend recollections of his own experiences with the fictional exploits of his hero garners praise from other reviewers of the work. "The physical details are fascinating," notes Zena Sutherland in *Bulletin of the Center for Children's Books*. The author's familiarity with the life he is writing about, according to Margery Fisher in *Growing Point*, gives "a stark reality" to the prose and allows him to let the reader enter "right into a boy's mind." "Drawing on his own World War II experiences as a child in the Warsaw ghetto," Kate M. Flanagan observes in *Horn Book*, enabled Orlev to produce "a first-rate survival story."

In Orlev's next work translated into English, *The Man from the Other Side*, the author again tells a story of a boy who must survive in a Polish ghetto during World War II. This time Orlev

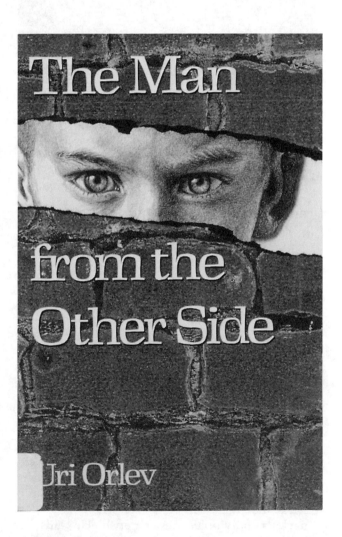

This 1991 novel tells the true story of a Polish journalist who grew up outside the Warsaw Ghetto.

brings to life a friend's story instead of drawing on his own background. In the prologue to the book, called "A Word about My Friend Marek," Orlev explains that the novel is a fictionalized version of the life of a Polish photojournalist whom he met in Israel. The photojournalist made Orlev promise not to tell his story publicly until after he was dead; the author wrote the novel after the man died in the crash of a Polish jetliner just months after their conversation. In *The Man from the Other Side*, Orlev presents the photojournalist as fourteen-year-old Marek, a boy who is finally deemed old enough to be of help to Antony, his stepfather. Antony smuggles food through the sewers of Warsaw to the Jews living in the ghetto. Marek dislikes Antony and wishes his father—who was killed in prison for being a communist—was still alive. One day Marek and two of his friends rob a Jew who has escaped from the ghetto. Marek's mother is enraged when she discovers what her son has done. Tearfully, she reveals to him that although he has not been raised a Jew, his biological father was Jewish. Marek is troubled by his mother's disclosure and he vows to make amends for his actions by giving his ill-gotten money to another Jew. Eventually, the boy befriends a Jew and ends up trapped in the Jewish ghetto during the uprising of 1943. Over the course of time, Marek finds his feelings towards his stepfather changing to admiration, and by the end of the story Marek agrees to let the man adopt him.

Many reviewers of *The Man on the Other Side* applaud Orlev's re-creation of Marek's story. "The scenes and dialogue come to life," Sue Rosenzweig maintains in *Voice of Youth Advocates*, "in a realistic portrayal of Marek's experiences and emotions." A *Kirkus Review* critic writes with special admiration of the characters Orlev develops in the book, calling them "sobering, believable blends." The reviewer also finds the book as a whole "subtle, beautifully crafted, altogether compelling." A *Publishers Weekly* reviewer in particular admires Marek, who is both Orlev's main character and his narrator, stating, "The voice of [the] 14-year-old narrator, Marek, would be gripping given any plot." Betsy Hearne in *Bulletin of the Center for Children's Books* and Dan Dailey in the *Five Owls* both highlight the gradual change in Marek's feelings towards Jews as well as the change in his relationship with his stepfather. "The sewers through which Marek travels," notes Hearne, "are a naturally apt metaphor for his journey through the under-world of self-knowledge." Putting even more emphasis on Marek's character development, Dailey praises Orlev's portrait "of the individual change of heart that is needed to erase prejudice, promote understanding, and foster cooperation and love in human affairs."

Stories of Survival

Like *The Man on the Other Side*, Orlev's next novel translated into English, *Lydia, Queen of Palestine*, is a retelling of a true story, in this case the life of Israeli poet Arianna Haran, whom Orlev met as a teenager. Like Marek, Lydia undergoes a change of heart in regard to her relationship with the adults in her life. "I was born in 1933 in Bucharest, Romania, and during the war I went to Palestine," Lydia summarizes her life in the first sentence of the novel. An only child, who seems to be alone much of the time, Lydia spends hours playing with her dolls in elaborate fantasy games in which she is the Queen of Palestine. When Lydia's parents begin to have marital difficulties and the child hears conversations between her mother and her grandmother about someone they call "That Woman," Lydia gives one of her dolls the same name and declares her an official enemy. She explains that even as a pre-schooler she knew—much like the Jews in the lands dominated by Hitler's armies—that "once you were an official enemy, anything could be done to you." "That Woman was my ugliest doll," she comments. "I liked to put her to death."

For Lydia, the break-up of her parents' marriage is much more devastating than any of the events of the war happening around her. Conditions in Romania for Jews worsen, however, so Lydia's mother decides to send her daughter to Palestine, where Lydia's father has already fled. There, Lydia lives on a kibbutz and eventually is reunited with her mother and father. While at first angry at them when she discovers they both have remarried, she learns to accept them. Now a spirited but thoughtful sixth grader, Lydia declares in an official ceremony with her dolls that both That Woman and That Man, her male counterpart, are no longer her enemies.

While Andrea Davidson in *Voice of Youth Advocates* describes Lydia as an "adult-sounding" child and doubts the book's interest for young adults, Mary M. Burns in *Horn Book* and Robin Tzannes

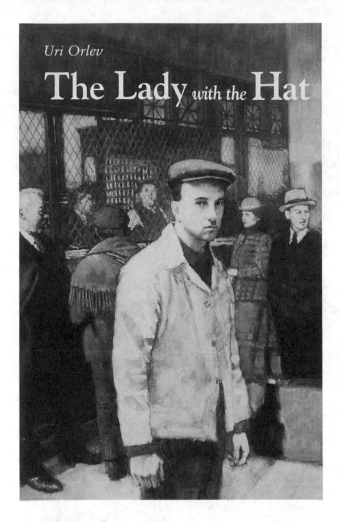

Uri Orlev

The Lady with the Hat

Finding his Polish homeland irrevocably changed after World War II, a young man tries to enter Palestine to begin a new life.

in the *New York Times Book Review* give Orlev high marks for his female creation. "Ingenious, self-confident, energetic, and bright, she is a force to be reckoned with—and a character no one can ignore," Burns writes of Lydia. "In Lydia," Tzannes maintains, "Mr. Orlev has created a real hero, one that wins our admiration but never our pity. Children will love her, will cheer her on in her battles and be uplifted by her triumphs." In all, the reviewer finds Lydia an "indomitable, free-spirited child, a genuine original." Schmidt, in *Twentieth-Century Young Adult Writers*, finds Lydia possesses, like characters from Orlev's other novels, characteristics that help her persevere where other less audacious individuals might perish. He calls her "manipulative, assertive, and dominant" and observes, "These are not qualities particularly useful on a kibbutz, but they are ones useful in surviving."

The Lady with the Hat, winner of the 1996 Batchelder Award, is another story of survival, but in several ways it is different from Orlev's previously translated works. Yulek, Orlev's main character in this novel, is older than the young protagonists encountered in either *The Lead Soldiers, The Man from the Other Side, The Island on Bird Street,* or *Lydia, Queen of Palestine.* In another contrast with those works, *The Lady with the Hat* deals with the post-war Jewish experience rather than the period of World War II itself. The novel begins two years after the end of the war when Yulek, whose family perished in concentration camps, decides to return to his former home in Poland. Once there, he finds another family living in the family house and all traces of the Jews eliminated. His only sense of hope comes when a former neighbor mentions that an Englishwoman in a hat had been looking for his family and him. Confused at first, Yulek realizes the woman must be his Aunt Malka, who had gone to England and married a British lord. As was the Jewish custom, his aunt's marriage to a Christian caused her to be pronounced dead by her conservative parents, and so Yulek's family and she had seldom had contact over the years. It had all happened so long ago, Yulek could not remember his aunt's married name, nor did he have any idea of how to get in touch with her.

The novel marks a departure from Orlev's typical straight-forward narration (deviated from only briefly in *The Lead Soldiers,* among his works in English translation). After the first couple of chapters of *The Lady in the Hat,* Orlev switches from Yulek's story to that of Lady Melanie Faulkner in her home in postwar London. Melanie, the reader learns, is actually Yulek's Aunt Malka and, as Yulek suspected, it had been she who was inquiring about his family in Poland. Throughout the rest of the story, the chapters alternate between Yulek's attempt to get into Palestine despite a British blockade around the area and Melanie's efforts to find her nephew after seeing his picture printed in a London newspaper article about young Jewish refugees. Melanie's encounters with holocaust survivors during her frantic search for Yulek causes her to examine her own Jewish identity and her relationship with her husband. Yulek, in the meantime, falls in love with Theresa, a Jewish girl brought up by a group of Catholic nuns

If you enjoy the works of Uri Orlev, you may also want to check out the following books and films:

Lois Lowry, *Number the Stars,* 1989.
Carol Matas, *Code Name Kris,* 1990.
Jane Yolen, *The Devil's Arithmetic,* 1988.
Schindler's List, Universal, 1993.

during the war, and stands by her as she similarly struggles to come to terms with her Jewish self. The novel ends with five letters written by important figures in the narrative, including Theresa, Yulek, and Melanie, telling how their experiences have changed their lives.

Several reviewers comment on the spirit of adventure present in the story, with Betsy Hearne in *Bulletin of the Center for Children's Books* comparing the events in the novel to a puzzle, stating: "there's suspense in the missing pieces. . . ." *Voice of Youth Advocates* contributor Bunni Union mentions other equally important elements of the work, noting, "A love story, a survival story, adventure, search and suspense all combine into the absorbing tale of a Holocaust survivor and his new friends and newfound relative." In *School Library Journal,* Marilyn Makowski compares *The Lady with the Hat* with *The Man from the Other Side* and maintains, "Both books go beyond the Jewish issues—they have non-Jewish characters who are crucial to plot development and who add balance." In this regard, *The Lady with the Hat* exemplifies the traits the Hans Christian Andersen Award jury praise so highly. While focusing on the Holocaust and its aftermath, Orlev creates characters who not only speak to Jewish readers as well as non-Jews but who also could move and act in a variety of scenarios. According to Khorana, in Orlev's works "readers . . . become aware of the duality of human beings: there are Germans who are good as well as Jews who betray, cheat, or rob. The humanity of Orlev's characters transcends the specifics of the historical situation."

■ Works Cited

Burns, Mary M., review of *Lydia, Queen of Palestine, Horn Book,* March, 1994, p. 200.

Dailey, Dan, review of *The Man from the Other Side, Five Owls,* May-June, 1991, pp. 104-5.

Davidson, Andrea, review of *Lydia, Queen of Palestine, Voice of Youth Advocates,* December, 1993, p. 297.

Epstein, Leslie, "Survivor's Story," *New York Times Book Review,* March 23, 1980, pp. 14, 31.

Fisher, Margery, review of *The Island on Bird Street, Growing Point,* May 1, 1985, p. 4435.

Flanagan, Kate M., review of *The Island on Bird Street, Horn Book,* April, 1984, pp. 197-98.

Hearne, Betsy, review of *The Man from the Other Side, Bulletin of the Center for Children's Books,* June, 1991, pp. 246-47.

Hearne, Betsy, review of *The Lady with the Hat, Bulletin of the Center for Children's Books,* June, 1995, p. 356.

Khorana, Meena, "Uri Orlev: Celebrating the Indomitable Spirit of Childhood," *Bookbird,* summer, 1996, pp. 6-8.

Review of *The Lead Soldiers, Publishers Weekly,* January 18, 1980, p. 130.

Makowski, Marilyn, review of *The Lady with the Hat, School Library Journal,* May, 1995, p. 122.

Review of *The Man from the Other Side, Kirkus Reviews,* May 1, 1991, p. 608.

Review of *The Man from the Other Side, Publishers Weekly,* May 31, 1991, pp. 75-76.

Neumark, Victoria, "Boiled Sweets," *New Statesman and Society,* July 6, 1979, p. 24.

Orlev, Uri, "Introduction" to his *The Island on Bird Street,* Houghton, 1984, pp. vii-xi.

Orlev, Uri, "A Word about My Friend Marek," in his *The Man from the Other Side,* Houghton, 1991, pp. 1-3.

Orlev, Uri, *Lydia, Queen of Palestine,* Houghton, 1993.

Orlev, Uri, author's comments in "Uri Orlev," *Twentieth-Century Young Adult Writers,* St. James Press, 1994, pp. 507-9.

Orlev, Uri, essay in *Something about the Author Autobiographical Series,* Volume 19, Gale, 1995, pp. 211-30.

Rosenzweig, Sue, review of *The Man from the Other Side, Voice of Youth Advocates,* October, 1991, p. 230.

Schmidt, Gary D., "Uri Orlev," *Twentieth-Century Young Adult Writers,* St. James Press, 1994, pp. 507-9.

Shipp, Randy, "Thread of Hope in Wartime Story," *Christian Science Monitor,* May 4, 1984, p. B4.

Sutherland, Zena, review of *The Island on Bird Street, Bulletin of the Center for Children's Books,* June, 1984, pp. 189-90.

Tzannes, Robin, "Audacity, Thy Name Is Lydia," *New York Times Book Review,* November 14, 1993, p. 60.

Union, Bunni, review of *The Lady with the Hat, Voice of Youth Advocates,* October, 1995, p. 222.

■ For More Information See

BOOKS

Children's Literature Review, Volume 30, Gale, 1993.

Contemporary Authors, New Revision Series, Volume 34, Gale, 1991.

Something about the Author, Volume 58, Gale, 1990.

PERIODICALS

Booklist, March 15, 1995.

School Library Journal, September, 1991.

Times Literary Supplement, February 22, 1985.*

—Sketch by Marian C. Gonsior

K. M. Peyton

■ Personal

Full name, Kathleen Wendy Peyton; also writes under name Kathleen Herald; born August 2, 1929, in Birmingham, England; daughter of William Joseph (an engineer) and Ivy Kathleen Herald; married Michael Peyton (a commercial artist and cartoonist), 1950; children: Hilary, Veronica. *Education:* Attended Kingston School of Art, 1947; Manchester Art School, Art Teacher's Diploma, 1952. *Hobbies and other interests:* Riding, walking in the mountains, airplanes, sailing, horseback riding, music.

■ Addresses

Home—Rookery Cottage, North Fambridge, Essex CM3 6LP, England.

■ Career

Northampton High School, Northampton, England, art teacher, 1952-56; writer, 1956—. *Member:* Society of Authors.

■ Awards, Honors

Carnegie Medal Commendations, British Library Association, 1962, for *Windfall,* 1964, for *The Maplin Bird,* 1965, for *The Plan for Birdsmarsh,* 1966, for *Thunder in the Sky,* 1967, for *Flambards,* 1969, for *Flambards in Summer,* and 1977, for *The Team;* American Library Association (ALA) Notable Books, 1963, for *Sea Fever,* 1967, for *Flambards,* 1969, for *Flambards in Summer,* 1971, for *Pennington's Last Term* and *The Beethoven Medal,* 1972, for *A Pattern of Roses,* and 1973, for *Pennington's Heir;* Horn Book Honor List, 1964, for *The Maplin Bird,* 1965, for *The Plan for Birdsmarsh,* 1973, for *Pennington's Heir,* 1975, for *The Team,* 1977, for *Prove Yourself a Hero,* and 1978, for *A Midsummer Night's Death.*

New York Herald Tribune Spring Book Festival Award Honor Book, 1965, for *The Maplin Bird;* Carnegie Medal, 1969, for *The Edge of the Cloud;* Boston Globe-Horn Book Award Honor Book, 1969, for *Flambards;* Child Study Association of America Children's Books of the Year selections, 1969, for *Fly-by-Night,* 1971, for *Pennington's Last Term,* 1974, for *Pennington's Heir,* and 1976, for *The Team;* Guardian Award, 1970, for the "Flambards" Trilogy; ALA Best Books for Young Adults selection, 1979, for *Prove Yourself a Hero;* School Library Journal Best Books of Spring selection, 1979, for *A Midsummer Night's Death.*

■ Writings

JUVENILES; UNDER NAME KATHLEEN HERALD

Sabre, the Horse from the Sea, illustrated by Lionel Edwards, A. & C. Black, 1947, Macmillan, 1963.

The Mandrake: A Pony, illustrated by Edwards, A. & C. Black, 1949.

Crab the Roan, illustrated by Peter Biegel, A. & C. Black, 1953.

JUVENILES

North to Adventure, Collins, 1958, Platt & Munk, 1965.

Stormcock Meets Trouble, Collins, 1961.

The Hard Way Home, illustrated by R.A. Branton, Collins, 1962, revised edition, Goodchild, 1986, published as *Sing a Song of Ambush,* Platt & Munk, 1964.

Windfall, illustrated by Victor Ambrus, Oxford University Press, 1962, published as *Sea Fever,* World Publishing, 1963.

Brownsea Silver, Collins, 1964.

The Maplin Bird, illustrated by Ambrus, Oxford University Press, 1964, World Publishing, 1965.

The Plan for Birdsmarsh, illustrated by Ambrus, Oxford University Press, 1965, World Publishing, 1966.

Thunder in the Sky, illustrated by Ambrus, Oxford University Press, 1966, World Publishing, 1967.

Flambards (first book in "Flambards" trilogy), illustrated by Ambrus, Oxford University Press, 1967, World Publishing, 1968.

(And illustrator) *Fly-by-Night,* Oxford University Press, 1968, World Publishing, 1969.

The Edge of the Cloud (second book in "Flambards" trilogy), illustrated by Ambrus, World Publishing, 1969.

Flambards in Summer (third book in "Flambards" trilogy), illustrated by Ambrus, Oxford University Press, 1969, World Publishing, 1970.

(And illustrator) *Pennington's Seventeenth Summer* (first book in "Pennington" trilogy), Oxford University Press, 1970, published as *Pennington's Last Term,* Crowell, 1971.

(And illustrator) *The Beethoven Medal* (second book in "Pennington" trilogy), Oxford University Press, 1971, Crowell, 1972.

(And illustrator) *A Pattern of Roses,* Oxford University Press, 1972, Crowell, 1973.

(And illustrator) *Pennington's Heir* (third book in "Pennington" trilogy), Oxford University Press, 1973, Crowell, 1974.

(And illustrator) *The Team,* Oxford University Press, 1975, Crowell, 1976.

The Right-Hand Man, illustrated by Ambrus, Oxford University Press (London), 1977, Oxford University Press (New York), 1979.

Prove Yourself a Hero, Oxford University Press, 1977, Collins World, 1978.

A Midsummer Night's Death, Oxford University Press, 1978, Collins World, 1979.

Marion's Angels, illustrated by Robert Micklewright, Oxford University Press, 1979, published as *Falling Angel,* Methuen, 1983.

The Flambards Trilogy (contains *Flambards, The Edge of the Cloud,* and *Flambards in Summer*), Puffin Books, 1980.

Flambards Divided, Oxford University Press, 1981, Philomel Books, 1982.

Dear Fred, Philomel Books, 1981.

Going Home, illustrated by Chris Molan, Oxford University Press, 1982, illustrated by Huck Scarry, Philomel Books, 1982.

Free Rein, Philomel Books, 1983, published as *The Last Ditch,* Oxford University Press, 1984.

Who, Sir? Me, Sir?, Oxford University Press, 1983.

Pennington: A Trilogy (contains *Pennington's Seventeenth Summer, The Beethoven Medal,* and *Pennington's Heir*), Oxford University Press, 1984.

Frogett's Revenge, illustrated by Leslie Smith, Oxford University Press, 1985, illustrated by Maureen Bradley, Puffin Books, 1987.

Downhill All the Way, Oxford University Press, 1988.

(And illustrator) *Plain Jack,* Hamish Hamilton, 1988.

Skylark, illustrated by Liz Roberts, Oxford University Press, 1989.

Darkling, Delacorte, 1989.

Poor Badger, illustrated by Mary Lonsdale, Doubleday, 1990, Delacorte, 1992.

The Boy Who Wasn't There, Delacorte, 1992.

(And illustrator) *Apple Won't Jump,* Hamish Hamilton, 1992.

The Wild Boy and Queen Moon, Doubleday, 1993.

(And illustrator) *The Swallow Summer,* Doubleday, 1996.

ADULT NOVELS

The Sound of Distant Cheering, Bodley Head, 1986.

No Roses Round the Door, Methuen, 1990.

Late to Smile, Methuen, 1992.

■ Adaptations

Flambards (television series), ITV (Yorkshire, England), 1976; *Going Home* (cassette), G.K. Hall,

1986; *The Right-Hand Man* was also adapted as a film, 1987.

■ Sidelights

The old, decaying turn-of-the-century hunting estate known as Flambards lay before twelve-year-old Christina after her long journey. Recently orphaned, the young girl finds herself living in an unfamiliar social world with relatives she does not know—her crippled Uncle Russell and her cousins, Mark, a strong hunter, and Will, who dreams of flying aeroplanes. This new world introduces Christina to what will become one of her life-long passions—horses—as well as to the man she falls in love with and eventually marries. Choosing Will over Mark, Christina and her husband-to-be leave Flambards and the dying class-driven society it stands for behind. The young couple elopes just before the start of World War I, and Will fulfills his dreams of becoming a pilot only to be killed during the war. Surviving this new tragic loss, Christina returns to Flambards as a twenty-one-year-old widow, heroically determined to give new life to the dying mansion, as well as to herself.

Within the pages of K. M. Peyton's Flambards trilogy, *Flambards, The Edge of the Cloud,* and *Flambards in Summer,* are showcased the young adult author's critically acclaimed skills: her accurate and powerful descriptions of physical activities and sensations, her detailed and realistic characterizations, and her perceptive narration of the social history of England. "It is clear that . . . Peyton's books deal with themes and interests of a rather wider and deeper kind than one finds in most children's books," maintains Dennis Butts in *The Use of English.* "The presence of death, the awareness of sexual love, the importance of money, give her novels an unusual texture for which their romantic structures provide a successful and accessible framework." Praising the author's storytelling abilities, Louis Claibourne asserts in *Spectator:* "Mrs. Peyton, you simply have to take my word for it, is what stumped reviewers call 'compulsively readable.' You *have* to turn the page, hear the next conversation, see the next bit of action." Peyton, contends M. S. Crouch in *Junior Bookshelf,* "is a born story-teller."

The first stories that emerged from Peyton's young imagination were born despite the suburban landscape into which she was born. Obsessed with horses from an early age, Peyton had to create her own imaginary horses because of the general lack of farm animals in her neighborhood. "Because of the dearth of real-life ponies in my childhood career, I had to make do with inventing imaginary ones, and this, I realize in retrospect, is what started my writing career," recalls Peyton in an essay for *Something about the Author Autobiography Series (SAAS).* "At least I never lacked for a vivid mental image: my bicycle was, in my mind, a liver chestnut hunter called Talisman. He carried me devotedly for miles in all directions, never putting a foot wrong. For the occasions when I went on foot, I chose one out of no less than two thousand horses that I had named and minutely described in several exercise books, and 'rode' accordingly, steadily if it was a youngster, with much gentling and soothing, or more wildly if it was of that nature, skittering in the gutters and galloping up the hills. In the evenings I wrote long tales about my invented ponies."

These stories were modeled after the numerous books Peyton checked out from the library, all of which included horses as part of the plot. "I knew all about pony-book heroines because I was an avid reader of the real thing," explains Peyton in *SAAS.* "My mother took me to the library every week, and while she chose her books I browsed in the children's section and borrowed pony books. Some I had out so many times I knew them by heart. My mother always tried to make me borrow different ones, but I wouldn't." Having had a difficult childhood, which included quitting school to work in an office and in her father's tobacconist shop at night, Peyton's mother always wanted her children to have a better start in life. And she knew that education was an important part of this, so she fought hard for Peyton and her brother to attend the best schools.

Among the schools Peyton attended was Wimbledon High School, which was halfway to London and six miles from home, requiring the young student to take the train every day. World War II was being fought at this time, and with the school being so close to London, Peyton and her classmates experienced many air raid disruptions during class, were on a train one morning that was machine-gunned by a German aeroplane, and left school one day to find the train station gone because of a bomb. "All this time I wrote books," remembers Peyton in *SAAS.* "I was never with-

A view of Peyton's yard—complete with ponies—in Essex, England.

out a current book on the go, although I always had a great deal of homework to do. I used to get very frustrated in the winter when we all had to huddle over the fire in one room, as coal was strictly rationed and the house was freezing. My father liked to play the radio, and although he respected silence while we did our homework, he didn't bother for my leisure activity, and I couldn't write with the radio on. Once I threw a pair of slippers at him in fury. That didn't go down very well."

An opportunity for Peyton to own a pony was also not well-received by her parents; they said no because the family had nowhere to keep it. Her friend Biddy, however, was able to take the pony Dolly Grey, so Peyton could still enjoy it. "Every Saturday morning I would ride my hunter/bike, Talisman, madly over to Biddy's, six miles away," Peyton relates in her autobiographical essay. "I felt that Dolly, by rights, was mine, but Biddy had a very bossy nature (and so did Dolly), so our threesome relationship was full of

ups and downs—literally." Among the many adventures Peyton and Biddy had with Dolly were Saturday shopping trips, a visit to Peyton's house, and a part in the school play for Dolly, during which she destroyed the shed roof and left a mess center stage. Sharing the pony led to a special friendship between the two young girls. "I loved going to her place and used to leave for home at the last minute to make the journey before it got dark," Peyton describes in SAAS. "I can remember pedalling madly along a stretch of dual carriageway, watching the huge red sun disappearing inexorably over the horizon, urging my hunter on with encouraging cries. My mother would be raging when I arrived in a collapsed heap at the front door."

Sweet Success at Sixteen

While she was enjoying her first real life pony, Peyton also wrote about fictional ones, sending every book she finished off to the publishers of her favorite readings. These manuscripts always came back, which Peyton expected, but she enjoyed the encouraging letters that were enclosed. "I never thought of becoming a writer, thinking it was just something one did in one's spare time," she explains in *SAAS*. "I intended to become a great artist, and all my endeavors in school were directed to going to art school." One of these art instructors suggested that Peyton try illustrating a book, and when the young writer said she would illustrate her current novel, the instructor asked to read it. Upon completion, she contacted Peyton's parents and urged them to type up the manuscript and send it to a publisher (no one knew of Peyton's own regular mailings to publishers). And so Peyton's parents gave the book to a neighbor who worked on a magazine in London, who in turn gave it to A. & C. Black.

Sabre, the Horse from the Sea was written the year that the war ended, when Peyton was fifteen; she was only sixteen when it became her first published novel. A London girl evacuated to the seaside is the main focus of the story; she leaves the war-torn city to find a beautiful grey thoroughbred and a young pilot who fights in the Battle of Britain. "I knew all about the Battle of Britain as a lot of it had happened over our heads, but I wasn't very good at plotting or plausibility," reveals Peyton in *SAAS*. "I killed off my young pilot as he got in the way at the end, taking too much of the responsibility of my heroine." Excited to have her first book published, Peyton was still determined to attend art school, even when her next book was published shortly after her first. At the same time, she enjoyed her last year at school and the peace and freedom brought on by the end of the war.

Following her first year at art school, Peyton was forced to transfer to the Manchester School of Art when her father was moved to this new location by his firm. Homesick for her friends and her old school, Peyton found solace in the nearby Pennines, the uplands of the Kinder Scout plateau. "I could find no one to go with so I went alone, sometimes cutting school on lovely autumn days and climbing up over the moors where the only sound was the rushing of the wind and the liquid, haunting cray of the curlew," describes Peyton in her autobiographical essay. "After my life in suburbia I was thrilled by this wild and lonely landscape." It was a common interest in the moors that brought Peyton and Mike, the ex-soldier who would become her husband, together.

Having met Mike at art school, Peyton soon discovered that he too spent his spare time exploring the countryside. "So, of course, I knew this was my sort of person, and we became friendly and began to spend our free time together," relates Peyton in *SAAS*. This new friendship evolved over the next three years, at which time Mike asked Peyton's father for permission to marry his daughter. In retrospect, Peyton describes the interview in *SAAS* as amusing: "My father asked him if he had any money, and he said no; a job?—no; any intention of getting a job?—no. Finally, my father asked when we wanted to get

This 1969 work is the second in the "Flambards" trilogy, set against the backdrop of World War I.

married, and Mike said, 'Next Saturday.' My mother had a fit but my father was amused and said we could get engaged if we liked, and wait and see what happened." Mike did not give Peyton the chance to wait, however, and the couple was married by the very next Saturday.

This marriage began a lifetime of travels and adventures for Peyton and her new husband, all of which served the author well by providing a continuous supply of new book ideas. "I have always felt that my marriage to Mike was very good for my development as a writer, for life has never been dull with him, and some of our adventures have given me great material," asserts Peyton in *SAAS*. Two daughters (and a number of sailboats) were eventually added to Peyton's family, and horses have also remained an important part of the author's life. "As writing is a sedentary occupation, I find the horses in my life make a wonderful balance," explains Peyton in *SAAS*. "Even the early morning chore of mucking out . . . is a

good physical start to the day, out in the cold and the rain, staggering to the muck heap with an overloaded wheelbarrow . . . it is far more stimulating to the brain than merely rolling out of bed to a cup of coffee by the fire before starting work."

The successful results of just such days of work can be found in Peyton's many young adult books, which include the author's popular Flambards series. It was the fiftieth anniversary of the First World War, as well as research done on early attempts of flying, that prompted Peyton to focus on the time period of 1912 to 1914. "I set the flying against the backdrop of Edwardian country life and a horsey (hunting) family, and, having been all at sea (in a literal sense) in my last five books, the joy of coming inland again and writing about my first love, the countryside— terra firma!—was very real," recalls Peyton in her autobiographical essay. "I never meant to write a sequel to *Flambards*, but after I finished it I felt

Peyton, a lover of the outdoors, walking in the Lake District.

so bereft that I could not leave the characters alone and approached my editor to see if I could write a sequel."

Two immediate sequels were published—*The Edge of the Cloud* and *Flambards in Summer*—followed several years later by *Flambards Divided,* the final book in the series. "While Peyton is enough of a realist to write about place in terms of the work that is done there, she is also enough of a romantic to create her most successful trilogy around a beautiful old country house, Flambards, and an orphaned heiress whose choices in marriage affect the fate of the house," points out Gwyneth Evans in an essay for *Twentieth-Century Young Adult Writers. Spectator* reviewer Leon Garfield also praises the settings and themes in Peyton's trilogy, writing that "the whole panorama of life at Flambards before and during the First World War is a major achievement in the genre of adolescent fiction. . . . Peyton's great skill in completing her spacious design leaves one with admiration and gratitude. Flambards and its inhabitants will be long remembered—and often revisited."

Pennington's Rebellion Begins

The critical and popular success of the Flambards series inspired Peyton to try her hand at a totally new subject matter. "I felt I was ready to turn to something quite different, something I thought might prove impossible: I decided to write the story of a very antisocial young thug," relates the author in *SAAS.* "I wanted to see if I could do something I knew nothing about, out of my imagination." And so the character of Patrick Pennington was created, a moody yet talented young man who excels at football, swimming, sailing, and playing the piano. The three novels that contain Penn's story, *Pennington's Seventeenth Summer, The Beethoven Medal,* and *Pennington's Heir,* begin with the humorous retelling of the somewhat reckless hero's last year at school. The following books are narrated by Ruth, the young woman who falls in love with Penn and eventually becomes pregnant and marries him. This relationship, as well as Penn's musical career and ever-increasing responsibilities, lend a more serious tone to the end of the young character's story.

"Penn is the most troubled and the most brilliant of all Peyton's characters, and his escapades, di-

This 1970 work begins Peyton's trilogy about a talented yet troubled young adult.

sasters, and triumphs are recounted with breathtaking excitement," asserts Evans. John W. Conner, writing in *English Journal,* similarly praises Peyton's characterization skills, concluding: "*Pennington's Last Term* will be read and reread by adolescents who search for a hero who sees life in their own terms. I urge adults to enjoy his adventures too!" Focusing on Penn's reckless side, Conner goes on to relate in his *English Journal* review of *The Beethoven Medal* that "Pat is what every adolescent sees and admires in his peers: a free spirit living a perilous existence because of adult-inspired regulations. . . . Human beings are a mass of contradictions. Mrs. Peyton has the considerable literary skill to portray this. She understands the emotional turbulence of adolescents and portrays this." A *Junior Bookshelf* contributor concludes in a review of *Pennington's Heir:* "Young readers will need no inducement to go back to the beginning of the Pennington story—and return to it many times. A masterly book."

Penn's wife Ruth, who provides much insight into her husband in the Pennington series, was not a new character for Peyton; she also appears in one of the author's earlier works—*Fly-by-Night.* In this classic English pony story, Ruth could be Peyton herself as a young girl; she struggles to save enough money to buy and train an unbroken pony. During the course of the story, she enters a new world when she is accepted into the Pony Club, and this world and its other inhabitants is examined again in Peyton's subsequent novels *The Team, Prove Yourself a Hero,* and *Free Rein.* The focus in these books is on wealthy Pony Club member Jonathan Meredith as he struggles to overcome the problems he experiences because of his overbearing and ambitious mother.

"That Peyton can write repeatedly about certain characters, such as Jonathan and Ruth, in very different situations and types of novels indicates both the vitality of the characters she has created and her versatility as a novelist," maintains Evans. This versatility is also evident in *Marion's Angels,* a story in which both Ruth and Penn reappear as secondary characters to Marion, a young girl who is dramatically changed by her mother's death. Devoted to her youthful father, Marion spends all of her time and energy trying to restore the village's decaying fifteenth-century church. When the church is used for a concert, Marion is enthralled with the playing of the young pianist, Penn, and she and her father grow close to him and his wife Ruth during their stay. So when a famous American violinist, who arranges a series of benefit concerts to save the church, invites Penn to accompany him back to the States, Marion is torn. She realizes this could be the end of the young couple's marriage, but the beginning of happiness for her father, who has fallen in love with Ruth.

Marion's Angels "is a book about architecture and music and human relationships, all tied up tightly together," describes a *Junior Bookshelf* reviewer, adding that "Peyton could clearly go on writing about Pennington and Ruth for ever; they are three-dimensional characters who will continue to grow and develop in response to inner convictions and external pressures. Marion and her father

---

If you enjoy the works of K. M. Peyton, you may want to check out the following books and films:

Patricia Harrison Easton, *Summer's Chance,* 1988.
Dick Francis's mystery novels, including *Whip Hand,* 1979, and *Comeback,* 1991.
Lynn Hall, *Flying Changes,* 1991.
Norma Fox Mazer, *After the Rain,* 1987.
Joyce Carol Thomas, *The Golden Pasture,* 1986.
The Black Stallion, United Artists, 1979.
Phar Lap, Twentieth Century-Fox, 1984.

Geoff are additions to the writer's gallery and they have this same quality." And a *Bulletin of the Center for Children's Books* contributor concludes that *Marion's Angels* "is one of Peyton's best: perceptive, beautifully constructed, serious in its concerns but lightened by a gentle humor, and outstanding in characterization and dialogue."

Just as the characters of Penn and Ruth have grown and changed throughout Peyton's novels, so has the author herself throughout her own writing career. Acquiring a share in her own race horse, for example, prompted Peyton to tackle this subject matter in her novels *Dear Fred* and *Darkling.* In *Dear Fred* thirteen-year-old Laura Keen is obsessed with the famous jockey Fred Archer and closely follows the events of his life. At the same time, she is growing older and maturing as events in her own life unfold. "Rich in emotion and scenic vigour, *Dear Fred* is the most satisfying novel for the young that I have read for a long time," asserts a *Growing Point* reviewer. *Darkling* also centers around horses, family situations, and first love. In this tale fifteen-year-old Jenny survives the eccentricities of her family while at the same time raising the difficult thoroughbred foal, Darkling, that her grandfather has given her. Jenny's growth into a mature young woman parallels the accomplishments of Darkling as he becomes a champion racing horse. "Peyton expertly creates the highs and lows of adolescent emotions," relates Charlene Strickland in *School Library Journal,* going on to conclude that *Darkling* is "typically Peyton and typically excellent storytelling."

Authentic portraits of young adults, including their actions and emotions, are the driving force of

Peyton's novels; her depth of characterization is what sets her apart. Evans concludes that Peyton's "greatest gift as an author for young adults . . . is the empathy with which she creates her characters, whether contemporary or from the past; while she retains a clear-sighted awareness of their limitations, she gives her often moody and difficult young people warm support in their determination to work out their own sense of what really matters in life."

■ Works Cited

Butts, Dennis, "Writers for Children: K.M. Peyton," *The Use of English*, Spring, 1972, pp. 195-202.

Claibourne, Louis, review of *The Beethoven Medal*, *Spectator*, November 13, 1971.

Conner, John W., review of *Pennington's Last Term*, *English Journal*, November, 1971.

Conner, review of *The Beethoven Medal*, *English Journal*, November, 1972.

Crouch, M.S., "Streets Ahead in Experience," *Junior Bookshelf*, June, 1969, pp. 153-59.

Review of *Dear Fred*, *Growing Point*, May, 1981, pp. 383-87.

Evans, Gwyneth, essay in *Twentieth-Century Young Adult Writers*, 1st edition, edited by Laura Standley Berger, St. James Press, 1994.

Garfield, Leon, review of *Flambards in Summer*, *Spectator*, November 1, 1969.

Review of *Marion's Angels*, *Bulletin of the Center for Children's Books*, March, 1980, pp. 139-40.

Review of *Marion's Angels*, *Junior Bookshelf*, April, 1980, pp. 87-88.

Review of *Pennington's Heir*, *Junior Bookshelf*, February, 1974.

Peyton, K.M., essay in *Something about the Author Autobiography Series*, Volume 17, Gale, 1994.

Strickland, Charlene, review of *Darkling*, *School Library Journal*, May, 1990, pp. 126, 128.

■ For More Information See

BOOKS

Children's Literature Review, Volume 3, Gale, 1978.
Something about the Author, Gale, Volume 15, 1979, Volume 62, 1990.

PERIODICALS

Bulletin of the Center for Children's Books, May, 1969, p. 148; November, 1971, p. 50; September, 1972, p. 14; February, 1979, p. 103; October, 1979, p. 36; March, 1982, p. 136; January, 1984, p. 95.

Growing Point, July, 1975, p. 2670; September, 1977, pp. 3158-61; January, 1983, pp. 4004-7; September, 1983, pp. 4131-35; May, 1990, pp. 5330-33.

Horn Book, December, 1969, p. 678; June, 1972, pp. 300-1; October, 1972, p. 475; April, 1980, pp. 177-78; September/October, 1990, pp. 608-9.

Junior Bookshelf, June, 1978, p. 159; August, 1984, pp. 178-79; August, 1986, pp. 145-46; June, 1996, p. 124.

Magpies, November, 1995.

New York Times Book Review, July 10, 1966, p. 38; May 28, 1967, p. 20.

School Library Journal, December, 1978, p. 63; January, 1980, p. 80; January, 1982, p. 90; March, 1983, p. 183; August, 1984, p. 86.

Times Literary Supplement, October 3, 1968, p. 1110; April 3, 1969, p. 354; October 16, 1969, p. 1199; October 30, 1970, p. 1258; December 5, 1975, p. 1454; July 15, 1977, p. 859; September 29, 1978, p. 1082; September 17, 1982, p. 1002; August 16, 1985, p. 910.

Voice of Youth Advocates, February, 1982, p. 36; August, 1982, p. 35; June, 1990, pp. 109-10.

Washington Post Book World, February 12, 1984, p. 10.*

—Sketch by Susan Reicha

Marjorie Kinnan Rawlings

■ Personal

Born August 8, 1896, in Washington, DC; died of a cerebral hemorrhage, December 14, 1953, in St. Augustine, FL; buried in Antioch Cemetery, Island Grove, FL; daughter of Frank R. (a patent attorney) and Ida May (Traphagen) Kinnan; married Charles A. Rawlings (a writer), May, 1919 (divorced, 1933); married Norton Sanford Baskin (a hotel owner), October, 1941. *Education:* University of Wisconsin, A.B., 1918.

■ Career

Young Women's Christian Association (Y.W.C.A.) National Headquarters, New York City, publicist, 1918-19; *Home Sector* (magazine), assistant service editor, 1919; newspaper writer with the *Louisville Courier-Journal*, Louisville, KY, and the *Rochester Journal*, Rochester, NY, 1919-23; United Features Syndicate, verse writer, 1925-27; author, 1931-53. Also owner and manager of a 72-acre orange grove in Florida. *Member:* National Academy of Arts and Letters (elected, 1938), Phi Beta Kappa, Kappa Alpha Theta.

■ Awards, Honors

Second place, *McCall's* Child Authorship Contest, 1912, for short story; second place, Scribner Prize Contest, 1931, for novella *Jacob's Ladder*; French Prix Femina Americana Award nomination, 1933, for *South Moon Under*; O. Henry Memorial awards, 1933, for short story "Gal Young Un," and 1946, for short story "Black Secret"; Pulitzer Prize for fiction, 1939, for *The Yearling*; LL.D., Rollins College, 1939; L.H.D., University of Florida, 1941; Newbery Medal Honor Book, 1956, for *The Secret River*; Lewis Carroll Shelf Award, 1963, for *The Yearling*; honorary degree, University of Tampa.

■ Writings

South Moon Under (novel), Scribner, 1933.
Golden Apples (novel), Scribner, 1935.
The Yearling (novel), illustrated by Edward Shenton, Scribner, 1938, illustrated by N. C. Wyeth, 1939, reissued with a study guide by Mary Louise Fagg and Edith Cowles, 1966.
When the Whippoorwill— (short stories; includes "Gal Young Un"), Scribner, 1940.
Cross Creek (autobiographical sketches), illustrated by Shenton, Scribner, 1942, new edition with introduction by Shirley Ann Grau, Time, 1966.
Cross Creek Cookery, illustrated by Robert Camp, Scribner, 1942, published in England as *The Marjorie Kinnan Rawlings Cookbook: Cross Creek Cookery*, Hammond, 1960.

Jacob's Ladder (novella), illustrated by Jessie Ayers, University of Miami Press, 1950.

The Sojourner (novel), Scribner, 1953.

The Secret River (novel), illustrated by Leonard Weisgard, Scribner, 1955.

The Marjorie Kinnan Rawlings Reader, edited with an introduction by Julia Scribner Bigham, Scribner, 1956.

Selected Letters of Marjorie Kinnan Rawlings, edited by Gordon E. Bigelow and Laura V. Monti, University Presses of Florida, 1983.

Short Stories by Marjorie Kinnan Rawlings, Roger L. Tarr, editor, University of Florida Press, 1994.

Author of syndicated column, "Songs of the Housewife," *Rochester Times-Union*, beginning 1926; contributor of short stories and articles to periodicals, including *New Yorker*, *Scribner's*, *Harper's*, *Atlantic*, *Collier's*, and *Saturday Evening Post*.

■ Adaptations

The Yearling was made into a film starring Gregory Peck and Jane Wyman by Metro-Goldwyn-Mayer (MGM), 1946; the 1948 MGM movie *The Sun Comes Up* was based on several of Rawlings's stories; "Gal Young Un" was adapted for film in 1980; *Cross Creek* was made into a film by Universal in 1983. A musical play version of *The Yearling* was written by Herbert E. Martin, Lore Noto, and Michael Leonard in 1973. A reading of *The Yearling* by David Wayne, Eileen Heckart and Luke Yankee is available on record and cassette from Caedmon; *Marjorie Kinnan Rawlings Short Stories* is available on cassette from Book Three Voices, 1995.

■ Sidelights

If Marjorie Kinnan Rawlings's name is remembered today it is because of her beloved 1938 children's novel, *The Yearling*. This classic tale about a boy and his pet deer won the Pulitzer Prize for fiction and made her a national celebrity. *The Yearling* is still read and enjoyed, more than a half century later. Although her most productive years were already over when she died in 1954, Rawlings's was still one of America's most beloved authors. An obituary in the *New York Times* lauded her as a literary figure on the rank of playwright Eugene O'Neill and poet Dylan Thomas, both of whom had also died recently.

Rawlings's writings, the *Times* obituary concluded, were "notable contributions to Americana." That assessment has proved valid, for literary historians now regard Rawlings as one of America's most interesting and important regional writers.

Marjorie Kinnan was born and raised in Washington, D.C., but spent a lot of time at the family's dairy farm in nearby Maryland and summers at her maternal grandparents' farm in Michigan. Years later, writing in her semi-autobiographical book *Cross Creek* (1942), Rawlings would recall the rural summers she and her brother Arthur enjoyed as some of her happiest times. Frank and Ida Kinnan were loving parents, but from the beginning young Marjorie enjoyed a special relationship with her father. She was a voracious reader and loved to write. By age six Marjorie was already scribbling stories. In 1907, at age eleven, she won a $2 prize in a *Washington Post* short story contest, and during her junior year at Western High School in Washington, she won a $75 second-place prize in a *McCall's* literary competition.

Marjorie Kinnan's idyllic childhood ended abruptly in 1913, when her father died from a kidney infection. "The loss of her father was the first deep tragedy and greatest betrayal in [her] young life," biographer Elizabeth Silverthorne writes in *Marjorie Kinnan Rawlings: Sojourner at Cross Creek*. "She remembered always 'the great and terrible stillness' that seemed to cover the earth on the day he died." Arthur Kinnan had been friends with prominent Washington politicians, one of whom was Wisconsin senator Robert La Follette. Kinnan so admired La Follette's progressive politics that he decided his children should attend the University of Wisconsin. Thus, following her husband's death, Ida Kinnan moved the family to Madison, Wisconsin, where in 1914 Marjorie enrolled at the university as an English major. Among her teachers was William Ellery Leonard, a well-known poet and critic. Leonard saw Kinnan's literary talents and encouraged her. One of her poems was included in an anthology entitled *Poets of the Future*, and she worked on the yearbook and campus literary magazine. It was through her involvement in the latter that she met and fell in love with classmate Charles ("Chuck") Rawlings, another would-be writer.

Upon graduating in 1918, Marjorie Kinnan moved to New York City, finding work as a YWCA publicist. In May of 1919, she and Chuck got married. The newlyweds found jobs as newspaper reporters at the Louisville *Courier-Journal.* They stayed two years, then moved to Rochester, New York, Chuck's hometown. He found work there as a sports reporter, while she wrote freelance articles and worked for an arts magazine called *5 O'clock.* Marjorie also put her poetic talent to work for the *Times-Union,* her husband's employer, when she created a syndicated series of light and humorous verses under the heading, "Songs of the Housewife." Years later, Rawlings told reporter Robert van Gelder in the *New York Times Book Review,* that her work as a journalism "sob-sister" was "a rough school," but "So long as you can avoid the stereotyping pattern, you learn a lot when you put down what people said and how they acted in great crises in their lives. And it teaches you objectivity."

Despite Rawlings's journalistic successes, her short stories continued to be rejected by magazine editors. Adding to her woes, her marriage was in trouble. Following a 1928 spring vacation in Florida, the couple decided to make a clean start. Marjorie used some money left to her by her mother as the down payment on a 74-acre orange farm. The rundown property was located in the sparsely settled "scrub country" at Cross Creek, Florida, about twenty miles southeast of Gainesville. From the beginning, Marjorie Rawlings felt a kinship with the people and the land, which she would describe in her book *Cross Creek* as having "an ancient and special magic." California State English professor Victor Lasseter, writing in the *Dictionary of Literary Biography,* has observed that "Like . . . Thoreau's move to Walden Pond, Rawlings's move [to rural Florida] allowed a literary concentration she might not have found in the city."

Initially, at least, the change of locale did nothing for Rawling's literary career. A novel she wrote went unpublished, and she still had no luck selling short stories. Finally, she told van Gelder, she began jotting down impressions of the life at Cross Creek, having resolved if she was going to write she should concern herself with her own experiences. Rawlings eventually crafted this material into a series of eight literary sketches she called "Cracker Chidlings: Real Tales from the Florida Interior"—"crackers" being a local term for the poor white residents of rural Florida. Gordon E. Bigelow, one of Rawlings's biographers, noted in *Frontier Eden: The Literary Career of Marjorie Kinnan*

Rawlings, that she began writing about the Crackers because they "appealed powerfully to her imagination and allowed her romantic sensibilities fullest exercise." Rawlings herself described them in a letter to a friend as "people of dignity . . . aloof," but "friendly and neighborly."

First Sales Spur Career

In March 1930, the editor of *Scribner's* magazine wrote to say he liked "Cracker Chidlings" and was willing to pay $150 for the story. He also asked Rawlings for some biographical information. She responded that the early years of her writing career were not important. "They are a shadow, against the satisfying substance that is our life in the heart of the Florida hammock," she told him in a letter. In some ways, Rawlings was right, for it was not until she settled at Cross Creek that she found the inspiration to create successful fiction. Legend has it she had vowed that if her "Cracker Chidlings" story was rejected she would quit writing forever. Though it's a good story, biographer Silverthorne says it is untrue; Rawlings had a self-described "incurable itch" to write and at this point in her life could never have stopped.

"Cracker Chidlings" attracted a lot of attention when it appeared in the February 1931 issue of *Scribner's,* not all of it favorable. Some locals reacted angrily to Rawlings's depiction of Cracker life. The editor of the Ocala *Evening Star,* for example, attacked the story as "libel against the citizens of Florida." Rawlings's fiery temper got the better of her, and in an angry letter she defended what she'd written. Furthermore, she said, she planned to write a lot more about the Crackers and to travel in the Florida wilderness, "where, alas, my dear sir, I am never likely to meet you."

True to her word, Rawlings next effort was a novella-length Cracker story she called "High Winds." The editor of *Scribner's* passed it along to Maxwell Perkins of Charles Scribner's and Sons publishing. Perkins, the legendary editor who harnessed the creative energies of such writers as Ernest Hemingway and F. Scott Fitzgerald, was a shrewd judge of literary talent. He thought Rawlings's story had promise and sent her several suggestions; one was that she give her story a happy ending. When Rawlings made the changes, her story was published in *Scribner's*

Jody Baxter discovers an abandoned fawn in this N. C. Wyeth illustration from *The Yearling*.

April 1931 issue. "Jacob's Ladder," as it was re-titled, is a tale about a young cracker couple whose love helps them overcome adversity. The story was a vital step in Rawling's literary development; as Rodger L. Tarr, the editor of *Short Stories by Marjorie Kinnan Rawlings*, noted in the introduction to that book, "much of the realism found in her portrayal of remote Florida in 'Jacob's Ladder' [later] found its way into her Pulitzer Prize-winning novel *The Yearling*."

Perkins began urging Rawlings to write a novel set in rural Florida. The idea excited her, for as she told him in a letter, she was "vibrating with material like a hive of bees in a swarm." But almost as important to Rawlings as the creative encouragement she received was the $700 she earned for "Jacob's Ladder." The money was badly needed. The Rawlingses had discovered putting their orange groves back into production was more costly and time-consuming than they had imagined. What's more, unlike his wife, Chuck Rawlings remained frustrated in his efforts to write fiction. As the frequency and intensity of the Rawlingses' quarrels increased, their marriage unraveled; Marjorie sought solace in her writing.

Scribner's published several more of her cracker stories, although one entitled, "Gal Young 'Un," appeared in two parts in the June and July issues of rival *Harper's* magazine. That story, which won Rawlings a reputation as an astute observer of the female experience, tells of a lonely middle-aged cracker widow named Mattie. When she gets involved with a no-good bootlegger, he uses and abuses her before she summons the courage to throw him out. "Rawlings's message is clear," Tarr observed, "those who sacrifice their dignity lose their identity. In the end, however, justice triumphs." Interestingly, *Scribner's* had rejected "Gal Young 'Un" because of its supposed bias *towards* men. Tarr viewed the story differently, describing it as "Rawlings at her best and most feminist." Other readers evidently agreed; "Gal Young 'Un" won the $500 first prize in the prestigious O.Henry Memorial Short Story contest for 1932.

Rawlings sold a few more stories to *Scribner's* before acting on Perkins's suggestion that she write a novel. To make her story as authentic as possible, Rawlings went to live in the scrub country with a cracker family. During the next ten weeks, she lived as her hosts did—hunting, fishing and learning all she could about moonshining.

When Rawlings returned to Cross Creek in mid-October 1931, she did so with "voluminous notes of the intimate type, for which the most prolific imagination is no substitute," as she told Perkins in one of her letters.

Out of Rawlings's experiences came the novel *South Moon Under* (1933). The title comes from a cracker expression describing the night sky when the moon is "under" the earth; that is supposedly the time when game are most active. *South Moon Under* is the story of a young cracker moonshiner who kills a cousin who betrays him to authorities. Perkins liked the book, although he shared Chuck Rawlings's opinion that the obscenities in the dialogue should be deleted in order to broaden the potential readership. Rawlings scoffed at the idea, telling Perkins in a letter that if she conceded, *South Moon Under* could be the first in a series of "The Rover Boys in Florida" books. Rawlings insisted the book be published as written. "If you like [it], I shall drink a quart of Bacardi [rum] in celebration," she wrote Perkins. "If you don't like it, I shall drink a quart of Bacardi."

Despite the salty language, *South Moon Under* was chosen as one of the Book of the Month Club selections for March 1932, and it received excellent reviews. Hirschell Brickell of *Books* termed the novel "a deftly handled piece of fiction," while Percy Hutchison of the *New York Times* praised it as "distinguished art." Foreign critics, no less impressed, nominated the book for the 1933 French Prix Femina Americana Award. It mattered not to Rawlings that the book did not win. "Prizes are relative, don't matter," she wrote Perkins. "All that does is coming as close as the limitations allow to re-creating the thing that stirs me." The only review for *South Moon Under* that really mattered to Rawlings was one given by Leonard Fiddia, the young cracker who had been the model for the book's moonshiner character. "You done a damn good job, for a Yankee," he told her.

Unfortunately for Rawlings, general release of her novel was delayed until early 1933. The very day it hit the stores was the same day President Franklin D. Roosevelt declared a bank holiday in an effort to halt a run on withdrawals caused by the deepening depression. With people preoccupied with that crisis, only about 10,000 copies of *South Moon Under* were sold; Maxwell Perkins felt the number should have been at least 100,000.

Gregory Peck was nominated for an Academy Award for Best Actor and Claude Jarman, Jr., received a special Oscar as outstanding child actor in this highly-praised 1946 film version of Rawling's classic tale of family love, *The Yearling*.

This was not Rawlings's only setback in 1933. After years of unhappiness, she and her husband Chuck separated that spring. Their divorce, finalized on November 10, left Rawlings more relieved than happy. "The first five years [of marriage] I cried; the next five I fought; the last four years I didn't give a damn," Silverthorne quoted her as telling a girlfriend. The divorce settlement left Rawlings broke. The $5,000 she earned in royalties from *South Moon Under* went to legal fees, taxes, and farm bills. The one "luxury" Rawlings bought was an indoor bathroom in the farmhouse at Cross Creek; she dreaded encountering snakes on her nocturnal visits to the outhouse. The day the $500 prize from the O. Henry short story competition arrived, Rawlings pantry was bare except for a tin of biscuits and one can of tomato soup.

Through all her personal problems, Rawlings continued to write. Her second novel appeared in the fall of 1935. *Golden Apples* was about two young cracker orphans, Luke and Alie Brinley, and their relationship with Richard Tordell, an ill-tempered young Englishman who's exiled to Florida in the nineteenth century. While the book's sales were encouraging, the reviews were mixed. Mary Ross of *Books* praised *Golden Apples* as a more ambitious novel than *South Moon Under*, one she felt proved "Mrs. Rawlings's ability to handle a more swiftly-moving and intricate web of emotion." A reviewer in the *Nation* described *Golden Apples* as "trite and quite harmless," and though Percy Hutchison of the *New York Times* felt the story was "honest, tender [and] enlightening," the critic also lamented the author had failed "to draw her many threads together and make a finished ending to her narrative." According to Silverthorne, Rawlings herself was disappointed with *Golden Apples*, dismissing it as "interesting trash, not literature."

It was now, with two novels to her credit, that Rawlings attempted the big novel Maxwell Perkins had been urging on her from the start of their working relationship—a story about a boy growing up in the Florida scrub country. What Perkins had in mind was character who was a cross between Mark Twain's *Huckleberry Finn* and Rudyard Kipling's *Kim*. "Do you realize how calmly you sit in your office and tell me to write a classic?" Perkins biographer A. Scott Berg reported Rawlings asking the editor in one of her letters. At one point, she threw away her first draft of the long book—because it was "sappy," Silverthorne quoted her as saying—and started all over again. Achieving the lofty goal Perkins had set for her was a daunting task and Rawlings "sweat blood," as she put it, in the long months she labored on the book, which was now called *The Yearling*.

An American Classic

Rawlings's efforts paid off. When the novel was published on April 1, 1938, critics hailed it as a modern American literary classic; that is an opinion most literary scholars still share. Set in northern Florida just after the Civil War, *The Yearling* recounts one year in the life of a sensitive twelve-year-old boy named Jody Baxter. During that year, Jody participates in a bear hunt, witnesses a devastating flood, sees a close friend die, and helps his father recover from a near-fatal rattlesnake bite. He also experiences the beauty of his surroundings and adopts an orphaned fawn, which he names Flag. When the pet cannot be restrained from eating the family's precious corn crop, it has to be killed. Jody himself must fire the final shot, an action that is his "final crossing from childhood to adulthood," according to Reese Danley Kilgo in the *Dictionary of Literary Biography*. Reviewer William Soskin of the *New York Herald Tribune Book Review* lauded *The Yearling* as "one of the most exquisite [stories of its kind] I have ever read." Lloyd Morris of the *North American Review* declared that the book vaulted Marjorie Kinnan Rawlings into a place "among our most accomplished writers of fiction."

Rawlings's treatment of timeless themes—human endurance, love, and beauty—struck a chord with readers young and old alike in a nation that by 1938 had suffered through nearly a decade of depression. *The Yearling* was the Book of the Month Club's main selection for April 1938, and

it shot to the top of the best-seller lists, staying there for several weeks. More than 60,000 copies were sold in the first sixty days after publication; and over the next two years, sales topped a half million. What's more, MGM studios purchased the movie rights to the book for $30,000, and it was awarded the Pulitzer Prize for fiction. Rawlings's life would never be the same again; after so many lean years, she had achieved fame and fortune with one novel. Asked by a reporter if she intended to travel around and become "the darling of the bookshops," Elizabeth Silverthorne recorded that Rawlings replied, "Hell, no, I'm going back to Cross Creek where people don't give a damn!"

Perkins followed up on the success of *The Yearling* with a collection of Rawlings's short stories entitled, *When the Whippoorwill—* (1940). Among the eleven selections in the volume were "Jacob's Ladder" and "Gal Young 'Un," two of Rawlings's best stories. Sales of the book and reviews of it were good. L. B. Salomon in the *Nation* praised *When the Whippoorwill—* as "a distinguished collection, with each story a gem." A reviewer for *Atlantic* magazine wrote, "[Rawlings] is one of the two or three *sui generis* storytellers we have, and we'd better thank God for her."

At Perkins's insistence, Rawlings now began working on a nonfiction book that enabled her to utilize her storytelling gift and to write in what Bigelow, writing in *Frontier Eden*, termed "the precarious idyllic tone she had sought in *The Yearling*." The result was *Cross Creek* (1942), a semi-autobiographical account of Rawlings's life in rural Florida. As expected, the book appealed to readers who had enjoyed *The Yearling*, and *Cross Creek* was a great success. Some enthusiastic critics even hailed Rawlings as the "female Thoreau." Reviewer Rose Feld of *Books* described *Cross Creek* as "Deeply honest and engaging," and Katherine Woods of the *New York Times* stated the book was filled with "beauty and laughter and poignancy and truth." Even so, Silverthorne noted that Rawlings was unhappy with *Cross Creek*, feeling many of the chapters fell short of what she had hoped to achieve.

Personal Woes

A few months after publication of *Cross Creek*, Scribner issued *Cross Creek Cookery*, a book of Rawlings's favorite regional recipes—cooking having long been one of the passions of Rawling's life. In some ways, these two books were a summation of her thirteen years in rural Florida, for on October 27, 1941, Rawlings had married Norton Sanford Baskin, a hotel and restaurant manager from St. Augustine. Thereafter Rawlings, who at age forty-five was already in declining health, spent much of her time in town with her husband. Rawlings was also upset by a libel action launched by a Cross Creek neighbor named Zelma Cason, who was upset at the way she'd been portrayed in Rawlings's book. Cason sought $100,000 in damages. The case pitted neighbor against neighbor and left Rawlings feeling depressed and hurt. What little creative energy she had virtually dried up when war with Japan broke out and her husband joined the American Field Service as an ambulance driver. With Norton overseas, Rawlings found it impossible to work. "Part of the trouble is that I cannot get my mind off the war in general and Norton in particular," Rodger Tarr quoted her as telling a friend in a letter.

Rawlings, always a staunch patriot, also supported the war effort by joining such prominent people as scientist Albert Einstein, publisher Bennett Cerf, and playwright Moss Hart in an organization called the Pledge Committee of the Writers War Board. However, her good intentions were soured when she became involved in an ugly controversy that arose when as part of her Board activities she wrote a 150-word sketch on a war theme. Rawlings provided an anecdote that spoke to the need for an end to racial inequality in America. When the syndicate distributing the anecdotes to newspapers rejected Rawlings's submission as too "controversial," she angrily refused to offer another.

The four years of war were a fallow period for Rawlings. Apart from a few short stories she wrote for the *New Yorker*, she produced little. Her ongoing health problems were worsened by heavy drinking. Yet even though she was not writing much, Rawlings remained in the public eye. In May 1946, the Cason libel action came to trail, with the jury finding for the plaintiff "on principle." Rawlings was ordered to pay $1 in damages, plus $1,000 of Cason's legal costs. Her own legal bills over the five-and-a-half years it took the case to make its way through the courts was another $18,000. While the total amount of money Rawlings spent defending herself was not incon-

---

If you enjoy the works of Marjorie Kinnan Rawlings, you may want to check out the following books and films:

Berlie Doherty, *White Peak Farm*, 1990.
Barbara Hall, *Dixie Storms*, 1990.
The works of John Steinbeck, including *Tortilla Flat*, 1935, *The Red Pony*, 1937, *Of Mice and Men*, 1937, and *The Grapes of Wrath*, 1939.
Mark Twain's *The Adventures of Tom Sawyer*, 1876, and *The Adventures of Huckleberry Finn*, 1884.
Old Yeller, Disney, 1957.

---

sequential, according to Elizabeth Silverthorne the real cost in terms of her emotional and physical health was incalculable, and "may have been a factor in her early death."

In the spring of 1947 Rawlings wrote a six-part serialized novella for the *Saturday Evening Post* entitled, "Mountain Prelude." MGM, which had produced a popular movie based on *The Yearling*, hired Rawlings to write a screenplay based on her story. In the end, the studio rejected her script and had it rewritten by another writer under a new title. An angry Rawlings vowed to have nothing more to do with Hollywood. Instead she again turned her attentions to a novel called *The Sojourner*, which she had been struggling with for more than ten years. The death of Maxwell Perkins in June 1947, not long after the conclusion of the Cason libel trial left Rawlings emotionally drained. She had difficulty writing, and it was only with a major effort that she finished *The Sojourner*, which she wrote in a house she had bought in the village of Van Hornesville in upstate New York.

The Sojourner, the only one of Rawlings's books set outside Florida, was a generational saga about a family from New York's Hudson River valley. Reviewers were disappointed by the book. Riley Hughes of *Catholic World* said it was an "astonishingly inept and wooden parable." Louis Bromfield of *Saturday Review* wrote that while it was "a good novel," *The Sojourner* "never quite attains the fire and feeling of the author's *The Yearling*. . . ." *The Sojourner* was the last book Rawlings wrote. She was stricken with a brain aneurism on the evening of December 12, 1953, and died the next day. She was fifty-seven.

Interest in Marjorie Kinnan Rawlings's writings did not end with her death. Two years later, in 1955, Scribner published a children's story called *The Secret River*, which she had written in 1947. The following year, Scribner issued an anthology entitled *The Marjorie Rawlings Reader*. Both books found favor with reviewers, as did the *Selected Letters of Marjorie Kinnan Rawlings* (1983) and *Short Stories by Marjorie Kinnan Rawlings* (1994), which were published at the University of Florida, where Rawlings's collected papers are archived.

Summing up Rawlings's career, Victor Lasseter wrote in *Dictionary of Literary Biography*, "Mar-jorie Kinnan Rawlings is more than a children's writer and more than a regionalist." Noting such works as "A Crop of Beans" and *Jacob's Ladder*, he declared that she "belongs to the tradition of such writers as John Steinbeck, Eudora Welty, and William Faulkner." Christian H. Moe, discussing the author in *Twentieth-Century Young Adult Writers*, stated that Rawlings "is a pastoral writer of percipience and power all of whose stories—besides her memorable *The Yearling*—can be enjoyed by young people."

■ Works Cited

Review of *When the Whippoorwill—*, *Atlantic*, June 30, 1940.

Berg, A. Scott, *Max Perkins: Editor of Genius*, Pocket Books, 1978.

Bigelow, Gordon E., *Frontier Eden: The Literary Career of Marjorie Kinnan Rawlings*, University Presses of Florida, 1966.

Bigelow, Gordon E., and Laura V. Monti, *Selected Letters of Marjorie Kinnan Rawlings*, University Presses of Florida, 1983.

Brickell, Hirschell, review of *South Moon Under*, *Books*, March 5, 1933, p. 5.

Bromfield, Lewis, review of *The Sojourner*, *Saturday Review*, January 3, 1953, p. 9.

Feld, Rose, review of *Cross Creek*, *Books*, March 15, 1942, p. 1.

Review of *Golden Apples*, *Nation*, December 25, 1935, p. 750.

Hughes, Riley, review of *The Sojourner*, *Catholic World*, March 1953, p. 471.

Hutchison, Percy, review of *South Moon Under*, *New York Times*, March 5, 1933, p. 7.

Hutchison, Percy, review of *Golden Apples*, *New York Times*, October 6, 1935, p. 3.

Kilgo, Reese Danley, *Dictionary of Literary Biography*, Volume 22: *American Writers for Children, 1900-1960*, 1983, pp. 282-85.

Lasseter, Victor, "Marjorie Kinnan Rawlings," *Dictionary of Literary Biography*, Volume 102: *American Short Story Writers, 1910-1945, Second Series*, pp. 248-253.

"Marjorie Kinnan Rawlings," *New York Times*, December 16, 1953, p. 34.

Moe, Christian H., "Marjorie Kinnan Rawlings," *Twentieth-Century Young Adult Writers*, edited by Laura Standley Berger, St. James Press, 1994.

Morris, Lloyd, "New Classicist," *North American Review*, autumn, 1938, p. 179.

Rawlings, Marjorie Kinnan, *Cross Creek*, Scribner, 1942.

Ross, Mary, review of *Golden Apples*, *Books*, October 6, 1935, p. 6.

Salomon, L. B., review of *When the Whippoorwill—*, *Nation*, June 8, 1940, p. 715.

Silverthorne, Elizabeth, *Marjorie Kinnan Rawlings: Sojourner at Cross Creek*, Overlook Press, 1988.

Soskin, William, "A Tom Sawyer of the Florida Scrub Lands," *New York Herald Tribune Books Review*, April 3, 1938, pp. 1-2.

Tarr, Rodger L., *Short Stories by Marjorie Kinnan Rawlings*, University of Florida Press, 1994.

van Gelder, Robert, "A Talk with Marjorie Kinnan Rawlings," *New York Times Book Review*, November 30, 1941.

Woods, Katherine, review of *Cross Creek*, *New York Times*, March 15, 1942, p. 1.

■ For More Information See

BOOKS

Bellman, Samuel I., *Marjorie Kinnan Rawlings*, Twayne, 1974.

Bigelow, Gordon E., *Frontier Eden: The Literary Career of Marjorie Kinnan Rawlings*, University of Florida Press, 1966.

Contemporary Authors, Volume 137, Gale, 1992.

Dictionary of Literary Biography, Volume 9, *American Novelists, 1910-1945, Part 2*, Gale, 1981.

Duke, Maurice, Jackson R. Bryen, and M. Thomas Inge, *American Women Writers: Biographical Essays*, Greenport Press, 1983, pp. 366-371.

Sammons, Sandra W., and Nina McGuire, *Marjorie Kinnan Rawlings and the Florida Crackers*, Tailored Tour Publications, 1995.

Twentieth-Century Literary Criticism, Volume 4, Gale, pp. 362-369.

PERIODICALS

New York Times Book Review, February 1, 1953.
Publishers Weekly, January 31, 1994, p. 25.

■ Obituaries

PERIODICALS

Newsweek, December 28, 1953.
Saturday Review, January 16, 1954.
Time, December 28, 1953.*

—Sketch by Ken Cuthbertson

Pamela F. Service

■ Personal

Born October 8, 1945, in Berkeley, California; daughter of Forrest Leroy (a dentist) and Floy (maiden name, Flemming) Horner; married Robert Gifford Service (a professor), July 8, 1967; children: Alexandra Floyesta. *Education:* University of California, Berkeley, B.A., 1967; University of London, MA, 1969. *Politics:* Democrat. *Religion:* Methodist. *Hobbies and other interests:* Acting, hiking, camping, canoeing.

■ Addresses

Home—419 North Washington, Bloomington, IN 47408.

■ Career

Writer. Indiana University, Bloomington, IN, art museum publicist, 1970-72; Monroe County Museum, Bloomington, IN, curator, beginning 1978; antique shop expert. Bloomington City Council, member, 1979—.

■ Awards, Honors

Honor Book, Golden Kite Awards, Society of Children's Book Writers and Illustrators, 1988, for *The Reluctant God.*

■ Writings

Winter of Magic's Return, Atheneum, 1985.
A Question of Destiny, Atheneum, 1986.
Tomorrow's Magic, Atheneum, 1987.
When the Night Wind Howls, Atheneum, 1987.
The Reluctant God, Atheneum, 1988.
Stinker from Space, Scribner, 1988.
Vision Quest, New York, Atheneum, 1989.
Wizard of Wind & Rock (children's picture book), illustrated by Laura Marshall, Atheneum, 1990.
Under Alien Stars, Atheneum, 1990.
Being of Two Minds, Atheneum, 1991.
Weirdos of the Universe, Unite!, Atheneum, 1992.
Stinker's Return, Scribner, 1993.
All's Faire, Fawcett, 1993.
Phantom Victory, Scribner, 1994.
Storm at the Edge of Time, Walker, 1994.
The Ancient African Kingdom of Kush (nonfiction; "Cultures of the Past" series), Marshall Cavendish, forthcoming.

Contributor to *Isaac Asimov's Science Fiction Magazine.* Author of a short story in a collection edited by Josepha Sherman, *Orphans of the Night.* Also author of a history column, *Bloomington Herald Times,* 1980—.

■ Work in Progress

A nonfiction book on Mesopotamia, for Marshall Cavendish; several fiction projects, including a story set in Indiana about high school students and the occult.

■ Sidelights

One night in the late 1980s, author Pamela Service sat down with anticipation (and snacks) to watch a science fiction movie on television. But soon after it began, Service realized that the movie would disappoint her. It had the same, tired old plot: aliens enter the bodies of humans to take over the world, but no one notices! Disgusted, Service began to think about what would happen if, instead of inhabiting human bodies, visiting aliens inhabited the bodies of animals. Service kept thinking about her idea, and after she and her family encountered a "large, odoriferous skunk," she developed the story which would become her most popular novel: *Stinker from Space*. The book, according to Betsy Hearne of *Bulletin of the Center for Children's Books*, is a "first-class, funny science fantasy that will hook middle-grade readers right from the first scene."

After the publication of *Stinker from Space* in 1988, Service did not intend to write a sequel. Encouraged by the letters of children asking "what happens next?" and requests from a publisher, Service wrote a sequel: *Stinker's Return*. This 1993 book, commented Hearne of *Bulletin of the Center for Children's Books*, is "fast-moving and lots of fun." What began as an attempt to poke fun at dull science fiction is now a gift to children who, like Service as a child, will not read unless they can get a hold of something engaging and fun.

Service's books, as she explains, are difficult to categorize. Some are mysteries involving the supernatural. Others, in which time travel, magic, and aliens are found, may be better described as science fiction or fantasy. Many of her works are based in one or more carefully researched settings. Most draw on her interests, which include politics, archaeology, Egyptology, and theater. Critics have lauded Service's integration of history, myth and original plots, her imagined future worlds, her sense of humor, and her ability to create suspense. According to Don D'ammassis of *s.f. chronicle*, Service can be counted among the "very few high

In this suspenseful sequel to *Winter of Magic's Return*, three teenagers are busy assisting King Arthur in his attempts to reunite what is left of Britain after nuclear destruction five hundred years earlier.

quality writers" of science fiction for young people.

A Reluctant Young Reader

Service loved to tell stories as a child, but she did not think about becoming a writer. She did not start reading until she was in the third grade, and even then, she read with difficulty. (Later, she learned that she was dyslexic.) Since reading was such a chore for Service, she read only those stories which captured her imagination. Fantasy, science fiction, unreal stories, and weird, offbeat tales kept her entranced, and kept her reading. Service loved science fiction novels, but her parents did not care for them. She found much easier access to science fiction through the medium of television, which seemed "safer" to her parents. Service also began to enjoy historical fiction as a child. Like science fiction, Service pointed out to *Authors and Artists for Young Adults* (*AAYA*), historical fiction presents "a world that doesn't exist and that you can't live in." One of her favorite books of this genre was *Mara: Daughter of the Nile,* by Eloise Jarvis McGraw. This book stirred Service's interest in Egypt and the Nile river.

Service watched science fiction shows like *The Twilight Zone* and *Star Trek.* (Although she doesn't watch much television these days, she still considers herself a "*Star Trek* enthusiast.") Television was not only "significant" for Service because it opened windows "to a lot of different worlds" and to things she "wouldn't have confronted" herself, it influenced her visual approach to writing. "I'll find myself creating a scene in my head

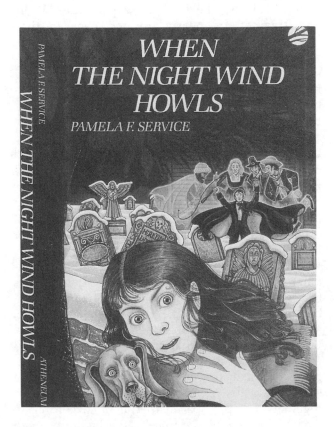

Service drew on her knowledge and love of theater to create this mystery novel about two friends who see ghosts at a local theater.

and then describing it," like "trying to describe" a movie there, she revealed.

In college, Service studied government inside as well as outside the classroom. She earned her bachelor's degree in political science while the famous free speech movement at Berkeley was in high gear. Service recalled that when the university forbade political and social organizations—from Republican and Democrat clubs to Christian fellowship and anti-nuclear groups—"we got upset." Service, along with Robert Service, the young man she married after graduation, served as members of the steering committee for free speech. They helped organize mass strikes and rallies which garnered nationwide attention and set a precedent for college protests in the United States.

After four years of studying politics and engaging in political activism, Service was "a little bit disillusioned." She decided she would like to study people long dead instead. In graduate school, Service indulged her love of archaeology and Egypt. At the University of London, she earned a master's degree in Egyptian history. When her husband, who had earned a degree in Mongolian language, history and culture, found graduate work at Indiana University, they moved to Bloomington, where they have lived ever since (with the exception of some time in Germany).

Service began work at the art museum at the university, as a publicist. As she once told *Something about the Author* (*SATA*), it was at this point in her life that she "spent bits of spare time writing stories, the sort of stories I enjoyed reading then or would have as a child. Mostly they were science fiction and fantasy with a sprinkling of political and historical fiction." Although Service's first attempts to get her work published failed, she kept working and submitting stories. Finally, in 1978, the same year she began to work for the Monroe County Museum as a curator, *Isaac Asimov's Science Fiction Magazine* bought one of her stories.

Service was encouraged, but she continued to receive rejection letters. She found herself with less time to write, especially after she won a seat on the Bloomington City Council in 1979. "Then in 1983," she once explained to *SATA*, "I ran for reelection to the City Council. I won my seat but lost my bid among my colleagues to be elected

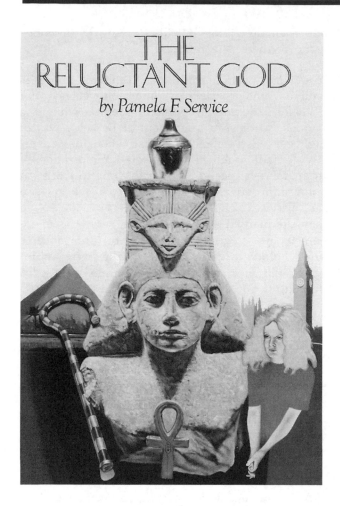

THE RELUCTANT GOD

by Pamela F. Service

This 1988 novel tells the story of a teenage girl who helps an Egyptian boy, buried alive 4000 years ago, find an urn stolen from his tomb.

Council President. In a huff I decided that if they didn't want me devoting my time to them, I'd just try writing another book. This time I had an idea that really excited me and I decided to try what was for me a new technique: I'd outline the story first rather than launching into a vague concept and expecting inspiration to carry me somewhere worth getting. It worked! In 1984 came the first acceptance letter."

Reviving Arthur

Although it was slow in coming, Service also received notice that she was to become a published novelist. *Winter of Magic's Return*, her first book, is set in a bleak and dreary post-nuclear holocaust Britain. The region is recovering from a five-hundred-year nuclear winter, and three teenagers in a boarding school (one of whom is really Merlin the magician) begin a mission to wake up the sleeping King Arthur in Avalon. Heather, Welly, and Earl (Merlin) make their way through war-torn kingdoms and confront mutants along the way. According to Holly Sanhuber of *School Library Journal*, Service's "action-filled plot and finely drawn characters will hold readers." A critic for *Booklist* found the "incorporation of the Merlin-Arthur-Morgana myth is smoothly realized" and Service provides "a fresh bridging of the post-nuclear debacle and high fantasy genres." "Service does an excellent job in establishing setting and her writing style is fluid," wrote a *Bulletin of the Center for Children's Books* critic.

Tomorrow's Magic, Service's third novel, continues the story of *Winter of Magic's Return*. The three teenagers are now busy assisting King Arthur in his attempts to civilize and govern what was Britain. In the process, they continue to battle Morgan La Fey, who wants to govern the land for her own purposes. Merlin comes to terms with his power, and Heather deals with her own magical talents. The book is suspenseful—"Welly and Heather are nearly trapped back in time on the day of the nuclear devastation," as a critic for *Booklist* noted. In the words of Ann A. Flowers of *Horn Book*, *Tomorrow's Magic* contains "humorous episodes and the excitement of hairsbreadth escapes and quick-witted magical confrontations."

Unlike her first and third novels, Service's second novel, *A Question of Destiny*, is set in contemporary America, in the middle of an election year; it is built on Service's understanding of American politics and her own experiences at presidential conventions as well as her imagination. Teenager Dan Stratton's father is a presidential candidate. When Dan suspects that one of his father's campaign staff advisors is hiding something, he checks his background and confronts him. The staff member finally admits that he is an alien in disguise, and that he wants Dan's father to win the election because he advocates environmentalism and the responsible use of technology. The alien especially wants to prevent earthlings from exploring space; Dan, his friend Carla, and the alien work together to stop a space experiment. According to Ann A. Flowers of *Horn Book*, "the highly charged atmosphere of the political campaign and convention and the science-fiction aspects of the story make for good adventure."

Born of Service's love of the theater, the mystery novel *When the Night Wind Howls* concerns the supernatural occurrences in a small town in Indiana. During the beginning of this novel, Sidonie Grant and her friend Joel think they've seen ghosts at the local theater; by the novel's end the pair have helped the theater groups' leading man win back his soul from the devil. *When the Night Wind Howls*, according to a critic for *Booklist*, is "spooky . . . Service's ability to create suspense keeps the pages turning." Like *When the Night Wind Howls, Phantom Victory* is another mystery set in the midwestern United States—South Bass Island in Ohio. Terri and Brian are led by ghosts to a treasure, and they save an old hotel at the same time. What makes this mystery rise "above

Jason Sikes, a boy who wants to rid Earth of its new Tsorian rulers, unexpectantly finds himself working with Aryl, a Tsorian warrior and the daughter of a Tsorian commander, to save the Earth's future.

most of the genre," asserted Carolyn Phelan of *Booklist*, is "its strong evocation of place" and "the past." Margaret Mary Ptacek of *Voice of Youth Advocates* concluded that *Phantom Victory* is a "winning and well written tale" and a "definite buy."

Travels through Time

The Reluctant God draws on Service's love of Egypt and archaeology, and her experience excavating in the Nile Valley. Its protagonist, Lorna, is helping her father, an archaeologist, on a burial site in Egypt. She finds Prince Ameni, the son of Pharaoh Senusert II, alive and hiding in a tomb; he voluntarily had himself buried alive 4000 years before to protect his people. But Ameni must return to the surface of the earth when an urn is stolen from the tomb, and Lorna travels with him to England to get it back from the thieves. "Because this tale is well written one is willing to suspend disbelief and enjoy the adventure," explained Susan H. Williamson of *Voice of Youth Advocates*. Kimberly Olson Fakih and Diane Roback of *Publishers Weekly* reported that "Service creates an impressive picture of daily life in Egypt at the time of the Pharaohs." Ironically, after accepting the Golden Kite Award for *The Reluctant God*, Service finally met Eloise Jarvis McGraw, the author of *Mara: Daughter of the Nile*—which had sparked her interest in Egyptology years before.

Many of Service's novels—like *Vision Quest* (in which a young woman communicates with long-dead Native Americans), *Weirdos of the Universe, Unite!* (in which a group of self-proclaimed weird teens find adventure with mythological beings), *Being of Two Minds* (in which a teen shares her mind with another)—involve time travel or the merging of minds across time and space. Similarly, *Storm at the Edge of Time*, set in the Orkney Islands of Scotland ("a marvelously dramatic place," explained Service) is a time-slip story full of fantasy, magic, and even space ships. Jamie, a girl from contemporary times, wanders into a circle of stones and slips into time with another teen (an ancient Viking) and a half-alien, half-human from a future, colonized earth. All three are descendants of a powerful "druid-type" being looking for a "significant magical thing that has been displaced," in each of the three different times in which the descendants were born, Service explained to *AAYA*, and because of this "the fate of

Pamela F. Service
Author of *Stinker from Space*

Though they live across the world from each other, they can read each other's minds and maybe save each other's lives....

BEING OF TWO MINDS

"An unusual idea sets the scene, and the plot moves quickly to a satisfying end." *School Library Journal*

FAWCETT JUNIPER

Connie Henricks, a typical American teenager, and Prince Rudolph, a teenage prince from a small European country, are able to exchange minds and souls with each other.

the universe is at stake." "From the opening paragraph Service grabs the reader . . . the story is fast paced and intriguing," commented Catherine M. Dwyer of *Voice of Youth Advocates.*

Throughout her career as a writer, Service has maintained her interest in archaeology and activism in politics. She has served as a delegate in two national presidential conventions. In 1996, she began her seventeenth year (fifth term) in the Bloomington City Council. There, she has developed a reputation as an advocate of tenants' rights, environmental causes, slow growth, and de-

velopment restrictions. In the mid-1990s, however, her determination to halt rampant development interfered with her work as a curator. When she voted against a project in which a major donor to the museum was involved, she had to leave the museum. Service now works part-time in an antique shop using the skills she developed as a curator.

If you enjoy the works of Pamela Service, you may want to check out the following books and films:

Lois McMaster Bujold, *The Warrior's Apprentice,* 1986.
Anne McCaffrey, *Pegasus in Flight,* 1990.
Gary Paulsen, *Canyons,* 1990.
Robert Silverberg, *Letters from Atlantis,* 1990.
Raiders of the Lost Ark, Paramount, 1981.
Phenomenon, Touchstone Pictures, 1996.

Service spends time with her family and indulges her love for acting and theater at the same time. "We do a lot of acting in community theatre groups," she stated, where they perform Shakespeare, comedy, and drama. Service, her husband, and their daughter Alexandra each take a part in the same play, so they can be together as they rehearse and talk about the play around the dinner table. Service told *AAYA* that she usually takes a small role, because she has so little time. Her favorite roles include Romeo in *Romeo and Juliet* (the cast Romeo dropped out, and she took up the part!) and the "vile villain" in an original Victorian melodrama.

With fifteen books to her credit and more on the way, Service is in a good position to advise aspiring writers. She told *AAYA* that "the best way to learn to write is to write." She thinks that writing courses can be helpful, especially for the "nitty gritty." If she'd taken such courses she thinks she may not have suffered such a long delay between the time she began writing and the time publishers began to accept her work. Service believes that it is also important for aspiring writers to keep in mind that they are always in the midst of a learning process. They must be willing "to make change and make revisions," and learn to look at their work with a critical eye. According to Service, writing "is a continual learning process"—she is still learning. Finally, encouraged Service, "continue to have faith in yourself and hang in there . . . keep writing, hoping, and submitting."

■ Works Cited

D'ammassis, Don, review of *Vision Quest* and *Stinker from Space, s.f. chronicle,* October, 1989, p. 45.

Dwyer, Catherine M., review of *Storm at the Edge of Time, Voice of Youth Advocates,* February, 1995, p. 351.

Fakih, Kimberly Olson, and Diane Roback, review of *The Reluctant God, Publishers Weekly,* March 11, 1988, p. 105.

Flowers, Ann A., review of *A Question of Destiny, Horn Book,* May/June, 1986, p. 334.

Flowers, Ann A., review of *Tomorrow's Magic, Horn Book,* January, 1988, p. 74.

Hearne, Betsy, review of *Stinker from Space, Bulletin of the Center for Children's Books,* March, 1988, pp. 144-45.

Hearne, Betsy, review of *Stinker's Return, Bulletin of the Center for Children's Books,* June, 1993, pp. 329-30.

Phelan, Carolyn, review of *Phantom Victory, Booklist,* May 15, 1994, p. 1679.

Ptacek, Margaret Mary, review of *Phantom Victory, Voice of Youth Advocates,* February, 1995, p. 341.

Sanhuber, Holly, review of *Winter of Magic's Return, School Library Journal,* December, 1985, p. 94.

Service, Pamela, interview with Ronie-Richele Garcia-Johnson for *Authors and Artists for Young Adults,* Volume 20, Gale, 1997.

Something about the Author, Volume 64, Gale, 1991, pp. 180-82.

Review of *Tomorrow's Magic, Booklist,* October 15, 1987, p. 400.

Review of *When the Night Wind Howls, Booklist,* June 15, 1987, pp. 1607-8.

Williamson, Susan H., review of *The Reluctant God, Voice of Youth Advocates,* June, 1988, p. 97.

Review of *Winter of Magic's Return, Booklist,* October 1, 1985, p. 269.

Review of *Winter of Magic's Return, Bulletin of the Center for Children's Books,* November, 1985, pp. 56-57.

■ For More Information See

PERIODICALS

Booklist, May 1, 1992, p. 1603.

Bulletin of the Center for Children's Books, May, 1989, p. 236.

Publishers Weekly, April 14, 1989, p. 69.

School Library Journal, May, 1986, p. 110; April, 1987, p. 113.

Voice of Youth Advocates, February, 1992, p. 387.*

—*Sketch by Ronie-Richele Garcia-Johnson*

Mary Shelley

■ Personal

Born August 30, 1797, in London, England; died of complications from a brain tumor, February 1, 1851, in Bournemouth, England; buried in the churchyard of St. Peter's Bournemouth; daughter of William (a philosopher and writer) and Mary (a writer; maiden name, Wollstonecraft) Godwin; married Percy Bysshe Shelley (a poet), December 30, 1816 (died, 1822); children: first child, a daughter (died in infancy), William (died, 1819), Clara Everina (died, 1818), Percy Florence. *Education:* Educated at home.

■ Career

Novelist, essayist, critic, and editor. Following the death of her husband, devoted herself to full-time writing to support herself and her surviving son.

■ Writings

Mounseer Nongtongpaw; or, The Discoveries of John Bull in a Trip to Paris, Juvenile Library, 1808.

History of Six Weeks' Tour through a Part of France, Switzerland, Germany, and Holland, with Letters Descriptive of a Sail round the Lake of Geneva, and of the Glaciers of Chamouni, with contributions by Percy Bysshe Shelley, Hookham, 1817.

Frankenstein; or, The Modern Prometheus (novel), three volumes, Lackington, Hughes, Harding, Mavor, & Jones, 1818, revised edition, one volume, Colburn & Bentley, 1831, two volumes, Carey, Lea, & Blanchard, 1833.

Valperga; or, The Life and Adventures of Castruccio, Prince of Lucca (novel), three volumes, Whittaker, 1823.

(Editor) Percy Bysshe Shelley, *Posthumous Poems of Percy Bysshe Shelley,* Hunt, 1824.

The Last Man (novel), three volumes, Colburn, 1826, two volumes, Carey, Lea, & Blanchard, 1833.

The Fortunes of Perkin Warbeck (novel), three volumes, Colburn & Bentley, 1830, two volumes, Carey, Lea, & Blanchard, 1834.

Lodore (novel), three volumes, Bentley, 1835, one volume, Wallis & Newell, 1835.

Falkner (novel), three volumes, Saunders & Otley, 1837, one volume, Harper & Brothers, 1837.

(Editor) P. B. Shelley, *The Poetical Works of Percy Bysshe Shelley,* four volumes, Moxon, 1839.

(Editor) P. B. Shelley, *Essays, Letters from Abroad, Translations and Fragments,* two volumes, Moxon, 1840.

Rambles in Germany and Italy in 1840, 1842, and 1843, two volumes, Moxon, 1844.

The Choice: A Poem on Shelley's Death, edited by H. Buxton Forman, [London], 1876.

The Mortal Immortal (short story,), Mossant, Vallon, 1910.

Proserpine and Midas: Two Unpublished Mythological Dramas, edited by A. Koszul, Milford, 1922.

Mathilda (novel), edited by Elizabeth Nitchie, University of North Carolina Press, 1959.

COLLECTIONS

Tales and Stories, edited by Richard Garnett, W. Peterson, 1891.

The Letters of Mary W. Shelley (Mostly Unpublished), edited by Henry H. Harper, Plimpton, 1918.

The Letters of Mary W. Shelley, edited by Frederick L. Jones, University of Oklahoma Press, 1947.

Mary Shelley's Journal, edited by F. L. Jones, University of Oklahoma Press, 1947.

My Best Mary: The Selected Letters of Mary Wollstonecraft Shelley, edited by Muriel Spark and Derek Stanford, Roy, 1953.

Collected Tales and Stories, edited by Charles E. Robinson, Johns Hopkins University Press, 1976.

The Letters of Mary Wollstonecraft Shelley, three volumes, edited by Betty T. Bennett, Johns Hopkins University Press, 1980.

The Journals of Mary Shelley, two volumes, edited by Paula Feldman and Diana Scott-Kilvert, Clarendon Press, 1987.

OTHER

Contributor to Volumes 86-88 and 102-103 in *The Cabinet of Biography*, Lardner's Cabinet Cyclopedia, 1835-1839. Also contributor of stories, reviews, and essays for *London Magazine*, *Blackwood's Edinburgh Magazine*, *Examiner*, and *Westminster Review*, and of stories to an annual gift book, *The Keepsake*, 1828-38. Collections of Shelley's works are housed in Lord Abinger's Shelley Collection on deposit at the Bodleian Library, the Carl H. Pforzheimer Library, New York Public Library, the Huntingdon Library, the British Library, and in the John Murray Collection.

■ Adaptations

FILMS, EXCEPT AS NOTED

Frankenstein, starring Colin Clive and Boris Karloff, Universal, 1931 (novel adaptation of movie by Richard J. Anobile, Pan Books, 1974); *Bride of Frankenstein*, starring Boris Karloff, Colin Clive, and Elsa Lanchester, Universal, 1935; *Son of Frankenstein*, starring Basil Rathbone, Boris Karloff, Bela Lugosi, Universal, 1939; *Frankenstein Meets the Wolf Man*, starring Lon Chaney, Jr., and Bela Lugosi, Universal, 1943; *The Curse of Frankenstein*, starring Peter Cushing and Christopher Lee, Warner Brothers, 1957; *Frankenstein 1970*, starring Boris Karloff and Tom Duggan, Allied Artists, 1958; *Frankenstein's Daughter*, starring John Ashley and Sandra Knight, Astor, 1958; *Frankenstein Meets the Space Monster*, starring James Karen and Robert Reilly, Allied Artists, 1965; *Frankenstein Conquers the World*, starring Nick Adams and Tadao Takashima, American International, 1966; *Frankenstein Created Woman*, starring Peter Cushing and Susan Denberg, Twentieth Century Fox, 1967; *Frankenstein's Bloody Terror*, starring Paul Naschy and Dianik Zurakowska, Independent International, 1968; *Frankenstein Must Be Destroyed*, starring Peter Cushing, Simon Ward, and Freddie Jones, Warner Brothers, 1970; *Frankenstein: The True Story*, starring Leonard Whiting, Michael Sarazin, David McCallum, and James Mason, MCA-TV, 1973; *Frankenstein and the Monster from Hell*, starring Peter Cushing, Shane Briant, and David Prowse, Paramount, 1974; *Young Frankenstein*, starring Mel Brooks, Gene Wilder, Teri Garr, Peter Boyle, and Marty Feldman, Twentieth Century Fox, 1974; *Frankenstein* (filmstrip; sound version, with guide), Listening Library, 1979; *The Bride*, starring Sting and Jennifer Beals, Columbia, 1985; *Gothic*, starring Natasha Richardson, Gabriel Byrne, and Julian Sands, Virgin Visions, 1986; *Mary Shelley's Frankenstein*, starring Kenneth Branagh, Robert De Niro, and Helena Bonham Carter, American Zoetrope, 1994.

PLAYS

H. M. Milner, *Frankenstein: or, The Man and the Monster* (two-act), Lacy's Acting Edition, c. 1850; David Campton, *Frankenstein: A Gothic Thriller* (two-act), Garnet Miller, 1973; Tim J. Kelly, *Frankenstein* (two-act), Samuel French, 1974; *Frankenstein: The Play*, Clark, Irwin, 1976.

RECORDINGS

Frankenstein (phonodisc), dramatization, with sound effects and music, directed by Christopher Casson, Spoken Arts, 1970; *Frankenstein* (phonotape), dramatization with sound effects and music, directed by C. Casson, Spoken Arts, 1974; *Frankenstein* (taken from a broadcast of the CBS program *Suspense*), starring Herbert Marshall, American Forces Radio and Television Service, 1976; *Frankenstein*, read by James Mason, Caedmon Records, 1977; *Weird Circle* (contains Edgar Allan Poe's *The Tell-Tale Heart* and *Frankenstein*; recorded from original radio broadcast), Golden Age, 1978; *Mary Shelley's Frankenstein* (audiotape), read by Kenneth Branagh, Simon & Schuster Audio, 1994.

■ Sidelights

Long after the event, Mary Shelley would recall the crucible out of which her most famous fictional progeny was fused. "In the summer of 1816, we visited Switzerland, and became the neighbors of Lord Byron. . . . But it proved a wet, ungenial summer, and incessant rain often confined us for days to the house. Some volumes of ghost stories, translated from the German and French, fell into our hands. . . ." After reading several of these tales of dead lovers and inconsolable ghosts, a better idea was struck upon by the gathered company. "'We will each write a ghost story,' said Lord Byron, and his proposition was acceded to."

As Mary Shelley wrote in her 1831 introduction to the revised edition of *Frankenstein; or, The New Prometheus*, the company—including herself, her soon-to-be husband, the poet Percy Bysshe Shelley, Byron, and his doctor, John William Polidori—all set to work coming up with fabulous stories, partly inspired by the Gothic tales of Ann Radcliffe, then so popular. Yet for Mary Shelley, the task at first proved fruitless. *"Have you thought of a story?* I was asked each morning, and each morning I was forced to reply with a mortifying negative." Then a conversation between her husband and Byron about galvanism and experiments of regenerating life with electrical charges started her thinking: "Perhaps a corpse would be re-animated . . . perhaps the component parts of a creature might be manufactured, brought together, and endued with vital warmth." This stimulus, together with a frightening dream that same night of a "pale student" who creates such a re-combined monster, set Shelley on course. "On the morrow I announced that I had *thought of a story.* I began that day with the words, *It was on a dreary night in November* . . . "

Frankenstein, like the monster created by the book's eponymous protagonist, has since its first publication in 1818 taken on a life of its own. In the introduction to the 1831 edition, Shelley wrote:

"Once again I bid my hideous progeny to go forth and prosper." She could have had no idea of how much it would prosper. The name itself has entered the vocabulary as synonymous with monster—though in fact Frankenstein was the name of the creator, not the monster. The novel was at once both "the apex and the last of Gothic fiction," as Muriel Spark noted in *Mary Shelley*. Its publication marked the death stroke of such an overblown genre, for "their mysteries [were] solved, by *Frankenstein*'s rational inquisition," according to Spark. The book has also inspired countless dramatizations—both plays and movies. The Frankenstein industry in Hollywood spans the gamut from pure horror films to comedy and attempts at high art. The theme of rational science versus romantic instinct has captured the imaginations of directors and cinema-goers alike. A 1994 addition to the list of such movies, *Mary Shelley's Frankenstein*, even incorporated the author's name into the title—a gentle reminder that the story ac-

The first published illustration of the monster, from the 1831 edition of *Frankenstein; or, The Modern Prometheus*.

tually had a creator: a woman barely nineteen years old at the time of its writing.

Literary Roots

Mary Shelley's personal life rivals anything she ever wrote. Her parents were Mary Wollstonecraft and William Godwin, both intellectual rebels of the closing of the eighteenth century. Wollstonecraft was the author of *A Vindication of the Rights of Women*, an early feminist tract with much influence in its day and still "required reading for studies in women's rights," according to Spark. Godwin was both a political philosopher and novelist, author of *Enquiry Concerning Political Justice* and the novel *Caleb Williams,* among others. These two did not simply write about a new society; they lived it. Wollstonecraft, spirited though often depressed, had a child, Fanny, out of wedlock during her years in Paris reporting on the French revolution. When Godwin met her in the summer of 1796, there was an immediate attraction. The couple at first set up separate houses near each other, then with the coming of a child, Godwin relented in his opposition to marriage, and they wed in March of 1797, just five months before the birth of Mary.

Her birth, however, was a mixed blessing for Godwin, for his wife died eleven days later from puerperal fever, and Godwin was left to care for the baby and her three-year-old half-sister. For the next several years he supervised all aspects of her care, and the two became inseparable. This tight bond was severed, however, when Godwin remarried to Mary Jane Clairmont in 1801. This stepmother brought a six-year-old son and four-year-old daughter into the union, and according to most accounts she had none of the finer sensibilities of Mary's biological mother. The new Mrs. Godwin was, according to such accounts, something of a dragon regarding Mary—making her do the housework while sending her own daughter Jane to boarding school. Mary was, in fact, educated at home but was fortunate to have her father's extensive library from which to choose volumes on topics from science to philosophy. There were also visitors to the house who provided intellectual stimulation—men such as William Wordsworth and Samuel Taylor Coleridge. She heard Coleridge recite his *Rime of the Ancient Mariner* while hiding in the parlor with her stepsister, Jane, an early influence that would effect

her later writing, most especially sections of *Frankenstein*. Other biographers have also noted that Mary inherited a pessimistic, depressed side to her character from her mother, spending many hours at her mother's grave reading from Wollstonecraft's works.

Godwin meanwhile, upon the insistence of his new wife, had begun a commercial enterprise in publishing with his Juvenile Library. One of Mary's favorite pastimes as a child was writing stories, and a reworking of a popular song into a long poem, *Mounseer Nongtongpaw*, became her first published work under her father's imprint. She was eleven at the time, and the work was popular enough to be republished in 1830 with illustrations by Robert Cruikshank, who illustrated much of Dickens's work. "It is not singular, that, as the daughter of two persons of distinguished literary celebrity, I should early in life have thought of writing," Shelley noted in her 1831 introduction to *Frankenstein*. In 1812, Godwin, influenced by his wife, sent Mary to friends in Scotland, where she remained until the summer of 1814, with only occasional visits to her home in London. These years helped nurture her literary imagination as well as give her a sense of freedom, away from her stepmother.

Percy Bysshe Shelley

Mary first met the poet, Percy Bysshe Shelley, in London on an 1812 visit home. Shelley, the son of a wealthy aristocrat, was a new disciple to Godwin's free-thinking creed, though it was not until Mary's final return home in 1814 that the two became attracted to each other. Shelley was married, the father of one child and another on the way, but he had grown weary of his wife and believed, as Godwin also espoused, in a higher morality than society's. The young poet visited Godwin's regularly, and Mary—chaperoned by her stepsister Jane—walked with him and paid visits to her mother's grave at St. Pancras Church. By the end of June they had declared their love for each other and when Godwin found out, he banned Shelley from the house. Young Mary was torn between love for her father and for Shelley, but soon followed her heart. An attempted suicide by the poet convinced her of his love and, accompanied by Jane, the couple fled to France on July 28, 1814. Mary was only sixteen at the time.

Villa Diodati, located near Geneva, Switzerland, was the home of Lord Byron, with whom Shelley was visiting when she created *Frankenstein*.

The next nine years, except for two interludes in England, were spent traveling in Europe, throughout Switzerland, Germany, and Italy. They were also characterized by poverty and domestic tragedy, by both romance and high melodrama. Living partnered without the benefit of marriage, Percy Shelley was cut off by his outraged father from any but a meager allowance, yet he and Mary, accompanied by Jane (who ultimately renamed herself Claire) travelled extensively in the summer of 1814 before returning to England in the fall, enough to give Mary Shelley material for a travel book, *History of Six Weeks' Tour,* ultimately published in 1817 and written largely from journals of the time and from letters sent home to her half-sister, Fanny.

Yet this was in the future: for the present Mary Shelley was pregnant, living in poverty in England with her common-law husband, often in hiding to avoid arrest for nonpayment of debts. In quieter times the couple continued their ambitious course of study in the classics and contemporary literature. Encouraged by her husband, Shelley also started a historical novel left unfinished as her pregnancy ended in a premature birth of a daughter in February, 1815. The baby died twelve days later. In her journal of March 19, 1815, Shelley recorded the following dream, a possible inspiration for *Frankenstein:* "Dream that my little baby came to life again—that it had only been cold & that we rubbed it before the fire & it lived." The reality was that the couple tried to pick up their old life again. "Read and talk," Shelley wrote in her journal. "Still think about my little baby—'tis hard, indeed, for a mother to lose a child." She would have more practice at such loss in the coming years. Complicating Shelley's life was the continual presence of her stepsister who had a decided affection for Percy Shelley, one that he, imbued with a passion for free love, did little to discourage. In fact, he urged Mary Shelley into an affair with his friend, Jefferson Hogg, not long after the death of their first child.

Frankenstein

A second child, William, was born in January of 1816 and in the following May the family departed for Geneva where they were to meet up with George Gordon, Lord Byron, stepsister Claire's new love interest and one of the most celebrated literary figures in all of Europe. And it was there that Mary Shelley began composition of her novel, first inspired by Byron's offhand remark. Initially the story of Victor Frankenstein and his creation seemed to her to be but a short tale, but encouraged by her husband, she developed the story at greater length.

For those familiar with the story of Frankenstein only from movie versions or anecdote, the novel will prove a surprise in its depth and breadth of detail and characterization. Told in retrospect, the novel opens with a ship frozen in the polar ice. Robert Walton, an English explorer, sees first a large misshapen creature drawn past his ship on sledge headed northwards. Later an ice flow carries a second sledge to his ship, and this contains Victor Frankenstein, severely weakened by exposure. Frankenstein manages to tell Walton his story before dying.

Raised in Geneva, Victor was early taken with the natural sciences; he was also in love with his adopted sister, Elizabeth. Sent to a university, Victor continued his studies in natural sciences and began to research how he might create life. After much work and many visits to the butcher shops and dissecting rooms, Victor managed to fashion an eight-foot creature and endow him with life, only to be frightened into a fever one night when the creature came lurking over his bed. Victor's best friend, Henry Clerval, helped to nurse him back to health; meanwhile the creature fled. Soon news reached Victor that his younger brother has been killed and that a family servant was found guilty of the crime. Depressed by these events, Victor went walking in the mountains where he once again encountered his creature who told him of his adventures since running away. Shunned by society for his hideous features, he learned to speak hiding in a hovel adjoining a farmer's cottage and listening to the family. He survived on what he could gather and on scraps, but each

time he tried to make human contact, he was met with such horror that his heart grew bitter. Finally he killed Victor's brother, making it look as though the servant had done the deed. Now he demanded that Victor create him a mate, which Victor reluctantly did, then destroyed. He could not in good conscience spawn a race of such monsters on the world. But the creature saw him destroy this female partner and vowed revenge, which he first took on Victor's friend Clerval, and then upon Elizabeth on Victor's wedding night.

Victor in turn vowed revenge, and has pursued his monster north to the polar regions where he now dies from exposure after telling an astonished Walton the entire tale. After Victor dies, the monster arrives at Walton's ship and tells Walton that Victor's was the greater crime, for he created life without a soul or a friend and it was right that he die. Upon saying this, the monster disappears upon the ice.

Shelley worked on the novel partially during the time of her third pregnancy. The book was finished in May of 1817, and her daughter, Clara Everina, was born in September of that year. During this same time she also put together the travel book, *History of Six Weeks' Tour,* published in late 1817. The couple had returned to England the year before, where more sadness awaited them. In October of 1816, Mary's half-sister Fanny killed herself, a terrible echo of her mother's two attempts at suicide, and Percy Shelley's wife died. This last event left the couple free to wed, which they did on December 30, 1816. The legitimacy of marriage improved their financial position somewhat with Percy Shelley's father.

Publication of *Frankenstein* occurred on New Year's Day of 1818. Its author's identity was at first unknown, though many assumed it to be by Percy Shelley. Critical response was mixed at the time, from those who thought the author had created a sensationalist and gruesome tract, to those who felt the anonymous author had great powers of imagination and description. Later critics tended to concentrate more on the philosophical impact of the novel, focussing on the subtitle, *The Modern Prometheus,* and examining the text for clues of unbridled creativity wreaking its own destruction. Still others have shown similarities in the novel to earlier Gothic horror novels such as Ann Radcliffe's *The Mysteries of Udolpho,* to books by Shelley's father, Godwin, including *Caleb Brown*

Boris Karloff played the monster in the classic 1931 film version of *Frankenstein*.

and *Saint Leon,* and allusions to John Milton's *Paradise Lost,* Goethe's *Faust,* and Coleridge's *Rime of the Ancient Mariner.*

Typical of the first category of reviewer is John Wilson Croker in the *Quarterly Review:* "Our taste and our judgement alike revolt at this kind of writing," Croker noted, and wondered "whether the head or the heart of the author be the most diseased." Yet no less a critic than Sir Walter Scott also saw the philosophical rather than sensational aspects of the novel: the destructive results of undeveloped affection and the pain and suffering caused by rejection. Scott commented in *Blackwood's Edinburgh Magazine* that "the author seems to us to disclose uncommon powers of poetic imagination," and concluded that "upon the whole, the work impresses us with a high idea of the author's original genius and happy power of expression."

Modern criticism has sided with Scott, and Shelley's novel has spawned not only a movie industry, but also a busy cottage industry in doctoral theses. Some have viewed the book from a feminist critique in which Shelley was exploring her ambivalent feelings for the entire belief in motherhood and the woman's role in procreation. Others have examined the book for clues to Mary Shelley's own troubled life at the time—the loss of her first child and writing the tale of Victor Frankenstein during the term of her second pregnancy. Anne K. Mellor in *Mary Shelley: Her Life, Her Fiction, Her Monsters,* postulated that the novel was created out of a "doubled fear, the fear of a woman that she may not be able to bear a healthy normal child and the fear of a putative author that she may not be able to write. . . . The book is her created self as well as her child."

The main theme of the book is that of overreaching ambition, as many critics have pointed out. In the case of Victor Frankenstein, however, it is interesting to note that his scientific inspiration results in death, a theme to be much developed in the twentieth century. As the critic Harold Bloom pointed out in *Partisan Review,* "Though Mary Shelley may not have intended it, her novel's prime theme is a necessary counterpoise to Prometheanism, for Prometheanism exalts the increase in consciousness despite all cost." Noting that though Frankenstein assumed God-like powers and apparently created life, Bloom went on to comment that "all he actually can give is death-

in-life." Victor Frankenstein himself, at the end of the novel, seems to understand this when he exhorts Walton to "seek happiness in tranquility and avoid ambition, even if it be only the apparently innocent one of distinguishing yourself in science and discoveries."

Spark, in her *Mary Shelley,* while noting the strengths of Shelley's book, also commented on its weakness in technique: "The story could have been better constructed," Spark wrote. "The chain which links the events together is weakened by improbable situations." A more serious defect for Spark was the "poverty of characterisation" in secondary characters, though she noted that the central characters, Frankenstein and the monster, were admirably developed. For Spark, as for many other critics, it is the development of these two main characters—twin sides of each other—that forms the core of the book. The monster is, in contrast to other thrillers of the day, fully developed and even sympathetic. "Mary Shelley was immature when she wrote, but she had courage, she was inspired," Spark concluded. "*Frankenstein* has entertained, delighted and harrowed generations of readers to this day."

To Europe Once Again

In 1818 the Shelleys returned to Europe, settling in Italy for Percy Shelley's health, yet the move proved disastrous. Clara Everina, just a year old, died in Venice in September, and the son, William, died the following year in Rome. "You see by our hap how blind we mortals are when we go seeking after what we think our good," Shelley wrote in a letter. "But the Climate is not [by] any means warm enough to be of benefit to him & yet it is that that has destroyed my two children— We went from England comparatively prosperous and happy—I should return broken-hearted and miserable—. . . . I can assure you I am much changed—the world will ever be to me again as it was—" At twenty-two, Mary Shelley had already experienced enough tragedy for one lifetime. In ways she blamed the deaths of her children on her husband and from that time on she withdrew from him.

She also kept writing. A novella, *Mathilda,* was written during the late summer and fall of 1819, but never published in Shelley's lifetime. Basically the story of a father and daughter's incestuous

A portrait of Shelley when she was about nineteen years old, the age she wrote her famous novel.

attraction for each other, *Mathilda* is told in the form of memoirs addressed to a poet named Woodville—a stand-in for Percy Shelley—and written by a young woman who expects to die at age twenty-two. Largely autobiographical, the story traces the course of Mathilda's life, from her birth—which caused the death of her mother—through the abandonment by her beloved father when she is sent to Scotland, and through her return sixteen years later and the admission by her father of his incestuous love for her. Writing about the novel, published in 1959, Mellor noted that *Mathilda* "calls into question the bourgeois sexual practices of her day." It was also full of anger and self-recrimination as Shelley was trying to come to terms with the deaths of her two children. The birth of her fourth and last child, Percy Florence, in November of 1819, in part helped to heal those emotional wounds.

By the spring of 1820, Shelley was hard at work on two blank-verse dramas from Ovid, *Proserpine* and *Midas*, as well as on another novel, *Valperga*. The latter was a historical novel about Castruccio, prince of Lucca, who returns to his native city after a life of exile and must chose between his love for Euthanasia and his search for absolute power. In this novel, Shelley once again takes up the exploration, begun in *Frankenstein*, of the costs of ambition. In the end, the book is a portrayal of a man who chooses power and fame over love. The writing of it filled three volumes, and her research took Shelley far beyond the bounds of what she had initially intended. Yet again, her writing was put on hold by tragedy. Settling in Pisa in 1821, the Shelleys were joined by Byron. Percy Shelley had formed liaisons with several other women, including stepsister Claire, since the time of his wife's cooling toward him. But with Byron's arrival at the end of the year, a spirit of literary camaraderie was once more established. This was cut short, however, with Mary Shelley's miscarriage in June, 1822, and then the death of her husband by drowning on July 8 while he was sailing in the Gulf of Spezia.

Mary Shelley was left now entirely on her own to raise her son. After a period of intense depression, she once again turned to writing not only for emotional succor but also for material sustenance. Her *Valperga* was published in 1823, the year she returned to England to live. The reception of her book was somewhat enhanced by a dramatic production of *Frankenstein* which had a prodigious success in London. None of Shelley's five other novels would be greeted with the critical success of her *Frankenstein*, however. Reviewers of the day could not help but compare *Valperga* to its author's first novel, as did a reviewer in *Blackwood's Edinburgh Magazine*: "*Valperga* is, for a second romance, by no means what its predecessor was for a first one." Most reviewers, then and now, agree that the novel is much too long. Her father, William Godwin, noted this defect in a letter to Shelley in 1822. "It appears, in reading," Godwin wrote, "the first rule you prescribed yourself was, I will let it be long. It contains the quantity of four volumes of *Waverly*. No hard blow was ever hit with a woolsack!"

In 1926 Shelley published *The Last Man*, something of an idealized picture of Percy Shelley in the guise of the last man left on earth after the destruction, by plague, of the human race in the twenty-first century. The book was also partly inspired by the death of Lord Byron in 1824. She wrote in her journal shortly after Byron's death: "The last man! Yes I may well describe that solitary being's feelings, feeling myself as the last relic of a beloved race, my companions extinct before me—" Recognized now as a prototype of the modern science fiction tale, *The Last Man* is Shelley's second-best known novel, and Shelley's "darkest and gloomiest," according to Eleanor Ty in *Dictionary of Literary Biography*. Spark commented that *The Last Man* "will hold more pertinent appeal for present-day readers than it did even in Mary's time, when it was regarded as an entertaining though highly fantastic story." In his 1972 study, *Mary Shelley*, William A. Walling noted that "*The Last Man* deserves serious attention in any assessment of Mary Shelley's career." Walling commented that though the book was "marred" by sentimentality, overwriting, and excessive length—defects in most of Shelley's fiction—it is a book "of real power," far surpassing any of her later fiction works. The book explores the theme of social and political change through its main character, Ryland, who champions—as did Percy Shelley and William Godwin—the republican ideal, though with disastrous consequences, heralding a "plague of liberty," as Walling put it. "Mary Shelley . . . has created a startlingly pessimistic allegory which identifies egalitarianism with a plague virulent enough to destroy civilization itself," Walling concluded.

In the 1820s, Shelley also turned her hand to journalism in an attempt to earn money, writing book reviews and cultural pieces for magazines such as *Examiner*, *London Magazine*, and *Westminster Review*. She also helped to edit the remaining manuscripts of Percy Shelley. However, the angry reaction of Sir Timothy Shelley to the appearance of his son's *Posthumous Poems* forced her to agree not to publish any more of her late husband's poems during the lifetime of Sir Timothy. In return, she won an annual allowance for her son.

A lesser known novel by Shelley is *The Fortunes of Perkin Warbeck* (1830), detailing the life of a man who claimed to have been the son of Edward IV, Duke of York, and thus a pretender to the throne. Shelley follows his fortunes from his escape from the Tower of London to his ultimate end on the scaffold. According to Ty in *Dictionary of Literary Biography*, *The Fortunes of Perkin Warbeck* was one of Shelley's "least successful" novels, inspired by

---

If you enjoy the works of Mary Shelley, you may want to check out the following books and films:

Vivien Alcock, *The Stonewalkers*, 1983.
Michael Bedard, *Redwork*, 1990.
Bram Stoker, *Dracula*, 1897.
The Fly, Brooksfilms, 1986.

Sir Walter Scott's historical romances, but suffering from uninspired writing. As Walling put it, *The Fortunes of Perkin Warbeck* is "essentially a lifeless novel, although it deserves our respect for the quality of the intelligence which is intermittently displayed in it."

More overtly autobiographical novels are *Lodore* (1835) and *Falkner* (1837). These two repeat the triangle of mixed emotions between father, daughter, and lover that was initiated in *Mathilda*. With *Lodore*, Shelley created for the first time a happy ending, though one which Ty concluded was "sentimentalized and unrealistic." *Falkner* is a more clearly autobiographical piece, in which the Byronic protagonist, Falkner, is the guardian of orphaned Elizabeth and is also haunted by secrets in his past. When Elizabeth falls in love with the son of a woman Falkner once helped destroy, he is beset by guilt. Elizabeth is thus caught between her lover, who seeks revenge, and her adoptive father's obsession. According to Ty, *Falkner*, Shelley's last novel, is also one of her "best works."

In 1831 came a revised edition of *Frankenstein* which helped Shelley's financial affairs, and beginning in 1834 she undertook a series of biographical sketches for the popular *Cabinet Cyclopedia* series, in addition to other journalistic chores. These mini-biographies increasingly became her bread and butter, and they included works on literary and scientific men of Italy, Spain, Portugal, and France. Indeed, Shelley's real skill as a journalist was in disseminating the cultural heritage of the continent to England. As John R. Holmes noted in *Dictionary of Literary Biography*, Shelley's biographical sketches "may be, as she thought they were, her very best writing; ironically, they are the least read. . . . The type of work these sketches form may best be termed 'serviceable.' They are lively and readable, but they are intended to be reference works." Shelley's own description of these years can be found in her journals: "Routine occupation is the medicine of my mind. I write the 'Lives' in the morning. I read novels and memoirs of an evening—such is the variety of my days and time flies so swift, that days form weeks and weeks form months, before I am aware."

With her son at Harrow and then at Trinity College, Shelley was much occupied with a literary life. She never married again, and in later years dedicated her life to keeping her dead husband's name before the public. Sir Timothy eventually relented regarding publication of his son's poetry, and Mary Shelley became a tireless editor and literary historian, writing notes and prefaces to editions of his work that "provide the most thorough and reliable biographical background to [Percy] Shelley's poems of any single source," according to Holmes. With the graduation of her son, Shelley's fortunes turned for the better—Sir Timothy endowed his grandson with a larger yearly stipend and he and his mother subsequently travelled together in Germany and Italy in the early 1840s, resulting in Shelley's final work, *Rambles in Germany and Italy*. By the time of its publication, however, Shelley was already suffering from poor health and beset by blackmailers who would plague her last years. After her son's marriage, Shelley lived with Percy Florence and his new wife. However, she soon began to exhibit symptoms of the brain tumor which eventually took her life on February 1, 1851.

Writing of Shelley's life, Leigh Hunt, poet and personal friend of Percy Shelley, once described the novelist as "four-famed." By this he meant her two famous parents, her poet husband, and the monster she had created. Alluding to this, Spark summed up Shelley's life, noting that she was not only the daughter of William Godwin and Mary Wollstonecraft, not only the wife of Shelley and mother of Sir Percy Shelley. "She was also a professional writer of lasting fame," Spark concluded, though, as Walling has pointed out, a "minor figure" in English literature.

■ Works Cited

Bloom, Harold, "*Frankenstein; or, The New Prometheus*," Partisan Review, Fall, 1965, pp. 611-18.

Croker, John Wilson, review of *Frankenstein; or, The Modern Prometheus*, Quarterly Review, January, 1818, pp. 375-85.

Godwin, William, letter to Mary Shelley, *The Life & Letters of Mary Wollstonecraft Shelley*, Volume 2, Marshall, Bentley & Son, pp. 50-52.

Holmes, John R. "Mary Wollstonecraft Shelley," *Dictionary of Literary Biography*, Volume 110: *British Romantic Prose Writers, 1789-1832*, Gale, 1991, pp. 209-220.

Mellor, Anne K., *Mary Shelley: Her Life, Her Fiction, Her Monster*, Routledge, 1988.

Scott, Sir Walter, "Remarks on *Frankenstein; or, The Modern Prometheus: A Novel*," Blackwood's Edinburgh Magazine, March, 1818, pp. 613-20.

Shelley, Mary W., *Frankenstein; or, The Modern Prometheus*, H. G. Daggers, 1845.

Shelley, Mary W., *The Letters of Mary W. Shelley*, Volume 1, edited by F. L. Jones, University of Oklahoma Press, 1944.

Shelley, Mary W., *Mary Shelley's Journal*, edited by F. L. Jones, University of Oklahoma Press, 1947.

Spark, Muriel, *Mary Shelley*, Constable, 1987.

Ty, Eleanor, "Mary Wollstonecraft Shelley," *Dictionary of Literary Biography*, Volume 118: *British Romantic Novelists, 1789-1832*, Gale, 1992, pp. 311-25.

Review of *Valperga; or, The Life and Adventures of Castruccio, Prince of Lucca*, Blackwood's Edinburgh Magazine, March, 1823, pp. 283-93.

Walling, William A., *Mary Shelley*, Twayne, 1972.

■ For More Information See

BOOKS

Bennett, Betty T., editor, *The Letters of Mary Wollstonecraft Shelley*, 2 volumes, Johns Hopkins University Press, 1980, 1983.

Bloom, Harold, editor, *Mary Shelley: Modern Critical Views*, Chelsea House, 1985.

Blumberg, Jane, *Mary Shelley's Early Novels*, University of Iowa Press, 1993.

Chernaik, Judith, *Love's Children* (fictional account), Knopf, 1992.

Dunn, Jane, *Moon in Eclipse: A Life of Mary Shelley*, Weidenfeld and Nicolson, 1978.

Feldman, Paula R., and Diana Scott-Kilvert, editors, *The Journals of Mary Shelley*, 2 volumes, Clarendon Press, 1987.

Gilbert, Sandra, and Susan Gubar, *The Madwoman in the Attic*, Yale University Press, 1979.

Hill-Miller, Katherine, *My Hideous Progeny: Mary Shelley, William Godwin, and the Father-Daughter Relationship*, University of Delaware Press, 1995.

Lyles, W. H., *Mary Shelley: An Annotated Bibliography*, Garland, 1975.

Nineteenth-Century Literary Criticism, Volume 14, Gale, 1988, pp. 245-309.

Nitchie, Elizabeth, *Mary Shelley: Author of Frankenstein*, Rutgers University Press, 1953.

Sunstein, Emily W., *Mary Shelley: Romance and Reality*, Little, Brown, 1989.

PERIODICALS

Booklist, April 15, 1983, p. 1070; March 15, 1985, p. 1031.

Kliatt, fall, 1983, p. 31; March, 1994, p. 50.

Library Journal, July, 1987, p. 79; November 15, 1993, p. 110; January, 1994, p. 172.

Los Angeles Times Book Review, August 28, 1994, p. 11.

New York Review of Books, November 19, 1987, pp. 35-38; June 29, 1989, p. 13.

Publishers Weekly, May 24, 1993, p. 83.

Times Literary Supplement, August 7, 1987, p. 842; July 29, 1988, p. 824; October 9, 1992, p. 23; June 25, 1993, p. 9.*

—*Sketch by J. Sydney Jones*

Jan Slepian

■ **Personal**

Surname is pronounced "*slep*-ee-an"; born January 2, 1921, in New York, NY; daughter of Louis (an engineer) and Florence (a housewife; maiden name, Elinger) Berek; married Urey Krasnopolsky, October, 1945 (divorced, 1948); married David Slepian (a mathematician), April 18, 1950; children: Steven, Don, Anne. *Education:* Brooklyn College, B.A., 1942; University of Washington, M.A. (clinical psychology), 1947; New York University, M.A. (speech pathology), 1964; attended University of California—Berkeley, 1979. *Hobbies and other interests:* Mycology, reading, music, swimming.

■ **Addresses**

Home and office—212 Summit Ave., Summit, NJ 07901. *Agent*—Sheldon Fogelman, 10 East 40th St., New York, NY 10016.

■ **Career**

Massachusetts General Hospital, Boston, language therapist, 1947-49; private speech therapist, 1952-58; Red Seal Clinic, Newton, NJ, speech therapist, 1953-55; Matheny School for Cerebral Palsy, Farhills, NJ, speech therapist, 1955-57; writer. *Member:* Society of Children's Book Writers and Illustrators, Authors Guild.

■ **Awards, Honors**

Best Book of the Year citation, *School Library Journal*, 1980, American Book Award finalist in children's fiction, and *Boston Globe-Horn Book* Honor for fiction, both 1981, and American Library Association (ALA) Notable Book citation, all for *The Alfred Summer;* author's awards, New Jersey Institute of Technology, 1981, for *The Alfred Summer*, 1983, for *The Night of the Bozos*, and 1988, for *Something beyond Paradise;* Best Books for Children citation, *New York Times*, and Notable Children's Book for Older Readers, *School Library Journal*, both 1981, and Notable Children's Trade Book in Social Studies, *Social Education*, Books for the Teen Age citation, New York Public Library, and Notable Book citation, ALA, all 1982, all for *Lester's Turn;* Best Books for Young Adults citation, ALA, Children's Book of the Year citation, Child Study Association of America, and Book of the Year citation, Library of Congress, all 1983, all for *The Night of the Bozos;* Ten Great Books of the Year for Teens citation, *Redbook*, 1987, for *Something beyond Paradise;* Notable Book citation, ALA, and *Booklist* Editor's Choice citation, both 1989, both for *The Broccoli Tapes;* Best Books citation, New York Public Library, and *Booklist* Editor's Choice citation, both 1990, both for *Risk 'n' Roses.*

■ **Writings**

YOUNG ADULT NOVELS

The Alfred Summer, Macmillan (New York City), 1980.

Lester's Turn (sequel to *The Alfred Summer*), Macmillan, 1981.

The Night of the Bozos, Dutton (New York City), 1983.

Getting on with It, Macmillan, 1985.

Something beyond Paradise, Philomel, 1987.

The Broccoli Tapes, Philomel, 1989.

Risk 'n' Roses, Philomel, 1990.

Back to Before, Philomel, 1993.

Pinocchio's Sister, Philomel, 1995.

"LISTEN-HEAR" PICTURE BOOK SERIES; WITH ANN SEIDLER

Alphie and the Dream Machine, illustrated by Richard E. Martin, Follett (New York City), 1964.

The Cock Who Couldn't Crow, illustrated by Richard E. Martin, Follett, 1964.

Lester and the Sea Monster, illustrated by Richard E. Martin, Follett, 1964.

Magic Arthur and the Giant, illustrated by Richard E. Martin, Follett, 1964.

Mister Sipple and the Naughty Princess, illustrated by Richard E. Martin, Follett, 1964.

The Roaring Dragon of Redrose, illustrated by Richard E. Martin, Follett, 1964.

"JUNIOR LISTEN-HEAR" PICTURE BOOK SERIES; WITH ANN SEIDLER

Bendemolena, illustrated by Richard E. Martin, Follett, 1967, published as *The Cat Who Wore a Pot on Her Head,* Scholastic, Inc. (New York City), 1981.

Ding-Dong, Bing-Bong, illustrated by Richard E. Martin, Follett, 1967.

An Ear Is to Hear, illustrated by Richard E. Martin, Follett, 1967.

The Hungry Thing, illustrated by Richard E. Martin, Follett, 1967.

The Silly Listening Book, illustrated by Richard E. Martin, Follett, 1967.

PICTURE BOOKS

(With Ann Seidler) *The Best Invention of All,* illustrated by Joseph Veno, Crowell-Collier (New York City), 1967.

(With Ann Seidler) *The Hungry Thing Returns,* illustrated by Richard E. Martin, Scholastic, Inc., 1990.

(With Ann Seidler) *The Hungry Thing Goes to a Restaurant,* illustrated by Elroy Freem, Scholastic, Inc., 1992.

Lost Moose, illustrated by Ted Lewin, Philomel (New York City), 1995.

Emily Just In Time, illustrated by Glo Coalson, Philomel, 1997.

OTHER

Building Foundations for Better Speech and Reading (teacher's training series; with cassette tapes), Instructional Dynamics Inc., 1974.

Also contributor of advice on speech problems, with Ann Seidler, to nationally syndicated newspaper column "Parents Ask." Slepian's works are included in the Kerlan Collection, University of Minnesota.

■ **Sidelights**

From her career as a speech therapist, Jan Slepian has brought an understanding of the dilemmas facing young people who suffer from physical, mental, and social handicaps to young adult fiction. Praised for novels that champion those people left outside the social mainstream—the ones not targeted by Madison Avenue advertisers, whose day-to-day lives are rarely, if ever, the subject of popular magazine articles, comic books, movies, television shows, short stories, or novels—her unlikely protagonists encounter events that challenge their perception of themselves as "not good enough" and force them to transcend their emotional, if not physical afflictions. Slepian "writes thought-provoking books," concludes *Twentieth-Century Young Adult Writers* contributor Carol Doxey, "stimulating young adults to think for themselves and to strive to overcome problems that have seemed like mountains until, after Slepian's characters, they seem like mere anthills."

Born in Manhattan, New York, in 1921, and raised in an immigrant neighborhood in the Bronx, Slepian was a shy child who gradually overcame her own mental handicap by playing the "Aziff" game. "Somehow I got the idea that if I could act as if I were confident and easy, people wouldn't know how I felt inside," she recalled in an essay for the *Something about the Author Autobiographical Series* (*SAAS*). "I found out that if you pretend something long enough, you wind up believing it yourself. . . . Believe me, this was a big help in my adolescent years and all the years since."

An Author by Chance

As a young woman, Slepian had no intentions of becoming an author. An avid reader as a child, she attended Brooklyn College where she majored in psychology for the simple reason that "I had the naive idea that I could find out why people do as they do." Graduate work in clinical psychology and speech pathology followed at the University of Washington. Married in 1950, she and her husband had three children to whom she dedicated much of her time, although continuing to work part-time while the kids were young. One day she and friend Anne Seidler, also a speech therapist, decided to write a series of articles on childhood speech problems for a newspaper column, "Parents Ask," which gratefully published them. Excited by the response to their work, the two women collaborated on a dozen picture books dealing with speech-related topics. Collected in the series "Listen-Hear" and "Jr. Listen-Hear," the books were published in 1964.

Over a decade later, Slepian decided to take an English class at the University of California at Berkeley, where she discovered the world of young adult novels. Her teacher, who had read some of Slepian's picture books, asked what writing projects her student was busy working on. "I told her that I was done, finished," Slepian recalled. But her teacher admonished her, "Oh no, you're not. You're just ready to go on to something else." Slepian sensed that her teacher was right, and soon enough, she found herself playing around with story ideas in the back of her mind.

Childhood Memories Converge in *The Alfred Summer*

Returning home, Slepian started working on a novel that had haunted her for a long time; it was published in 1980 as *The Alfred Summer*. Finishing that book was an important milestone in

her life. As she revealed in *SAAS:* "I've had many golden moments in my life, but this was something quite different. More than anything in the world I had wanted to write a decent book, and that night I knew that I had. I said to myself, 'You are fifty-seven years old and this is one of the most happy moments of your life.' It seemed to me remarkable that I could say that at my age."

Taking place during the mid-1930s, *The Alfred Summer* recounts one summer in the lives of four children: Alfred, Claire, Lester, and Myron. Lester Klopper, who is afflicted by cerebral palsy, and Alfred Burt, who is mentally retarded, become friends and, along with the tomboyish Claire, help their clumsy friend Myron finish building a boat

This 1980 novel about four unlikely friends was inspired by the author's memory of her younger retarded brother Alfred.

that he has been struggling with. They call the boat, which ultimately sinks, *The Getaway*, "a name they all understand, each in his own terms," notes Natalie Babbitt in her review of the book in the *New York Times Book Review*, "for they are all prisoners of one kind or another." The title character was inspired by Slepian's mentally retarded brother, who had been a source of both joy and anguish for Slepian and her family. "Only aware that Alfred was the cause of fights between my parents, I hated him," the author confessed. "People acted funny around him, and he made my mother cry and my father angry. Yet at the same time I was attached. He was sweet and laughed at my jokes and he was my brother. I learned early that you can hold within yourself contradictory feelings."

The Alfred Summer had its germ in an event that its author recalled from her childhood. In an effort to find Alfred a playmate, Slepian's mother asked the mother of a child with cerebral palsy if their two sons could spend some time together. The other boy's mother refused to let her son even associate with the mentally retarded Alfred: "she wanted her son to play only with normal kids." Slepian realized that within this memory was an intriguing what-if story. "What if Lester and Alfred had become friends?"

After its publication *The Alfred Summer* received several awards, including being named a *Boston Globe-Horn Book* Award Honor Book and one of the best books of the year by *School Library Journal*. Her novel's positive reception cast its author's relationship with her brother in a new light. "My mother and father thought his life was blasted, wasted," she explained of her brother in *SAAS*. "In a sense it was, of course. He still sits in a hospital like a bundle from the lost and found. But in another sense his life wasn't a waste. Because of this book, that's all turned around. He has reached and affected many, many people, more than most of us 'normals' have. Such is the power of words."

Her pleasure over *The Alfred Summer* encouraged Slepian to write a sequel. 1981's *Lester's Turn* takes place after Alfred's mother dies and his father places his mentally retarded and epileptic son in the hospital. Distraught over the effect of institutionalization on his friend, Lester quits school, finds a job, and then tries to kidnap Alfred. His first attempt fails, but with the help of Claire and

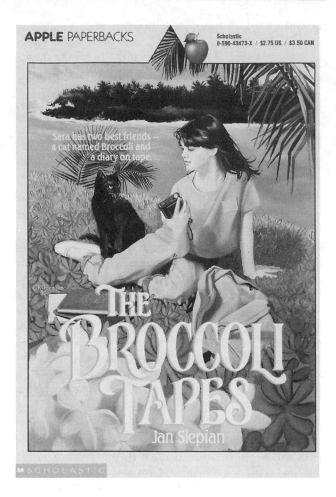

In this 1989 novel, Sara becomes homesick after her family moves to Hawaii for five months; befriending a cat and sending tapes to her old classmates help her pass the time.

a nurse from the hospital, a concert to benefit his friend is organized. The doctors allow Lester to take Alfred out of the hospital for the day, but tragically, the retarded young man suffers a burst appendix and must be hurried back to the hospital, where he dies. The death of his friend means more than the loss of a loved one for Lester. He comes to realize that his preoccupation with Alfred's needs was also a means of avoiding his own problems. "*Lester's Turn* was needed," its author explained, "because I wanted to find out more about some characters I had met in the first novel." Taken together, both books impressed critics: Babbitt noted that the novels' "language is rich, often funny, always fresh, and both stories are worth telling, a condition that has become increasingly rare in novels for young readers."

Hiding behind Unseen Masks

Slepian often draws upon characteristics of her own life and the places that she has visited to flesh out her stories. Her first two novels were both set in the Brighton Beach community where she spent her own childhood. She set her third novel, *The Night of the Bozos*, near a lake in up-state New York where she and her family spent Christmas vacations as a teenager. Slepian explained in *SAAS* that *The Night of the Bozos* "is a good example of how I put together people, or parts of people, I have known from different eras of my life." The character of the reclusive, obsessive thirteen-year-old musical prodigy George Weiss, who immerses himself in the study of sound to the exclusion of almost everything else, was modeled after her own son, Don. The fictional

Going back in time, two teenage cousins try to correct the bad things that happened to them over the past year, but find they can't and fear they may have to relive the bad year over.

George lives with his mother and his Uncle Hibbie, a character based on a speech patient whom Slepian met while working at Massachusetts General Hospital before her children were born. Because of his speech impediment, Hibbie is very retiring and feels comfortable around few people besides his immediate family. George takes it upon himself to act as Hibbie's protector.

George and Hibbie eventually meet Lolly, a teenage girl with a tattoo on her arm—unusual in those days—who takes them to meet her family, an eccentric entourage of traveling carnival workers. Hibbie is entranced by the life of the carnival; with Lolly's encouragement, he dons a clown costume and becomes a "Bozo" who sits above a tank of water and jeers at the crowd, taunting them into paying for balls to throw at a target that will dunk him when hit. When he becomes the Bozo Hibbie's stuttering problem disappears, and a fun-loving, extroverted personality is freed. "The story, which celebrated quiet determination and the restorative energy of friendship, is at once humorous, grotesque, and poignant," notes a *Horn Book* reviewer.

Both *Something beyond Paradise* (1987) and *The Broccoli Tapes* (1989) take place on the islands of Hawaii where Slepian, her husband, and their children spent their summers for over a decade. Sixteen-year-old Franny Simone is given the opportunity to train as a dancer, but it would mean leaving Honolulu and moving to New York City. Afraid to leave her mother alone to care for her ailing grandmother, and distracted by a new love affair, Franny's dilemma in *Something beyond Paradise* is portrayed in a manner that "clearly delineates the ambivalence, built-up feelings, and agonizing that accompany decision making," according to Mary Ojibway in *Voice of Youth Advocates*. In *The Broccoli Tapes*, Sara and her brother have the opposite problem: five months in paradise is a tough adjustment, especially while their father is busy teaching and their mother takes care of their ailing grandmother. It isn't until she befriends a wild cat, dubbed Broccoli, that Sara finds a way to deal with her homesickness. With Broccoli as the audience, she begins to tape-record her impressions of her time in Hawaii, and sends them back to her classmates in Boston; these tapes provide the novel's text. Befriending a native boy, Eddie Nutt, who is undergoing problems with his parents, Sara also watches as the grandmother she loves slowly dies in what *Booklist* reviewer Ilene

Cooper calls "a rich, robust story that encompasses all of life's themes—birth, death, joining, letting go, and, of course, love."

At Home in the Bronx

Returning to a New York setting, Slepian published *Risk 'n' Roses*, a novel about two sisters whose close relationship starts to fall apart after their family moves to a new neighborhood in the Bronx. Fifteen-year-old Angela Berman, who is mentally handicapped, becomes friends with Mr. Kaminsky, a reclusive old man who lives across the street. Mr. Kaminsky spends his time caring for a rose garden in which each bloom is named after a member of his family killed in the Nazi Holocaust. Meanwhile, Angela's younger sister Skip, who had always cared for her older sister, becomes intrigued by the wild and flamboyant Jean Persico, an older girl who seems to run the neighborhood and who encourages Skip to join her secret gang of friends. Jean leads her willing followers in wildness and takes a personal delight in taunting Mr. Kaminsky. The test of Skip's loyalty to her best friends in the gang comes when the clever Jean tricks naive Angela into debudding all of the old man's prized roses with a pair of scissors. In a strong conclusion, Skip begins to understand the sacrifices that must be made in choosing between a loyalty to friends or family. While noting that the novel's conclusion is perhaps too tidy, Martha V. Parravano praises *Risk 'n' Roses* in *Horn Book:* "The book's examination of the nature of power . . . is strong and lucid, while the references to 'Snow White and Rose Red' and 'Snow White and the Seven Dwarves' inform the story with the truth and force of a folk tale."

The element of magic finds its way into 1993's *Back to Before*, when Linny Erda and his cousin Hilary, each resentful of the loss of a parent, find a brass ring that transports them a year backward in time. Instead of Hilary's Vermont home, the two find themselves in their old Bronx neighborhood. In Linny's case, his ailing mother, who had died right after an argument in which he stormed out of the house, is still alive; Hilary's alcoholic father has not yet walked out on her and the rest of his family. The tragedies they know will come have not happened yet; the teens believe they have been given the power to change the course of events. Ultimately, though, the changes they

If you enjoy the works of Jan Slepian, you may want to check out the following books and films:

Daniel Keyes, *Flowers for Algernon*, 1966.
Hazel Krantz, *For Love of Jeremy*, 1990.
Jane Yolen, *The Devil's Arithmetic*, 1988.
Rain Man, United Artists, 1988.

make are only within themselves, through coming to terms with their own responsibility for the realities of their parents' lives. While problems in the science-fiction premise of the novel remain, Betsy Hearne notes in *Bulletin of the Center for Children's Books* that "Slepian animates her characters with a natural immediacy and lets us see inside them without getting too didactically therapeutic."

Marionettes as a Mirror of Humanity

Slepian's next novel was inspired by the relationship between actress Candace Bergen and her father, the famous ventriloquist Edgar Bergen. Bergen, with his puppets Charlie McCarthy and Mortimer Snerd, was well known to vaudeville audiences in the early decades of the twentieth century. *Pinocchio's Sister*, published in 1995, is a psychological thriller set against the eerie backdrop of the vaudeville circuit. Mr. Rosedale, a famous ventriloquist, his dummy, and his daughter, Martha, travel from city to city to perform. Martha's mother has long since died, and the ten-year-old girl begins to feel jealousy and resentment against the beautifully clothed and painted wooden dummy, Iris, upon which her distraught father seems to lavish most of his time and attention. With the help of a young acrobat named Stashu, Martha plots to kidnap and destroy Iris, but finds she cannot bring herself to complete the deed. Instead she seeks to become the much-loved Iris, steals the puppet's blonde wig, and adopts its mannerisms. It is only after Stashu convinces others of Martha's problems that she is provided the companionship that she has so desperately needed. *Voice of Youth Advocates* contributor Ruth K. J. Cline notes that the book raises powerful moral questions" that may encourage "thoughtful dialogue with readers," while Martha Davis Beck adds in the *New York Times Book Review* that "The shadowy world of vaudeville allows Jan Slepian rich ground in which to explore the distinctions between fantasy and reality, love and need, acting a part and living ones's life."

Despite the many diverse settings and situations that comprise her stories, Slepian acknowledges that much of her work comes from within herself. "I know there are bits and pieces of my life in all my books," she wrote in an essay published in *Speaking for Ourselves, Too*, "my experiences, my concerns, and above all my feelings. No matter how disguised, in a certain sense, novel writing is autobiographical." By beginning her career as a novelist at the relatively late age of fifty-seven, Slepian is able to lavish upon her readers a broad range of experiences, interesting personalities, and colorfully drawn settings, which she incorporates into her novels. But for this author writing is definitely a two-way street between her and the appreciative young readers who have allowed her to continue her craft; as she noted in *SAAS*, "Sometimes, when the writing is going well, when a character has come alive on the page, or I have found the right 'taste,' the right sentence or even the right word, then, I can tell you that there is nothing in the world to match it. I'm like a bystander watching a miracle. I count myself blessed that I'm a writer and think that that is the best possible thing to be."

■ Works Cited

Babbitt, Natalie, review of *The Alfred Summer, New York Times Book Review,* April 27, 1980, p. 52.

Babbitt, Natalie, review of *Lester's Turn, New York Times Book Review,* May 27, 1981, p. 38.

Beck, Martha Davis, review of *Pinocchio's Sister, New York Times Book Review,* July 30, 1995.

Cline, Ruth K. J., review of *Pinocchio's Sister, Voice of Youth Advocates,* August, 1995, p. 165.

Cooper, Ilene, review of *The Broccoli Tapes, Booklist,* April 15, 1989, p. 1472.

Doxey, Carol, "Jan Slepian," *Twentieth-Century Young Adult Writers,* St. James Press, 1995, pp. 594-96.

Hearne, Betsy, review of *Back to Before, Bulletin of the Center for Children's Books,* September, 1993, p. 24.

Review of *Night of the Bozos, Horn Book,* February, 1984, pp. 65-66.

Ojibway, Mary, review of *Something beyond Paradise, Voice of Youth Advocates,* June, 1987, p. 84.

Parravano, Martha V., review of *Risk 'n' Roses, Horn Book,* January, 1991, p. 70.

Slepian, Jan, essay in *Something about the Author Autobiographical Series,* Volume 8, Gale, 1989, pp. 263-73.

Slepian, Jan, essay in *Speaking for Ourselves, Too,* compiled and edited by Donald R. Gallo, National Council of Teachers of English, 1993, pp. 192-93.

■ For More Information See

BOOKS

Fifth Book of Junior Authors and Illustrators, edited by Sally Holmes Holtze, H. W. Wilson, 1983.

Something about the Author, Gale, Volume 51, 1988, Volume 85, 1996.

PERIODICALS

Best Sellers, October, 1981, p. 279; May, 1986, p. 80.

Booklist, July 15, 1980, p. 1677; April 1, 1987, p. 1199; January 15, 1990, p. 1914; May 1, 1992, p. 1612; October 1, 1993, p. 335; March 1, 1995, p. 1250.

Bulletin of the Center for Children's Books, March, 1986, p. 138; July, 1987, p. 219; April, 1989, p. 205; November, 1990, p. 70.

Childhood Education, March, 1981, pp. 208, 235; March, 1984, p. 289.

Growing Point, January, 1982, p. 4013.

Interracial Books for Children, No. 4, 1982, p. 10.

Junior Bookshelf, June, 1982, p. 109.

Kirkus Reviews, November 1, 1983, p. 208; May 1, 1987, p. 725; March 1, 1989, p. 384; July 15, 1990, p. 1006; June 1, 1993, p. 728.

Library Journal, January 15, 1968, p. 285; January 15, 1969, p. 290.

Locus, July, 1993, p. 46.

Los Angeles Times Book Review, April 23, 1989, p. 10.

New Advocate, winter, 1990, p. 72; spring, 1991, p. 135; spring, 1994, p. 153.

New York Times Book Review, September 12, 1982, p. 55; January 20, 1991, p. 28.

Publishers Weekly, June 19, 1981, p. 100; May 29, 1987, p. 80; July 13, 1990, p. 56; August 10, 1992, p. 72; May 24, 1993, p. 89; July 18, 1994, p. 248; February 27, 1995, p. 39.

Quill & Quire, February, 1995, p. 39.

School Librarian, June, 1982, p. 137.

School Library Journal, April, 1987, p. 113; April, 1989, p. 104; April, 1990, p. 97; November, 1990, p. 118; October, 1993, p. 130.

Times Educational Supplement, November 20, 1981, p. 33.

Voice of Youth Advocates, February, 1991, p. 358.

Washington Post Book World, November 8, 1981, p. 14.*

—Sketch by Pamela L. Shelton

Robert Swindells

■ Personal

Born March 20, 1939, in Bradford, Yorkshire, England; son of Albert Henry (in sales) and Alice (Lee) Swindells; married, August, 1962; wife's name, Cathy (divorced, c. 1976); married Brenda Marriott, 1982; children: (first marriage) Linda, Jill. *Education:* Huddersfield Polytechnic, teaching certificate, 1972; Bradford University, M.A., 1988. *Politics:* "Ecology." *Hobbies and other interests:* Reading (almost anything), walking, travel, watching films.

■ Addresses

Home and office—3 Upwood Park, Black Moor Rd., Oxenhope, Keighley, West Yorkshire BD22 9SS, England. *Agent*—Jennifer Luithlen, "The Rowans," 88 Holmfield Rd., Leicester LE2 1SB, England.

■ Career

Telegraph and Argus, Bradford, Yorkshire, England, copyholder, 1954-57, advertising clerk, 1960-67; Hepworth & Grandage (turbine manufacturer), Bradford, engineer, 1967-69; Undercliffe First, Bradford, elementary school teacher, 1972-77; Southmere First, Bradford, part-time teacher, 1977-80; full-time writer, 1980—. *Military service:* Royal Air Force, 1957-60. *Member:* Society of Authors.

■ Awards, Honors

Children's Books of the Year selection, Child Study Association of America, 1975, for *When Darkness Comes;* National Book Award nomination, children's category, Arts Council of Great Britain, 1980, for *The Moonpath and Other Stories;* Other Award, 1984, Children's Book Award, Federation of Children's Book Groups, and Carnegie Medal runner-up, British Library Association, both 1985, all for *Brother in the Land;* Children's Book Award, 1990, for *Room 13;* Carnegie Medal, 1994, for *Stone Cold;* Earthworm Award, senior fiction category, 1995, for *Timesnatch.*

■ Writings

When Darkness Comes, illustrated by Charles Keeping, Brockhampton Press, 1973, Morrow, 1975.
A Candle in the Night, illustrated by Gareth Floyd, David & Charles, 1974, published as *A Candle in the Dark,* Knight, 1983.
Voyage to Valhalla, illustrated by Victor Ambrus, Hodder & Stoughton, 1976, Heinemann Educational, 1977, Knight Books, 1994.

The Very Special Baby, illustrated by Ambrus, Hodder & Stoughton, 1977, Prentice-Hall, 1978.

The Ice Palace, illustrated by June Jackson, Hamish Hamilton, 1977.

Dragons Live Forever, illustrated by Petula Stone, Prentice-Hall, 1978.

The Weather-Clerk, illustrated by Stone, Hodder & Stoughton, 1979.

The Moonpath and Other Stories, Wheaton, 1979, published as *The Moonpath and Other Tales of the Bizarre,* illustrated by Reg Sandland, Carolrhoda Books, 1983.

Norah's Ark, illustrated by Avril Haynes, Wheaton, 1979.

Norah's Shark, illustrated by Haynes, Wheaton, 1979.

Ghost Ship to Ganymede, illustrated by Jeff Burns, Wheaton, 1980.

Norah and the Whale, illustrated by Haynes, Wheaton, 1981.

Norah to the Rescue, illustrated by Haynes, Wheaton, 1981.

World Eater, Hodder & Stoughton, 1981, Knight, 1983.

The Wheaton Book of Science Fiction Stories, illustrated by Gary Long, Wheaton, 1982.

Brother in the Land, Oxford University Press, 1984, Holiday House, 1985.

The Thousand Eyes of Night, Hodder & Stoughton, 1985.

The Ghost Messengers, Hodder & Stoughton, 1986.

Staying Up, Oxford University Press, 1986.

Mavis Davis, illustrated by Amelia Rosato, Oxford University Press, 1988.

The Postbox Mystery, illustrated by Kate Rogers, Hodder & Stoughton, 1988.

A Serpent's Tooth, Hamish Hamilton, 1988, Holiday House, 1989.

Follow a Shadow, Hamish Hamilton, 1989, Holiday House, 1990.

Night School, illustrated by Rob Chapman, Paperbird, 1989.

Room 13, illustrated by Jon Riley, Doubleday, 1989.

Daz 4 Zoe, Hamish Hamilton, 1990.

Tom Kipper, illustrated by Scoular Anderson, Macmillan, 1990.

Dracula's Castle, illustrated by Riley, Doubleday, 1991.

Hydra, Doubleday, 1991.

Rolf and Rosie, illustrated by David McKee, Andersen Press, 1992.

You Can't Say I'm Crazy, illustrated by Tony Ross, Hamish Hamilton, 1992.

Fallout, Morrow, 1992.

The Go-Ahead Gang, illustrated by M. Bradley, Hamish Hamilton, 1992.

Inside the Worm, illustrated by Riley, Doubleday, 1993.

Sam and Sue and Lavatory Lou, illustrated by Val Biro, Simon & Schuster, 1993.

The Secret of Weeping Wood, illustrated by Carolyn Dinan, Scholastic, 1993.

The Siege of Frimly Prim, illustrated by Anderson, Methuen, 1993.

We Didn't Mean to, Honest!, illustrated by Dinan, Scholastic, 1993.

Stone Cold, Hamish Hamilton, 1994.

Timesnatch, Doubleday, 1994.

Kidnap at Denton Farm, illustrated by Dinan, Deutsch, 1994.

Jacqueline Hyde, Transworld, 1996.

Last Bus, illustrated by Mark Edwards, Hamish Hamilton, 1997.

"ALFIE" SERIES; TRANSLATOR

Gunilla Bergström, *Alfie and His Secret Friend,* Wheaton, 1979.

Bergström, *Who'll Save Alfie Atkins?,* Wheaton, 1979.

Bergström, *Alfie and the Monster,* Wheaton, 1979.

Bergström, *You're a Sly One, Alfie Atkins,* Wheaton, 1979.

Bergström, *Is That a Monster, Alfie Atkins?,* Farrar, Straus, 1989.

OTHER

Contributor to books, including the short story "Moths" to *The Methuen Book of Strange Tales,* edited by Jean Russell, illustrated by Tony Ross, Methuen, 1980, and *Haunting Christmas Tales,* Scholastic, 1991.

■ Sidelights

Historical fact and supernatural elements often intermingle in the contemporary young adult novels of Robert Swindells. Perhaps best known for his anti-nuclear novel *Brother in the Land,* Swindells's other works realistically portray young adults dealing with family problems and social issues while also experiencing visits from shadowy figures and creatures from other planets. "His stories exhibit sheer narrative energy to a high degree: common assent among readers is that few writers' pages are more compulsively turned over," declares Dennis Hamley in an essay for *Twentieth-Century Young Adult Writers*. "Through an acute historical sense, profound understanding and unease about today's social conditions, and logical projection of them into convincing and disturbing dystopias, Swindells uses narrative to dramatise human failings and young adult possibility highly effectively." A *Junior Bookshelf* reviewer similarly states that "here is a writer who can tell a tale forcefully and clearly, and can put the young person's viewpoint on topical matters without the intrusion of adult overtones."

Born on March 20, 1939, in Bradford, Yorkshire, England, Swindells was the eldest child in his family; he was later joined by three brothers and a sister. In the meantime, however, important historical events were just beginning, including the start of World War II. Six months old at the time, Swindells didn't really understand that his father, a salesman for a wholesale floor covering company, had been drafted into the Royal Air Force. "He'd driven the company's vans for many years so they made him a driver and he left us," remembers Swindells in an essay for *Something about the Author Autobiography Series* (*SAAS*). "I was too young to really know him then, and for me he became someone who dropped by now and then to make a fuss of Mum and me before roaring off to wherever it was he went in his big smoky truck."

It was during the Luftwaffe bombing of the city on August 28, 1940, that Swindells's brother Donald was born. Having walked through the raid to be with his new son, Swindells's father decided soon after to move the family to a rented cottage ten miles outside the city. "We were to live there till I was nearly five, though Bradford was never bombed again, and my earliest conscious memories are centred around that tiny community which was called Spring Wells," relates Swindells in *SAAS*, adding: "Those first memories include a ginger cat named Toscanini who lived next door and lived on cheese, Mum slicing her weekly egg in halves for Donald and me to share, and the excitement generated by the arrival of parcels from Canada." By this time Swindells's father was stationed overseas in Calgary, and every so often he sent glorious packages filled with sweets and other supplies.

Aside from the celebrations surrounding the arrivals of the Canadian packages, there wasn't much in the way of entertainment out in the country. Swindells's mother had a radio, and she also passed the time by taking her two young sons for long walks in the surrounding moorland: "As we walked, Mum would tell us the names of the birds and the wildflowers we'd see along the way, and this gave me a love of and interest in nature which is with me to this day."

It was during this time in the country that Swindells also developed his first images of the German enemy as he listened to his mother and her friend Mrs. Applegate talk about the war. These discussions, combined with images of characters from two popular commercials of the day, had Swindells imagining Germans to be large, black, hairy creatures with fangs who dropped bombs from aeroplanes. "I was four when I found out that Germans were people," reveals Swindells in *SAAS*. "I sat there on the floor and thought, People! Germans are people. I remember to this day what the shock of that realisation felt like. It was a mingling of enormous surprise and sweet relief: relief because, no matter what sort of people Germans were, they were just people, and couldn't possibly be anywhere near as terrifying as the hairy, razor-fanged monstrosities who had haunted my dreams for so long."

When Swindells turned five in 1944, he and his mother and brother moved back to the city so he could start school, even though the war was still nearly a year from being over. "And so I went to school," states Swindells. "Each child had a peg on the classroom wall to hang his gas mask on. We did gas drill and shelter drill, but we were only five so we didn't really know what it was all about." School assemblies were also filled with air raid drills, and every time an aeroplane flew over the school yard all the children scattered and ran to the high walls surrounding the school. There was even a visit from a policeman who showed the first movie Swindells had ever seen. In this film two young boys find a shiny object in a ditch, which turns out to be a bomb that explodes. "Apparently there were rumours at this time that the Nazis were dropping small, brightly coloured bombs which exploded, not on impact but in response to body heat," explains Swindells in *SAAS*. "I don't believe it now, but I did then, and it must've been about 1948 before I picked anything up off the road."

It was while in school that Swindells learned of the end of the war. In August of that same year his brother David was born and his father came home for good; the house was now full and Swindells found it difficult to find a quiet place in which to read. "I learned to sink so deeply into whatever fantasy I was reading about that mayhem might erupt all around and I wouldn't even notice," he points out in *SAAS*. "Books became an escape route for me. A way out of the house. Out of the city. Out of my very ordinary life."

Swindells's life became more complicated with the end of the war. A new brother, Peter, was born. His parents began to have problems as they struggled to provide for their newly expanded family. Swindells's father was away for long periods of time for his sales job, which only brought in a fluctuating income, and his mother seemed resentful of being left to deal with the kids alone again as she had during the war. "Anyway, the strain began to cause rows between them which distressed me greatly," reveals Swindells in *SAAS*. "I retreated even further into my fantasy world, reading all day when I wasn't in school and often, with the aid of a flashlight, far into the night." It was at this point that Swindells began making up his own stories. "In these stories I was a six-foot-tall hero, a child-genius, a red-deer stag. I'd play these stories back endlessly on my long walks to and from school, and at night in my bed. It was better than dwelling on the ceaseless bickering, the thousand shabby little economies of home. Better than reality."

Childhood Disappointment

When Swindells reached the age of eleven reality proved disappointing for him once again: he failed the eleven-plus examination, which meant he would only get an elementary education before leaving school at the age of fifteen to work. While dealing with his own shattered dreams of becoming a teacher, Swindells was also forced to face the disapproval of his father, who had left school at the age of twelve. "He began to mock my constant reading, and frequently gave it as his opinion that I'd never amount to anything," Swindells relates in *SAAS*. "Sometimes he'd say this in front of other people—people I cared about. I had no defence. I was filled with a sort of helpless rage. He'd been no good at school—what reason had he to expect his kid to be any different? And any-

way I'd show him. I'd be something he wasn't. I'd never empty dustbins, that's for sure."

The school Swindells did attend was Lapage Street Secondary Modern, and it was here that he met Mr. Gledhill, an inspirational English teacher. "He didn't just teach it—he loved it and cared about it, and he cared about us too," remembers Swindells in *SAAS*. "We weren't failures to him. He taught us with flair and with energy, and at the end of each day he read to us, and this was where his greatest talent lay. He didn't just read— he did all the voices and a lot of the actions too. . . . He lost himself in the story—forgot where he was—fenced and ran and wrestled, right there in front of the class. He mesmerized us and then he told us we could be anything we wanted—all we had to do was believe." It was Mr. Gledhill who entered Swindells in an essay contest during his last year at school. Organized by the Royal National Lifeboat Institution, the contest consisted of writing an essay on the lifeboat service, and Swindells won, giving him a well-needed boost of confidence in his intellectual abilities.

Just a few days after his fifteenth birthday, Swindells got his first job in a silk-screen printing factory as a trainee. The wages and the work suited him fine, but he became interested in another job when he saw an advertisement for a copyholder in the local newspaper. And so for the next two years Swindells worked for this newspaper, reading original copy aloud to a proofreader who checked it against the proofs. "The proofreaders were bright, literate types who enjoyed playing with the language—solving crosswords, inventing puns, composing satirical verses about the boss—stuff like that," describes Swindells in his autobiographical essay. "They discussed the news stories too, pointing out to us kids examples of political bias in the reporting and answering our questions when we read something we didn't understand. Those two years were a continuation of my education, though I didn't spot that at the time."

While satisfied with his work life, Swindells's home life was quickly deteriorating; he and his brothers were growing up and the house became even more crowded. In addition to the privacy problems, there was still a lack of money and Swindells could not get along with his father anymore. At the same time, his mother was ill, in the early stages of multiple sclerosis, though this

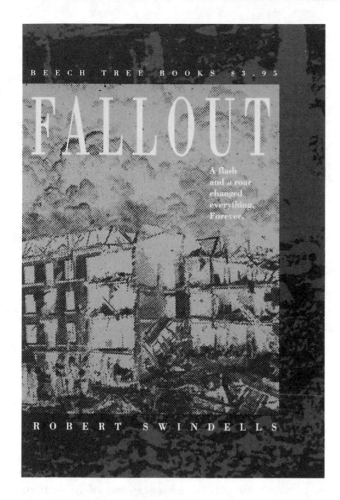

This powerful 1992 work places Danny and his brother in a position of survival after a nuclear device explodes, killing their mother and cutting off communication to the outside world.

remained undiagnosed until seven years later. The situation worsened when Swindells got into a physical fight with his father one night in defense of his mother. It was now impossible for him to live at home any longer, so a couple of days later he enlisted in the Royal Air Force for three years.

Early Fatherhood

Although he originally wanted to fly, Swindells was unable to qualify as a pilot because of his poor vision and lack of academic qualifications; he was made a clerk instead and sent to Germany. "It was okay, especially abroad, but I didn't like it enough to extend my engagement, and so in 1960, at twenty-and-a-half I came out, went back to the local paper, and started looking round for

a girl," states Swindells in *SAAS*. He found this girl in the spring of 1961 when he was twenty-two and she was only approaching sixteen. "Her name was Cathy, and we fell for each other on our first date," remembers Swindells. "We saw each other almost every night after that. It was the dawn of the swinging sixties—the beginning of the sexual revolution—and our discovery a year later that we were about to become parents obliged us to advance our marriage plans by several months."

Married in 1962, the couple welcomed their daughter Linda in January of 1963 and managed to put a deposit down on a small house soon thereafter. "It was a tight squeeze financially and I suppose we were too young really for parenthood, but we were happy," Swindells describes in *SAAS*. This new life brought new friends as well, including the Horner couple next door, who were both in their eighties and had been active in the South African War and the two world wars. One day Mrs. Horner told Cathy an old wives' tale about avoiding pregnancy; however, the Swindells were soon expecting their second child. "We believed her (well—old folks are wise, right?) and as a result Linda got a sister when she was just one year and three days old," states Swindells in *SAAS*. "Cathy and I were now eighteen and twenty-three respectively, and parents twice over."

For the next few years life was hard and hectic for the Swindells family. The new baby, Jill, suffered from colic, which caused many sleepless nights, as did the dog who lived down the street and began yapping at six every morning. To make matters worse, by 1964 Swindells's mother's disease had been diagnosed, and it progressed rapidly until 1966 when she died. Feeling depressed and responsible for his mother, Swindells only found relief after visiting a psychiatrist who told him that it was actually parents who were responsible for their children, not the other way around. "The relief was unbelievable," remembers Swindells in *SAAS*. "I felt like I was floating six inches clear of the ground all the time. That man's words, together with his prescription, preserved my sanity through the final weeks of my mother's life and enabled me to cope with her death which, in the absence of help, would probably have killed me too."

Several months after the pain of his mother's death, Swindells found new hope when he discovered that his insurance collector was going off to college to become a teacher. "It was a turning point in my life: the moment I realised it wasn't too late," observes Swindells in *SAAS*. "If I started now and stuck at it, I might rescue my dream after all. That September I went along and enrolled for some GCE classes." Two years later, after giving up his job at the paper for a more convenient one at a factory, Swindells passed all the necessary exams and applied at a teacher training college in Hudderfield. "I couldn't believe it," continues Swindells in *SAAS*. "I'd gone in a factory hand and come out a student: the first college student we'd ever had in our family. I'd made it. I was going to be a teacher after all."

College Dreams Fulfilled

Although Swindells's wife was equally as excited for him, she was also a bit uneasy about the changes to come. "A whole new world had opened its doors to me, and she couldn't help wondering how it might affect us," explains Swindells in *SAAS*. "I wasn't worried. I couldn't see past the golden glow in my head. I gave notice at the factory, threw away my greasy coveralls, and decked myself in jeans and gaudy scarf. I was twenty-nine, but I bought a guitar and started to grow my hair." College life turned out to be everything Swindells expected it to be, and he enjoyed every minute of it. Choosing English as his major subject, he spent his time at lectures, tutorials, and the theatre, later discussing his studies over coffee for hours on end.

Although he originally expected to struggle in comparison to the young students around him, Swindells instead excelled in college, earning A's for most of his essays and moving to the top part of his class. "It was a good feeling," he continues in *SAAS*. "A healing feeling, if you'll pardon the alliteration. Accustomed from the age of eleven to regard myself as a failure, I was finding success. 'Mum,' I'd sometimes whisper, though I had no religion, no belief in afterlife, 'do you see me? Do you know?' It mattered to me then, and it matters now."

Also among Swindells's studies in college were children's novels, of which he read several. "I loved them," he states in *SAAS*. "I thought, These are much more fun than most of the stuff I read when I was a kid. These writers don't talk down.

It's not about fairies. They assume intelligence in the reader. I also thought, I bet I could write one of these." During his third year Swindells attempted to do just this. Required to write a Long Study, or thesis, he requested permission to instead write a children's novel, which he was allowed to do after submitting a sample chapter for approval. Over the next three months Swindells completed this novel, titled "Aftermyth," turning in chapters as he finished them and keeping a journal to record his thought processes along the way. Once complete, the novel was reviewed by a lecturer from another university, Dr. Atkinson, who summoned Swindells to suggest that he submit his finished product to a publisher. "I think I must've gaped," recalls Swindells. "I mean come on. This wasn't real. It was like one of the fantasies I used to make up about myself when I was a kid. Any minute now I was going to wake up in the factory and find I'd been dozing at my bench."

Becomes Published Teacher

Dr. Atkinson proceeded to give Swindells the names of several publishers, and he mailed the manuscript off to the first one on the list. As soon as the package was in the mail he forgot about it, concentrating instead on the end of his schooling and the beginning of his teaching career. Only a week later, however, there was a response from a Brockhampton Press editor who wanted Swindells's book. "So. It was a case of the right place at the right time, and I was in," observes Swindells in *SAAS*. "When I started teaching that September my book was in course of preparation, and it would be published the following spring while I was still doing my probationary year. It was a heady time for me. Suddenly here I was a teacher and a writer too. My life was changing with alarming rapidity."

One of the consequences of these changes came in the form of an invitation to a publisher's party in London. Both Swindells and his wife were terrified that they would not fit in at such a party. With his second novel underway, though, Swindells didn't want to jeopardize his chances of getting it published, so he decided to go. Calling in advance about the dress, he was told to wear whatever he liked, but decided to wear his best suit anyway. "When I walked in the room it was full of people in jeans and jumpers," Swindells recalls in *SAAS*. "In my dark suit I stood out like a Mormon at a convention of Hell's Angels. Somebody put a drink in my hand and steered me towards a group in the middle of the room. They were talking about reviewers. I didn't have a book out yet, so I couldn't contribute much to this conversation. After a minute or two I moved on. Nobody noticed. I couldn't bring myself to muscle in on another group so I stood alone, wondering how soon it'd be okay for me to leave." At this point, an elderly gentleman sitting nearby invited Swindells to sit down and proceeded to put him at ease, asking about his book and pointing out various people in the room. Swindells's rescuer turned out to be H. E. Todd, the author of the "Bobby Brewster" books who traveled around the world telling his stories to children.

This first publishing party behind him, Swindells continued work on his second novel, which he finished just as his first one was published. "I sent it in, expecting the same sort of praise I'd gotten the last time," he relates in *SAAS*. "Not only did I not get it, but the thing was rejected outright." The editor of Swindells's first book had moved on to a new publisher, though, and when he heard of the rejection he asked the author to send him the book, and then proceeded to publish it. "So. Two written, two published," continues Swindells in *SAAS*. "I thanked my lucky stars and started work on a third. Teaching was okay, too, but things at home were not."

Swindells's new life brought with it new interests and new friends, all of which contributed to the disintegration of his marriage. He was no longer the man his wife had married and she resented it, which in turn made him angry. The relationship continued to deteriorate until 1976, when Swindells met Brenda Marriott during a trip to visit Beatrix Potter's cottage. Both were in marriages that had already begun to disintegrate and they started seeing each other, eventually leaving their homes and moving in together. "We seized our chance of happiness and in so doing, made others unhappy," reveals Swindells in *SAAS*. "We knew this at the time, and we know it now."

During these changes in his personal life, Swindells continued to write in the mornings while he taught full time for six years. Most of his writings were published, and he was steadily building up a body of work, so he began to receive invitations to speak to children about his books.

If you enjoy the works of Robert Swindells, you may want to check out the following books and films:

Eileen Charbonneau, *The Ghosts of Stony Clove*, 1988.
Barry Faville, *The Keeper*, 1988.
Jill Paton Walsh, *A Parcel of Patterns*, 1983.
George Miller's "Mad Max" trilogy, including *Mad Max* (1980), *The Road Warrior* (1981), and *Mad Max Beyond Thunderdome* (1985).
Testament, Paramount, 1983.

Because of his own teachings, he could only accept the weekend and evening invitations. Frightened at first, Swindells gradually learned how to talk to audiences of adults and children, and since he was getting fees for these engagements, he eventually decided to quit full-time teaching in order to do more of it. "It was a risky thing to do, especially just then," points out Swindells in his autobiographical essay. "That same year, one of my editors left children's publishing, saying it had no future. Thanks a lot, I thought. And to bolster my confidence still further, my publisher turned down the first two books I wrote as a full-timer. They must have known this was a make or break time for me, and yet they acted without apparent compunction, and this shattered a couple of illusions I'd had regarding the nature of the relationship between publisher and author. It's a lesson I've never forgotten."

Anti-Nuclear Sentiments Bring Success

The next four years were a struggle for the new couple, during which they had to rely heavily on Brenda's salary as a teacher. Then, in 1984, Swindells's antinuclear novel *Brother in the Land* was published to great critical acclaim, bringing the author the Children's Book Award among other honors. "Almost overnight my name became a familiar one in the little world of children's books, and I knew I wouldn't be returning to the classroom," states Swindells in *SAAS*. Written in the form of a diary, *Brother in the Land* describes the effects of a nuclear bomb dropped on England. Danny, the teenage author of the diary, survives with his father and brother Ben; his father is killed soon after, though, when their cellar is raided by the new rulers of the land. This forces Danny and Ben to join an agricultural commune, where new hope for the future is soon crushed when the crops fail and women give birth to monstrous babies because of the radiation. As the commune breaks up, Danny and Ben set off with their new friend Kim in one final attempt for survival.

"In *Brother in the Land,* . . . Robert Swindells has created a horrifyingly credible picture of the aftermath of the bomb in a Yorkshire town," asserts a *Junior Bookshelf* reviewer. Eugene La Faille, writing in *Voice of Youth Advocates,* similarly maintains that *Brother in the Land* "realistically chronicles the life of a family and community after a nuclear war." And Hamley points out that "few post-nuclear holocaust novels are as grim and uncompromising," going on to conclude: "Swindells looks fearlessly at the overwhelming nature of his subject: a deserved award-winner, the novel has had great effect in schools and must rank at the top of its particular sub-genre."

Writing of his anti-nuclear beliefs in his autobiographical essay, Swindells explains that "the insights I acquired through study have helped me use my writing to promote, without didacticism, ideas about peace, tolerance, and cooperation. It is, I believe, a sad commentary on the state of our society that a concern for these civilising ideals tends still to make enemies for a writer: my hope for the future resides in the fact that these enemies are always adults, never the young people for whom the books are written. . . . There will arise a generation, gentler and more wise than my own, and they will inherit the earth."

The world Swindells portrays in his novels previous to *Brother in the Land* is one of ghosts and other supernatural inhabitants from the earth and other planets. There is a Viking ghost in *Voyage to Valhalla,* a family who breeds baby dragons for a living in *Dragons Live Forever,* and a horrible space creature that is threatening to swallow the earth in the black hole that is its mouth in *World Eater.* In this last novel, published in 1981, it is only young Orville Coppelstone, engrossed in his new pigeon, that realizes the threat a new egg-shaped planet poses to earth. This planet is in actuality a large egg, and when it hatches the organism it produces will in fact swallow the earth in one big black hole. With the help of a journalist friend, Orville comes up with a scheme that

is successful in saving the earth from the giant space egg. *World Eater* "is a most ingenious tale, observes a *Junior Bookshelf* reviewer, adding that it "shows just how far-reaching is the author's imagination and just how much in tune he is with the types of story that children like to read."

Returning to his outer space and supernatural themes after *Brother in the Land,* Swindells creates a new race of creatures to invade earth in *The Thousand Eyes of Night.* The book's prologue provides the background—as the thirteenth planet that orbited Betelgeuse is about to be destroyed, its life-forms are dispatched to find a new home. These life-forms are actually super-mice that end up on earth in a railway tunnel where the local children like to play. Through a series of discoveries the children figure out what is happening, but can get no help from the adults in their lives (who don't believe their story), and so must conquer the invaders on their own. In *The Thousand Eyes of Night,* asserts a *Junior Bookshelf* contributor, "Swindells's plot is tight and to a degree *unsensational* while his child and adult characters are deftly sketched within the space allowed him. There is a very full ration of plot within only 120 pages. It has nightmare potential, though."

Ghosts, often the makings of nightmares themselves, play major roles in both *The Ghost Messengers* and *A Serpent's Tooth.* The young protagonists in both stories must deal with their visions of people from the past while fighting such present-day problems as conservation and nuclear waste disposal at the same time. *The Ghost Messengers* is a "well-plotted book [that] makes the ghost messengers credible and proceeds at a disciplined pace to a genuinely exciting climax," concludes a *Junior Bookshelf* reviewer. And another reviewer for *Junior Bookshelf* sums up *A Serpent's Tooth* by writing: "The story provokes thought all through its high drama. It may speak directly to many children distressed with family troubles or concerned about conflicts in society."

Swindells's 1989 novel *Follow a Shadow* mixes in themes of loyalty and choices with the supernatural elements of many of his previous stories. In this tale teenager Tim South finds a portrait of a man who looks amazingly like him. He later learns that the man is referred to as the "wicked man" who seduced his great-great-great-great grandmother when she was an innocent young girl. During a class trip to the Yorkshire moors

Tim and his friends are rescued during a strong storm by a ghostly figure who turns out to be the man in the drawing—Branwell Bronte. This leads Tim to realize that he has been following down the same wicked path to despair that Branwell did (he has been torn between the values of his gang and the stability of his girlfriend Dilys). *Follow a Shadow* is an "intriguing story, with a clever historical tie-in" and "sustains suspense throughout," states Bruce Anne Shook in *School Library Journal*. Hamley writes that "the contemporary narrative is handled surely," adding that *Follow a Shadow* ends with "a brilliantly realised climax."

The same could be said for Swindells's career; he has achieved far more than he ever hoped for on that day long ago when his father told him he would amount to nothing. "And so, there it is," the author and teacher concludes in *SAAS*. "I've neither worked particularly hard nor lived a particularly virtuous life and yet I have everything I need: everything I ever truly wanted. Why? How do these things happen? Partly of course it's being born in the right place. . . . Partly it's the talents you're born with. . . . Mostly, though, it's other people. Parents. Teachers. An understanding employer somewhere along the way. A rich old uncle. Some we remember with gratitude and affection. Most we don't remember at all, or never even knew, so that we're tempted to think of ourselves as self-made men, when in truth there's no such thing. . . . I hope you can hear me, Mum. You, and all the others, because I want to say thanks. I mean it. It's been fantastic, and it never would have happened without you."

■ Works Cited

Review of *Brother in the Land*, *Junior Bookshelf*, October, 1984, p. 222.

Review of *The Ghost Messengers*, *Junior Bookshelf*, February, 1986, p. 41.
Hamley, Dennis, essay for *Twentieth-Century Young Adult Writers*, St. James Press, 1994.
La Faille, Eugene, review of *Brother in the Land*, *Voice of Youth Advocates*, August, 1985, p. 190.
Review of *A Serpent's Tooth*, *Junior Bookshelf*, June, 1988, p. 153.
Shook, Bruce Anne, review of *Follow a Shadow*, *School Library Journal*, October, 1990, p. 145.
Swindells, Robert, essay in *Something about the Author Autobiography Series*, Volume 14, Gale, 1992.
Review of *The Thousand Eyes of Night*, *Junior Bookshelf*, June, 1985, p. 147.
Review of *World Eater*, *Junior Bookshelf*, February, 1982, p. 38.

■ For More Information See

PERIODICALS

Booklist, April 1, 1984, p. 1122; August, 1988, pp. 1915-16.
Books for Keeps, September, 1993, p. 17; November, 1993, p. 26; January, 1994, p. 9; January, 1997.
Growing Point, March, 1982, pp. 4024-26; March, 1985, pp. 4406-7; July, 1988, p. 5001.
Junior Bookshelf, October, 1977, p. 293; February, 1979, p. 42; August, 1994, p. 151; October, 1994, pp. 190-91.
School Library Journal, April, 1984, p. 120; April, 1988, p. 114.
Times Educational Supplement, September 30, 1994, p. 19.
Times Literary Supplement, July 16, 1976, p. 885; April 13, 1984, p. 414; April 12, 1985, p. 418.*

—Sketch by Susan Reicha

Mark Twain

onym, 1864; *Sacramento Union*, Sacramento, CA, correspondent under Twain pseudonym, 1866-69; *Buffalo Express*, editor under Twain pseudonym, 1869-71. Owner of Charles L. Webster & Co. (publishers) in early 1880s. *Military Service:* Confederate Army during Civil War; became second lieutenant.

■ Personal

Real name, Samuel Longhorne Clemens; born November 30, 1835, in Florida, MO; died of heart disease, April 21, 1910, in Redding, CT; buried in Elmira, NY; also wrote under pseudonyms Sieur Louis de Conte, Josh, S. L. C., Quentin Curtius Snodgrass, and Thomas Jefferson Snodgrass; son of John Marshall (a lawyer) and Jane (Lampton) Clemens; married Olivia Langdon, February 2, 1870 (died, 1904); children: Langdon, Olivia Susan, Clara, Jean Lampton.

■ Career

Writer. Worked as a printers' apprentice and typesetter in Hannibal, MO, 1847-50; associated with *Hannibal Journal*, 1850-52; typesetter, 1853-57; apprentice riverboat pilot, 1857-59; riverboat pilot, 1859-60; secretary and government worker in Nevada, 1860-62; miner, 1862; *Territorial Enterprise*, Virginia City, NV, reporter (sometimes under pseudonym Mark Twain), 1862-64; *Morning Call*, San Francisco, CA, reporter under Twain pseud-

■ Awards, Honors

Honorary M.A., Yale University, 1888; Litt.D., Yale University, 1901; LL.D., University of Missouri, 1902; named to American Academy of Arts and Letters, 1904; D.Litt., Oxford University, 1907.

■ Writings

NOVELS UNDER PSEUDONYM MARK TWAIN, EXCEPT WHERE NOTED

(With Charles Dudley Warner) *The Gilded Age: A Tale of Today*, illustrated by Augustus Hoppin and others, American Publishing, 1873, Twain's portion published separately as *The Adventures of Colonel Sellers*, edited by Charles Neider, Doubleday, 1965.

The Adventures of Tom Sawyer, illustrated by True Williams, American Publishing, 1876.

The Prince and the Pauper, Chatto & Windus, 1881, Osgood, 1882.

The Adventures of Huckleberry Finn, Tom Sawyer's Comrade, illustrated by Edward Windsor Kemble, Chatto & Windus, 1884.

A Connecticut Yankee in King Arthur's Court, illustrated by Dan Beard, Webster, 1889, published in England as *A Yankee at the Court of King Arthur*, Chatto & Windus, 1889.

The American Claimant (adapted from the play by Twain and William Dean Howells; also see below),Webster, 1892.

Tom Sawyer Abroad, by Huck Finn, illustrated by Dan Beard, Webster, 1894.

Pudd'nhead Wilson: A Tale, Chatto & Windus, 1894, expanded as *The Tragedy of Pudd'nhead Wilson, and the Comedy of Those Extraordinary Twins*, American Publishing, 1894.

(Under pseudonym Sieur Louis de Conte) *Personal Recollections of Joan of Arc*, illustrated by E. V. Du Mond, Harper, 1896.

Extract from Captain Stormfield's Visit to Heaven, Harper, 1909.

The Mysterious Stranger: A Romance, illustrated by N. C. Wyeth, edited by Albert Bigelow Paine and Frederick A. Duneka, Harper, 1916.

Simon Wheeler: Detective (unfinished novel), edited by Franklin R. Rogers, New York Public Library, 1963.

Novels also published in various multi-title volumes, reprints, and selected editions. Selections also included in anthologies.

SHORT STORIES AND SKETCHES UNDER TWAIN PSEUDONYM

The Celebrated Jumping Frog of Calaveras County, and Other Sketches, edited by John Paul, C. H. Webb, 1867.

Screamers: A Gathering of Scraps of Humor, Delicious Bits, and Short Stories, J. C. Hotten, 1871.

Eye Openers: Good Things, Immensely Funny Sayings, and Stories, J. C. Hotten, c. 1871.

A Curious Dream, and Other Sketches, Routledge, 1872.

Mark Twain's Sketches, illustrated by R. T. Sperry, American News, 1874.

Mark Twain's Sketches: New and Old, American Publishing, 1876.

Merry Tales, Webster, 1892.

The 1,000,000 Pound Bank-Note, and Other New Stories, Webster, 1893.

Tom Sawyer, Detective, as Told By Huck Finn, and Other Stories, Chatto & Windus, 1896.

The Man That Corrupted Hadleyburg, and Other Stories and Essays, 1900, revised edition, Chatto & Windus, 1900.

A Double Barrelled Detective Story, illustrated by Lucius Hitchcock, Harper, 1902.

A Dog's Tale, illustrated by W. T. Smedley, Harper, 1904.

Extracts from Adam's Diary (also see below), illustrated by F. Strothmann, Harper, 1904.

Eve's Diary Translated from the Original Ms (also see below), illustrated by Lester Ralph, Harper, 1906.

The $30,000 Bequest, and Other Stories, Harper, 1906.

A Horse's Tale, illustrated by Lucius Hitchcock, Harper, 1907.

The Curious Republic of Gondour, and Other Whimsical Sketches, Boni & Liveright, 1919.

(With Bret Harte) *Sketches of the Sixties*, Howell, 1926.

Short Stories of Mark Twain, Funk & Wagnall, 1967.

The Diaries of Adam and Eve (contains excerpts from *Adam's Diary* and *Eve's Diary*), American Heritage, 1971.

Early Tales and Sketches, Volume 1: *1851-1864*, edited by Edgar M. Branch and Robert H. Hirst, Volume 2: *1864-1865*, edited by Edgar M. Branch, Robert H. Hirst, and Harriet Elinor Smith, University of California Press, 1979-81.

Short stories and sketches also published in various multi-title volumes, reprints, and selected editions. Selections also included in numerous anthologies.

PLAYS UNDER TWAIN PSEUDONYM

Colonel Sellers (five-act), produced in New York, 1874.

(With Bret Harte) *Ah Sin*, produced in Washington, DC, 1877.

Also author, with G. S. Densomore, of *The Gilded Age* (adapted from the novel by Twain and Warner), 1873; author, with William Dean Howells, of *The American Claimant; or, Mulberry Sellers Ten Years Later*, 1887. Plays also published in various multi-title volumes, reprints, and selected editions. Selections also included in numerous anthologies.

TRAVEL BOOKS UNDER TWAIN PSEUDONYM

The Innocents Abroad; or, The New Pilgrims' Progress, illustrated by True Williams, American Publishing, 1869, published in England as Volume 1: *Innocents Abroad*, Hotten, 1870, Volume 2: *The New Pilgrims' Progress*, Hotten, 1870.

The Innocents at Home (also see below), Routledge, 1872.

Roughing It, Routledge, 1872, revised edition (includes *The Innocents at Home*), American Publishing, 1872.

An Idle Excursion, Rose-Belford, 1878, revised as *Punch, Brothers, Punch!, and Other Sketches*, Slote, Woodman, 1878.

A Tramp Abroad, illustrated by Twain and others, American Publishing, 1880, excerpt published as *Jim Baker's Bluejay Yarn* (also see below).

Following the Equator: A Journey around the World, American Publishing, 1897, published in England as *More Tramps Abroad*, Chatto & Windus, 1897.

Europe and Elsewhere, edited by Albert Bigelow Paine, Harper, 1923.

Traveling with the Innocents Abroad: Mark Twain's Original Reports from Europe and the Holy Land, edited by Daniel Morley McKelthan, University of Oklahoma Press, 1958.

Jim Baker's Bluejay Yarn, illustrated by Fred Brenner, Orion Press, 1963.

Travel writings also published in various multi-title volumes, reprints, and selected editions. Selections also included in numerous anthologies.

ESSAYS UNDER TWAIN PSEUDONYM

How to Tell a Story, and Other Essays, Harper, 1897.

English as She Is Taught, Mutual Book Co., 1900.

King Leopold's Soliloquy: A Defense of His Congo Rule, P. R. Warren, 1905.

Editorial Wild Oats, Harper, 1905.

My Debut as a Literary Person, with Other Essays and Stories, American Publishing, 1906.

(Originally published anonymously) *What Is Man?*, De Vinne Press, 1906, revised as *What Is Man?, and Other Essays*, Harper, 1917.

Christian Science, with Notes Containing Corrections to Date, Harper, 1907.

Is Shakespeare Dead?, Harper, 1909.

In Defense of Harriet Shelley, and Other Essays, Harper, 1918.

Concerning the Jews, Harper, 1934.

Essays also published in various multi-title volumes, reprints, and selected editions. Selections also included in numerous anthologies.

CORRESPONDENCE UNDER TWAIN PSEUDONYM

Mark Twain's Letters (two volumes), edited by Albert Bigelow Paine, Harper, 1917.

Mark Twain, the Letter Writer, edited by Cyril Clemens, Meador, 1932.

Mark Twain's Letters to Will Bowen, edited by Theodore Hornberger, University of Texas Press, 1941.

The Love Letters of Mark Twain, edited by Dixon Wecter, Harper, 1949.

Mark Twain to Mrs. Fairbanks, edited by Dixon Wecter, Huntington Library, 1949.

Mark Twain to Uncle Remus, 1881-1885, edited by Thomas H. English, Emory University, 1953.

(With William Dean Howells) *Mark Twain-Howells Letters* (two volumes), edited by Henry Nash Smith and William M. Gibson, Belknap Press, 1960.

Mark Twain's Letters to Mary, edited by Lewis Leary, Columbia University Press, 1961.

Mark Twain: Letters from the Earth, edited by Bernard De Voto, preface by Henry Nash Smith, 1962.

Mark Twain's Letters from Hawaii, edited by A. Grove Day, Appleton-Century, 1966.

Mark Twain's Letters to His Publishers, edited and with an introduction by Hamlin Hill, University of California Press, 1967.

Mark Twain's Letters to Henry Huttleston Rogers, edited by Lewis Leary, University of California Press, 1969.

Mark Twain's Letters, Volume 1: *1853-1866*, edited by Edgar Marquess Branch, Michael B. Frank, and Kenneth B. Anderson, Volume 2: *1867-1868*, edited by Harriet Smith, et al, Volume 3: *1869*, edited by Victor Fischer, Michael Frank, and Dahlia Armon, Volume 4: *1870-1871*, edited by Victor Fischer, et al, University of California Press, 1988-1995.

Correspondence also published in other volumes, collections, and anthologies. The Twain Project at the University of California, Berkeley, is compiling the complete letters of Twain.

AUTOBIOGRAPHICAL WORKS UNDER TWAIN PSEUDONYM

Old Times on the Mississippi, Belford, 1876, reprinted as *The Mississippi Pilot*, Ward, Lock & Tyler, 1877, revised as *Life on the Mississippi*, Osgood, 1883, excerpt published as *The Boy's Ambition*, Lerner, 1975.

Mark Twain's Autobiography (two volumes), edited by Albert Bigelow Paine, Harper, 1924, edited as one volume by Charles Neider, Harper, 1959.

Autobiographical works also included in other multi-title volumes, collections, and anthologies.

COLLECTED JOURNALISM UNDER TWAIN PSEUDONYM

Letters from the Sandwich Islands Written for the Sacramento Union, edited by G. Ezra Dane, Grabhorn, 1937.

The Washoe Giant in San Francisco, edited by Franklin Walker, Fields, 1938.

Mark Twain's Letters in the Muscatine Journal, edited by Edgar M. Branch, Mark Twain Association of America, 1942.

Mark Twain of the Enterprise: Newspaper Articles and Other Documents, 1862-1864, edited by Henry Nash Smith, University of California Press, 1957.

Contributions to the Galaxy, 1868-1871, edited by Bruce R. McElderry, Jr., Scholars' Facsimiles and Reprints, 1961.

Mark Twain's San Francisco, edited by Bernard Taper, McGraw, 1963.

Clemens of the "Call": Mark Twain in San Francisco, edited by Edgar M. Branch, University of California Press, 1969.

ANTHOLOGIES UNDER TWAIN PSEUDONYM

The Family Mark Twain, Harper, 1935.

Mark Twain's Wit and Wisdom, edited by Cyril Clemens, Stokes, 1935.

The Portable Mark Twain, edited by Bernard De Voto, Viking, 1946.

Mark Twain on the Art of Writing, edited by Martion B. Fried, Salisbury Club, 1961.

Selected Shorter Writings of Mark Twain, edited by Walter Blair, Houghton, 1962.

Great Short Works of Mark Twain, edited by Justin Kaplan, Harper, 1967.

"What Is Man?," and Other Philosophical Writings, edited by Paul Baender, University of California Press, 1973.

Twain Unabridged, Running Press, 1976.

Mark Twain Speaking, edited by Paul Fatout, University of Iowa Press, 1976.

The Comic Mark Twain, Doubleday, 1977.

Mark Twain Speaks for Himself, edited by Paul Fatout, Purdue University Press, 1978.

The Devil's Race-Track: Mark Twain's "Great Dark" Writings, edited by John S. Tuckey, University of California Press, 1979.

Work also collected and represented in numerous other anthologies.

OTHER WORKS UNDER TWAIN PSEUDONYM, EXCEPT WHERE NOTED

Mark Twain's (Burlesque) Autobiography and First Romance, Sheldon, 1871.

(With others) *Practical Jokes with Artemus Ward*, J. C. Hotten, 1872.

A True Story [and] *The Recent Carnival of Crime*, Osgood, 1877.

"1601"; or, Conversation as It Was by the Social Fireside in the Time of the Tudors, [Cleveland], 1880.

The Stolen White Elephant, Etc., Osgood, 1882, published in England as *The Stolen White Elephant*, Chatto & Windus, 1882.

(Editor with William Dean Howells and others) *Mark Twain's Library of Humor*, illustrated by E. W. Kemble, Webster, 1888.

Mark Twain's Speeches, edited by F. A. Nast, Harper, 1910.

Mark Twain's Speeches (two volumes), edited by Albert Bigelow Paine, Harper, 1924.

(Under pseudonym Thomas Jefferson Snodgrass) *The Adventures of Thomas Jefferson Snodgrass*, edited by Charles Honce, Pascal Covici, 1928.

Mark Twain's Notebook, edited by Albert Bigelow Paine, Harper, 1935.

Mark Twain's Travels with Mr. Brown, edited by Franklin Walker and G. Ezra Dane, Knopf, 1940.

Mark Twain's First Story, Prairie Press, 1952.

Life as I Find It, edited by Charles Neider, Hanover House, 1961.

Mark Twain's "Mysterious Stranger" Manuscripts, edited by William G. Gibson, University of California Press, 1969.

Mark Twain's Notebooks and Journals, Volume 1: *1855-1873*, edited by Frederick Anderson, Michael B. Frank, and Kenneth Anderson, Volume 2: *1877-1883*, edited by Frederick Anderson, Lin Salamo, and Bernard L. Stein, Volume 3: *1883-1891*, edited by Robert Pack Browning, Michael B. Frank, and Lin Salamo, University of California Press, 1975-79.

Work also included in multi-title volumes and anthologies.

Contributor—sometimes under pseudonyms Quentin Curtius Snodgrass, Josh, and S. L. C.—to periodicals, including *Alta California, Atlantic Monthly, Californian, Century, Forum, Golden Era, Harper's, McClure's Weekly, New York Saturday Press, New York Tribune, North American Review,* and *Youth's Companion.*

COLLECTED WORKS

The Writings of Mark Twain (twenty-five volumes), American Publishing, 1899-1907.
The Writings of Mark Twain (twenty-five volumes), edited by Albert Bigelow Paine, Harper, 1906.
The Writings of Mark Twain (thirty-seven volumes), edited by Albert Bigelow Paine, Wells, 1922-1925.

Works also published in other multi-volume collections. The Mark Twain papers are mainly collected at the Bancroft Library, University of California, Berkeley. The Mark Twain Project at Berkeley is engaged in the publication of all of Twain's published and unpublished Papers and Works, projected at eighty volumes.

■ **Adaptations**

The Adventures of Huckleberry Finn was adapted as a motion picture titled *Huckleberry Finn,* in 1931 by Paramount, in 1939 by Metro-Goldwyn-Mayer (MGM), as a musical adaptation in 1974 by United Artists, and as a motion picture of the same title in 1960 by MGM and in 1993 by Disney Productions; *The Adventures of Tom Sawyer* was adapted as *Tom Sawyer* in 1930 by Paramount, as *Tom Sawyer, Detective* by Paramount in 1939, and as a motion picture of the same title in 1938 by Selznick International and in 1973 by United Artists; *A Connecticut Yankee in King Arthur's Court* was adapted as the film *A Connecticut Yankee* in 1931 by Twentieth Century-Fox, and as a motion picture of the same title in 1949 by Paramount; *The Prince and the Pauper* was adapted as a film of the same title in 1937 by Warner Brothers and as a motion picture titled *Crossed Swords* in 1978 by Warner Brothers; *A Double Barrelled Detective Story* was adapted as a film of the same title in 1965 by Saloon Productions; *The Celebrated Jumping Frog of Calaveras County, and Other Sketches* was adapted as a film titled *Best Man Wins* in 1948 by Columbia; *The 1,000,000 Pound Bank-Note, and*

Other New Stories was adapted for a film titled *Man with a Million* in 1954 by United Artists.

Among the many stagings of Twain's works are *Tom Sawyer* and *Huckleberry Finn;* some of Twain's writings have also been adapted as radio plays; *Huckleberry Finn* has also been staged as a musical. Twain's own life inspired *The Adventures of Mark Twain,* filmed by Warner Brothers in 1944, and such stage productions as *Mark Twain Tonight!*

■ **Sidelights**

At the end of a long and prolific career with the pen, America's favorite humorist grew reflective about his craft, yet kept his tongue firmly planted in his cheek: "I have always been able to gain my living without doing any work; for the writing of books and magazine matter was always play, not work. I enjoyed it; it was merely billiards to me." Thus could Samuel Clemens, writing in *Mark Twain's Autobiography,* sum up a half century of authorship and the penning of such classics as *The Adventures of Tom Sawyer, The Adventures of Huckleberry Finn,* and *Life on the Mississippi* as "Billiards." But as with so much else about Clemens, what was meant for public consumption was a very different matter from what went on in private.

Clemens's pseudonym, Mark Twain, is perhaps the most appropriate one in literature to date. Adapted from riverboat parlance to warn of shallow water—two fathoms or twelve feet—the term as a name fitted its bearer to perfection. There was always a "twaining" involved with Clemens, a paradoxical duality of dark and light. He was America's favorite humorist, yes, but also the author of such bleak and bitter works as *The Mysterious Stranger, Pudd'nhead Wilson,* and "The Man That Corrupted Hadleyburg." A great success in his day with mansions and servants and world travel, Clemens also suffered through the deaths of his wife of forty years and three of his children, the nervous collapse of the fourth, and bankruptcy at an age when most authors are hoping for comfortable retirement. A great innovator, using the vernacular in literature in a manner in which it had never been used before, Clemens gave birth to a peculiarly localized narrative fiction, prompting Ernest Hemingway's much later remark that all American literature derives from

Loosely based on the author's life, *The Adventures of Tom Sawyer* has become an American classic.

Huckleberry Finn. Yet Clemens was as much reviled as praised for this use of spontaneous speech patterns in his books and journalism. Such language was too much for genteel readers of the day, it was thought. And of this day, too, it would seem, for Clemens is still under the microscope in the late twentieth century for his language, though now such criticism is leveled in the name of political correctness. One of the most written about literary personages of American literature, Clemens held his chosen profession to be mere "billiards." Even his identity is fogged: was he Clemens or Twain? Several biographies have been written to discover the answer to that conundrum, yet the fact remains that Clemens left a literary legacy that is as beloved by young readers as by adults; he created characters such as Tom Sawyer and Huck Finn who continue to live independent lives from their creator.

A Missouri Upbringing

Clemens was born in Florida, Missouri, in 1835. This was the year of Halley's Comet; he would die seventy-five years later, the next time that comet was visible. At age four, young Clemens moved with his family of three brothers and two sisters to Hannibal, a small town on the Mississippi. Clemens's father, John Marshall Clemens, was on the slide from genteel life. He had moved repeatedly—from Kentucky to Tennessee and from Tennessee to Missouri—but nothing could prevent the financial debacle ahead, nor restore his good health. His father's penchant for costly business speculation was inherited by Clemens's son, Samuel, as well as an older brother, Orion. Elected a justice of the peace in Hannibal, John Clemens died in 1847. His father's death put an end to Clemens's formal education. At the age of twelve he set to work as a printers' apprentice in the office of the local newspaper, the Hannibal *Courier*.

But life was not all tragedy in Hannibal; in fact much of it was an idyll of youth that Clemens would replay through his fiction the rest of his life. The river was churning with riverboats, an average of three a day which called at the little town of Hannibal. Young Clemens used the river and its banks as his playground, constructing rafts and discovering swimming holes. There were also the woods and a nearby cave to add spice to his life. But increasingly boyhood was left behind, and Clemens began to work for his brother on the newspapers Orion owned. He also began writing, using the easy vernacular of the day that he had ingested from articles he had typeset. His first publication, "The Dandy Frightening the Squatter," appeared under his initials, S. L. C., in a Boston magazine, *Carpet-Bag*, in 1852. Clemens was just seventeen.

Orion Clemens, unfortunately, had little better business sense than his father had, and over the next years managed to bankrupt a succession of newspapers along the Mississippi. Clemens, the young typesetter, stayed with his brother until 1853, absorbing the rough humor of the day in the pieces he set, and finally left for several years of wandering, in St. Louis, New York, Philadelphia, Washington, D.C., and Cincinnati. By this time he was sending back dispatches to whatever newspaper Orion owned at the time. These were years of apprenticeship in a different trade—the billiards game of writing.

From the River to the West

In 1857, Clemens had a new scheme in mind: he would take a ship from New Orleans to South American and the Amazon where he was determined to make his fortune growing cocoa. But other events interceded: Clemens met a riverboat pilot, Horace Bixby, who agreed to take on the twenty-two-year-old as a cub pilot. Ever since his youth in Hannibal, Clemens had dreamed of becoming a riverboat pilot, much as a youth a century later might dream of becoming a fireman. For the next two years, Clemens apprenticed under Bixby, finally earning his pilot's license in 1859. Until the beginning of the Civil War and the subsequent curtailment of riverboat traffic, Clemens

revelled in his new job and prestige. With the coming of the war, however, Clemens joined the Confederate forces. As he noted in his autobiography, "I was a *soldier* two weeks once in the beginning of the war, and was hunted like a rat the whole time." He was soon out of the army and accompanying his brother Orion to Nevada Territory where the latter has been appointed secretary to the governor. In Nevada, Clemens panned for gold for a year, an experience he would later incorporate in the book *Roughing It*, just as he would utilize material from Hannibal and his riverboat piloting days in other popular books. If Clemens proved unsuccessful at ore mining, he was a wizard at mining his own life for material for his books.

By late 1862 Clemens had joined the staff of the Virginia City *Territorial Enterprise*, writing both humorous pieces as well as conventional news, using for the most his pseudonym of Mark Twain. His humorous pieces included elaborate hoaxes—fabricated news that scooped his competition—as well as slang-filled "first-person" accounts. A challenge to a duel sent Clemens on his way, however, with his next stop San Francisco. Here he contributed humorous sketches to various papers, including the *Alta California, San Francisco Call, Golden Era, California*, and *Sacramento Union*. A libel suit issued by the San Francisco police department sent Clemens on the move again, this time to the Sierras for a few months until the suit was forgotten. And it was in the rough and tumble mining camps of the Sierras where Clemens heard the story of a jumping frog contest that would make his fame.

Upon returning to San Francisco, Clemens discovered that Artemus Ward, the well-known humorist, wanted a piece from him for a humor anthology. Clemens wrote down his tale of a jumping frog filled with lead shot and first titled it "Jim Smiley and His Jumping Frog," and later retitled it "The Celebrated Jumping Frog of Calaveras County." Too late for inclusion in the Ward anthology, Clemens's story was published in the *New York Saturday Press*, then pirated, then published along with other tales in Clemens's first book, *The Celebrated Jumping Frog of Calaveras County, and Other Sketches*. It was a tale, according to Pascal Covici, Jr., in *Dictionary of Literary Biography*, which spread Clemens's, or rather Twain's name "across the country, preparing the way for the national reputation he held for the rest of his life." Both a humorous regional tale as well as a comment on the Easterner's vision of the West, Clemens's tale is, as Covici noted, "about telling the frog's story; that is, about 'celebrating' the frog, about the process by which the frog becomes a celebrity," and displays the point-of-view technique that is at the heart of Clemens's humor.

Throughout the 1860s, Clemens travelled in California and other points West, including Hawaii, logging stories in local newspapers and magazines. It was in this same period that he began what would become a large part of his income—speaking on the lecture tour, then a popular form of entertainment. Clemens proved an excellent raconteur, his blend of sardonic humor and grit charming audiences. This oral literature proved helpful in his writing, as well, especially as he developed the casual spoken form of narrative so much associated with him. The *Alta California* commissioned Clemens in 1866 to sail down the West coast to Nicaragua and thence to New York, filing travel letters along the way. Once in New York, Clemens learned of the sailing of the *Quaker City* on a five-month cruise to Europe and the Holy Land and convinced his editors at the *Alta California* to foot the bill for his passage in exchange for more travel letters.

An Innocent Abroad

The first of such cruises, the *Quaker City* was a far cry from the *Love Boat*. Clemens did all he could during the voyage to shake up his dour fellow-passengers, all so hell-bent on gaining Culture. It was, as he later wrote, "a funeral excursion without a corpse." The subtitle of the subsequent book of dispatches tells the story: *The Innocents Abroad; or, The New Pilgrims' Progress.* Clemens proceeded to shock his Pilgrims at every opportunity, lighting his cigar from the lava of Vesuvius, ready to scoff at the great works of art and the religious relics displayed to them. His letters home and the book he compiled from them formed the standard Yankee response to the Old World: a sardonic "show-me" attitude that once again pleased readers. Clemens, working his material into book form after returning from his voyage, decided on publication by subscription, which demanded lengthy manuscripts. Such subscription books, sold door-to-door, reached an audience left largely untouched by the bookstores, and the tale told by Mark Twain did remarkably well, selling

some 70,000 copies in its first year, making it a bestseller in its day and securing Clemens's reputation as a writer of note.

A second reward for the voyage was marriage. On board ship, Clemens had become friends with a fellow passenger, Charles Langdon, son of a wealthy family. Clemens later met Charles's sister, Olivia, and the two fell in love. The success of *The Innocents Abroad* helped to make Clemens an eligible suitor, and upon marriage, the couple received a mansion as a wedding present from Olivia's father, as well as a sizeable share in the *Buffalo Examiner.* For several years, Clemens stayed on in Buffalo, contributing pieces to the newspaper, editing a magazine, and writing what would become his second book, *Roughing It,* about his

Two boys from opposite ends of the class ladder get to see how the other half lives in this 1881 story of mistaken identity.

adventures in Nevada. In 1871, after the death of his father-in-law, the Clemens family moved to Hartford, Connecticut, into the bosom of literary America—Harriet Beecher Stowe was a neighbor—and built a magnificent home. New friends were made, significantly William Dean Howells, editor of the *Atlantic Monthly*. Clemens had arrived in the genteel world he had so long parodied. The family would remain in Hartford for the next twenty years, though the death of Clemens's son in the first years added sorrow to the joy of his successes.

Mr. Twain and the Two Toms

Roughing It was also sold on a subscription basis, and like its predecessor, proved successful with this new segment of the American reading public. Clemens capitalized on the success by a lecture tour to England. Then, settled once again in Hartford, Clemens collaborated with another neighbor, Charles Dudley Warner, on the novel *The Gilded Age*, a love story and political satire set during the administration of President Ulysses S. Grant. More lecture tours took Clemens back to England, and then he returned to a book that he had been playing with since 1870, one that began as a sort of burlesque of an adult romance, told from the point of view of an adolescent infected with puppy love: a story about a boy named Tom Sawyer.

The story, Clemens's first solo novel, is based loosely on the author's own boyhood in Hannibal. The tale follows the exploits of Tom over the course of one summer in the fictional town of St. Petersburg on the Mississippi. Told in the episodic style which Clemens had perfected in his earlier works, *The Adventures of Tom Sawyer* joins several story lines together to stand the traditional preachy juvenile novel of the day on its head. With Tom Sawyer it is not so much virtue that is rewarded as it is adventure and play. One thread of the story involves Tom's love for Becky Thatcher and his rebellious exploits at school. These typical childhood adventures are contrasted with the more elaborate ones Tom shares with his pal, Huck Finn. Together the two witness grave-robbing and the murder of Dr. Robinson by Injun Joe late one night; Tom eventually must testify in court to save the life of the falsely accused Muff Potter; and Tom and Huck run away from St. Petersburg for Jackson's Island. Homesickness brings them back to town, however, where the local populace are holding a funeral for the boys, who are thought to have drowned. In the finale, Tom attends a picnic held by Becky's father, he and the girl become lost in McDougal's Cave, Tom finally finds their way out after three days of searching, and he has suddenly become the hero of the town. Meanwhile, Injun Joe has starved to death within the very same cave, and Tom and Huck subsequently recover the villain's stolen loot which they had earlier seen him hiding. In the end, Tom seems to have joined the world of propriety, insisting that Huck must place himself under the care of Widow Douglas. Tom tells his disappointed friend, "Huck, we can't let you into the gang if you ain't respectable, you know."

Clemens wrote in the preface to the novel that "Although my book is intended mainly for the entertainment of boys and girls, I hope it will not be shunned by men and women on that account, for part of my plan has been to try to pleasantly remind adults of what they once were themselves and of how they felt and thought and talked, and what queer enterprises they sometimes engaged in." Indeed, critics over the past century have recognized the dual audience for the book. The critic Diana Trilling in her *Claremont Essays* noted that "Much more than it is now thought to be a book *for* children, it is regarded as a classic *of* childhood, especially to be read by adults of college age with an interest in the American past." As recently as 1982, the American novelist John Seelye, himself the author of a Huck Finn pastiche, noted in the *Sewanee Review* that "few readers, of any age, can set *Tom Sawyer* aside once they start to read it." Reviewers of Clemens's day were no less enthusiastic. "The story is a wonderful study of the boy-mind," commented a reviewer in the *Atlantic Monthly* in 1876. "The tale is dramatically wrought, and the subordinate characters are treated with the same graphic force that sets Tom before us."

Tom Sawyer quickly entered the American idiom—a mischievous youth with a good heart. Many have noticed how Tom can be compared to other quintessential juvenile heroes of the time such as Ragged Dick, created by Horatio Alger. But where Alger's youthful protagonists were all piety and goodness, Tom exalted in laziness, play, and profanity, and was nonetheless heroic and successful. Clemens's ending, however, with Tom neatly fitting in as a respected member of the

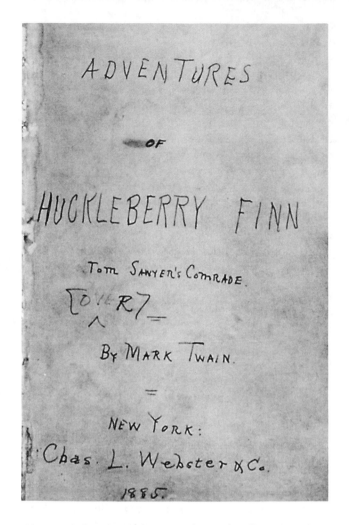

Clemens' dummy title page from the first American edition of his popular classic.

society he once affected to despise, has rankled some. Hamlin Hill, writing in *Dictionary of Literary Biography*, noted that "Tom is a conformist pretending to be a rebel, with one eye closely on the limits which his society would permit for token assaults on its institutions." The same might be said for Clemens, himself.

Other critics have called attention to the episodic quality of the writing, some criticizing, some applauding. Lewis Leary, however, in the *Virginia Quarterly Review*, felt that "There is another artistry, of theme and structure, which makes *Tom Sawyer* more than a charming narrative which transcends its own weaknesses." For Leary that theme is simply "that innocent boyhood adventure, the brave curiosity of the imaginative boy, leads from innocence to knowledge of evil. . . .

In the final part we discover that adventure . . . and not common sense, leads finally to the wiping out of evil." Much has been made of the mythic symbolism in *The Adventures of Tom Sawyer*, of Clemens's feelings toward women and matriarchal society; many doctoral theses have been churned out of meaning supposedly found between the lines of the book. Yet in the final analysis it is the readability of the book, the lasting power of the story that matters; it is the hymn-like quality of the story as a fond remembrance of youth. As John C. Gerber wrote in his *Mark Twain*, "as an idyll of boyhood it has no peer anywhere." And Barry A. Marks in *English Journal* summed up nicely the hymn-like quality that Clemens himself noted about the book: "Inherent in its structure is a song praising mankind—praising his weakness and need for love and security as well as his strength and capacity for achievement, but mostly praising the life which permits man's conflicting motives to exist together in ultimate harmony."

The popular success of *Tom Sawyer* convinced Clemens to prepare a sequel, this time focusing on the character of Huck Finn, though this writing would occupy him for the next seven years. Meanwhile he had a family and house to support. More European travels inspired a new travel book, *A Tramp Abroad*, similar in many aspects to *The Innocents Abroad*. And then in 1881 came the publication of another book popular among young readers, *The Prince and the Pauper*, featuring yet another streetwise Tom in the character of young Tom Canty. Set in sixteenth-century England, the book has as its plot engine the device of mistaken identities so popular in the novels of Charles Dickens, among others. Tom Canty, a poor boy mistreated by his father, attempts to sneak into the castle to see Prince Edward the day before the death of King Henry VIII. Edward, seeing the ragged boy being dealt with harshly by his guards, invites Tom into the palace. As a joke, the two switch clothing, but still wearing Tom's rags, the Prince goes to reprimand his guard and is promptly thrown out of the palace as a pauper. Clemens then alternately follows the lives of the two who have accidentally changed places. Tom claims he is no prince and is treated as if he is crazy, while Edward gets equal treatment for claiming he is the Prince. Slowly, however, Tom adapts to the life of royalty and takes his duties seriously, earning the respect of the people for his compassion. Prince Edward also undergoes a change because of new circumstances. Come face to face with the poor, he develops empathy for their circumstances. Ultimately, after surviving many adventures, Edward is able to break into Westminster Abbey and exchange places before the coronation of the false Tudor. Edward rewards Tom for his services, and in the end it appears he will become an enlightened monarch.

The Prince and the Pauper was a stylistic departure for Clemens, written as it was with much archaic period language and a dearth of humor. Many critics at the time (and later) noted that Clemens seemed to be appealing to a genteel audience with his historical novel, and disappointing sales with his own subscription house confirmed that opinion. A critic in the *Atlantic Monthly* noted this in his review of the book. While praising Clemens for his new direction, the reviewer also commented that "It will be interest-

Illustrator Steven Kellogg's version of Huck Finn and Miss Watson from the 1994 version of *The Adventures of Huckleberry Finn.*

ing to watch for the popular estimate of this fascinating book." In the *New York Tribune* William Dean Howells, dean of American writers and a close personal friend to Clemens, called the new novel "a very remarkable book." While American critical response was generally favorable, British reviewers of the day tended to focus on the fact that Clemens played freely with historical fact. One reviewer for the *British Quarterly Review* is typical of this criticism: "[Twain] has written a story which gives a vivid idea of a historical period, but which outrages history at every point in the most bare-faced manner." Later reviewers and critics have noted the fact that the positive critical reception in its day was probably a result of the novel fitting more closely to literary conventions than had earlier creations by Mark Twain. Gerber, in his *Mark Twain*, goes so far as to call it "the most conventional and blandest" book Clemens ever wrote. Yet another modern critic, Roger B. Salmon in his *Twain and the Image of History*, praises *The Prince and the Pauper* for its development of themes and imagery that would play crucial parts in Clemens's larger works such as *Life on the Mississippi, The Adventures of Huck Finn,* and *A Connecticut Yankee in King Arthur's Court.* Whatever the critical response, the fact was that *The Prince and the Pauper* was a financial disaster, partly due to the inexperience of the newly formed publishing house which distributed it, and partly because the book did not speak to a subscription audience.

A Return to the Mississippi

Clemens next gathered together sketches he had done for the *Atlantic Monthly* about his days as a riverboat pilot, "Old Times on the Mississippi," and padded them out to fill the required pages of a badly needed subscription book. Clemens had inherited his father's and brother's penchant for unwise investments, and with the financial failure of *The Prince and the Pauper*, was greatly in need of new royalties. The subsequent book, *Life on the Mississippi*, was a nostalgic look at life on that great river. Clemens made a return visit in 1882 to the haunts of his boyhood, sailing from St. Louis to New Orleans with his former teacher, Horace Bixby. Clemens gathered new visions to pair with his recollections. The result, however, was greatly padded to fit the subscription book formula, and once again Clemens was faced with commercial failure. Critical opinion of the book is mixed to this day. Hill in *Dictionary of Literary Biography* commented that "The modern river was as colorless as Mark Twain's prose, and only the 'Old Times on the Mississippi' opening has literary merit." The opposite view is taken by Robert Kith Miller, who, in his book *Mark Twain*, declared that *Life on the Mississippi* heralded "Twain's emergence as a great modern writer" and "established Twain as something more than a western humorist." The book is generally considered, despite its bloated size, to be among Clemens's more lasting works.

But lasting or not, it did not help his financial position. Clemens returned to the long ignored manuscript about Tom Sawyer's friend, Huck Finn. Clemens had written 400 pages of it in 1876 after the success of *The Adventures of Tom Sawyer*. Work on the manuscript had been desultory after that time, interrupted as it was by other literary projects and financial schemes. It seemed that Clemens's travels of 1882 researching his *Life on the Mississippi* rekindled his interest in the book, and in 1883 he finished the novel. *The Adventures of Huckleberry Finn* essentially picks up Huck's tale where it was left off in *The Adventures of Tom Sawyer*. But the book is no mere sequel. In fact it charted new ground in literary technique, being completely told from the point of view of the uneducated Huck and in the language of the people, not of some literary narrator.

Huckleberry Finn

The opening of the novel finds Huck having somewhat adapted to the "sivilizin'" influences of Widow Douglas and even attending school. But then one day Huck learns that his brutal father has returned to St. Petersburg. Fearful that his father will take his share of the treasure recovered by him and Tom Sawyer in the earlier book, Huck entrusts his with Judge Thatcher. True to form, Huck's father does take his son off to the woods where he beats him, but Huck manages to escape, making it look as though he is dead. The rest of the book is an elegy to the river and the freedom it represents. On the island where Huck has escaped to, he discovers Jim, a runaway slave. They stay there together for a few days and then Huck returns to the mainland, in disguise, to learn that his father has left again and that his, Huck's, death has been attributed to Jim. Returning to the island, Huck tells the events to Jim,

who decides to escape to the north. Huck accompanies him on a raft, but it is not long before they crash into a riverboat. Jim disappears as Huck saves himself. On shore, Huck is taken in by the Grangerford family, representatives of old debased southern aristocracy who are continually feuding with their neighbors, the Sheperdsons. Huck once again discovers Jim, hiding in the woods, and together the two escape to the river again, leaving the feuding families shooting at each other on shore. More adventures ensue when the duo encounter the Duke and the King, two con-artist carpetbaggers. Ultimately the Duke turns Jim in for reward money, but Huck once again plans to help him escape. This time, however, toward the end of the book, Tom Sawyer is called in to help. It is Tom who develops a convoluted scheme to set Jim free, a scheme made unnecessary by the deathbed granting of Jim's freedom by the slave's owner. All turns out well in the end, with Huck's father dying off stage and Tom's Aunt Sally offering to adopt Huck.

Considered one of the classics of American literature, it is interesting to note that Clemens himself, though pleased with his creation, in no way thought he had created a masterpiece, and that reception of the book at the time was cool, even hostile. It was not until the early twentieth century that *The Adventures of Huckleberry Finn* started to gain the stature of greatness it maintains today. Once again, Clemens employed an episodic structure in the writing, but the book maintained an artistic cohesiveness because of the central theme of the development of Huck's moral code as well as the sustained use of vernacular speech throughout the novel. Huck slowly comes to see the runaway slave, Jim, as an individual, and just as slowly begins to take a stance independent of traditional attitudes towards slavery. In the end, Huck ruminates on the religious implications of what he has done, that is, setting free someone else's "property," and decides he would rather suffer the fires of hell than turn his friend in. Huck and Jim's journey down the Mississippi is viewed by critics as being a metaphor for freedom and a refutation of the corrupt life on land or of civilized life in general. Such thematic and structural techniques lend this novel a unity that his earlier books had not achieved, and some critics of the day recognized this. "In no other book has the humorist shown such artistic restraint," noted Brander Matthews in a 1885 *Saturday Review* article, "for there is in *Huckleberry Finn* no

Clemens based Huck Finn's character on Tom Blankenship, a neighbor from Hannibal, Missouri, whose barnlike house (since demolished) is shown here.

mere 'comic copy,' no straining after effect; one might almost say that there is no waste word in it."

Other contemporary critics were not so kind, and the novel was banned in many libraries, including that of Concord, Massachusetts. Such criticism derided the book as too rough and coarse, for Clemens had unflinchingly told the book in the spoken idiom of the South. Though Clemens joked at the time that the banning of his book could only help sales—and it did, the novel was an overwhelming popular success—such criticism stung and may have had a lasting effect on his work. Several decades after publication however, critical opinion began to swing the other way. The well known American critic William Lyon Phelps pointed out in his 1910 *Essays on Modern Novel-*

ists that both *Tom Sawyer* and *Huck Finn* were "prose epics of American life," and that the latter was not "really a child's book at all. Children devour it, but they do not digest it. It is a permanent picture of a certain period of American history." By 1919, the novelist and critic Waldo Frank in his *Our America* could wax quite eloquently about *The Adventures of Huckleberry Finn* as "a voice of American chaos, the voice of a precultural epoch," and dubbed its protagonist "the American epic hero." The editor and satirist H. L. Mencken jumped on the critical bandwagon the same year in a *Smart Set* essay, calling the book "a masterpiece that expands as year chases year. There, if I am not wrong, he produced the greatest work of the imagination that These States have yet seen." And in an earlier *Smart Set* essay, Mencken had declared that Clemens ranked "well above Whitman and certainly not below Poe. I believe that he was the true father of our national literature, the first genuinely American artist of the blood royal." Other influential writers and critics, including Ernest Hemingway, T. S. Eliot, and Carl van Doren, helped to canonize the work into the received masterpiece of today. Bernard De Voto, in his 1932 *Mark Twain's America*, declared that "The book has the fecundity, the multiplicity, of genius," and Clifton Fadiman noted in his introduction to a 1940 edition of *Huck Finn* that "Here, in this rambling tale about the unimportant adventures of a boy . . . are the matters, the myths, the deep conflicts of the American people." As the years passed, so did the depth of critical interpretation.

Reaction breeds reaction, however, and other critics began to examine the book for flaws, especially in its rather miraculous ending. Leo Marx led the charge in the *American Scholar* by noting that "the ending of *Huckleberry Finn* makes so many readers uneasy because they rightly sense that it jeopardizes the significance of the entire novel." Until this ending, Huck has denied the rules of society, has found his own morality. Suddenly, however, with the introduction of Tom Sawyer and the traditional happy ending, this biting edge to the novel is dissipated. Other critics counter that Huck's decision in the end to "light out for the Territory" vindicates his free will and rebelliousness. Yet as Clemens himself noted, none of us are really free from some form of determination. Ironically, the real-life model for Huck, Tom Blankenship, later became a justice of the peace in Montana and a respected member of "civilized" society. Other modern critics have attacked the book on racial grounds, saying that Clemens portrays a stereotyped minstrel-show black man in Jim. The African American novelist Ralph Ellison, author of the acclaimed *Invisible Man*, noted in his *Shadow and Act* that Jim was "a white man's inadequate portrait of a slave." Still other modern critics wonder at the prestige the novel has achieved. Novelist Jane Smiley in *Harper's* commented that after re-reading the novel she was stunned. "Yes, stunned. Not, by any means, by the artistry of the book but by the notion that this is the novel that all American literature grows out of, that this is a great novel, that this is even a serious novel." Smiley posits that the fame of the novel is due to a good old boys club of reviewers who ignored the women writers of the same period. Clemens, were he

alive, would surely be amused at all the controversy a century and more after publication of his yarn.

The Later Years

Sales of *The Adventures of Huckleberry Finn* were encouraging, as were those of the *Memoirs of Ulysses S. Grant*, which Clemens convinced the former U.S. president and Union general to publish through his newly founded publishing house. Yet Clemens was pouring ever more money into the development of a typesetting machine; that and the upkeep on his Hartford mansion combined to drain his coffers as quickly as he could fill them. In 1889 he published *A Connecticut Yankee in King Arthur's Court*, a novel of life in sixth-century England. A factory foreman in America named Hank Morgan, suffering a blow to the head, awakens to find himself in the time of King Arthur. Through his Yankee ingenuity, he "sets out to enlighten the kingdom," according to Hill in *Dictionary of Literary Biography*. Wreaking havoc with inventions from the nineteenth century, Hank is ultimately put into a trance by Merlin and sent back to his own time, where he finally awakens from his adventures to discover it has all been a dream.

Variously seen as a diatribe against the technological world or as a critique of English culture, the book had a bleak tone, and the biting humor did not win a large readership. Critics of the day recognized the social satire inherent in the novel, and many, including Howells, commended the work. Over the years, the novel has been assigned to the handful of Clemens books that critics count among his best, though interpretation of it is still divided between those who see it as realistic entertainment and those who view it as a scathing indictment of society and technology. As James D. Williams concluded in an *American Literature* essay of 1964, "the novel survives neither as a theory of history nor as an 'inverted satire,' but rather as a giddy, shrewd, and violent realization of that ordinary fantasy in which a hostile world is reduced to impotence before the unchanged yet unconquered dreamer."

Clemens's financial problems grew ever worse until he and his publishing house finally went bankrupt. But realizing that the only barter a writer has is his character, he vowed to pay off

If you enjoy the works of Mark Twain, you may want to check out the following contemporary novels:

Cynthia Blair, *The Banana Split Affair,* 1985.
Paul Fleischman, *The Whipping Boy,* 1986.
Walter Dean Myers, *The Mouse Rap,* 1990.
Ann Rinaldi, *Wolf by the Ears,* 1991.
Ruth Thomas, *The Runaways,* 1989.

all his debts. Leaving the United States with his family in 1894, Clemens set off on a world-wide lecture tour and several years of living cheap in Europe. His later works included *The Tragedy of Pudd'nhead Wilson,* perhaps best known for the aphorisms that begin each chapter. That which begins the book—"Tell the truth or trump—but get the trick."—sets the tone for this novel of mistaken identity, of twins confused at birth, and of a lawyer who uses fingerprints to untangle a murder. As with *Connecticut Yankee,* the humor here is grim. "Beneath the contrivances and melodrama of the novel runs the darkest vein of Mark Twain's thought," commented Hill in *Dictionary of Literary Biography.* Sales, though, were good, and helped to pull the family out of debt. However, Clemens soon learned of worse tragedies than bankruptcy, when his beloved daughter Susy died in 1896. Another daughter, Jean, was diagnosed with epilepsy, and his wife, Olivia, always of delicate health, also began failing. There was nothing triumphant about his return to the United States in 1899. The writing of this later period, especially "The Man that Corrupted Hadleyburg," and *The Mysterious Stranger,* thus reflect an increasing misanthropy in Clemens. In the posthumously published latter novel, Satan appears in human form to show up the citizens of a sixteenth-century Austrian town for the hypocrites and cheats they are. Miller, in his study *Mark Twain,* comments that *The Mysterious Stranger* is "the most important of Twain's shorter works," but also adds that it is "the most contemptuous."

The last decade of Clemens's life added more tragedy: the death of his wife in 1904 in Italy and of his daughter Jean in 1909, and the breakdown of a third daughter, Clara. Clemens spent much of the decade writing his autobiography, living first in a house on Fifth Avenue in New York, and then at the end in a villa near Redding, Con-

necticut. It is, ironically, these final years which are most vividly documented in scores of photographs and which made him into a literary icon. Clemens became the dapper little man in a white linen suit—he only began wearing this trademark toward the end of his life, his hair and moustache thick and white. An elder and revered literary lion, there was still some humor in him, as can be read in the pages of *Mark Twain's Autobiography.* When he died, on April 21, 1910, a nation mourned. Clemens was both symbol and recorder of a country coming of age. As Hill noted in *Dictionary of Literary Biography,* "[Clemens's] experiences ranged by good fortune through the exact events that captivated the American imagination—the river during its golden age, the Far West of its bonanza days, the first waves of middle-class American tourists to Europe, the mania for material wealth. . . . He captured, with amazing fidelity, essential aspects of the American experience and the American stance." Clemens took literature out of the academy and put it into the hands of Everyman. Some critics never forgave him that. Perhaps the most fitting epitaph would come from the mouth of his most beloved character, Huck, in the opening sentences of *The Adventures of Huckleberry Finn:* "You don't know about me, without you have read a book by the name of *The Adventures of Tom Sawyer,* but that ain't no matter. That book was made by Mr. Mark Twain, and he told the truth, mainly. There was things he stretched, but mainly he told the truth."

■ Works Cited

Review of *The Adventures of Tom Sawyer, Atlantic Monthly,* May, 1876, pp. 617-29.

Covici, Pascal, Jr., "Mark Twain (Samuel Langhorne Clemens)," *Dictionary of Literary Biography.* Volume 11: *American Humorists, 1800-1950,* Gale, 1982, pp. 526-55.

De Voto, Bernard, "The Artist as American," *Mark Twain's America and Mark Twain at Work,* Houghton, 1967, pp. 288-322.

Ellison, Ralph, "Change the Joke and Slip the Yoke," *Shadows and Acts,* Random House, 1964, pp. 45-59.

Fadiman, Clifton, "Lead-Ins: A Note on 'Huckleberry Finn'," *Party of One,* World Publishing, 1955, pp. 129-31.

Frank, Waldo, "The Land of the Pioneer," *Our America,* Boni and Liveright, 1919, pp. 13-58.

Gerber, John C., *Mark Twain*, Twayne, 1988.

Hill, Hamlin, "Samuel Langhorne Clemens (Mark Twain)," *Dictionary of Literary Biography*, Volume 12: *American Realists and Naturalists*, Gale, 1982, pp. 71-94.

Howells, William Dean, review of *The Prince and the Pauper*, *New York Tribune*, October 25, 1881.

Leary, Lewis, "Tom and Huck: Innocence on Trial," *Virginia Quarterly*, Summer, 1954, pp. 417-30.

Marks, Barry A., "Mark Twain's Hymn of Praise," *English Journal*, November, 1959, pp. 443-48.

Marx, Leo, "Mr. Eliot, Mr. Trilling, and Huckleberry Finn," *American Scholar*, Autumn, 1953, pp. 423-40.

Matthews, Brander, "Huckleberry Finn," *Saturday Review*, January 31, 1885, pp. 153-54.

Mencken, H. L., *Smart Set*, February 2, 1915.

Mencken, H. L., "Final Estimate," *H. L. Mencken's "Smart Set" Criticism*, edited by William H. Nolte, Cornell University Press, 1968, pp. 182-89.

Miller, Robert Kith, *Mark Twain*, Ungar, 1983.

Phelps, William Lyon, "Mark Twain," *Essays on Modern Novelists*, Macmillan, 1910, pp. 99-114.

Review of *The Prince and the Pauper*, *Atlantic Monthly*, December, 1881, pp. 843-45.

Review of *The Prince and the Pauper*, *British Quarterly*, January, 1882, p. 118.

Salmon, Roger B., *Twain and the Image of History*, Yale University Press, 1961.

Seelye, John, "What's in a Name: Sounding the Depths of *Tom Sayer*," *Sewanee Review*, Summer, 1982, pp. 408-29.

Smiley, Jane, "Say It Ain't So, Huck," *Harper's*, January, 1996, p. 61.

Trilling, Diana, "Tom Sawyer, Delinquent," *Claremont Essays*, Harcourt, 1964, pp. 143-52.

Twain, Mark, *The Innocents Abroad; or, The New Pilgrim's Progress*, American Publishing, 1869.

Twain, Mark, *The Adventures of Tom Sawyer*, American Publishing, 1876.

Twain, Mark, *The Adventures of Huckleberry Finn, Tom Sawyer's Comrade*, Chatto & Windus, 1884.

Twain, Mark, *The Tragedy of Pudd'nhead Wilson, and the Comedy of Those Extraordinary Twins*, American Publishing, 1894.

Twain, Mark, *Mark Twain's Autobiography*, edited as one volume by Charles Neider, Harper, 1959.

Williams, James D., "Revisionism and Intention in Mark Twain's 'A Connecticut Yankee'," *American Literature*, November, 1964, pp. 288-97.

■ For More Information See

BOOKS

Benson, Ivan, *Mark Twain's Western Years*, Stanford University Press, 1938.

Branch, Edgar M., *The Literary Apprenticeship of Mark Twain*, University of Illinois Press, 1950.

Budd, Louis J., *Mark Twain: Social Philosopher*, Indiana University Press, 1962.

Clemens, Cyril, *My Cousin Mark Twain*, introduction by Booth Tarkington, Rodale, 1939.

De Voto, Bernard, *Mark Twain's America*, Little, Brown, 1932.

Dictionary of Literary Biography, Gale, Volume 23: *American Newspaper Journalists, 1873-1900*, 1983, pp. 31-46, Volume 64: *American Literary Critics and Scholars, 1850-1880*, 1988, pp. 34-47, Volume 74: *American Short-Story Writers before 1880*, 1988, pp. 54-83.

Emerson, Everett H., *The Authentic Mark Twain: A Literary Biography*, University of Pennsylvania Press, 1984.

Fatout, Paul, *Mark Twain in Virginia City*, University of Indiana Press, 1964.

Gale, Robert L., *Plots and Characters in the Works of Mark Twain* (two volumes), Shoe String, 1973.

Gibson, William M., *The Art of Mark Twain*, Oxford University Press, 1976.

Hearn, Michael Patrick, essay in *Writers for Children*, edited by Jane Bingham, Scribner's, 1988.

Hill, Hamlin, *Mark Twain: God's Fool*, Harper, 1973.

Kaplan, Justin, *Mr. Clemens and Mr. Twain*, Simon and Schuster, 1966.

Lauber, John, *The Inventions of Mark Twain*, Hill and Wang, 1990.

Macnaughton, William R., *Mark Twain's Last Years as a Writer*, University of Missouri Press, 1971.

Masters, Edgar Lee, *Mark Twain: A Portrait*, Scribner's, 1938.

Neider, Charles, *Mark Twain*, Horizon, 1967.

Paine, Albert Bigelow, *Mark Twain: A Biography; the Personal and Literary Life of Samuel Langhorne Clemens* (four volumes), Harper, 1912.

Rasmussen, Kent R., *Mark Twain A to Z: The Essential References to His Life and Writings*, Facts on File, 1995.

Sanborn, Margaret, *Mark Twain: The Bachelor Years*, Doubleday, 1990.

Seelye, John, *The True Adventures of Huckleberry Finn*, Northwestern University Press, 1970.

Smith, Henry Nash, *Mark Twain: The Development of a Writer*, Belknap Press, 1962.

Wagenknecht, Edward, *Mark Twain: The Man and*

His Work, 3rd edition, University of Oklahoma Press, 1967.

Wecter, Dixon, *Sam Clemens of Hannibal*, Houghton, 1952.

Wilson, James D., *A Reader's Guide to the Short Stories of Mark Twain*, Hall, 1987.

PERIODICALS

American Quarterly, Winter, 1964, pp. 595-601; Spring, 1967, pp. 86-103.

College English, October, 1955, pp. 6-10.

English Journal, October, 1935, pp. 615-27.

International Books for Children, 1984, pp. 4-13.

Journal of American Folklore, April, 1952, pp. 407-26.

Mark Twain Journal, Winter, 1972, p. ii.

Midwest Quarterly, Winter, 1967, pp. 181-97; January, 1972, pp. 201-12.

Modern Language Quarterly, September, 1962, pp. 254-62.

New Quarterly, April, 1876, pp. 198-200.

New Republic, August 15, 1955, pp. 17-18; August 22, 1955, pp. 16-18.

Nineteenth-Century Fiction, March, 1964, pp. 383-91; March, 1982, pp. 452-70.

Partisan Review, June, 1948.

Sewanee Review, Summer, 1954, pp. 389-405.

Southern Review, Winter, 1982, pp. 100-10.

Yale Review, September, 1934, pp. 118-29; Spring, 1958, pp. 421-31.*

—Sketch by J. Sydney Jones

Kate Wilhelm

shop, Michigan State University, beginning 1968. *Member:* Science Fiction Writers of America, Authors Guild, Authors League of America, PEN.

■ Personal

Born June 8, 1928, in Toledo, OH; daughter of Jesse Thomas and Ann (McDowell) Meredith; married Joseph B. Wilhelm, May 24, 1947 (divorced, 1962); married Damon Knight (a writer and editor), February 23, 1963; children: (first marriage) Douglas, Richard; (second marriage) Jonathan. *Education:* Attended high school in Louisville, KY.

■ Addresses

Home—1645 Horn Lane, Eugene, OR 97404. *Agent*—Brandt & Brandt, 101 Park Ave., New York, NY 10017.

■ Career

Employed as a model, telephone operator, sales clerk, switchboard operator, and insurance company underwriter; full-time writer, 1956—. Co-director, Milford Science Fiction Writers Conference, 1963-76; lecturer at Clarion Fantasy Work-

■ Awards, Honors

Nebula Award of Science Fiction Writers of America, 1968, for best short story, "The Planners"; Hugo Award of World Science Fiction Convention, 1977, Jupiter Award, 1977, and second place for the John W. Campbell Memorial Award, 1977, all for *Where Late the Sweet Birds Sang*; American Book Award nomination, 1980, for *Juniper Time: A Novel*.

■ Writings

More Bitter Than Death, Simon & Schuster, 1962.
The Mile-Long Spaceship (short stories), Berkley Publishing, 1963, published in England as *Andover and the Android*, Dobson, 1966.
(With Theodore L. Thomas) *The Clone*, Berkley, 1965.
The Nevermore Affair, Doubleday, 1966.
The Killer Thing, Doubleday, 1967, published in England as *The Killing Thing*, Jenkins, 1967.
The Downstairs Room, and Other Speculative Fiction (short stories), Doubleday, 1968.
Let the Fire Fall, Doubleday, 1969.
(With Thomas) *The Year of the Cloud*, Doubleday, 1970.

Abyss: Two Novellas, Doubleday, 1971.

Margaret and I, Little, Brown, 1971.

City of Cain, Little, Brown, 1973.

(Editor) *Nebula Award Stories,* Number 9, Gollancz, 1974, Harper, 1975.

The Clewiston Test, Farrar, Straus, 1976.

Where Late the Sweet Birds Sang, Harper, 1976.

The Infinity Box: A Collection of Speculative Fiction (short stories), Harper, 1976.

Fault Lines: A Novel, Harper, 1976.

Axoltl (multimedia science fantasy), first produced in Eugene, OR, at University of Oregon Art Museum, April 6, 1979.

Juniper Time: A Novel, Harper, 1979.

(With husband, Damon Knight) *Better Than One,* New England Science Fiction Association, 1980.

A Sense of Shadow, Houghton, 1981.

Oh, Susannah!: A Novel, Houghton, 1982.

Welcome Chaos, Houghton, 1983.

The Hindenberg Effect (radio play), first broadcast by KSOR (Ashland, OR), 1985.

Huysman's Pets, Bluejay Books, 1986.

(With Richard Wilhelm) *The Hills Are Dancing,* Corroboree Press, 1986.

The Hamlet Trap, St. Martin's, 1987.

The Dark Door, St. Martin's, 1988.

Crazy Time, St. Martin's, 1989.

Smart House, St. Martin's, 1989.

Children of the Wind, St. Martin's, 1989.

Cambio Bay, St. Martin's, 1990.

Sweet, Sweet Poison, St. Martin's, 1990.

Death Qualified: A Mystery of Chaos, St. Martin's, 1991.

State of Grace (short stories), Pulphouse, 1991.

And the Angels Sing: Stories, St. Martin's, 1992.

Seven Kinds of Death, St. Martin's, 1992.

Justice for Some, St. Martin's, 1993.

The Best Defense, St. Martin's, 1994.

Malice Prepense, St. Martin's, 1996.

CONTRIBUTOR

Samuel R. Delany and Marilyn Hacker, editors, *Quark No. 3,* Popular Library, 1971.

Harlan Ellison, editor, *Again, Dangerous Visions: 46 Original Stories,* Doubleday, 1972.

Thomas M. Disch, editor, *Bad Moon Rising: An Anthology of Political Foreboding,* Harper, 1973.

Damon Knight, editor, *A Shocking Thing,* Pocket Books, 1974.

Roger Elwood and Robert Silverberg, editors, *Epoch,* Berkley Publishing, 1975.

Femmes au Futur: Anthologie de nouvelles de science-fiction feminine (short stories), Marabout, 1976.

Also contributor to "Orbit" anthology series, edited by Damon Knight: *Orbit 1,* Putnam, 1966, *Orbit 2,* Putnam, 1967, *Orbit 3,* Putnam, 1968, *Orbit 4,* Putnam, 1968, *Orbit 5,* Putnam, 1969, *Orbit 6,* Putnam, 1970, *Orbit 7,* Putnam, 1970, *Orbit 8,* Putnam, 1970, *Orbit 9,* Putnam, 1971, *Orbit 10,* Putnam, 1972, *Orbit 11,* Putnam, 1972, *Orbit 12,* Putnam, 1973, *Orbit 13,* Putnam, 1974, *Orbit 14,* Harper, 1974, *Orbit 15,* Harper, 1974, *Orbit 18,* Harper, 1976, *Orbit 19,* Harper, 1977, *Orbit 20,* Harper, 1978.

OTHER

Contributor to periodicals, including *Fantastic, Future, Magazine of Fantasy and Science Fiction, Amazing, Cosmopolitan,* and *Strange Fantasy.* A manuscript collection is located at Syracuse University.

■ Sidelights

"For the first five years of my life no one could understand a thing I said," remarked prolific author Kate Wilhelm in an essay in *Contemporary Authors Autobiography Series* (CAAS). Perhaps that is why Wilhelm has spent most of her adult life putting her voice forward in an array of award-winning novels and short stories, primarily science fiction. Wilhelm outgrew her speech impediment, but fortunately for her many readers, never outgrew her desire to write.

Wilhelm was born the fourth of six children in Toledo, Ohio. She spoke quite a bit, but her mother and father were the only ones who could interpret her noises. "Very early I stopped trying to communicate, thinking, I suppose, there was little point to it," Wilhelm commented in *CAAS.* "To a certain extent I became an invisible child, and this continued for most of my life before I left home. When I got very good grades in school, no one noticed. When I stayed home from school for no particular reason, no one noticed. As a teenager I was never severely questioned about the hours I kept, the many activities I was engaged in. I don't think anyone noticed."

Wilhelm's private world provided her with a rich inner life. When she was put in charge of taking care of her younger brothers, she told stories to entertain them, and they were transfixed. As a child, Wilhelm's mother read to her a lot, and although people couldn't understand her speech, she began to read on her own without being taught. Her mother's dedication to reading helped Wilhelm grow as a reader. She related in *CAAS* that "I cannot remember a time when I could not read. Every week my mother went to the library with a shopping bag and brought home the world."

In kindergarten Wilhelm was cured of her disabling speech impediment. There was a speech therapist who worked there; Wilhelm was sent in for an evaluation. "The teacher listened to me for a few minutes and knew exactly what was wrong. She made me slow down and pronounce each syllable. My tongue had been put on fast forward at birth, and it was relatively simple to change it

A husband and wife—Constance Liedl, a psychologist, and Charlie Meiklejohn, a private detective—team up to clear the name a young set designer accused of murder.

to normal speed," Wilhelm told *CAAS*. After her sudden conversion, Wilhelm became very fond of the teacher, although they did not cross paths often. "She saw me, heard me, understood me, made me feel special; she opened the world to me."

A precocious child in many ways, Wilhelm would create castles and other buildings with blocks while the other children were struggling to learn how to read. At home, she poured over the newspaper, read popular magazines of the day, and often stole into her brothers' room to borrow a book or magazine. "I never prowled through their other belongings, or snooped generally, although they suspected that someone was doing that," Wilhelm told *CAAS*.

Wilhelm had many strong likes and dislikes. She loved playing hide and seek and was not afraid of the dark; however, a trip to the carnival and a ride on the Ferris wheel was enough to cause a screaming fit. She enjoyed sweets and cookies, but refused to eat anything doughy, such as pasta, dumplings, and noodles. She also didn't like gravy or butter, and was turned off to duck when her housekeeper "gave me the duck neck and insisted it was a leg. I started to eat it and pulled out a very long thing that looked to me like a worm. I ran shrieking from the table and would not touch duck or chicken again for many years," she related to *CAAS*. However, she loved the many different kinds of bread that her mother would bake: "Coming home from school in cold weather to a house scented with freshly baked yeast bread was one of the greatest pleasures of childhood."

Family Misfortunes

Although Wilhelm grew up during the Great Depression, her family had been well-off. Her father, a millwright, had found work in factories during the worst years. However, as Wilhelm became a teenager, her father's health declined. Lung infections he had suffered during World War I resulted in long-term damage that did not surface until many years later. He tried to keep his jobs, moving the family to Kentucky, Kansas, and back to Kentucky, but eventually his health declined to the point that he couldn't work anymore. Wilhelm's world was turned around. The many moves split the family apart. Wilhelm had to take on more of the family duties, like cooking dinner and watch-

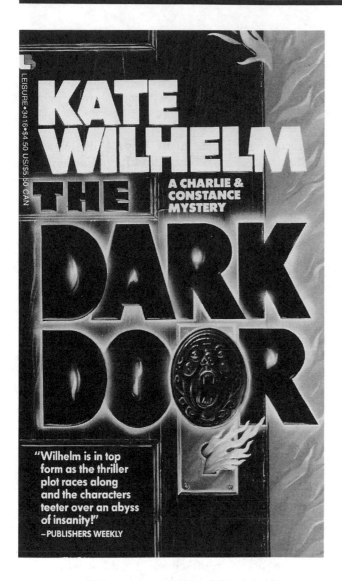

"Wilhelm is in top form as the thriller plot races along and the characters teeter over an abyss of insanity!" —PUBLISHERS WEEKLY

In this 1988 thriller, Meiklejohn and Liedl find themselves searching for an arsonist who sets fire to abandoned buildings filled with murdered people.

ing over the younger children. Wilhelm's mother took a job, which helped stabilize the family finances. "Childhood crashed in many ways that year," Wilhelm commented to *CAAS*. "Our family was totally disrupted, totally different." Her older siblings were working and dating, so they were seldom around.

When she babysat for her younger siblings, Wilhelm used her imagination to keep them amused. "I told them the stories of books I had read, of movies I had seen, and when those ran out, I began to make up stories. I reinvented the serial, every day leaving our hero in an impos-

sible situation, to be continued the following day. I held my audience." Another delight for Wilhelm was that she was able to get an adult library card. "I read everything in the branch library," Wilhelm related in *CAAS*. "For several years I think I was intoxicated with words. I judged nothing and read everything with equally rapt attention. Mysteries, travel books, westerns, classics, best-sellers. I loved them all."

Wilhelm's parents allowed her grandfather to move in with the family during that time, a decision that was unfortunate for Wilhelm. Her parents contended that they didn't want the children to be unsupervised. "We all hated him. . . ." Wilhelm contended to *CAAS*. "He wanted someone to get up and make his breakfast before seven, and he wanted a real lunch at eleven, and supper at five." It wasn't his particular habits though, that made Wilhelm hate him—it was his cruelty and inappropriate behavior. "If he found me reading the newspaper, he simply picked it up and walked away with it, to the porch or the living room where he dozed with it on his lap. Eula and I both tried to keep all the way out of his way. He would sidle up to one or the other of us every chance he got and drop his arm on our shoulder, let his hand fall as if by accident on our breast, and then feel us, squeeze a little," Wilhelm recalled in *CAAS*.

The children formulated a plan to retaliate; they were able to create a series of household disruptions without being detected. Her grandfather suspected that her brother Russ was behind all the mischief and raised his cane to him in front of Wilhelm's mother. Fortunately, her mother had noticed the children's change in attitude, and after witnessing this affront to her son, she asked the grandfather to leave, despite his protests. However, the memory of his abuse was there a long time. "He was a vigorous man in his mid-sixties when he lived with us, and for the next fifteen years until his death I made certain I was never alone in a room with him. When he came to visit, I went to my room, or left the house altogether. So did my brothers," Wilhelm told *CAAS*.

Wilhelm did well in her classes in high school, especially English, math, and science. "All through high school, teachers encouraged me to write. I was the editor of the school paper, and sometimes wrote the entire issue," she told *CAAS*. Wilhelm showed proclivity towards science and math, but unfortunately, there were few acceptable career paths for a woman with her talents in those times. "When I told the dean I wanted to be a chemist, she discouraged me. She said I would end up teaching chemistry, and I knew very well I did not want to be a teacher. I believed her although I did not believe any of the teachers who told me to work at becoming a writer," Wilhelm reminisced. Wilhelm earned a scholarship to a local university, and went to investigate, but the lack of classes that were interesting to her kept her from pursuing that path.

What's in a Name?

It was during a job held in high school that Wilhelm found out about one of the most confounding episodes in her life. She was working as a telephone operator and having difficulties mastering the job. Called into her supervisor's office, she was scared that she would be fired. When asked to supply her name, she replied "Catherine Meredith." Her supervisor told her that that wasn't her correct name. She was shocked because her family had always called her Catherine. She was told her name officially was Kate; however even that proved to be incorrect. After locating her birth certificate, she learned that her given name was actually Katie.

Wilhelm married shortly after high school and pursued several different kinds of jobs before she decided to become a full-time writer. "When I began to write at the age of twenty-eight, it was like going home, as if all my life I had been lost and speechless, and was only then finding my way back home, finding I could talk," she told *CAAS*. She was reluctant to become a writer for many years, despite words of encouragement. "Possibly I was intimidated by the teachers who urged me to be a writer because I was afraid they expected great works from me, and I did not for a minute believe I could do great things."

In *Contemporary Authors*, Wilhelm commented further on one of her motivations to write. "If I could sum up my philosophies and compulsions in a few paragraphs, there would be no need to write books, and there is a need. I believe we are living in an age of cataclysmic changes; we are living in an age that is the end of an era. My work is my attempt to understand how we got

"The Girl Who Fell into the Sky," which won the 1986 Nebula Award for best novelette, is included in this collection.

here, why we stay, and what lies ahead if anything does."

Wilhelm tackled the subject of cloning in her novel *Where Late the Sweet Birds Sang* (1976), which went on to win the Hugo and Jupiter awards for science fiction. The novel centers around the Sumner family, who survive a nuclear disaster and decide to make clones to re-populate the earth. However, the clones are telepathic and think they are superior to humans; they want to take over civilization. Their fatal flaw is that since they are born in groups and are telepathic, they never experience loneliness, which in turn keeps them from becoming creative, independent, and powerful.

Anne Hudson Jones praised the novel in the *Dictionary of Literary Biography*, contending that it "offers a poignant reminder that human strengths and weaknesses are inextricably bound together." Gerald Jonas, writing in the *New York Times Book Review,* commended Wilhelm's technique and the power of her narrative voice: "Her cautionary message comes through loud and clear: giving up our humanity to save our skins is a bad bargain no matter how you look at it."

Environmentalism is the primary theme of *Juniper Time: A Novel* (1979). A drought comes to the United States that devastates its residents; hope rests on an alien message discovered in space. A young linguist is sent to decode it; however, she decides that what is needed is a lesson in using the earth's treasures wisely, and she chooses to learn from an American Indian tribe.

"A probing revelation of human character, a pulsing mystery, and a lucid model of chaos theory."
—Katherine Dunn, author of Geek Love

Death Qualified
A MYSTERY OF CHAOS
Kate Wilhelm

In this 1991 work, Barbara Holloway is asked to defend a woman accused of murdering her husband who had been missing for seven years.

In *The Clewiston Test* Wilhelm interweaves gender relations with a science-laden plot. Anne Clewiston Symons is a scientist whose career has eclipsed her husband's. Her discovery of a factor in the blood that can quell all pain is exciting, but threatening—the chimpanzees in the test study have shown signs of violence. After a terrible car accident, where she appears withdrawn, her husband suspects she has taken the serum. As tensions mount, it becomes increasingly less clear if Anne's problems are being caused by a jealous husband or by her scientific discovery. Christopher Lehmann-Haupt, writing in the *New York Times*, claims that "whatever is bothering Anne serves as a nice little litmus test for the chauvinism of the male ego." In the *New York Times Book Review,* Jerome Charyn comments on the skill of Wilhelm's storytelling in the novel: "Written in a style that never calls attention to itself, 'The Clewiston Test' is a horror story that avoids the usual trappings of its genre. Kate Wilhelm isn't interested in futuristic nightmares."

The Plots Thicken

Death Qualified: A Mystery of Chaos (1991) was a departure for Wilhelm, with a stronger mystery theme than many of her other works. Lucas Kendricks has been kept in prison in a scientific research project for seven years. He is able to escape and make his way home. Kendricks's jailer, convinced he holds important evidence, kills him just as he arrives home. Kendricks's wife ends up being charged for his murder. This book introduces the character of Barbara Holloway, a disillusioned lawyer who takes the case because of the mystery it provides. Holloway delves deep into the intrigue of the scientific experiment Lucas was involved in, which leads to revelations about fractals and chaos theory. Lucinda Snyder, writing in *Voice of Youth Advocates* thinks that Wilhelm has crafted an interesting novel, but finds the book "ultimately comes up short." *Los Angeles Times Book Review* reviewer Sherry Gershon Gottleib praises the novel for its apt characterizations and thrilling pace, concluding that *Death Qualified* "is an unqualified success."

Wilhelm returns to the life of Holloway in the 1994 release *The Best Defense*. This novel follows Paula Kemmerman, a woman who is accused of killing her daughter and burning down the domestic violence shelter where she had been stay-

---

If you enjoy the works of Kate Wilhelm, you may want to check out the following books and films:

David Brin, *Earth,* 1990.
Mary Higgins Clark, *The Cradle Will Fall,* 1980.
Anne McCaffrey, *The Ship Who Sang,* 1969.
2001: A Space Odyssey, MGM, 1968.

---

ing. Kemmerman becomes disgusted with the legal system after being unjustly accused; she is almost ready to give up on herself. Holloway, unable to refuse hard-luck cases, throws herself into this one. In the end, Holloway finds that Kemmerman is being framed by right-wing activists who oppose women's rights. Elsa Pendleton, writing in *Library Journal,* believes that Wilhelm has handled this mainstream mystery novel with skill, claiming that Wilhelm "brings a competent voice and a thoughtful eye to her new territory." *Booklist* reviewer Emily Melton believes that the work will "create many new Wilhelm converts."

"In her science fiction, Kate Wilhelm holds a mirror to our world, and in her work we can see the dilemmas present in our uneasy, late-20th-century lives," wrote Pamela Sargent in *Twentieth-Century Science Fiction Writers.* Wilhelm has also become known for her versatility; she writes both novels and short stories with ease, and transverses easily between science fiction and more mainstream works. Widely praised for her adept characterizations and detailed plots, Wilhelm has remained a very readable writer. Sargent concludes that "her stories are easily accessible, but they are not escapist entertainments which one can read and then put aside; the issues she raises are present in our lives."

■ Works Cited

Charyn, Jerome, review of *The Clewiston Test, New York Times Book Review,* February 22, 1976.

Gottleib, Sherry Gershon, review of *Death Qualified: A Mystery of Chaos, Los Angeles Times Book Review,* June 30, 1991, p. 6.

Jonas, Gerald, review of *Where Late the Sweet Birds Sang, New York Times Book Review,* January 18, 1976.

Jones, Anne Hudson, essay on Wilhelm in *Dictionary of Literary Biography,* Volume 8: *Twentieth-Century American Science Fiction Writers,* Gale, 1981.

Lehmann-Haupt, Christopher, review of *The Clewiston Test, New York Times,* May 13, 1976.

Melton, Emily, review of *The Best Defense, Booklist,* June 1 & 15, 1994, p. 1780.

Pendleton, Elsa, review of *The Best Defense, Library Journal,* May 1, 1994, p. 140.

Sargent, Pamela, essay on Wilhelm in *Twentieth-Century Science Fiction Writers,* 3rd edition, St. James Press, 1991, pp. 863-4.

Snyder, Lucinda, review of *Death Qualified: A Mystery of Chaos, Voice of Youth Advocates,* October, 1991, p. 234.

Wilhelm, Kate, autobiographical essay in *Contemporary Authors Autobiography Series,* Volume 8, Gale, 1989, pp. 297-310.

Wilhelm, Kate, comments in *Contemporary Authors, New Revision Series,* Volume 36, Gale, 1992.

■ For More Information See

BOOKS

Dream Makers: The Uncommon People Who Write Science Fiction, Volume 1, Berkley Publishing, 1980.

PERIODICALS

Booklist, May 15, 1995, pp. 1635, 1638.

Chicago Tribune Book World, February 16, 1986.

Globe and Mail (Toronto), March 4, 1989.

Kirkus Reviews, April 15, 1994, p. 510; May 15, 1995, p. 674.

Los Angeles Times, May 8, 1981; November 15, 1983.

Los Angeles Times Book Review, December 19, 1982.

Locus, August, 1992, p. 55; September, 1992, pp. 13, 64; September, 1993, p. 67; July, 1994, p. 61; August, 1994, p. 57.

Magazine of Fantasy and Science Fiction, November, 1971; April, 1979; January, 1980.

Newsweek, November 29, 1971; February 9, 1976.

New York Times Book Review, March 10, 1974; August 26, 1979; March 9, 1986; October 25, 1992, p. 36.

Publishers Weekly, May 16, 1994, p. 53; May 22, 1995, p. 51; May 27, 1996, p. 66.

Psychology Today, October, 1975.

Saturday Review, April 30, 1977.

Voice of Youth Advocates, April, 1993, p. 9; October, 1995, p. 226.
Washington Post, September 21, 1982.*

—*Sketch by Nancy Rampson*

Acknowledgments

Acknowledgments

Grateful acknowledgment is made to the following publishers, authors, and artists for their kind permission to reproduce copyrighted material.

LOUISA MAY ALCOTT. Alcott, Louisa May, photograph. Corbis-Bettmann. Reproduced by permission./ McKendry, Kenny, illustrator. From a cover of *Good Wives*, by Louisa M. Alcott. Puffin Classics, 1994. Reproduced by permission of Penguin Books Ltd./ McKendry, Kenny, illustrator. From a cover of *Little Men*, by Louisa M. Alcott. Puffin Classics, 1994. Reproduced by permission of Penguin Books Ltd./ Marmee, with the March girls, illustration by Rene Cloke. From *Little Women*, by Louisa May Alcott. P. R. Gawthorn Ltd., n.d.

RUDOLFO ANAYA. Virgil, Bernadette, illustrator. From a cover of *Bless Me, Ultima*, by Rudolph A. Anaya. Warner Books, 1972. Copyright © 1972 by Rudolfo A. Anaya. All rights reserved. Reproduced by permission./ Virgil, Bernadette, illustrator. From a jacket of *Jalamanta: A Message from the Desert*, by Rudolfo Anaya. Warner Books, 1996. Cover © 1996 Warner Books. All rights reserved. Reproduced by permission./ Anaya, Rudolfo, photograph. Reproduced by permission of Rudolfo Anaya.

MAYA ANGELOU. Jacket of *I Know Why the Caged Bird Sings*, by Maya Angelou. Random House, 1969. Copyright © 1969 by Maya Angelou. All rights reserved. Reproduced by permission of Random House, Inc./ Jacket of *On the Pulse of Morning*, by Maya Angelou. Random House, 1993. Copyright © 1993 by Maya Angelou. All rights reserved. Reproduced by permission of Random House, Inc./ Jacket of *Phenomenal Woman: Four Poems Celebrating Women*, by Maya Angelou. Random House, 1994. Copyright © 1995 by Maya Angelou. All rights reserved. Reproduced by permission of Random House, Inc./ Angelou, Maya, photograph. AP/Wide World Photos. Reproduced by permission.

T. ERNESTO BETHANCOURT. Jacket of *The Dog Days of Arthur Cane*, by T. Ernesto Bethancourt. Holiday House, 1976. Copyright © 1976 by Thomas Paisley. All rights reserved. Reproduced by permission./ Jacket of *Dr. Doom: Superstar*, by T. Ernesto Bethancourt. Holiday House, 1978. Copyright © 1978 by Tom Paisley. All rights reserved. Reproduced by permission./ Jacket of *Instruments of Darkness*, by T. Ernesto Bethancourt. Holiday House, 1979. Copyright © 1979 by Tom Paisley. All rights reserved. Reproduced by permission./ Deraney, Michael, illustrator. From a jacket of *The Me Inside of Me*, by T. Ernesto Bethancourt. Lerner Publications, 1985. Copyright © 1985 by Tom Paisley. All rights reserved. Reproduced by permission./ Paisley, Tom (T. Ernesto Bethancourt), photograph by Bob Campbell. Reproduced by permission.

GWENDOLYN BROOKS. Taylor, Cledie, illustrator. From a cover of *Riot*, by Gwendolyn Brooks. Broadside Press, 1969. Copyright © by Gwendolyn Brooks 1969. All rights reserved. Reproduced by permission./ Cover of *The World of Gwendolyn Brooks*, by Gwendolyn Brooks. Harper & Row, Publishers, 1971. Copyright © 1971 by Gwendolyn Brooks Blakely. Reprinted by permission of HarperCollins Publishers, Inc./ Brooks, Gwendolyn, photograph by Myles De Russey. Harper & Row. Reproduced by permission of HarperCollins Publishers, Inc.

JOHN DONOVAN. Brundage, Avery, illustrator. From a jacket of *Family*, by John Donovan. Harper & Row, Publishers, 1976. Copyright © 1976 by John Donovan. All rights reserved. Reproduced by permission of HarperCollins Publishers, Inc./ Jacket of *I'll Get There. It Better Be Worth the Trip*, by John Donovan. Harper & Row, Publishers, 1971. Copyright © 1969 by John Donovan. Reproduced by permission of HarperCollins Publishers, Inc./ Jacket of *Wild in the World*, by John Donovan. Harper & Row, Publishers, 1971. Copyright © 1971 by John Donovan. All rights reserved. Reproduced by permission of HarperCollins Publishers, Inc./ Donovan, John, photograph by Teri Slotkin. Reproduced by permission of the Estate of John Donovan.

MICHAEL DORRIS. Robbins, Ken, illustrator. From a jacket of *A Yellow Raft in Blue Water*, by Michael Dorris. Henry Holt and Company, Inc. Jacket design copyright © 1987 by Henry Holt and Company, Inc. Reproduced by permission of Ken Robbins./ Dorris, Michael, photographer. From a jacket of *The Broken Cord*, by Michael Dorris. Harper & Row, Publishers, 1989. Jacket photograph © 1989 by Michael Dorris. Reproduced by permission of HarperCollins Publishers, Inc./ Dorris, Michael, photograph by Jerry Bauer. © Jerry Bauer. Reproduced by permission.

ANNE FINE. Jacket of *Alias Madame Doubtfire*, by Anne Fine. Little, Brown and Company, 1988. Copyright © 1988 by Anne Fine. All rights reserved. Reproduced by permission of Little, Brown and Company./ Mujica, Rick, illustrator. From a jacket of *My War with Goggle-Eyes*, by Anne Fine. Little, Brown and Company, 1989. Copyright © 1989 by Anne Fine. All rights reserved. Reproduced by permission of Little, Brown and Company./ Cover of *Flour Babies*, by Anne Fine. Laurel-Leaf, 1992. Copyright © 1992 by Anne Fine. Reproduced by permission of Bantam Doubleday Dell Books for Young Readers./ Fine, Anne, photograph. Reproduced by permission of Anne Fine.

BRIAN JACQUES. Howell, Troy, illustrator. From a jacket of *Redwall*, by Brian Jacques. Philomel Books, 1986. Jacket illustration © 1986 by Troy Howell. Reproduced by permission of Philomel Books./ Howell, Troy, illustrator. From a jacket of *Mossflower*, by Brian Jacques. Philomel Books, 1988. Jacket illustration © 1988 by Troy Howell. Reproduced by permission of Philomel Books./ Canty, Thomas, illustrator. From a cover of *Mattimeo*, by Brian Jacques. Avon Books, 1990. Reproduced by permission of Avon Books, New York./ Howell, Troy, illustrator. From a cover of *The Bellmaker*, by Brian Jacques. Philomel Books, 1995. Cover art copyright © 1995 by Troy Howell. Reproduced by permission of Philomel Books./ Jacques, Brian, photograph. Radio Merseyside. Reproduced by permission.

MIKE JUDGE. Judge, Mike (with Beavis and Butt-head), photograph by Frank Ockenfels. Frank Ockenfels/Outline Press. Reproduced by permission.

R. R. KNUDSON. Egielski, Richard, illustrator. From a jacket of *Rinehart Shouts*, by R. R. Knudson. Farrar, Straus & Giroux, 1987. Jacket illustration copyright © 1987 by Richard Egielski. Reproduced by permission of Farrar, Straus and Giroux, Inc./ Hale, Christy, illustrator. From a jacket of *The Wonderful Pen of May Swenson*, by R. R. Knudson. Macmillan Publishing Company, 1993. Jacket illustrations copyright © 1993 by Christy Hale. Reproduced by permission of Christy Hale./ Knudson, R. R., photograph. Reproduced by permission of R. R. Knudson.

MAYA LIN. Vietnam Memorial Wall, photograph by S. Scott Applewhite. AP/Wide World Photos. Reproduced by permission./ Lin, Maya Ying, photograph. AP/Wide World Photos. Reproduced by permission.

JOHN MARSDEN. Cover of *So Much to Tell You . . .*, by John Marsden. Fawcett Juniper, 1987. Copyright © 1987 by John Marsden. Reproduced by permission of Random House, Inc./ Hillenbrand, Will, photographer. From a jacket of *Tomorrow, When the War Began*, by John Marsden. Houghton Mifflin Company, 1995. Jacket art © 1995 by Will Hillenbrand. Reproduced by permission./ Marsden, John, photograph by David Furphy. Photo © 1994 by David Furphy. Reproduced by permission of John Marsden.

WILLIAM MAYNE. Tuckley, Shirley, illustrator. From a jacket of *All the King's Men*, by William Mayne. Delacorte, 1988. Copyright © 1982 by William Mayne. All rights reserved. Reproduced by permission of Delacorte Press, a division of Bantam Doubleday Dell Publishing Group, Inc./ Sizemore, Ted, illustrator. From a jacket of *Gideon Ahoy!*, by William Mayne. Delacorte Press, 1989. Jacket illustration copyright © 1989 by Ted Sizemore. Reproduced by permission of Delacorte Press, a division of Bantam Doubleday Dell Publishing Group, Inc./ Bailey, Brian, illustrator. From a jacket of *Antar and the Eagles*, by William Mayne. Delacorte Press, 1990. Jacket illustration © 1990 by Brian Bailey. Reproduced by permission of Delacorte Press, a division of Bantam Doubleday Dell Publishing Group, Inc./ Mayne, William, photograph. © Carole Cutner. Reproduced by permission of Walker Books Ltd., London.

JIM MURPHY. A man sitting on a flying machine, illustration. From *Guess Again: More Weird & Wacky Inventions*, by Jim Murphy. Bradbury Press, 1986. Copyright © 1986 Jim Murphy. Reproduced by permission of Simon & Schuster Books for Young Readers, an imprint of Simon & Schuster Children's Publishing Division./ Jacket of *The Boy's War: Confederate and Union Soldiers Talk about the Civil War*, by Jim Murphy. Clarion Books, 1990. Reproduced by permission of Houghton Mifflin Company./ Thompson, John, painter. From a jacket of *The Great Fire*, by Jim Murphy. Scholastic Inc., 1995. Jacket painting © 1995 by John Thompson. Reproduced by permission of Scholastic Inc./ Murphy, Jim, photograph. Clarion Books. Reproduced by permission.

GEORGIA O'KEEFFE. O'Keeffe, Georgia, photograph. UPI/Corbis-Bettmann. Reproduced by permission./ "Calla Lillies," painting by Georgia O'Keeffe. Private Collection. Reproduced by permission of the Gerald Peters Gallery, Sante Fe./ O'Keeffe, Georgia (standing next to her painting "Life and Death"), photograph. UPI/Corbis-Bettmann. Reproduced by permission.

URI ORLEV. Titherington, Jean, illustrator. From a jacket of *The Island on Bird Street*, by Uri Orlev. Translated by Hillel Halkin. Houghton Mifflin Company, 1984. Jacket illustration © 1984 by Jean Titherington. Reproduced by permission of Houghton Mifflin Company./ van der Schans, Roelof, illustrator. From a jacket of *The Man From the Other Side*, by Uri Orlev. Translated by Hillel Halkin. Houghton Mifflin Company, 1991. Jacket art © 1990 by Roelof van der Schans. Reproduced by permission of Houghton Mifflin Company./ Doney, Todd, illustrator. From a jacket of *The Lady with the Hat*, by Uri Orlev. Translated by Hillel Halkin. Houghton Mifflin Company, 1995. Jacket art © 1995 by Todd Doney. Reproduced by permission of Houghton Mifflin Company./ Orlev, Uri, photograph by Aliza Auerbach. Copyright by Aliza Auerbach. Reproduced by permission.

K. M. PEYTON. Barrett, Robert, illustrator. From a cover of *The Edge of the Cloud*, by K. M. Peyton. Oxford University Press, 1989. Text copyright © 1969 by K. M. Peyton. Cover illustration © 1989 by Robert Barrett. Reproduced by permission of Robert Barrett./ Morris, Tony. From a cover of *Pennington's Seventeenth Summer*, by K. M. Peyton. Oxford University Press, 1970. Copyright © 1970 by K. M. Peyton. Reproduced by permission of K. M. Peyton./ Peyton, K. M., photograph. Reproduced by permission./ Home of K. M. Peyton, K. M. Reproduced by permission.

MARJORIE KINNAN RAWLINGS. Boy approaching a fawn sitting on the ground, illustration by N. C. Wyeth. From *The Yearling*, by Marjorie Kinnan Rawlings. Charles Scribner's Sons, 1967. Copyright, 1939, renewed © 1967 by Charles Scribner's Sons. Reproduced by permission of Atheneum Books for Young Readers, an imprint of Simon & Schuster Children's Publishing Division./ Rawlings, Marjorie Kinnan (with dog), photograph. Reproduced by permission.

PAMELA F. SERVICE. Gowing, Toby, illustrator. From a jacket of *Tomorrow's Magic,* by Pamela F. Service. Atheneum, 1987. Jacket illustration copyright © 1987 by Toby Gowing. Reproduced by permission of Toby Gowing./ Sargent, Claudia Karabaic, illustrator. From a jacket of *When the Night Wind Howls,* by Pamela F. Service. Atheneum, 1987. Jacket illustration © 1987 by Claudia Karabaic Sargent. Reproduced by permission of Claudia Karabaic Sargent./ Pettingill, Ondre, illustrator. From a jacket of *The Reluctant God,* by Pamela F. Service. Atheneum, 1988. Jacket illustration copyright © 1988 by Ondre Pettingill. Reproduced by permission of Ondre Pettingill./ Pettingill, Ondre, illustrator. From a jacket of *Under Alien Stars,* by Pamela F. Service. Atheneum, 1990. Jacket illustration copyright © 1990 by Ondre Pettingill. Reproduced by permission of Ondre Pettingill./ Cover of *Being of Two Minds,* by Pamela F. Service. Fawcett Juniper, 1991. Copyright © 1991 by Pamela F. Service. All rights reserved. Reproduced by permission of Random House, Inc./ Service, Pamela F., photograph by Robert Talbot. Macmillan. Reproduced by permission of Atheneum Books for Young Readers, an imprint of Simon & Schuster Children's Publishing Division.

MARY WOLLSTONECRAFT SHELLEY. Shelley, Mary Wollstonecraft, painting by Richard Rothwell, photograph. The Granger Collection. Reproduced by permission./ Karloff, Boris (in the 1931 motion picture "Frankenstein"), photograph. The Granger Collection. Reproduced by permission./ Villa Diodati near Geneva (the Shelley home), illustration. The Granger Collection. Reproduced by permission./ First illustration of the Frankenstein Monster, by Mary Shelley. Source unknown./ Shelley, Mary Wollstonecraft, illustration. Source unknown.

JAN SLEPIAN. Allen,Tom, illustrator. From a jacket of *The Alfred Summer,* by Jan Slepian. Macmillan Publishing Company, 1980. Copyright © 1980 Macmillan Publishing Co., Inc. Reproduced by permission of Simon & Schuster Books for Young Readers, an imprint of Simon & Schuster Children's Publishing Division./ Cover of *The Broccoli Tapes,* by Jan Slepian. Apple Paperbacks, 1990. Illustration copyright © 1990 by Scholastic Inc. Reproduced by permission./ Cover of *Back to Before,* by Jan Slepian. Apple Paperbacks, 1994. Illustration copyright © 1994 by Scholastic Inc. Reproduced by permission./ Slepian, Jan, photograph. Reproduced by permission of Jan Slepian.

ROBERT SWINDELLS. Cover of *Fallout,* by Robert Swindells. Beech Tree Books, 1992. Copyright © 1984 by Robert Swindells. Reproduced by Beech Tree Books, a division of William Morrow and Company, Inc./ Swindells, Robert, photograph. © N. K. Howarth.

MARK TWAIN. Tom Sawyer leaning on a barrel, looking at other children, illustration by Walter C. Hodges. From *Tom Sawyer,* by Mark Twain. J. M. Dent & Sons Ltd., 1955. Reproduced by permission./ Keane, Gary, illustrator. From a cover of *The Prince and the Pauper,* by Mark Twain. Puffin Classics, 1994. Reproduced by permission of Penguin Books, Ltd./ Huckleberry Finn, hiding behind a tree, illustration by Steven Kellogg. From *The Adventures of Huckleberry Finn,* by Mark Twain. William Morrow, 1994. Illustrations copyright © 1994 by Steven Kellogg. All rights reserved. Reproduced by permission of William Morrow and Company, Inc./ Tom Blankenship's home in Hannibal, MO, photograph. Mark Twain Home Board, Hannibal, MO. Reproduced by permission./ Title page of "Adventures of Huckleberry Finn: Tom Sawyer's Comrade," by Mark Twain, photograph. Source unknown./ Twain, Mark, photograph. Corbis-Bettmann. Reproduced by permission.

KATE WILHELM. Cover of *The Hamlet Trap,* by Kate Wilhelm. St. Martin's Press, 1987. Copyright © 1987 by Kate Wilhelm. All rights reserved. Reproduced by permission./ Pickard, Morgan, painter. From a jacket of *Children of the Wind: Five Novellas,* by Kate Wilhelm. St. Martin's, 1989. Copyright © 1989 by Kate Wilhelm. All rights reserved. Reproduced by permission./ Espenak, Fred, illustrator. From a jacket of *Death Qualified: A Mystery of Chaos,* by Kate Wilhelm. St. Martin's Press, 1991. Copyright © 1991 by Kate Wilhelm. All rights reserved. Reproduced by permission./ Cover of *The Dark Door,* by Kate Wilhelm. Leisure Books, 1993. Copyright © 1988 by Kate Wilhelm. All rights reserved. Reproduced by permission./ Wilhelm, Kate, photograph by Richard Wilhelm. Reproduced by permission.

Cumulative Index

Author/Artist Index

The following index gives the number of the volume in which an author/artist's biographical sketch appears.